D1560806

THE BENTHOS OF LAKES

THE BENTHOS OF LAKES

RALPH O. BRINKHURST

Department of Zoology
University of Toronto
Toronto, Ontario
Now at, Department of the Environment
Fisheries and Marine Services
Biological Station, St. Andrews, N.B.

With
the collaboration of
R. E. BOLTT, M. G. JOHNSON, S. MOZLEY,
and A. V. TYLER

ST. MARTIN'S PRESS NEW YORK

St. MARTIN'S PRESS, INC.,
175 Fifth Avenue, New York, N.Y. 10010

Printed in Great Britain

Library of Congress Catalog Card Number: 74-16826

First published in the United States of America in 1974

AFFILIATED PUBLISHERS: Macmillan Limited, London
also at Bombay, Calcutta, Madras and Melbourne

To all those who have hauled an Ekman by hand from 50 m in a small boat on a windy day to find a stone caught between the jaws.

PREFACE

The purpose of this introduction is to establish the limits of the subject matter that my assistants and I have sought to cover, and to indicate the sort of readers for whom it has been written.

The benthos of a lake is not an harmonious unit, clearly defined by morphometric or functional considerations. To some, the fauna of a lake includes both a littoral and a benthic fauna, as though the bottom-dwelling organisms along the shore were distinct from the spatially identified sublittoral and profundal regions. In this volume we treat the benthos as being *that assemblage of animals living in or on the sediments and dependent upon the decomposition cycle for most if not all of its basic food supply*. The shore fauna is here considered to be comprised of three basic assemblages: that dependent upon wave action on a stony shore, particularly for respiratory needs; that dependent upon the shelter of macrophytic vegetation from which it derives its food supply, the aufwuchs or overgrowth on the weed surface; and the true fauna of the shallow water sediments. Part of the in-fauna may exist in the shallowest parts of the lake in and upon the sediment immediately beneath the weed-associated littoral assemblage, but it is clearly less likely to find suitable accumulations of decomposing organic material on a wave washed stony shore.

Hence the benthos is here considered as the true in-fauna, and especially that inhabiting substrates ranging from sand through mud to silt. This definition underemphasises the problem of the epibenthic forms, particularly the crustaceans, and transitory forms such as *Chaoborus*, which will have to be dealt with later.

The distinction between a pond and a lake is, of necessity, an artificial one that reflects the difficulty faced by the ecologist in trying to set up categories as reference points for study of what is, essentially, a continuum. The use of the word 'pond' can even be seen to vary regionally, as the ponds of the Atlantic coast of North America would undoubtedly be called lakes by most visitors to the region. Again, we will not endeavour to clarify this, but will draw from information on what would generally be conceded to be lakes, referring to ponds where it is imperative to do so as, for instance, in the section on production studies.

The students of lake benthos have adopted a number of distinct approaches, which will be discussed in detail later on. Two distinct themes can be identified here, however. There are those who have investigated the benthos of a lake or lakes as limnologists, and those who have undertaken to follow their study of a group of organisms (usually a taxonomic unit) into whatever habitat they occupy. Here we are primarily concerned with studies of lakes *per se*, particularly those in which there is some chemical/physical background data available, and a fairly complete identification of the species involved. Such studies are few, despite the voluminous literature in the field and a general feeling among students that this approach is long outdated. Even scarcer are studies that extend over more than one or two seasons, and it is unfortunately necessary to state that *there has never been a study of the benthos of a lake in which, in the senior author's opinion, the sampling methodology and schedule have been properly evaluated, most of the major species identified, and which extended over all seasons for a consecutive number of years.*

Despite this total lack of a properly described benthos, we have enough partial accounts, clues, hypotheses and studies of specific components to enable us to lay the plans for such a study. This cannot be done with the resources of any one individual within the academic community, however, hence the most useful contribution that can be made from such a position is to present this review of just what we do and do not know about this aspect of limnology.

It should now be clear that the volume is intended to be, first and foremost, a detailed review for those scientists and senior students working in the field. It may, at the same time, act as a source book for graduate students, as well as for those responsible for shaping programmes in research institutes. If it does nothing else, it may serve to convince a number of students that ecological research proceeds on many fronts simultaneously. There are architects that conceive structures, and there are those that build brick by brick.

In the direct sense, this is not a book about pollution but the senior author believes that we will never learn to manage our ecosystems until we understand how they work. In the hurried expansion of research activity in lacustrine ecosystems, there has been a gross overdependence on technology and engineering, and far too little attention paid to the living components of the systems that are involved in all the multitude of undesirable pollution symptoms, but there are signs that at least some administrations have recognised this deficiency. What is even worse, living systems have been subject to study as though they were predictable machines—algae are algae regardless of species, eutrophication is equated to ageing as though this were a well-established limnological law. It is to be hoped that some degree of constructive pessimism about the state of the art of benthic research will be communicated to those responsible for many current projects, so that the biologist will be invited to join as an equal in the complex team that will be required to bring about the Ecological Revolution that must supersede the Industrial Revolution.

Finally, the production of a book in such a specialised area may be justified by the need to stimulate benthic research, a field that seems to be languishing compared with more classical limnological and fisheries investigations. Few standard texts concern themselves with the benthos in any detail, and few good contributions to its study appear in current journals. The authors hope that, by reviewing some of the progress in the field to date, a number of younger limnologists may be stimulated enough to remedy some of the deficiencies in our knowledge.

Although the title page indicates a single authorship, this is no more than a matter of convenience. The work of organising my first set of reprints and references was undertaken by Mr. M. Burley who spent a year working with me at Liverpool University. The long delayed project was reactivated in Toronto in 1970, when Dr. S. Mozley translated and abstracted most of the German benthic literature, as well as that dealing with chironomids and lake typology. The section on vertical distribution of benthos, and much of the rest, was researched by Dr. R. E. Boltt; and the production section was prepared and written by Dr. M. G. Johnson; and Dr. A. V. Tyler authored the section on community analysis. I have attempted to draw all these pieces of information together into a single account, and hence bear the responsibility for any errors and omissions arising from the process of rearranging material. I cannot fully express my gratitude to my collaborators and the many assistants who have, in one way or another, contributed so generously to the production of this work. My particular thanks must be expressed to Mr. Frank Miller, who organised a team of students (Cathie Klink, Pauline Barnucz, Diana Nielson and Paul Hagan) at Sheridan College, Oakville, to draw up the illustrations, and especially to Mr. Ted Pulford of The Macmillan Company of Canada Limited, who thoroughly reviewed my manuscript and made many suggestions for the improvement of both content and style.

Contents

Glossary

Some terms may cause difficulty for the reader, and so an attempt is made here to explain (rather than define) terms. See also *Fundamentals of Limnology*, 3rd Ed., Ruttner trs., Frey and Fry, Toronto, 1963.

Allochthonous	Organic material formed primarily by photosynthesis, outside the system under consideration (cf. Autochthonous).
Aufwuchs	Microscopic plant and animal forms which encrust submerged surfaces, both living and non-living; a rich food source for grazers.
Autochthonous	Organic matter which originates within the system under consideration, primarily by photosynthetic activity (cf. Allochthonous).
Community (Biocenosis)	Groups of organisms found in a habitat, more closely related to each other ecologically than they are to other such groups.
Degree-days	Where a biological process is related to temperature, such that completion would be achieved in 20 days at 10° or 10 days at 20°, either being equal to 200 degree-days.
Dy	A bottom deposit of precipitated humic colloids (cf. Gyttja).
Dystrophic	*See* Trophic Gradient.
Emergent Vegetation	Plants with leaves and other parts above water level but with submerged roots (cf. submerged and floating vegetation: plankton).
Epibenthic	Superficially benthic organisms of the mud/water interface.
Epideictic	Adapted for display.
Eutrophic	*See* Trophic Gradient.
Glacial Relict	Survivors of the Pleistocene biota restricted to particular localities by reason of glacial history and/or temperature tolerance.
Gyttja	Finely divided organic detritus on lake bottoms; sediment typical of aerobic lake bottoms (seemingly most organic muds as opposed to peaty muds, or Dy).
Humus (humic)	Partly decomposed organic material, soil tending to peat.
Indicator Organisms	Organisms supposedly with narrow environmental tolerance used as indicators of environmental stress. Sensitive species may indicate stress by their absence, tolerant species confuse people by living in small numbers in 'clean' or natural localities. Indicator communities are preferred (*see* Saprobien System).
Internal Seiche	A standing wave in a lake; the result of piling up of warm surface water at one end of the lake and consequent displacement of cool bottom water at the other and the subsequent oscillations of the discontinuity layer in restoring itself to the horizontal in thermally stratified lakes.
Lacustrine	Pertaining to lakes.
Littoral	(Also sublittoral). Relative to depth distribution. In marine biology usually that area exposed by rise and fall of tide. In limnology usually the shallowest part of the lake variously defined, equivalent to sublittoral of marine biology (*see* chapter 3).
Macrobenthos	(Microbenthos, meiobenthos). Organisms visible to the naked eye. Microbenthos may be restricted to bacteria *et al.* but may include all forms not visible to the naked eye (i.e. nematodes).
Meromictic	A lake in which the water mass does not mix or circulate (*see* Mixis).
Monomictic	A lake in which the water is mixed or circulates once a year (*see* Mixis).
Mesohumic	Moderately humic (or peaty) as opposed to poly, oligo humic, etc., *see also* Dystrophic—chapter 2 (table 2.4).
Mesosaprobic	*See* Saprobien System.

Mesotrophic	*See* Trophic Gradient.
Mixis	The annual frequency with which a lake 'turns over' or stratification breaks down (amictic, dimictic, meromictic, monomictic, polymictic, etc. q.v.).
Oligosaprobic	*See* Saprobien System.
Oligotrophic	*See* Trophic Gradient.
Poisson Distribution	In statistics, a series which gives the frequency with which groups of zero, one, two etc., organisms will be encountered together if distribution is random.
Polysaprobic	*See* Saprobien System.
Profundal	Of the deeper part of a lake; not definable (*see* chapter 3) cf. littoral.
R.Q.	Respiratory quotient; the ratio of CO_2 evolved to O_2 used in respiration.
Saprobien System	A system akin to that of the Trophic System or Trophic Gradient, by which organisms are related to degree of pollution (usually organic) or lack of oxygen in an ecosystem. An attempt to schematise the indicator species concept, now tremendously elaborated (Sladecek. *Arch. J. Hydrobiol.* 7: 1973). A pseudoquantitative construct as fallible as the Trophic System with the same rudiments of common sense. Grades of Oligo-Meso-Polysaprobic minutely subdivided in some schemata.
Secondary Production	Energy or materials stored by photosynthesis referred to as primary production; the quantities stored by consumers are hence secondary production. Standing stock (often miscalled standing crop) often misused for secondary production, i.e. the static measure may not reflect the dynamic concept.
Stenothermy	Having a narrow temperature tolerance (cold s., warm s.).
Trophic Gradient	The lake series oligotrophic (superficially meaning unproductive)—mesotrophic—eutrophic (or highly productive) properly overlaid with a second dimension in relation to humic content or degree of Dystrophy (usually ignored in recent literature or thought of as fourth lake type), often assumed to represent evolutionary phases in lake history as in the transition to dry land. The terminal phases of this process lead to morphometric eutrophy-enhanced plant production, warm turbid water, rich in nutrients, coarse fish instead of game fish, deoxygenated mud, etc. Lake basins may, in fact, run low in nutrients and lakes become oligotrophic (less productive) with time. Never properly defined. See chapter 2.
Turnover Ratio	Ratio of throughput to content; in the production sense, the relationship between standing stock and production per unit time; production per unit biomass per unit time.
Voltine	Number of generations in a year (Univ., Biv.).

PART I

THE DISTRIBUTION AND ABUNDANCE OF LAKE BENTHOS

1 THEMES IN BENTHIC RESEARCH

Any attempt to trace discrete streams of thought in benthic research is confounded by the tendency of workers in this field to carry out a largely descriptive survey, followed by a discussion of several theoretical concepts in the light of the results obtained. Only rarely do we find examples of specific tests of hypotheses; thus it is not surprising to find we have no real body of theory upon which to predict the effects of environmental stress on the distribution and abundance of benthic species.

Any effort to untangle this Gordian knot in order to arrive at some understanding of the structure and function of benthic communities may be looked upon with some suspicion by those prepared to sever it by force. We refer, of course, to those who would put their faith in mathematical models concerned only with quantities of matter or energy, or who seek correlations at the expense of any attempt to understand causal relationships, perhaps even resorting to the use of data established on the basis of a single visit to each site. Because sound management of aquatic systems will require decisions concerning the *quality* of the ecosystem, and hence the preservation of particular species of economic value such as the Atlantic salmon, which is usually preferred over carp as a table item in northern latitudes, we surely need to develop the best of *both* approaches. The trouble with so much of the classical study of the benthos is not the absence of models, expressed verbally instead of symbolically, but the almost complete lack of any attempt to validate them with laboratory experiments and/or cleverly designed field-sampling programmes. There are, if anything, too many rather than too few hypotheses; most of them arrived at by a process of post-rationalisation from data collected for what were, at best, ill-defined reasons. An examination of the past, then, may not yield much hard information, but it may enable us to save some time in the future by suggesting themes for research and identifying blind alleys for what they are.

Interest in the benthic fauna of lakes began in Switzerland with the discovery of a nematode in the deep water of Lac Léman by Forel in 1869. The original line of work thus stimulated was, of course, faunistic–zoogeographical in emphasis. *The Catalogue des Invertèbres Suisse*, *Die Susswasserfauna Deutschlands*, and books by Carpenter, Furneaux, Hentschel, Mellanby, Morgan, Needham, Ward and Whipple and all the others represent the products of this study. Probably most of today's limnologists were introduced to their field by reading in these classical works.

Early descriptive accounts of lakes, such as that on Lake Neuchatel (Switzerland) by Monard (1919) refer to systematic treatises on Protozoa, Turbellaria, Nematoda, Oligochaeta, Mollusca, Ostracoda, and Phyllopoda which were used to support the identifications of the fauna. Few recent studies can boast so wide a systematic base, nor can they refer to many recent systematic reviews of such wide generality. Our knowledge of the systematics of the freshwater fauna, particularly of the immature stages of insects, especially in North America, is still sadly deficient.

The study of groups of animals, some of which may happen to inhabit lakes (and particularly the shallow edges of lakes) continues, of course, down to the present time, involving people who are primarily zoologists rather than limnologists (although the distinction may not always be clear cut).

The focal point of this type of study seems to have passed from Switzerland, through Scandinavia (climaxed perhaps by the publication of two volumes on aquatic animals by Wesenberg Lund) into Britain. Here, stimulated by the approach adopted by T. T. Macan at Windermere, a tradition of group-oriented studies produced a series of biologists who have used their basic taxonomic and biological orientation to move into broader ecological and limnological studies of a more theoretical nature. Among this group we could site H. B. N. Hynes, K. H. Mann, T. B. Reynoldson, W. D. Williams and many others including, perhaps, the author.

This trend toward a more ecological approach was often stimulated by contact with, or migration to, North America, where finances and manpower were obtained more readily to promote collaborative field studies or the creation of research teams. The lack of a systematic base caused by the complexity of the fauna, and by the large size of the politico–geographical units often used as a context for the publication of systematic reviews, may also have promoted the search for non-taxonomic approaches to the study of lakes in North America. It would be pretentious to hold that the British tradition is unique in its attention to systematics, but the accident of geographic rather than mere political boundaries, small size and a relatively simple fauna, perhaps led to the development of a middle course between the recent 'energy and matter' approach of many Americans and the ardent lake typologists of Europe. This is reflected by the production of recent books by Macan (1963) and Hynes (1970) in which the organisms and their distribution and abundance are the primary focus of attention. That North America is not devoid of systematic studies may be evidenced by reference to the revision of Ward and Whipple by Edmondson (1959) and the systematic survey by Pennak (1953).

Such biological studies lead naturally into physiology, as do the predictions that could be made as a result of distributional and typological studies, but few freshwater biologists have been willing to study benthic organisms in the laboratory in order to test some of the assumptions based on their observations. Respiratory physiology is, as we shall see, particularly important in this respect and has received some attention. The studies of Alsterberg, Ambühl, Berg, Harnisch, Mann and Walshe, are exceptions to the general lack of association between field observations and laboratory experiments. Even so, few if any satisfactory explanations of the observed distribution and abundance of species have been proffered to date. All too often the observations of those concerned with benthic lake typology, the Saprobien System, or other successional changes in benthic fauna, have failed to stimulate, propose or conduct the laboratory tests necessary to their further refinement by developing good comparative studies. Many of the studies that have been made involve the use of resistant or tolerant species, and scant attention has been focused on the animals found in systems less noticeably affected by man.

Studies on the feeding of benthic invertebrates have been even scarcer than those on respiration. In this area we may cite Reynoldson, Marzolf, Hargrave, and Walshe as the basis of a small but select company. Many more specific studies have been done using benthic animals, but the primary aim of these has often been physiological rather than limnological. Some of the physiological work that has been done to date, however, suggests a word of caution to those tempted to reach into the literature for physiological demonstrations of the limits of tolerance of even these hardy species. As a result, discussion of this data will appear in a later section of the book devoted to the complex reality that tends to confound the creation of simplified theories.

Another of the main thrusts of early lake studies relates to zoogeography and the origin of lake faunas. Part of the early view of the lake as a microcosm was as much a consideration of the supposed separateness of the lake fauna from that of the surrounding land as it was an early appreciation of the complex interrelationships within the lake itself. The actual origins of lakes were described by Monard (1919) as having been the basis of a lively polemic for 50 years, and it was only the common agreement of a glacial origin of lake basins in Switzerland and northern Europe that led to an acceptance of the concept that much of the fauna must be of post-glacial origin and hence quite recent in the basins under consideration.

The concept of the glacial relict soon arose, beginning with a lecture by Loven to the Royal Swedish Academy in 1860 (Segerstrale, 1962), and has been pursued by a number of authors, often as a discrete zoogeographical problem. Ekman (1920, 1959), Holmquist (1959), Ricker (1959) and Segerstrale (1962) are among the most notable and recent contributors to this field, and the Swiss tradition is maintained by Juget (1967) who retains an interest in the problem. This area of concern does overlap more general limnological thought, however, in that once it was recognised that the fauna of lakes was not composed of unique higher taxa but merely a series of lacustrine species of well-known classes and orders (if not often those same species found in rivers and ponds), the question of the existence of two faunal elements became the focus of attention. The debate between Zschokke, Monard, Ekman and others over the existence of an upper and lower fauna inhabiting the shallow and deep regions respectively was related to the problem of vertical zonation that seemed to be obvious on the basis of a number of physical/chemical parameters and the distribution of plants. The existence of cold stenotherms (with temperature tolerances that do not appear to have been examined in the laboratory) seemed to suggest the existence of a group of early colonists or pre-glacial survivors that migrated around the receding ice fronts and are now trapped in hypolimnetic waters, and a still later set of immigrants moving from the shore into deeper water. This old concept is maintained by those who persist in regarding a littoral and a profundal fauna as though they were distinct entities, without realising that the microhabitats in some parts of the shallow areas of a lake differ from anything available in deep water, whereas silt-inhabiting deep water species can also be found in shallow water silts.

Discussion of the origins of faunas, and the probable marginal origin of recent immigrants (though aerial insects did not need to walk in from the edge in order to deposit eggs) led to a consideration of the numbers of species in relation to depth and, with the advent of quantitative methodology related to production studies by Ekman and Petersen, the total number of individuals and even the correlation of biomass with depth. Vertical distribution studies, the effect of migrations of the fauna on the kinds of patterns obtained, and the relationship of the patterns to certain types of lakes as defined by the typologists, formed the theoretical basis of much benthic limnology. Three of the major contributors to this discussion were Lundbeck, Eggleton and Deevey.

The older lake typology study as it relates to benthic organisms was developed by Thienemann along lines somewhat similar to those of the Saprobien System—the recognition of certain ecosystems by virtue of the presence of special indicator organisms. In this instance the chironomid larvae were the preferred group, although this turned out to be an unfortunate choice. The taxonomy of the immature stages of the aquatic Diptera is by no means complete even now, and much of the weakness of the system in the eyes of modern limnologists may be due more to the inadequacy of its systematic basis than to the intellectual shortcomings of the method, which can be modified to include relative abundance and the concept of indicator associations.

The typologists, and those concerned with vertical distribution, were attempting to relate the differences and similarities between lakes on the basis of regional descriptive studies, and so they provide a basic pair of themes to consider in reviewing the literature on benthos that has a limnological rather than zoological emphasis. Many of the best known limnologists have contributed to the debate on Thienemann's original classification and its subsequent modifications. Among these we should recognise Lundbeck, Deevey, Berg, and Brundin.

There are those who, assuming that the typologists were trying to set up a taxonomy of lakes akin to a series of distinct pigeon holes, would point out that lakes exist in a continuum rather than in discrete groups, and hence the basis of the typological approach is faulty. Those who adopt this view have not, perhaps, read the typologists, who continually emphasised that their lake types were, in fact, best looked upon as abstract ideals representing zones along a continuum. They also admitted the existence of several such sets of variables, however, and it is of interest to note that few remember the limitations set upon the use of the oligotrophic–mesotrophic–eutrophic array to which current limnologists are so fond of referring. In fact, before the engineers got hold of the term 'eutrophication', the limnologists had just about dispensed with the search for definable lake types, no matter how abstract, because of the complexity of those classification schemes that did emerge. An examination of these concepts may therefore be justified because we continue to use the terms developed in 'trophic-lake typology', and because our understanding of the function of aquatic systems may be aided by recognising the successional status of the species associations that can be detected in nature.

While the typologists and those concerned with vertical profiles may be said to focus their attention on distribution, the production biologist focuses on biomass or abundance. He may be concerned with the estimation of standing stock, or with the flow of energy (less often the flow of material), but he should, of course, be concerned with the *sizes of pools of material as well as the flow rates between them.* With the invention of a quantitative methodology of sorts, the estimation of production began, especially in terms of the needs of fishery biologists. Ekman, Alm, Lang, Lundbeck, Rawson, Northcote and Larkin, Deevey and Hayes may be mentioned as major contributors to this work, the latter in terms of the attempt to relate secondary production (usually measured as standing stock estimates obtained on the basis of one visit) to a few simple parameters of a lake such as morphometric ratios and total dissolved solids. Where these relationships appeared to be applicable to plankton and fish populations, they seemed to hold little promise where studies of the benthos were concerned, perhaps because the decomposition cycle was not precisely tuned to primary production, but a re-examination of the data makes us a little more optimistic. In any event, our third main theme will emphasise production biology. We do this while recognising that many of these studies have referred to the typological system which is supposed to be based on productivity, although it was defined by just about any other factor until such time as productivity estimates became feasible.

The focus of the subsequent discussion, then, is on the work of the synecologists in benthic limnology rather than the autecological studies of species. While it has become popular in recent times for 'reductionists' to be denigrated at the expense of 'holists' it is worth bearing in mind that the two approaches do, in fact, sustain one another. The detailed work of the autecologist is given direction and focus by reference to the sweeping generalisations of the holists, and the critical constraints of the grand theoretical schemata that should serve to modify and improve the ideas are frequently derived from the awkward facts of the specialist. Hence, while it is not possible to review the many disconnected facts about benthic species gathered by autecologists (who may have to adopt that approach by virtue of space, time and financial considerations), it is perhaps worth our while looking at the sources of variation that complicate the life of a would-be holist who might wish to make some use of the accumulated wisdom rather than adopting an entirely empirical approach to the search for correlations. For this reason, having reviewed the existing literature on the basis of the three main themes of typology, vertical distribution and production, we will then turn our attention to sources of variation as they apply to the type of information that has been accumulated, including the methodological questions of selection of sampling gear, sampling sites, time regimes and other key points so frequently ignored. Having examined the past and commented on recent developments, it seems logical to propose some of the ways in which benthic research may now progress.

2 LAKE TYPOLOGY

One of the single most important tasks undertaken in the earliest phases of any science is the reduction of a mass of empirical descriptive material to fit a logical scheme of classification. If the classification is soundly based on causal relationships, it may prove to be of immense predictive value as well as being a convenient shorthand. The Periodic Table of the chemical elements is probably the most obvious example of such a predictive classification. Such classifications of ecological entities have usually been beset by such a huge diversity of material that few logical schemata have emerged, but complexity *can* be accommodated in classification, as evidenced by the classification of the animal kingdom as a whole. The Linnaean system of nomenclature has been successfully applied to both animals and plants throughout a 200-year explosion of species descriptions. This binominal system, with its dendritic superstructure of successively finer divisions, foreshadowed the theory of Organic Evolution, and has absorbed modifications in methodology such as the advent of computers and the legalistic codification of the practice of nomenclature. The theoretical basis of the system, as stated in the Biological Species definition, has been seriously challenged because it is derived from the theory of evolution itself, and is 'non-operational' in today's terminology. Nonetheless, the system has enabled us to use a single word, such as 'mammal', to categorise and compress a mass of complex and voluminous data to a manageable concept. Despite our lack of an operational definition, it is possible to observe a group of individuals, such as Polar Bears, that are more like each other than the members of any other group, although each of these groups is composed of discrete individuals made up of a series of integrated morphological and physiological systems. The difficulty in moving to classifications of lakes is that we are forced to accept the view that they function as units as do single organisms. This is essentially the view proposed by Forbes (1887) in his classic description of the lake as a microcosm, but this view has been refuted by those who have demonstrated that a lake is part of an entire watershed system, affected not only by climate but by the geology, morphology and ecology of the catchment basin, and also by man. We might, therefore, have a drainage basin classification, but one further problem has to be examined. While the classification of the living world is in accord with evolutionary theory, it depends upon the recognition of real discontinuities between the basic units at any given point in time. As species change with time, it is apparent that these discontinuities may be blurred in some instances where speciation is incipient. The science of geomorphology indicates that lakes are relatively transient features of the landscape in the light of a geological time scale, and the concept of lake maturation has been imposed upon ideas of lake classification in an attempt to add an evolutionary component to the problem. The establishment of discrete groups of lakes has always proved difficult.

It is, perhaps, ironic that—as the focus shifts from structure to function in any biological discipline—the feedback to classification is often neglected and the older discipline is often made an object of scorn. The backlash is not long delayed, however, as students of function discover that perplexing discrepancies in data may be attributed to faulty identifications. Urgent cries are soon heard from applied biologists required to manage farms, forests, and fisheries, and to resolve conflicts arising from the need to preserve endangered wildlife while still controlling pest problems, when they find they cannot identify key components of their systems.

The most discussed question in limnology today may be the vexed issue of eutrophication, a 'physiological' response to overfertilisation of lakes (and perhaps rivers too) that has become confused with the geological evolutionary process. Its name is derived from a classification system that has survived despite a totally inadequate theoretical basis. While limnologists of 20–30 years ago were hoping to have sidetracked the vexed typology question, it has bounced back into the limelight as an article of faith, particularly among engineers lacking adequate limnological training. Hence the point in resurrecting the issue here. A causally-based classification would bring order out of chaos, and assist our attempts to manage aquatic systems.

From the outset, there were three different approaches involved. The major foundation was the system derived by Naumann (1919) from terminology first coined by Weber (1907) for bog soils. In the first source the terms 'eutrophic' and 'oligotrophic' were suggested to describe the quantity of plant nutrients present. Ironically, in view of subsequent developments, the contemplated evolutionary sequence ran from rich (eutrophic) to poor (oligotrophic), due to the process of leaching. Naumann was not concerned with benthic fauna, but was more interested in available plant nutrients, particularly nitrogen, phosphorus and calcium, the quantity of phytoplankton produced at the height of the season, as well as the type of sediments generated (gyttja in eutrophic lakes, dy in oligotrophic lakes). The colour of the water, due to humic material present, subdivided the oligotrophic category into clear and brown water systems. The classification implied that it was of regional application in that it reflected local edaphic factors, and it was also made abundantly clear that the lake types were abstract concepts. According to a translation of Naumann by W. Kretschmar:

> the three types distinguished by me are standard or ideal cases, which may occur under natural conditions in altered or intermediate forms (the establishment of lake types and a serial arrangement of lakes are quite different problems). Since the general appearance of a lake depends on all metabolic processes occurring within its water, this has been the basis for the establishment of lake types. In every lake type, metabolic processes are principally different! Thus, the lake types are defined according to their particular metabolic processes or . . . according to their particular biological production. Hence lake type is an abstract conception, representing a somewhat ideal classification of lakes with similar metabolic processes or similar biological production.

This 'primary economy' system was thoroughly reviewed by Elster (1958, 1962) and as it pays little attention to benthos, we will not dwell upon it at length.

The second approach is related to the system used for the detection of pollution, known as the Saprobien System (Kolkwitz and Marson, 1908, 1909) which is still used, in highly modified form, in river biology. This system attempted to codify the observed changes in dominant organisms related to organic pollution, more precisely to the organic content of the sediment and the depletion of oxygen created by its breakdown. According to this scheme, heavily polluted rivers were classified as polysaprobic, unpolluted waters as oligosaprobic, and there were, of course a mesosaprobic region and other subdivisions of these basic three. The system has become more and more complex by moving towards the recognition of the diagnostic value of species associations that take into account relative abundance rather than the mere presence of a few indicator species.

Any experienced field biologist familiar with one or two groups of organisms can make a rapid general assessment of a given habitat by checking on the commonest species that come to hand by taking a few qualitative samples. One can quickly tell if a lake bottom contains mostly oligochaetes, or *Chaoborus*, red chironomids or others, or a truly diverse fauna, by looking at the residue on a screen after washing a couple of Ekman grabs through it. Such a quick, crude estimate of dominance still has value in an initial survey to establish sampling points, but the results cannot be expressed statistically. Sampling with somewhat greater intensity complicates the picture, adds species, shows up local variation, and it is not until a really rigorous sampling procedure is adopted that a new perspective can be obtained. One then finds that the dominant species that are used to name the association are usually those same ones that are revealed by the first random cast. When Dr. M. G. Johnson was studying the Bay of Quinte it was necessary to select sites for intensive study long before it was possible to analyse all the extensive survey data. The sites he picked turned out to be in the middle of the associations delimited by the objective analyses performed later on that survey data.

The fault with the Saprobien System, and the Benthic Lake Typology system which mimics it, is that the user has to have a remarkable degree of professional status to have his experienced diagnosis accepted simply because he has seen the symptoms before (akin to the pronouncement of the medical consultant after the most superficial examination) or there has to be a huge detailed and costly survey done (just as the young houseman has to have a battery of laboratory tests to support his hypothesis) before anyone will act on the findings. Most critics of such schemata lack the security of a Thienemann but are not prepared to do the truly hard work needed to bring the study out of the confusing mediocrity created by using inappropriate statistics on inadequate data. A rough analysis of the relative abundance of the most important members of the fauna, particularly the relatively immobile macrobenthic organisms that live longer than microbiota (so that the speed of recovery from environmental change is not too great), can be used as a very valuable and quite sensitive monitoring system in studies of polluted rivers (Hynes, 1960) but it has not often been applied to lakes and the vexed issue of eutrophication. While the original Saprobien System as it applied to the microbiota was extended to the macrobenthos of rivers, it may also have been a prime source for the recognition of Baltic and sub-alpine lake types by Thienemann (1913, 1918, *et al.*). At first, the classification was based on differences between adjacent volcanic sink-hole lakes in the Eifelmaare region of southern Germany and their correlation with Baltic area and sub-alpine lakes. The relatively shallow lakes of the Baltic type suffer oxygen depletion in the hypolimnion during summer stratification, a phenomenon related to the production of phytoplankton blooms, and generate bottom faunas dominated by *Chironomus* larvae. The deeper, colder lakes contain *Tanytarsus* larvae rather than *Chironomus*, and retain high oxygen concentrations in the hypolimnion even during summer stagnation. These two 'lake types' again were abstractions . . .

> the ideal case brought into workable form, the essential pattern, which is never represented in nature in its simplification, but always uniquely developed. The individual expressions never correspond in all particulars to the type. If one investigates a lake typologically, one cannot expect the impossible from nature who, *if she is ever to be scientifically comprehended to any degree* in all her peculiarities, patterns and processes, *must be categorized*—(Thienemann, 1925, 1954).

On the basis of morphometry, oxygen content, sediment quality and the 'maturity' of the system, but above all the fauna (at first the Chironomidae, later many different organisms) this causal–ecological approach was steadily widened until a huge diversity of lake types was defined. This area has been reviewed by Järnefelt (1953), Deevey (1941), and Brundin (1949), as discussed below.

In the third system, regional studies attempted to demonstrate serial arrangements of lakes (Pearsall, 1921), but many scientists attempted to apply the 'trophic standard' nomenclature to general regions of the gradient. In benthic terms this often involved the quantity of benthos (Alm, 1922; Lundbeck, 1926; Deevey, 1941) in addition to the purely qualitative considerations raised earlier. Implicit in this is the assumption that the benthos responds more or less directly to the chemical/physical conditions that determine algal production in the photic zone.

The Benthic Lake Typologies

The supposed causal relationship between the factors determining summer and winter oxygen concentrations in stratified lakes (morphology, thermal regime, primary production and allochthonous materials of high BOD) and the ability of benthic organisms to survive these conditions (particularly their respiratory physiology) led Thienemann to classify lakes first into Baltic and alpine types, later equated to the eutrophic–oligotrophic (clear water) nomenclature developed by Naumann. The Thienemann system as developed by

TABLE 2.1. Lake types according to Thienemann (1925) (modified)

	Oligotrophic	Eutrophic	Dystrophic
Distribution	alpine and foot hills	Baltic lowlands and alps	mostly Scandinavia
Morphology	deep, narrow littoral	shallow, broad littoral	variable
Hypolimnion/Epilimnion	hypolimnion large	hypolimnion small	—
Water colour	blue-green	brown–green, green–yellow	yellow–brown
Transparency	great	small–very small	small
Water chemistry	poor in N and P humic material absent Ca variable	rich in N and P humic material slight Ca usually high	poor in N and P humic substances abundant Ca low
Suspended detritus	minimal	rich, planktogenic	rich, allochthonous
Deepest mud	non-saprobic	saprobic (gyttja)	peaty (dy)
O_2 in summer	60–70% minimum decrease even with depth	0–40% minimum decrease sharp in metalimnion	0–?% minimum decrease sharp in metalimnion
O_2 under ice	as above	shallow—as above deep—as oligotrophic	strongly depleted in deeper parts
Littoral plant production	low	rich	low
Plankton	low quantity, present at all depths, large diurnal migration, seldom blooms	large quantity, small diurnal migration often blooms	low quantity, rarely blooms
Benthos	diverse, *Tanytarsus* fauna, no *Chaoborus* 300–1000 animals/m² 1–4 g dry weight/m²	restricted, *Chironomus* fauna, *Chaoborus* usually present 2000–10 000/m² 100 g dry weight/m²	very restricted, *Chironomus* (no *C. anthracinus*) or none, *Chaoborus* probably always present 10–20/m² or none
Distribution with depth	constant	decreasing	
Further succession	to eutrophy	to pond or meadow	to peat–moor

1925 (table 2.1) is much more complex than the *Tanytarsus*/*Chironomus* division originally suggested. *Chironomus anthracinus* (= *bathophilus*, *liebelibathophilus*) is taken to be sensitive to winter deoxygenation, *C. plumosus* to summer stagnation. The system included only stratifying lakes, and included *Chaoborus* (as *Corethra*), but the latter was rejected first by Lundbeck (1926) and eventually by Lang (1931) because of its questionable affiliation with the true benthos and the sampling problems that this engenders. The larval systematics of the chironomids was later reviewed by Lenz (1954) and a simplified version of the classification was outlined by Berg (1938) in a form somewhat like the adaptation in table 2.2.

Alm (1922) was interested in the relative standing stocks of fish and benthos, but he applied his quantitative as well as his qualitative data on chironomids and other organisms to the subject of lake typology (table 2.3). Again, the simple oligotrophic–eutrophic division was further subdivided according to the fauna present, using such broad categories as oligochaetes and amphipods. Subsequent authors consider his *Tanypus* type to be compound. The amphipod type approaches Thienemann's *Tanytarsus* type, and the oligochaete lakes are merely polluted or meromictic according to Deevey (1941), who also referred the *Otomesostoma* type to the *Orthocladius* or *Stictochironomus* lakes of others.

In an extensive monograph that treated many aspects of benthic biology, Lundbeck (1926) derived the system outlined in table 2.4. It is apparent that we now have a *two-dimensional* scheme, allowing for the interaction of the trophic lake typology (seen as related to ageing, as expressed by the development of organically rich sediments with time, and hence proceeding from oligotrophy to eutrophy) with the complex question of the influence of the degree of dystrophy, or humic acid content of the sediment. This humic factor was a major cause of conflict between the views of Thienemann and Naumann, who proposed essentially one-dimensional schemes, which conflicted both with each other and with that of Lundbeck.

TABLE 2.2. The lake classification of Thienemann (1925) according to Berg (1938)

(1) *Tanytarsus* (oligotrophic) lakes	(2) *Chironomus* (mostly eutrophic) lakes			(3) *Chaoborus* lakes without *Chironomus*
Tanytarsus characteristic, *Chaoborus* absent, deep water oxygen levels always high (>58% in summer, >77% in winter). Relict crustacea present in baltic regions	*Chironomus* larvae with tubuli characteristic, summer oxygen values <40%, winter oxygen variable			*Chironomus* is absent from all regions, oxygen concentrations in deep water 6–12%, below ice 5–20%
	(a) No *Chaoborus*. Summer oxygen about 30–60%. Relict crustacea present in Baltic regions	(b) *Chaoborus* present. Summer oxygen values <40%, winter oxygen variable		
		(b) (i) *anthracinus* (*Bathophilus*) lakes—with *Chironomus anthracinus* (*liebeli-bathophilus*) in profundal: 3 further subtypes dependent upon relative abundance of *C. anthracinus* and *C. plumosus* and oxygen values	(b) (ii) *plumosus* lakes—with *C. plumosus* in the profundal: 2 types depends upon presence of *C. anthracinus* and oxygen values	

While the eventual completion of the ageing process was thought to lead to the formation of first semi-terrestrial and then terrestrial conditions, Lundbeck held that the endpoint differed depending upon the humic acid component of the accumulated sediments. He compared his data with those of Koppe and Utermöhl (cited in Lundbeck, 1926) on the ranking of the same lakes according to sediments and phytoplankton, and with the earlier studies by Thienemann. He found the agreement generally good, but some lakes (such as Ukleisee, Germany) differed as the type species (*C. anthracinus*) found by Thienemann could no longer be found—an early indication that lake typology should not be based on short visits and few samples. Lundbeck rejected several of Thienemann's more complex subdivisions, omitted *Chaoborus* from the system and noted that Alm's categories included relict species of limited geographical range, along with some categories defined on a broad systematic base (such as oligochaetes as a whole) but nonetheless he did attempt to correlate Alm's lake types with his own. He found only two *Tanytarsus* lakes in northern Germany, one of which Koppe and Utermöhl (cited in Lundbeck, 1926) had called eutrophic on the basis of their evidence, but he was aware of the fact that meso- and polyhumic lakes, in the early stages of maturation are not *Tanytarsus* lakes. He also found some lakes with irregular oxygen/depth curves which contained *C. anthracinus* (= *bathophilus*) plus *Tanytarsus*, and used transitional designations for them. Lenz (1925, 1928*a*, 1928*b*) also described intermediate lake types on the basis of chironomids sent to him from Norway

TABLE 2.3. Summary of the Swedish lake types according to Alm (1922)

	Eutrophic	Oligotrophic				
	Chironomus (*Plumosus*) type	Oligochaete type	*Tanypus* type	Amphipod type	*Chaoborus* (*Corethra*) type	*Otomesostoma* type
Water colour	muddy grey–green–brown at times clear	usually muddy grey–green–brown	yellow–green–brown at times clear colourless	clear colourless	brown to dark brown	clear or grey–green
Phyto-plankton production	high; often blooming	usually high; often blooming	moderately low; often no blooms	low; never blooming	low; usually no blooms	extraordinarily low; seldom blooming
Acidity in the depth	summer time and at times late winter usually low, often none	often low during the summer	varying however most often high	always high	varying often low or none	probably always high
Bottom composition	typical sludge at times clay or lime rich. Pyrit frequent	sludge often mixed with clay, sand, etc.	brownish sludge or miry clay, often rich in plant fragments (detritus)	sludge, sand, clay	typical mire or peat mire at times sludge supersaturated with plant compost	stone, sand, clay, sludge
Size and depth	small or large; usually shallow and warm lakes	larger or medium large; deeper but nevertheless warm lakes	small to large; shallow or deep, warm or cold lakes	usually large and always deep lakes	most often smaller peat-bog lakes or lakes that are overgrown	larger or smaller mountain lakes cold deep or shallow
Benthic production	high 20–60 or more animals and least 0.1–0.2 gram often considerably more per 10 dm^2	moderately high, however varying; 15–16 animals and 0.06–0.3 gram per 10 dm^2	medium high; 6–50 animals and 0.03–0.1 gram per 10 dm^2	probably high, however to a great extent changeable with the bottom composition	particularly low, only isolated animals and highest ca. 0.03 gram per 10 dm^2	probably low, in southerly mountain lakes, however relatively high
Faunal composition	most important *Chironomus plumosus*. Oligochaetes constantly present *Ceratopogon* increase with content of pyrit *Valvata* and others with content of lime	*Chironomus* of different types and besides most often dominant. Large oligochaetes and *Pontoporeia*	*Chironomus* of many types however probably always *Tanypus* oligochaetes rather common *Pisidium* often in abundance and *Ephemera* at times rather common	species-rich fauna of *Eutanytarsus*, oligochaetes, Turbellaria and most often relicts are common	*Chironomus* of different types *Ceratopogon* and oligochaetes and most often *Corethra* in large abundance	at times fairly species-rich *Chironomus* of different types oligochaetes, Turbellaria and among them *Otomesostoma*, *Pisidium*, etc.

TABLE 2.4. Lake typology from Lundbeck (1926) (after Naumann, 1931)

			Oligohumic		Mesohumic		Polyhumic	
			A true gyttja	A′ leaf gyttja	B′ dy gyttja	B leaf dy	C′ dy	C dy
Oligotrophic	*Tanytarsus* lake	I	*Tanytarsus* community	—	—	—	—	unknown *Chironomus* community
Oligotrophic	*Tanytarsus-Bathophilus* lake	I′	*Tanytarsus-Bathophilus* community		unknown *Tanytarsus* or *Bathophilus* community	—	—	unknown *Chironomus* community
Eutrophic	*Bathophilus* lake	II	*Bathophilus* community		*Bathophilus* community		—	—
Eutrophic	*Bathophilus-Plumosus* lake	II′	*Bathophilus-Plumosus* community			—	—	—
Eutrophic	*Plumosus* lake	III	*Plumosus* community			unknown *Chironomus* or *Plumosus* community	—	—

TABLE 2.5. Lake typology of Decksbach (1929) (after Naumann, 1931)

			Oligohumic		Mesohumic		Polyhumic	
			A true gyttja	A′ leaf gyttja	B′ dy gyttja	B leaf dy	C′ dy	C dy
Oligotrophic	*Tanytarsus* lake	I	*Tanytarsus* community	—	—	—	—	unknown *Chironomus* community
Oligotrophic	*Tanytarsus Bathophilus* lake	I′	*Tanytarsus–Bathophilus* community		—	—	—	unknown *Chironomus* community
Oligotrophic		I″	—	—	unknown *Chironomus*— or *Bathophilus* community		—	*Plumosus* community
Intermediate	*Sergentia Stictochironomus* lake	UI	*Sergentia Stictochironomus* community	—	—	—	—	—
Intermediate	*Stictochironomus-Sergentia* lake	UI′	*Stictochironomus Sergentia* community	—	*Sergentia-Plumosus* community	—	—	—
Intermediate	*Sergentia Bathophilus Plumosus* lake	UII	*Sergentia Bathophilus Plumosus* community	—	—	—	—	—
Eutrophic	*Bathophilus* lake	II	*Bathophilus* community			*Bathophilus* community	—	—
Eutrophic	*Bathophilus Plumosus* lake	II′	*Bathophilus–Plumosus* community			—	—	—
Eutrophic	*Plumosus* lake	III	*Plumosus* community			—	—	—

(the *Stictochironomus* type is mesotrophic, and there is also a *Sergentia* type) and concluded that chironomid genera (or larvae) with a similar morphology must represent ecological equivalents. This view was effectively refuted by Brundin (1949). Decksbach (1929) extended Lundbeck's system somewhat (table 2.5) by studying lakes in the infertile moor areas of the Russian steppes. He indicated that some dystrophic lakes sometimes start as shallow moor pools, rather than by the gradual filling in of a deeper lake.

The intermediate, mesotrophic type was recognised by Valle (1927), but he categorised the three basic trophic types into a large number of subdivisions according to their benthos (table 2.6 a–c). Like Alm, he included organisms other than chironomids, and he also noted the influence of the local soils and plant associations in the watersheds of his Karelian lakes. Further, he recognised the paucity of benthos in Fennoscandian lakes, and the discussed causal relationship between temperature and benthos. Some of his lakes do not stratify (*vide* Thienemann), but he seemingly overlooked the differences between what became known as harmonic and disharmonic oligotrophy (see below). Other terms were coined for special types of lakes. Pesta (1929) studied shallow, high-alpine lakes and described a panoligotrophic type (table 2.7), while Järnefelt (1925, *et seq.*) extended the schemes of Alm and Valle in Finland, and in 1929 described a paramixo–eutrophic type. Lastockin (1931) studied Russian lakes, again calcium-poor moor lakes, all small and shallow, and felt that Järnefelt's eutrophic lakes with humic features were essentially eutrophic, but he pointed out that some lakes showed horizontal heterotrophy (often the effect of bays or river deltas) or vertical heterotrophy where benthos from various parts of the lake does not correspond to the more uniform

TABLE 2.6*a*. The lake typology of Valle (1927): Eutrophic type

	Plumosus	Tubifex	Tubifex–Corethra	Tubifex–Pontoporeia
Soil type	fertile, clay rock	fertile, clay, morraines	fertile, clay, rocky	fertile, clay, very rocky
Morphometry	steep shore rather shallow	broad shore with deep locales	broad shore with deep locales	relatively deep, 22 m maximum steep shores
Transparency and colour	variable, vegetational	turbid, vegetational	turbid, vegetation and humus (red–brown)	variable, relatively turbid, vegetational
Stratification	2-layered, cool depth epi- and meta-limnion	2-layered, cool depth epi- and meta-limnion	temporarily 2-layered, cool in summer	3-layered, hypolimnion cold
O_2	low near bottom	low near bottom	low near bottom	low near bottom, a decrease in metalimnion relatively high in hypolimnion
Sediments	coarse-detritus gyttja	clay, fine-detritus gyttja iron ore	clay, fine detritus gyttja, iron ore	clay, fine detritus gyttja, no iron
Abundance of profundal fauna	abundant, species-poor	abundant, diverse	relatively rich, diverse	notably abundant
Kinds of benthos	chironomids, fewer oligo-chaetes, a few *Corethra*, no *Pisidium*	oligochaetes, chironomids, fewer *Pisidium*, no *Corethra*	oligochaetes, chironomids, *Corethra*, fewer *Pisidium*	oligochaetes, chironomids amphipods, all else rare
Characteristic forms	*C. plumosus*	*Tubifex*, *C. plumosus*, *Polypedilum*, *Monodiamesa*, *Cryptochironomus*	*Tubifex*, *Corethra*, *C. batho-philus*, *Polypedilum*, *Pisidium casertaneum*, *Tanypus*	*Tubifex*, *Pontoporeia*, *Ch. salinarius Stictochironomus*, *Monodiamesa*, *Sergentia*
	1 lake	1 lake	1 lake	1 lake

TABLE 2.6*b*. The lake typology of Valle (1927): Mesotrophic type

	Pisidium–Corethra	Lumbriculus–relict	Pisidium–Sergentia
Soil type	moderately fertile, rocky, morraines and clay	moderately fertile, rocky, morraines and clay	sand, moderately fertile near some parts of lakes
Morphometry	shallow, steep-shored	deep, steep-shored	rather shallow
Transparency and colour	turbid, clear to red or rust-brown, temporary vegetational colour	clear–very clear, yellow-brown, humus variable	very clear, yellow–green to brown–yellow, humus very to moderately low
Stratification	2-layered, small metalimnion	3-layered, cold hypolimnion	1-layered, warm
O_2 in summer	moderately to very low in metalimnion	only very near bottom, if ever, low	decreases near bottom
Sediments	dy-gyttja, less humidified dy	dy-gyttja, less humidified dy	dy-gyttja, less humidified dy, sand underlayer
Abundance of profundal fauna	variable, rather great, diverse	variable, rarely sparse, diverse	variable, very abundant, *not* diverse
Benthos	*Pisidium*, chironomids, fewer oligochaetes	oligochaetes, relict crustacea, chironomids, *Pisidium*	*Pisidium* and chironomids, few oligochaetes
Characteristic forms	*Pisidium lilljeborgi*, *P. casertaneum*, *P. henslowanum*, *Corethra*, *Limnodrilus udekemianus*, *Tanypus*, *Stictochironomus*, *Monodiamesa* sometimes common	*Mysis*, *Pontoporeia*, *Pallasea*, *Pisidium conventus*, *Lumbriculus* —*Stictochironomus* and *Monodiamesa* rather abundant	*P. lilljeborgi*, *Sergentia*, sometimes *P. casertaneum* is common
	2 lakes	3 lakes	2 lakes

TABLE 2.6*c*. The lake typology of Valle (1927): Oligotrophic type

	Pisidium	Stictochironomus–Pisidium	Sialis–Chironomid	Stictochironomus
Soil type	poor Ås, sandy morraine	dry Ås	sterile moor and morraines	very sterile moor and Ås
Morphometry	relatively to very shallow	composite basin, locally deep	shallow	rather shallow
Transparency and colour	turbid, more or less red–brown	turbid, very red–brown	turbid, very red–brown	turbid, very red–brown
Stratification	1 to 2-layered, warm or cool	3-layered, cold hypolimnion	1-layered, warm or cool	1-layered, rather cold
O_2	high to very high	decrease in epilimnion; in deeper water, fairly high	at least temporarily low	decrease near surface of water, not very low at bottom
Sediments	iron, dy, over sand	iron, dy, over sand	iron, dy, over sand	iron, dy, over sand
Littoral vegetation	sparse, shallow	sparse, shallow	sparse, shallow	sparse, shallow
Abundance of profundal fauna	relatively or very sparse	poor, not diverse	poor, not diverse	absent from deeps, patchy poor
Kinds	*Pisidium*, few chironomids	chironomids, fewer *Pisidium*, a few *Corethra*	chironomids, *Sialis*, *Pisidium* and *Corethra* rare	only chironomids
Characteristic forms	*P. lilljeborgi*, *P. casertaneum*, *P. carelicum*, *Stictochironomus*, *Monodiamesa* or *Didiamesa*, occasionally *P. conventus*	*Stictochironomus*, *Pisidium lilljeborgi*, others rare	*Sialis flavilatera*, fewer *C. bathophilus*, *Tanypus*, *Cladopelma* (*Limnochironomus*)	*Stictochironomus* others rare
	4 lakes	1 lake	1 lake	1 lake

TABLE 2.7. The panoligotrophic (later ultraoligotrophic) lake type
Pesta (1929)

Character	Oligotrophic	Panoligotrophic
Geography	alps and sub-alps	high alps
Morphometry	deep, narrow littoral shelf, hypolimnion ≫ epilimnion	shallow, mainly narrow littoral, hypolimnion ⩽ epilimnion
Colour and transparency	blue to green; great	blue to green; great
Water chemistry	nutrient and humus poor Ca variable	nutrient and humus poor Ca variable
Suspended detritus	very little or none	if present, mineral or allochthonous
Sediments	low in organics, not gyttja	little or no organic matter
Oxygen	abundant, down to 70 or 60% above bottom	everywhere > 90 (or 80)%
Littoral plants	sparse	sparser
Plankton	sparse, wide daily vertical migration, blooms rare, green algae > blue greens	sparse, migration limited by depth, blooms absent, diatoms > green algae
Littoral limits	weakly expressed by plants, no sublittoral	no true profundal, sublittoral poorly defined
Deep water fauna	stenoxybiontic, diversity high, *Tanytarsus*	diversity low, euryoxybiont (?) identity unknown, ? Paratanytarsus
Benthos	*Chaoborus* absent	*Chaoborus* rare
Abundance	300/m^2, 1–4 mg	relatively poor, amount unknown
Deepwater *Coregonus* spp.	usually present	absent
Maturation, filling in	to eutrophic lake	? through shallow oligotrophic lake to eutrophic 'Tümpel'

trophic classification based on algae. Despite this insight into one of the most serious criticisms of lake typology, see p. 88, he simply defined a mixotrophic category for non-classifiable lakes!

The lake typology system was criticised by Alsterberg (1930) who emphasised the importance of transient microstratifications of chemical conditions at the mud/water interface, as well as the weakness of assessing the trophic status of a lake on the basis of only a few samples. By 1931, Naumann had extended the general theory, separating harmonic from disharmonic lakes—the latter being lakes in which the quantity of a single

TABLE 2.8*a*. Chemical characteristics of some lake types according to Naumann (1931)

Type	Ca	N and P	Fe	Humic acids	Suspended clay	pH
Alkalitrophic	polytypic	oligotypic	oligotypic	oligotypic	oligo- to mesotypic	8
Argillotrophic	oligo- to polytypic	oligo- to polytypic	?	oligo- to polytypic	polytypic	7
Eutrophic	oligo- to polytypic	meso- to polytypic	oligotypic	oligo-meso-typic	oligo- to mesotypic	7
Oligotrophic in a strict sense	oligotypic	oligotypic	oligotypic	oligo-meso-typic	oligo- to mesotypic	7
Acidotrophic	oligotypic	oligotypic	oligotypic	oligo-meso-typic	oligo- to mesotypic	7
Dystrophic	oligotypic	oligotypic	meso- to polytypic	meso- to polytypic	oligo- to mesotypic	7
Siderotrophic	oligotypic	oligotypic	meso- to polytypic	oligo- to polytypic	oligo- to mesotypic	7

TABLE 2.8*b*. Biological characteristics of various lake types after Naumann (1931)

Type	Water	Phytoplankton	Higher plants	Bottom deposits
Alkalitrophic	clear; colour never yellow or brown	low production	typically luxuriant	lake-chalk, partly calcareous gyttja, shell-gyttja
Argillotrophic	turbid from clay	low to high production	typically luxuriant	clay-gyttja, partly gyttja-clay, probably also algal gyttja
Eutrophic	turbid from algae	high production	typically luxuriant	fine-detritus gyttja, partly coarse-detritus gyttja, partly shell-gyttja
Oligotrophic S.Str.	clear; colour never yellow or brown	low production	weakly developed	fine-detritus gyttja, coarse-detritus gyttja
Acidotrophic	clear	low production	weakly developed	?
Dystrophic	clear; colour yellow to brown	low production	weakly developed	lake-dy
Siderotrophic	clear; colour often yellow to brown	low production	weakly developed	diatomaceous 'ochre', lake-ore

chemical element detracts from the trophic potential of the lake (table 2.8) and ended up with twenty subdivisions. The terms paraeutrophic and paraoligotrophic were used for the disharmonic lake series. He objected to the Thienemann–Lundbeck school because they tended to downplay the role of primary production, but he felt that his scheme could be applied to all freshwater systems. Lang (1931) felt that the existing classifications were premature, and reckoned that there were already more than sixty lake types, but he proceeded to employ a new scheme—his inadequate sampling method probably accounting for the lack of diversity of benthos described in those of his lakes which did not fit any of the existing lake types. When Brundin (1949) revised Lang's study of Lake Straken in Sweden, he found a much more diverse fauna than that reported earlier. Lang, however, did attempt to test some predictions about the respiratory abilities of *Chironomus* species.

Thienemann (1931) decided that the division between harmonic and disharmonic lakes was even more fundamental than the oligotrophic–eutrophic division. He did not find the diversity of dystrophic lakes revealed in later studies, although by now he had extended the chironomid system to include tropical lakes. Lenz (1933) defended the system, and Miyadi (1933) employed chironomids and other organisms in his classification of Japanese lakes (table 2.9) with a system based on the causal-ecological concept. He then compared this to data on the trophic standard typology, acknowledging the difference between the two systems. His mollusc lake type is aberrant in that there is no true profundal zone in such lakes. His *Chaoborus* lakes are very small, moderately shallow, and suffer severe oxygen depletion in summer, but as (1) iron is not limiting, (2) the benthos is abundant, and (3) there is little humic material, they do not correspond with the European lakes so named. Again, the polytrophic-*plumosus* type is probably aberrant in that it is polymictic and is shallow with readily decomposable organic sediments. Blue-green algae bloom repeatedly, and very high standing stocks of benthos are recorded in comparison with other Japanese lakes. In general, these Japanese lakes are low in calcium, nitrogen and phosphorus and are weakly buffered. Among the oligotrophic types it is odd to note an oligotrophic-*plumosus* category, which Deevey (1941) discussed in relation to the effect of iron on this nitrogen-phosphorus-poor lake with a morphometrically determined eutrophic type oxygen curve.

TABLE 2.9. Lake types as defined by Miyadi (1933)

Yoshimura's type	Names of lakes	Locality	Max. depth (m)	Type of bottom fauna
Poly- or eutrophic	Suwa-ko	Nagano	7	polytrophic *plumosus*
	Kasumiga-ura	Ibaraki	7	polytrophic *plumosus*
	Kita-ura	Ibaraki	9	polytrophic *plumosus*
	Tôro-ko	Hokkaidô	6	polytrophic *plumosus*
	Inba-numa	Tiba	2	mollusca (with *plumosus*)
	Kawaguti-ko	Yamanasi	15	mesotrophic *plumosus*
	Takasuka-numa	Saitama	6	*Corethra* (with *plumosus*)
Mesotrophic	Nakatuna-ko	Nagano	13	*Corethra* (with *plumosus*)
	Yogo-ko	Siga	14	*Corethra* (with *plumosus*)
	Konuma	Hokkaidô	5	mesotrophic *plumosus*
	Onuma	Hokkaidô	13	mesotrophic *plumosus*
	Yuno-ko	Totiki	13	mesotrophic *plumosus*
	Yamanaka-ko	Yamanasi	15	mesotrophic *plumosus*
	Syôzi-ko	Yamanasi	16	mesotrophic *plumosus*
	Hibara-ko	Hukusima	31	mesotrophic *plumosus*
	Akimoto-ko	Hukusima	34	mesotrophic *plumosus*
	Yukunaki-numa	Hukusima	18	*Tanytarsus–Endochironomus*
	Kizaki-ko	Sinano	29	*Tanytarsus–Endochironomus*
	Aoki-ko	Sinano	58	*Tanytarsus–Endochironomus*
Oligotrophic	Numazawa-numa	Hukusima	92	*Tanytarsus–Endochironomus*
	Odaira-numa	Hukusima	36	*Tanytarsus–Endochironomus*
	Asino-ko	Kanagawa	43	*Tanytarsus*
	Nisino-umi	Yamanasi	73	*Tanytarsus*
	Inawasiro-ko	Hukusima	96	*Tanytarsus*
	Motosu-ko	Yamanasi	133	*Tanytarsus*
	Tyûzenzi-ko	Totiki	166	*Tanytarsus*
	Tazawa-ko	Akita	425	*Tanytarsus*
	Sikotu-ko	Hokkaidô	363	oligochaeta
	Kurata-ko	Hokkaidô	146	oligochaeta
	Tôya-ko	Hokkaidô	183	oligochaeta
	Kirigome-ko	Totiki	16	oligotrophic *plumosus*
	Karigome-ko	Totiki	15	oligotrophic *plumosus*
	Saino-ko	Totiki	19	oligotrophic *plumosus*

Lundbeck's second major contribution (1936) tabulated data on surface area depth, sediment, transparency, water colour, distribution of littoral vegetation and benthos of some deep alpine lakes, as a result of which he modified his classification (table 2.10), and indicated the number of lakes in each category (table 2.11). He proposed two oligotrophic benthic subtypes—the *Orthocladius* and *Tanytarsus* lakes. In the former, *Orthocladius* dominated *Tanytarsus* which was, in turn, more abundant than *Pisidium*, the association being apparently sensitive to the effect of river-transported allochthonous material or its accumulation in bays and near habitations. Berg and Petersen (1956) stated that the category was recognised by Thienemann and other authors prior to Lundbeck, and it is now generally understood that orthocladiine species increase in number with decreasing annual mean temperature, and are found particularly in lakes of high altitude or latitude. Within this category Lundbeck placed the Bodensee (Germany/Switzerland) and Lago Maggiore (Italy) as well as Vättern and Lac Léman (Switzerland). His *Tanytarsus* lakes, (which are shallower, and have a more organic sediment than *Orthocladius* lakes) are found in the peripheral valleys farther from the alps themselves. Lakes such as Lago di Como and Zürich See in Switzerland were held to be affected by river inflow or by man (see page 97) so that they were artificially created *Tanytarsus* lakes

TABLE 2.10. Morphological and hydrographical characteristics of individual lake type according to Lundbeck (1936) (modified)

Lake type	Surface area (ha) mean	max.	min.	Max. depth (m) (of all lakes) mean	max.	min.	Mean depth (m) mean	max.	min.	Type of bottom	Trans-parency (m)	Forel-Ule scale water colour	Max. depth (m) of littoral vegetation
A Ia (*Orthocladius*)	15 774	47 548	2423	250	372	151	138	176	90	<5% organic, semisolid, clayey loam	4–7 (1–20)	4–6 (3–7)	20–30
A Ib (*Tanytarsus*)	4236	8014	924	123	214	73	50	104	24	similar, slightly higher organic content	6–10 (2–13)	6–9 (4–10)	8–18
A I/IIa (*Stictochironomus*)	98	129	68	30	34	25	17	20	14	mineral gyttja, Ca. 20% organic content	3–12	9 (5–10)	12–15
A I/IIb (*Sergentia*)	513	856	219	30	33	23	15	17	13	same as A I/IIa	4–5 (2–9)	10–11 (9–13)	6–10
A IIa (*Ch. anthracinus*)	(321) (1 lake)	—	—	32	36	25	17	19	13	mineral-poor gyttja >50% organic content	2–3	11 (8–11)	?
A IIb (*Chir.*) *anthracinus* + *plumosus*	352	765	193	19	35	11	8	11	5	same as A IIa	3–4 (3–8)	11–12 (10–13)	4–6
A′ I/IIb	53	780	(20)	42	59	(34)	—	26	—	H_2S more abundant, Ca higher, sediment with leaf detritus	6–7 (4–12)	4–8 (6–7)	15
B′ I/IIb (*Sergentia*)	(177)	1 lake		(35)						soft, humus-brown mud low in Ca and other minerals	10–13	9	8
B′ IIc *Ch. plumosus* ?	99	186	12	14	17	12	—	6	—	soft, humus-brown mud low in Ca and other minerals	3	12	7
B IIc *Ch. plumosus* ?	19	33	8	10	15	6	5	7	4	soft, humus-brown mud low in Ca and other minerals	2–5	12–15	3–4

I = oligotrophic; I/II = mesotrophic; II = eutrophic. A = harmonic; A′ = harmonic with much leaf detritus; B = mesohumic.

TABLE 2.11. Numbers of lakes of each type in northern Germany and the alpine peripheral region modified from Lundbeck (1936)

Type (step)		Northern Germany Series A	B	together	%	Alps Series A	B	together	%
I	*Orthocladius*	—	—	—	10	7	—	7	43
	Tanytarsus	6	—	6		11	—	11	
I/II	*Stictochironomus*	—	—	—	2	3	—	3	24
	Sergentia	1	—	1		6	1	7	
II	*Chironomus anthracinus*	1	8	9	88	4	—	4	33
	anthrac.-plum.	14	3	17		4	—	4	
	plumosus	17	8	25		—	6	6	

that were originally (from morphometrical evidence) *Orthocladius* lakes. Later evidence also suggested changes in the classification of lakes such as Bodensee and Lago Maggiore, and one difficulty in using a series of fragmentary studies of a lake to compile a composite picture of it for classification purposes is that seemingly conflicting information may be created by temporal or spatial heterogeneity as well as taxonomic errors or sampling inadequacies. The terms 'primary' and 'secondary' were used to express the difference between lakes in which the benthos conformed to predictions made from morphometry and those in which it did not. Despite the recognition that a long list of species would categorise lakes better than one or two 'types' which might be missing for a variety of reasons, limitation of larval taxonomy and inadequate sampling equipment and programmes prevented the establishment of such lists.

Although he was critical of Lundbeck, Pagast (1943) also can be regarded as of the Thienemann school. He did point out a need to extend the sampling period to include more than one season, and that associated species are of value, as well as the fact that alpine lakes almost invariably have the same chironomids at the same absolute depth zones regardless of trophic standard. It was therefore obvious that the depth at which samples are taken may unduly influence one's views.

The complexity of faunal associations, and the varying ecology of each species, caused Wesenberg-Lund (1943) to reject the whole concept of a simple typological series of lakes categorised by their faunal elements. He pointed out the degree to which valuable concepts had become enshrined as articles of faith by those unwilling to reappraise them critically in the light of experience. The British seem to have inherited the Wesenberg-Lund approach and have remained sceptical of both the European systems and the American preoccupation with energy flow and material cycling without a firm base in taxonomy. This view finds expression in Macan's valuable survey of the studies of the English lakes (1970) as well as in his earlier volume (1963) where the subject of energy flow is minimised. There is here, however, an emphasis on the difference between the sequence of lakes as envisaged by Pearsall (1921) and the European categorisation of lakes—but if Pearsall was prepared to group lakes together, and the Europeans emphasised the abstract quality of their groupings, there is, in fact, little difference between the two schools of thought as expressed by the originators. It commonly happens that disciples codify and adhere rigidly to a formalised version of what had been only a working hypothesis of its creator—and one he would probably have modified in the light of later experience.

Deevey (1941), in a comparative limnological study of thirty-six Connecticut and New York lakes, reviewed and criticised benthic lake typology up to this point and, like Miyadi, he used a system based primarily upon chironomids, a group that appears to be more diverse in North America than in other parts of the world. His attempt to correlate benthos with oxygen curves was less successful than the dogmatic assertions of the European school of thought would suggest, but the redox potential of the sediment surface appeared to be a better guide. It was suggested that the influence of iron was particularly noticeable in some of these Connecticut lakes—and a brief comment reminds the reader that the harmonic series alone has been discussed in terms of benthos. The fundamental distinction between *Chironomus* and *Tanytarsus* lakes is well illustrated by Deevey's data, as for instance in the detailed comparison of Job Pond and Lake Quarsapaug, and there is a correlation between benthic biomass and total lake chlorophyll. The latter was judged to be related to the influence of mean depth on total versus trophogenic zone chlorophyll, but mean depth alone was not closely correlated with biomass. All of the lakes of this region are reasonably similar, and the whole assemblage is somewhat mesotrophic in character. Chironomid larval systematics has so far bedeviled any attempt to relate American lake types to European lakes of the same designation and only Stahl (1959, 1966) has managed to fit American lakes into the European schemata, finding *Sergentia coracina* in three Indiana lakes which had the best oxygen supply of the sixteen examined, and in one of these *Tanytarsus* was found. The other lakes contained *Chironomus* or, where oxygen levels were exceedingly low at times, only *Chaoborus*. In Myres lake, and in Tippecanoe, which now contain *Chironomus* and *Chaoborus*, *Sergentia* heads were found in the sediment, but Stahl suggested that gradual diminution of the hypolimnion had led to the increasing severity of oxygen stress, not changes in productivity over time.

After studying a number of shallow lakes on the border between Finland and Sweden, Brundin (1942) demonstrated a rough correspondence between depth, iron concentration, suspended humus and benthos. While his lakes had much in common with those of Valle, Lenz and Järnefelt, discrepancies between his work and that of Lang were attributed to the limitations of Lang's methodology. In a second contribution (1949) several major advances were made (table 2.12). The importance of stenothermy in geographical distribution of chironomid species was added to the concept of oxygen limitation, and the significance of barriers to dispersal, such as mountain ranges, was indicated. Such difficulties, as well as problems related

TABLE 2.12. The lake classification of Brundin (1949)

Ultraoligotrophic	Oligotrophic	Oligotrophic–humic	Eutrophic lakes
Very cold profundal, inorganic sediments Arctic—cold temperate, larger and deeper with lower latitude, categorised by *Heterotrissocladius subpilosus*, other species include *Protanypus caudatus*, *Procladius barbatus*, *Paracladopelma obscura*	In gymnosperm boreal forests and mountains, clearest examples being calcium deficient oligohumic lakes. Type species mostly regional (1) stably stratified: *Stictochironomus rosenschöldi* association: *T. lugens*, *Monodiamesa ekmani*, *Heterotrissocladius määri*, ? *H. subpilosus*, *Sergentia coracina*, *Paracladopelma obscura* (2) polymictic–oligotrophic: *Tanytarsus* association: *H. määri*, *Tanytarsus* spp. *Monodiamesa bathyphila*, *Protanypus morio*, *H. grimshawi et al.* (3) metastable oligotrophic: *Chironomus anthracinus* (small numbers)	Low production, high humus, low oxygen concentrations (1) mesohumic or polymictic –polyhumic: *Stictochironomus rosenschöldi* association, with Tanytarsini excluded with increasing humic content (2) stratified polyhumic: *Chironomus tenuistylus*, *Trissocladius naumanni*, *Sergentia longiventris*	discussed from the literature

to the volume of the hypolimnion in relation to the quantity of decomposable material received by it and hence the oxygen deficit or lack of it, led Brundin to dissociate trophic standard from benthos indicators. Furthermore, he preferred species associations (based on properly identified adults rather than vaguely named larvae) to type species, because of the stability of the system generated thereby. He felt that chironomids had been overvalued as indicators of lake typology, as each association had been held to represent a new lake type; zoogeography was often ignored, environmental requirements were studied only superficially, and poorly identified larvae were employed to group lakes with 'the same' benthic fauna. In addition, it was suggested that the much emphasised relationship between specific composition of the benthos and oxygen concentration was not attributable solely to primary production, but that the standing stock of benthos might be more indicative of trophy than might the presence of certain species.

Mesotrophic lakes were held to have no positive indicators. Brundin had little personal familiarity with eutrophic lakes, but made reference to examples of them described in the literature. His oligotrophic lakes were ranked according to humic content of both water and sediment, although the term dystrophic was not favoured. Mesotrophic and mesohumic lake types were held to be negatively characterised, lacking any extreme cases against which unique characteristics could be evaluated.

Another valuable point to emerge here was the true identity of the '*Chironomus plumosus*' of polyhumic lakes. This one species was formerly held to be characteristic of both highly eutrophic and polyhumic lakes, though these have quite distinct faunas in other respects. With the discovery that two chironomid species were actually involved, this 'false' problem was removed, and the polyhumic lake could now be categorised by reference to *C. tenuistylus*. This is but one example of the utterly inadequate taxonomic basis of the system, so heavily dependent on the identification of immature chironomids. By 1956, Brundin had changed several of his categories, and apparently some of his views (table 2.13). The name *Tanytarsus*

TABLE 2.13. Lake classification of Brundin (1956)

I	II	II/III	III		IV
Heterotrissocladius subpilosus lakes (ultraoligotrophic)	*Tanytarsus lugens* lakes (*S. rosenschöldi* lakes of 1949) (oligotrophic)	*Stictochironomus rosenschöldi–Sergentia coracina* (mesotrophic)	a. *Chironomus anthracinus* (moderately eutrophic)	b. *Chironomus plumosus* (strongly eutrophic)	*Chironomus tenuistylus* (dystrophic)

lugens association was used for the single oligotrophic category recognised, being easier to remember and more in accord with the original terminology than *Stictochironomus rosenschöldi*. The community includes ten species in all, including those listed in table 2.12. Again, the polymictic (or mesohumic) subdivision was abandoned in the section formerly termed oligotrophic-humic which others would call dystrophic. Although a mesotrophic category was recognised, its II/III rating suggests that it is an intermediate, rather than a real, category.

Brundin was concerned with oxygen levels at the mud/water interface, accurate species identification based on reared adults, and the role of zoogeography. Moreover, he echoed Deevey's view that the profundal environment rather than the trophic standard determines the occurrence of chironomids. Some of these points had been made by others, but many lake typologists seemed content to go on searching for synthetic classifications based on occasional visits to a large number of lakes. Järnefelt (1953), for instance, sampled each of a series of over a hundred lakes at one point on one date and tried to fit the results to every existing classification as though the criticisms discussed above had never been aired. He used both chironomid and wider ranging systems of benthic characterisation, and again demonstrated a relatively poor correlation between benthos and trophic standard as otherwise defined, emphasising causal ecology instead. The two systems attributable to Järnefelt (1925, 1953) are summarised in highly condensed form in tables 2.14 and 2.15. It is clear that most of his eutrophic lake types in the second system would simply be dubbed *Chironomus* lakes by others taking a broader view of what dominance means. Others are clearly shallow water associations.

TABLE 2.14. Bottom-fauna typology according to Järnefelt (1925)

Eutrophic	Oligotrophic
(1) Chironomids (±oligochaetes)	(1) Ephemerid–sialid–chironomid
(2) *Chaoborus* (+chironomids + oligochaetes)	(2) *Pisidium*–chironomid–ephemerid
(3) Ephemerid (+chironomids + oligochaetes)	(3) *Pisidium*
	(4) Amphipod–*Pisidium*–chironomid

TABLE 2.15. Bottom-fauna typology according to Järnefelt (1953)

Eutrophic–harmonic	Oligotrophic–harmonic
(1) Ephemerid (*E. vulgata, C. plumosus, C. salinarius, Polypedilum*, ceratopogonids)	(1) Ephemerid (*Stictochironomus, Monodiamesa bathyphila*, Tanypodinae
(2) Relict type with chironomid associates (*Pontoporeia, Pallasea, Mysis, C. plumosus, C. salinarius, C. anthracinus, Monodiamesa*)	(2) *Sialis*
(3) *Pisidium*	(3) Relicts with *Stictochironomus* and Tanypodinae
(4) Culicid with *Chaoborus, C. plumosus, C. anthracinus*	(4) *Gammarus*
(5) *Chironomus*	(5) *Pisidium*
(a) *C. plumosus*	
(b) *Glyptotendipes*	
(c) Ceratopogonid	
(6) *Valvata*	(6) Chironomids
	(a) *Stictochironomus*
	(b) *Sergentia*
	(c) Tanytarsini
	(d) Orthocladiinae

At this late stage of the game another new term was introduced by Steinböck (1953, 1958)—the kryo-eutrophic type—an alpine system with practically no plankton but a very abundant (unidentified) benthos apparently dependent upon wind borne detritus which is sufficient to cause complete oxygen depletion beneath the winter ice cover. Brundin (1956) noted that the benthic densities cited were not extraordinary as compared with shallow arctic lakes, and that glaciers might well be a source of the organic detritus. Andean lakes have simple but abundant benthos as well, and the chironomids, while different, show similar trends to those of European species so far as the fundamental *Chironomus*/*Tanytarsus* division is concerned. The term 'guanotrophy' was used by Leentvaar (1967) and by Brinkhurst and Walsh (1967) to describe lakes affected by bird guano, but the latter, at least, were being a little facetious.

In a late review of the topic, Thienemann (1954) reiterated the abstract nature of ideal lake types—valuable concepts for expressing certain general features that may not be combined in any given natural situation, but which enable broad comparisons to be made, and function to be understood more clearly. Nonetheless, he failed to consider the problems related to dystrophy and winter ice cover.

Berg and Petersen (1956) found mixed characteristics of dystrophic, eutrophic and other types in the Danish Lake Gribsø and, in an attempt to destroy the approach, attacked the eccentricities of typologists.

This particular lake has been affected by human interference in the form of peat bog drainage, which may explain much of the confusion when trying to compare it to lakes in less settled or remote areas. In a long series of studies of Danish Lake Esrom (Berg, 1938; Jonasson, 1963; Jonasson and Kristiansen, 1967) we have the best description of a classical Baltic-eutrophic lake (Thienemann type II [*Chironomus*] b. [with *Chaoborus*] 1. [*anthracinus*] a. [*anthracinus* abundant]). It is a very simple lake, morphometrically, and is sited in the region in which the Thienemann scheme was first evolved. Later studies attempt to demonstrate an actual relationship between epilimnetic production and benthic production—something long claimed but not demonstrated (Jonasson, 1964).

As Stahl (1959) pointed out, the work of Brundin is about the most precise in this field, but it was largely limited to ultra-oligotrophic to oligotrophic lakes. He reviewed the characteristics of *Sergentia* lakes (Stahl, 1966), pointing out that few had been carefully investigated and hence the mesotrophic condition is only poorly categorised. Even *Chironomus* lakes have been studied in less detail than the oligotrophic type, and so it is not possible to add associated species to the names *C. anthracinus* and *C. plumosus* as one can with *T. lugens*. *Chaoborus* may succeed *Chironomus* under severe stress, of course. Stahl points out a number of drawbacks in the scheme employing chironomids. They are not always the dominant organisms, being replaced by *Chaoborus*, or oligochaetes, or *Pontoporeia* for example; factors other than oxygen supply may limit the chironomid fauna (especially the nature of the sediment) and the scheme is heavily oriented to the Palaearctic fauna.

As recently as 1968, Hilsenhoff and Narf attempted to correlate the species of chironomids and other benthos with an assortment of chemical and physical data, and found no real statistical correlations beyond those attributable to chance alone.

Few other groups have been studied with sufficient intensity to rival the classifications based on chironomids, although the systematic basis for such studies may be more secure than that for the midges! In the last decade the taxonomy and distribution of aquatic Oligochaeta has been clarified, and one might suggest that these, plus the Sphaeriidae, would have provided the better basis for this study. These groups are widely distributed among and within lakes; there are no confusing problems of sexual dimorphism or immature phases, leading to duplicate nomenclatural systems; and the temporal fluctuations in representation in the benthos so characteristic of midges are absent. The personal interest of a few students probably set forth a whole train of studies on chironomids at the expense of other groups, probably because larval exoskeletons can be found readily in fish guts, and the aerial phase was known to entomologists before limnologists became involved.

An initial attempt to find a series of tubificid species related to the well-known array of lakes in the English lake district failed as soon as it was recognised that each lake was a mosaic of local environments and that no one set of samples would suffice to obtain a characteristic set of worms (Brinkhurst, 1964). The production of a list of species known from European lakes (Brinkhurst and Jamieson, 1971) did not reveal any simple correlation between lake type and worm species present, partly because the lakes had probably changed in character over the years, but also because of intralacustrine variation. Working with the identity of worm species in relation to organic pollution in rivers soon demonstrated that the *relative abundance* of worm species and the degree of dominance of worms over other benthos was, in fact, a useful diagnostic tool. Where *Tubifex tubifex* and/or *Limnodrilus hoffmeisteri* dominated not only the worm population but all the benthos, conditions were often too limiting even for *Chironomus* species—as in Ditton Brook, Liverpool (Brinkhurst and Kennedy, 1965) and Toronto Harbour (Brinkhurst, 1970). Other *Limnodrilus* species could join this assemblage (very occasionally *L. udekemianus* replacing it) until *T. tubifex* was replaced by *Potamothrix* and *Aulodrilus* species. The clean water assemblage of *Rhyacodrilus* species *Peloscolex variegatus*, *Tubifex kessleri* still has some *L. hoffmeisteri* with it and *T. tubifex* may reappear at this opposite extreme of the spectrum. In some genera, nice replacement sequences can be found, such as the *Peloscolex multisetosus*–

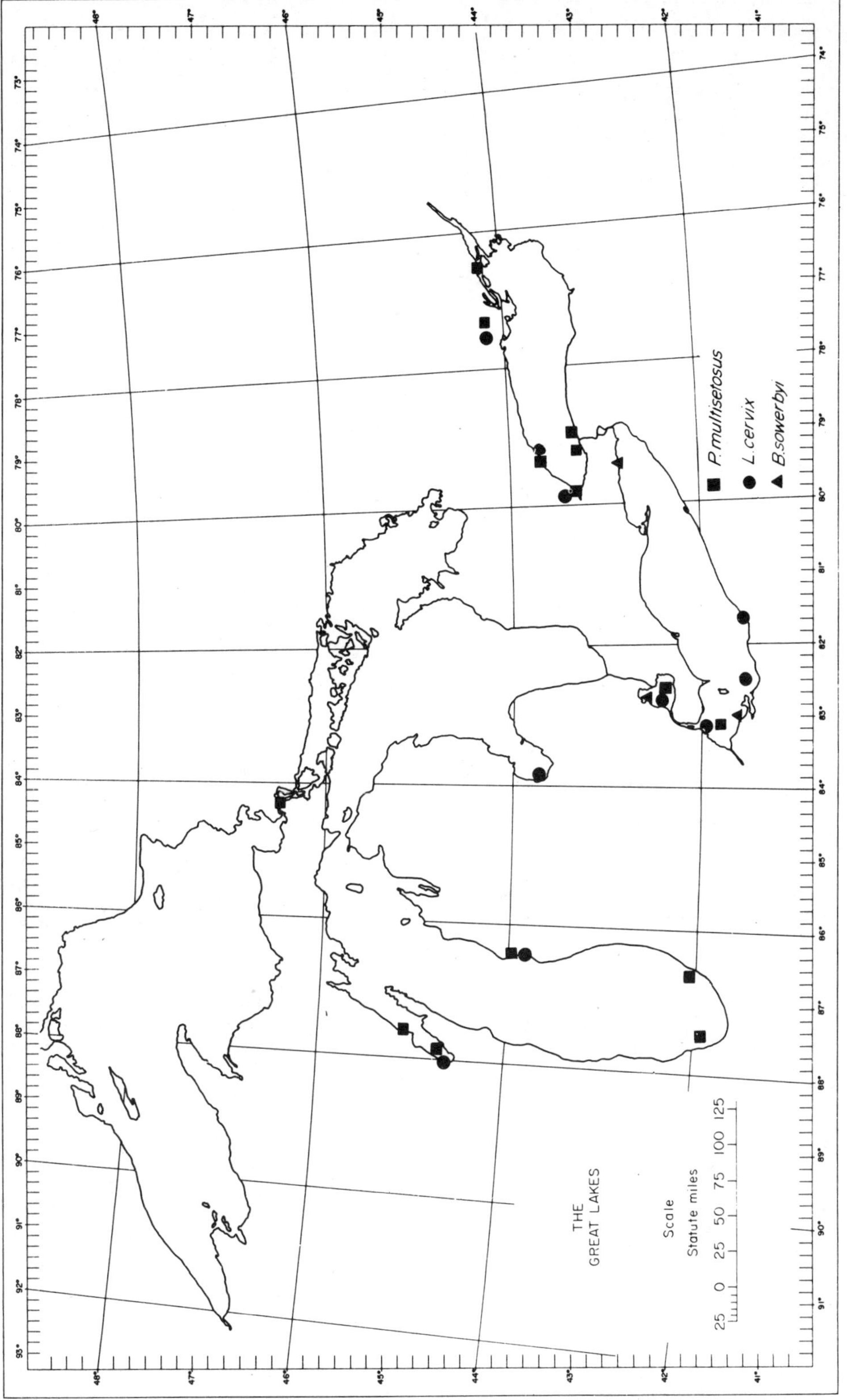

FIGURE 2.1. The distribution of three species of Tubificidae in the Great Lakes. In most instances points refer to specific localities. Only a single specimen of *Branchiura sowerbyi* was found in eastern Lake Erie.

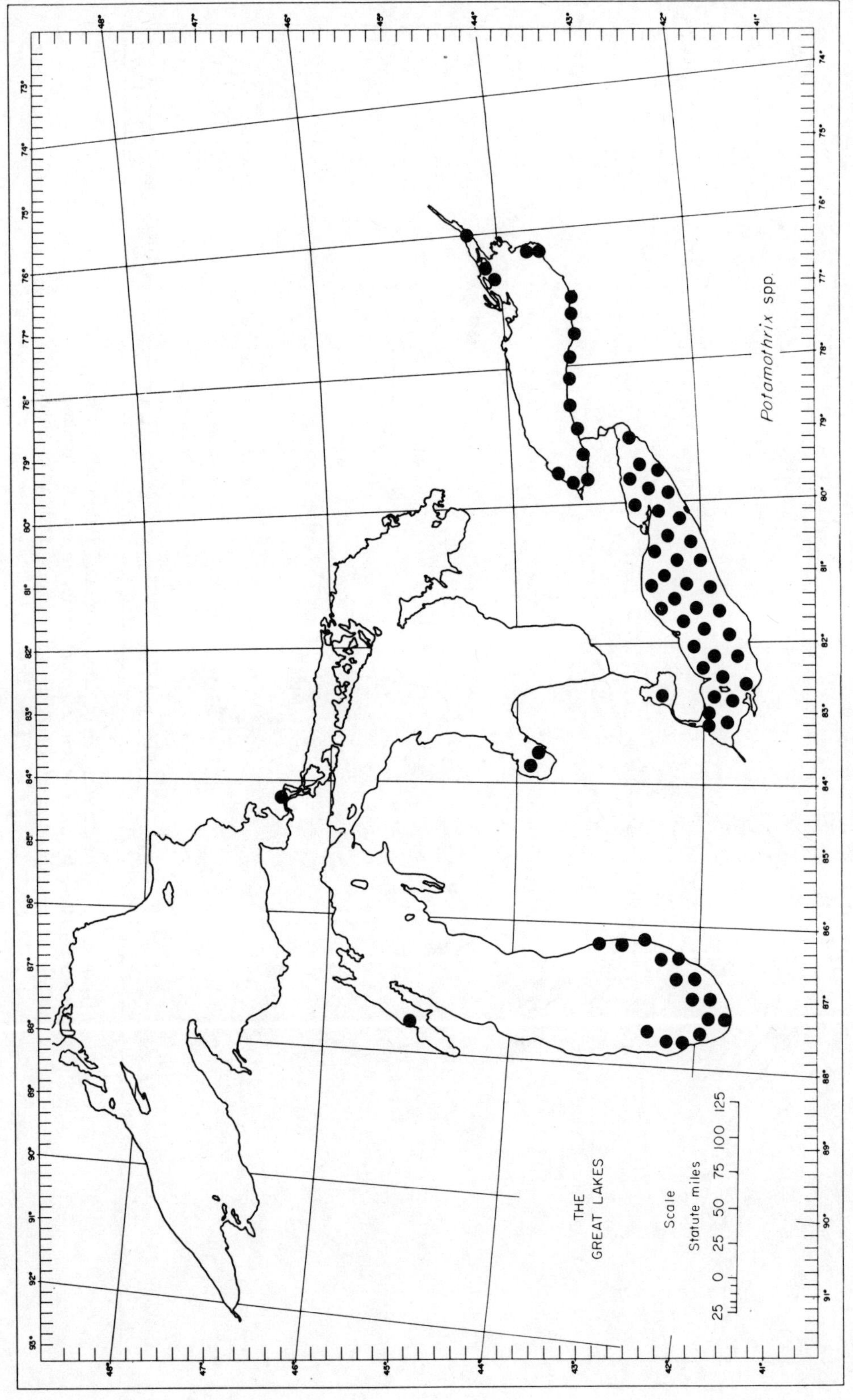

FIGURE 2.2. The distribution of *Potamothrix* species (mostly *P. moldaviensis*) in the Great Lakes. In many instances points refer to broad areas of distribution rather than specific localities.

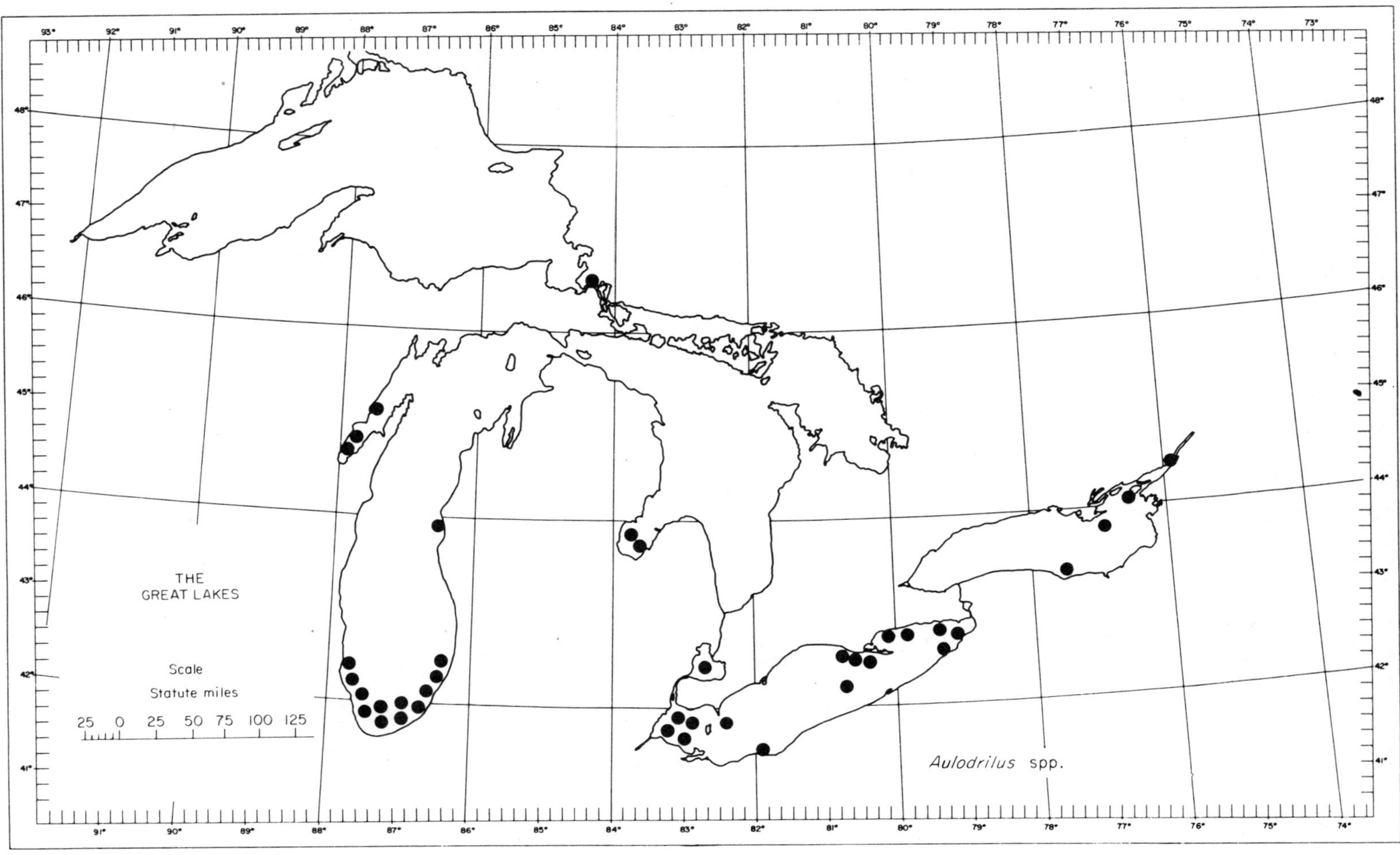

FIGURE 2.3. The distribution of *Aulodrilus* species (*A. pluriseta*, *A. piqueti*, *A. limnobius*, *A. americanus*) in the Great Lakes. Points refer to broad areas of distribution rather than specific localities.

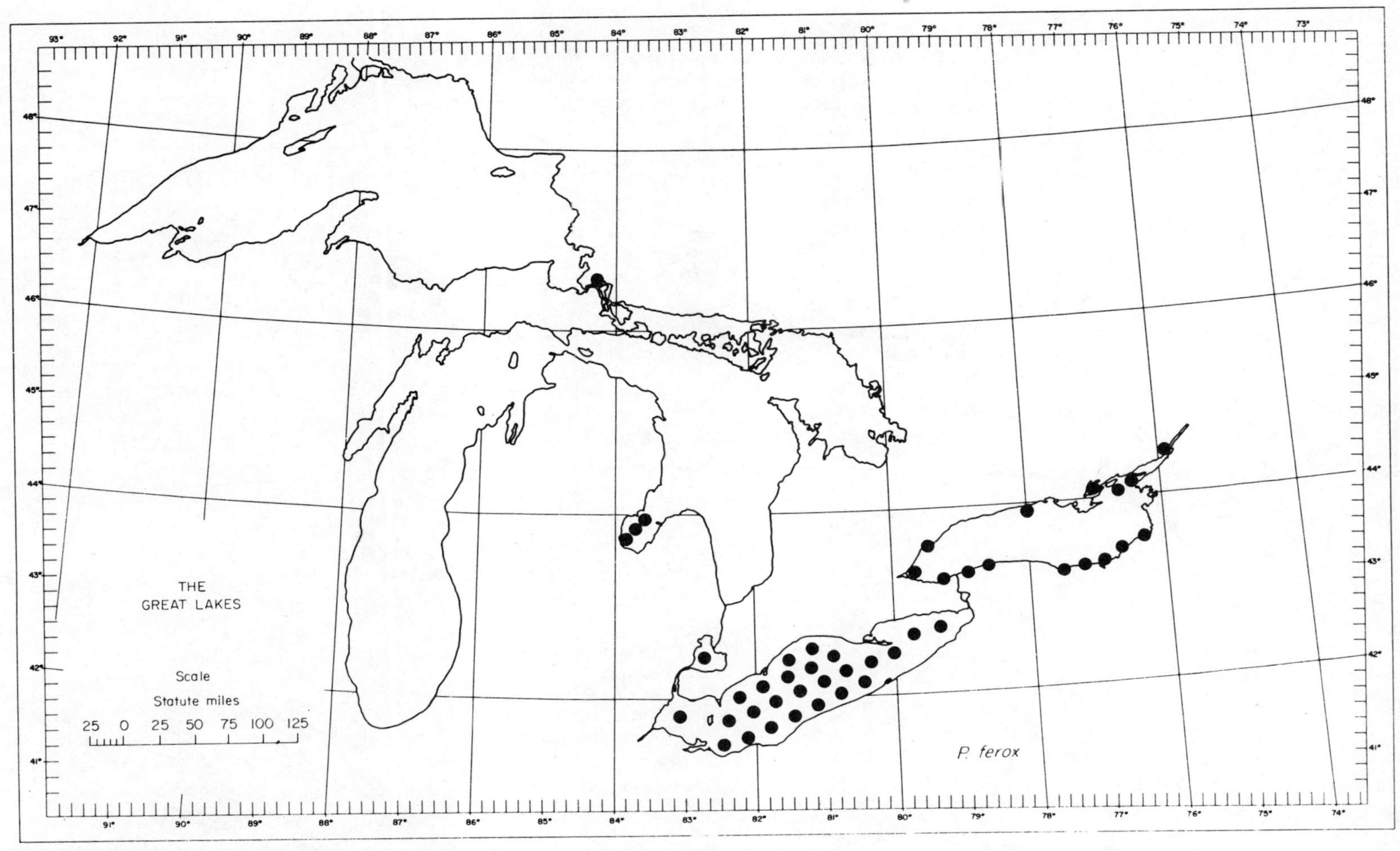

FIGURE 2.4. The distribution of *Peloscolex ferox* in the Great Lakes. Points refer to broad areas of distribution rather than specific localities.

ferox–variegatus series of very eutrophic to oligotrophic conditions in the St. Lawrence Great Lakes (figures 2.1 and 2.4 in which the unmarked areas contain the clean water assemblage). Many of the distribution patterns observed to date have been established using previously gathered material or rapidly obtained samples taken as part of a pollution survey. More precise sampling soon shows that species lists can usually be lengthened by both extensive and intensive sampling, but the proportional representation of worm species so revealed suggests the same story—the species found at a given spot in quick surveys are those that prove to be the most abundant at that site when proper samples are taken. Both the Saprobien System and Lake Typology sampling may be done *very* superficially, when the less abundant species are overlooked altogether, or very carefully in order to establish relative abundance of species rather than lengthy species lists. Perhaps it takes a Thienemann to see the simplicity of the indicator association concept! In modern terms, however, it should be possible to obtain careful analysis of communities for research purposes, such as those revealed in the study of the Bay of Quinte above Kingston in Lake Ontario (Johnson and Brinkhurst, 1971*a*), in which the chironomids, oligochaetes, sphaeriids and crustaceans were all employed in determining statistical evaluations of community or association limits.

Some authors have attempted to relate the abundance (standing stock) or production of benthos to lake type or to fish yield, while others have sought to establish correlations between morphometry, total dissolved solids and quantitative estimates of plankton, fish and benthos in order to establish a new set of empirical yardsticks with which to replace the old typological system (though they are in fact seeking an alternative classification). These matters are discussed in chapter 4, along with the general considerations of standing stock and production.

3 BATHYMETRIC DISTRIBUTION

Even the most cursory examination of a lake suggests that there is a difference between conditions on the bottom in the shallow water and those that apply to the deep lake bed owing to wave action, surface warming and the penetration of light. A lake shore exposed to wave action may be sandy or rocky, whereas sediments beneath deeper water usually consist of silt, clay, or organic mud. Inflows, outflows and shallow bays supporting stands of emergent vegetation create local conditions. Stratification of the lake during summer divides it into at least two, and usually more zones in relation to depth. This, in turn, may lead to chemical as well as thermal gradients, with dissolved oxygen gradients being particularly evident in productive lakes. The penetration of light may limit the distribution of vascular plants although, below about 10 m, other physiological problems may become involved (Gessner, 1952; Ferling, 1957).

A lake's organisms may be distributed in response to these and other factors that limit their vertical distribution, and this became apparent to the earliest limnologists, but the emphasis placed on their findings differed in a number of ways. There is a small body of literature concerned with the number of species present in relation to depth, but it is more concerned with the factors and the fauna that can be used to define zones in the lake. Finally, there is that literature concerned with the number of organisms in relation to depth and the contribution that a knowledge of such distributions might bring to the discussion of lake typology.

The number of taxa clearly falls with depth in a number of arbitrarily selected lakes as indicated by Welch (1935) and in figure 3.1, and there are several obvious reasons for this. Adult and immature insects with need for access to the air/water interface for respiratory requirements will presumably be confined to inshore waters. Although some fully aquatic larvae of species that are aerial as adults (chironomids for example) do not seem to be depth limited despite the length of the journey undertaken prior to emergence from great depths, others are, and hence this limitation is presumably due to factors other than access to the atmosphere. Mayfly larvae, for instance, are not generally present much beyond the 15–20 m depth recorded in Lake Simcoe (Rawson, 1930). In totally aquatic groups such as the amphipods, some forms seem limited to the shallows where others penetrate the whole of a lake. For example, while *Pontoporeia affinis* is abundant at depths in lakes such as Lake Nipigon (Canada), *Gammarus lacustris* and *Hyalella azteca* are limited to the upper 30 m (Adamstone and Harkness, 1923). There is a wider diversity of microhabitats in the littoral zone, of course, hence more species may be recorded there *in toto*, though not all will be found at any given spot. The number of species recorded at a particular location is, of course, dependent upon the samples taken, in that an inexhaustible list of rare species will be found if the collector perseveres long enough, or includes enough taxa in his samples. To be meaningful, these analyses should be based on indices of diversity, which combine relative abundance with species lists.

A number of species may be unable to inhabit the cold region of the lake beneath the summer thermocline, especially if this becomes deficient in oxygen, while other species may be restricted to deep-water situations. The presence of animals restricted to the cold, deep water of large lakes has interested zoogeographers from the earliest time, and one of the primary aims of early benthic studies was an attempt to decide whether or not the benthos consisted of two distinct elements, the 'littoral' and 'profundal' faunas, or of one fauna that diminished with depth, or of some intermediate between these two extremes. The discussion is an extension of the earliest debates about the origin of organisms found to inhabit lakes. Did this fauna penetrate lakes from the littoral or was there an isolated, specially evolved benthic fauna—each part of a 'microcosm', and

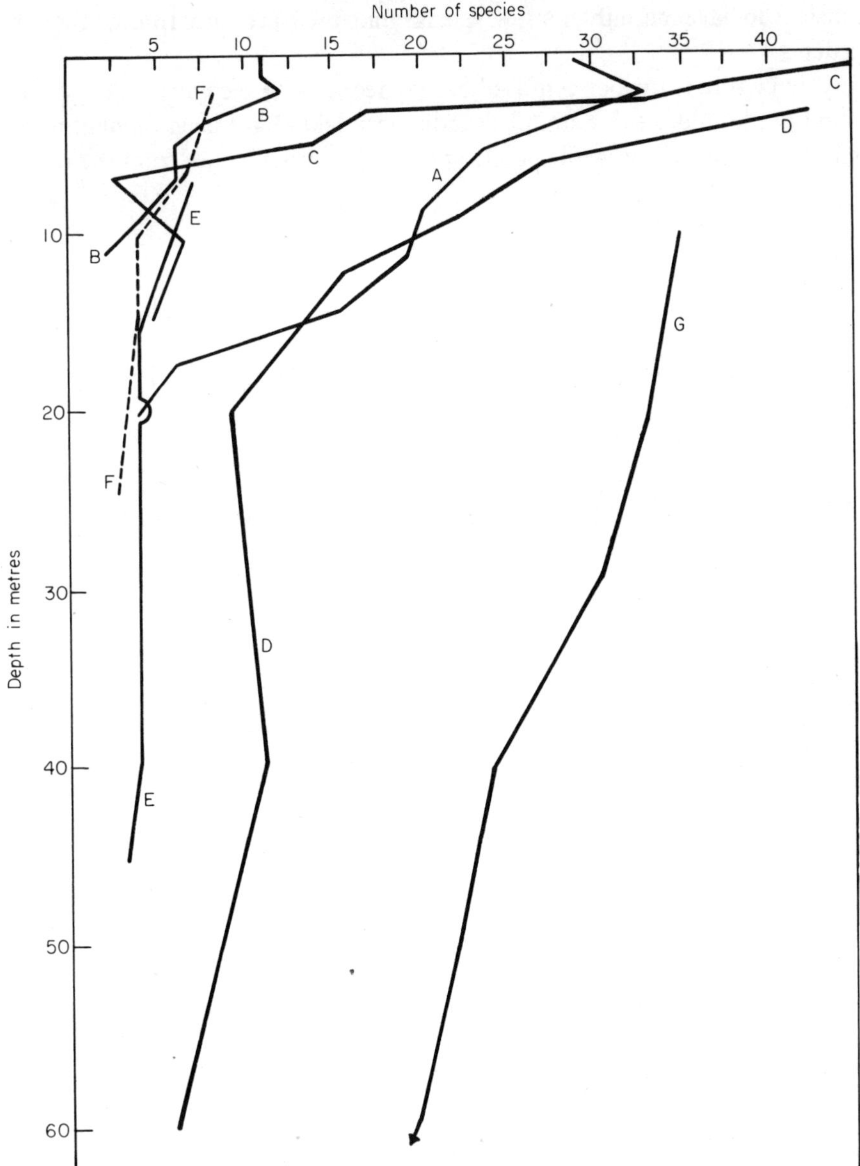

FIGURE 3.1. Number of species in relation to depth in various lakes. A—Esrom Lake, Denmark; B—Gribsø Lake, Denmark; C—L. Borrevann, Norway; D—Windermere, Britain; E—Opeongo Lake, Canada; F—Redrock Lake, Canada; G—Lake Neuchatel, Switzerland (number/10).

each isolated from other islands of such fauna? The special nature of very large lakes such as Russian Baikal is reflected by the long list of endemic species, and the same is true of many of the African Rift Valley lakes (especially Tanganyika), but similar phenomena in smaller Macedonian lakes such as Ochrid, Prespa, Dojran and Skadar, and the Japanese Lake Biwa, indicate that the phenomenon is due to the antiquity of the lakes rather than their size. Time has permitted speciation in these and other ancient lakes, whereas the majority of lakes are too transient to have more than a few specially adapted profundal forms that are distinct from their littoral antecedents.

This already complex picture is further confused by the necessity to recognise relict species. Some of the forms originally found in the cold, deep water of Scandinavian lakes have been thought to be relicts of pre-glacial faunas that survived the ice age, while others apparently invaded lakes from the estuaries of the cold

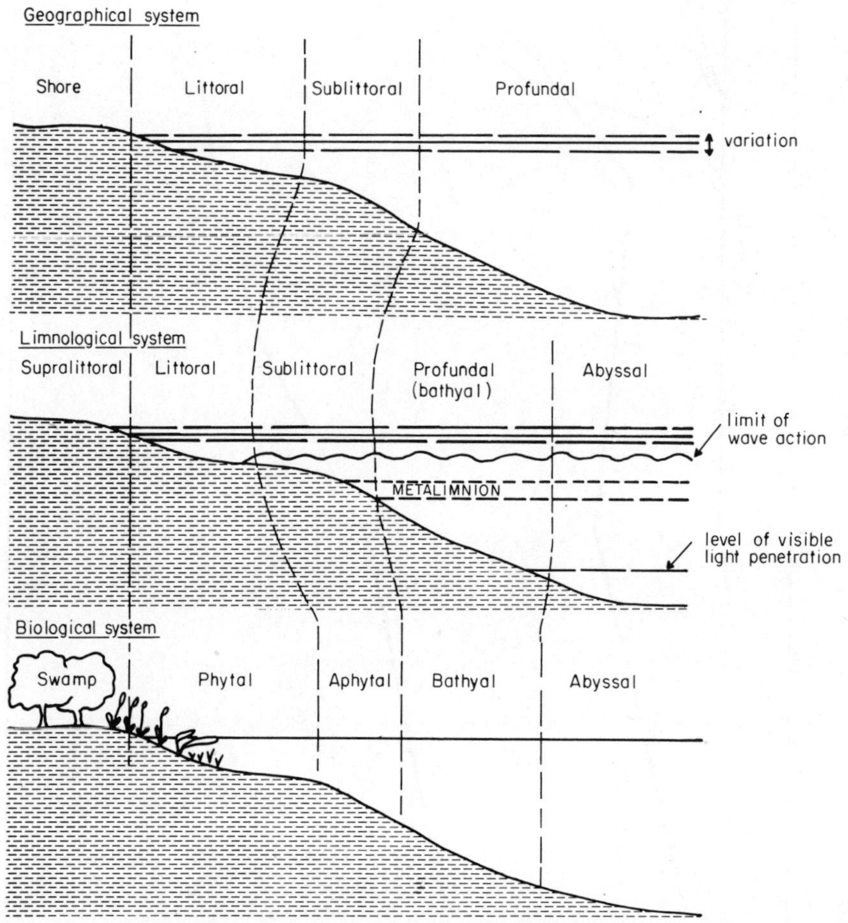

FIGURE 3.2. Geographical, Limnological and Biological lake zonations (after Dussart).

arctic sea owing to complex changes in water level and direction of flow created by ice dams. These forms, then, may actually be prevented from inhabiting the shallower water because of the conditions there, and so they may only be found in deep water (or in cold spring-fed streams) whereas the benthic forms originating in the margin are commonly found at most depths even when they reach their maximum abundance in deeper water.

With these factors in mind, we may now proceed to examine the problem of zonation in lakes. From the outset it is clear that zonations can be built up within the framework of a number of disciplines. Dussart (1966) indicated the correspondence, or lack of it, between zones defined according to three disciplines (figure 3.2). The terminology employed in the limnological system (littoral, sublittoral, upper and lower profundal) was supported by Eggleton (1931) and has been fairly generally accepted ever since.

Zschokke (1911) suggested that the fauna could be divided into two groups—Ufertiere (or shallow water species) and Tiefentiere (deep water species)—but that these co-existed at many depths because of an overlap in their distribution. In one lake, for instance, he recognised eleven Ufertiere and thirteen Tiefentiere species at a depth of 200 m. Von Hofsten (1911) was more concerned with the question of evolutionary antecedents, discussed earlier. He recognised:

(1) Cosmopolitan eurytherms
- 1^{y}—those perfectly like their littoral ancestors
- 2^{y}—profundal species derived from these

(2) Profundal species missing from the littoral
- 1^{y}—cold stenotherms
- 2^{y}—pre-glacial relicts
- 3^{y}—ancient freshwater species of non-glacial origin.

Ekman (1915) returned to a simple depth based system of three divisions for the fauna:

Littoral/sublittoral
Sublittoral/profundal
Eurybathial

He noted, however, that the zonation was indistinct, and was affected by exposure to wind and wave action in the main basin. The effect of substrate on the density of benthos within any one zone was noted, as was the presence of certain so-called profundal species in the littoral zone where the substrate was suitable. The faunal zonation did not correspond to the normal zonation based on the presence of rooted plants, however. In 1917 he defined a euprofundal fauna—animals always limited to the depths even in arctic or alpine lakes—and then proceeded to eliminate most species from this category other than forms in ancient lakes where they have had time to evolve.

Lake St. Moritz (Switzerland) was divided into the following zones by Borner (1917):

(1) littoral (0–4 m)
- (a) fauna of the stony surf zone
- (b) fauna of the littoral sand
- (c) fauna of still water
  - (i) shore overgrown with plants
  - (ii) outermost shore
  - (iii) steep slopes or rock and sand

(2) sublittoral (4–22 m)
- (a) littoral–sublittoral (4–10 m)
  - (i) Characetum
  - (ii) Potametum
- (b) sublittoral–profundal (10–22 m)

(3) profundal (22–40 m)—with a profundal central basin up to 45 m deep.

Borner agreed with earlier authors (Zschokke, 1900; Steinman, 1906, 1907; Wesenberg-Lund, 1908) who had suggested that the fauna of the stony lakeshore was essentially like that of stony streams, presumably being dependent upon wave action in lieu of current to maintain a high oxygen concentration, low silt load and a changing water supply to the respiratory surfaces. He also established the relative poverty of the sandy substrate noted by Wesenberg-Lund (1908) and indicated that it was more like that of deeper zones than the rest of the shore, a point of some significance to be discussed below. The still water fauna was found to be richer than either of these other two faunas and many pond species were found.

The sublittoral zone was divided into sub-zones dominated either by *Chara* or *Potamogeton*, the former sub-zone being much richer in benthic species than the latter, where the 'true mud dwellers' were absent. Only eleven of the fifty-five species present reached their maximum development within this zone, however, so that a simple plot of number of species in relation to depth did not indicate the extent of the change which has taken place in moving into this zone. The fauna of the steep sandy slopes was not readily associated with either the littoral or sublittoral.

The profundal contained mostly oligochaetes, *Pisidium*, chironomids, and bryozoans. The profundal basin, as defined, was thought to be polluted, even at this early date, as the fauna was restricted to a lot of tubificids and a few, often stunted, specimens of a small number of other species.

The problem of the origin of the profundal fauna of Lake Neuchatel (Switzerland) was discussed by Monard (1919) who recognised that apart from transients there were those species that were essentially eurybathic while, at the same time, being particularly adapted to and dominant in the profundal, while others were specialised species restricted to the profundal despite the lake edge origin accorded to all. Schmassman (1920) used the stenothermy concept but classified the fauna of high alpine lakes into:

(1) Littoral (and sublittoral) fauna.
(2) Eurybathic fauna.
(3) Cavernicolous forms that reach the lake from groundwater.
(4) Incidental fauna typical of rivers and ponds.

Noting that several authors (for example, Lundbeck, 1926) had divided lakes into a number of regions with respect to depth, and eschewing the problem of tidying up the different ideas that had been introduced, Eggleton (1931) divided his lakes as follows:

	Littoral zone	Sublittoral zone	Profundal zone
Douglas Lake (Michigan)	0–9 m	9–15 m	15–28 m
Third Sister Lake (Michigan)	0–3 m	3–10 m	10–18 m
Kirkville Green Lake (NY)	0–3 m	3–6 (or 8) m	8–61 m

In general terms, his littoral region extends from shore to the approximate limit of the vegetation (presumably rooted macrophytes), while the profundal zone is that part of the lake from the deepest point up to somewhat above the average upper limit of the hypolimnion. The sublittoral consists of the region left over. Eggleton then pointed out that the limits differed from lake to lake, as evidenced by his study of the three lakes mentioned above.

A number of earlier schemes were summarised by Welch (1935), and these are presented in tabular form (table 3.1) without further comment. The abyssal zone (that beyond 600 m) was added to a classification scheme essentially similar to that used by Eggleton, but the gradual nature of the transitions was emphasised, as well as the shifting nature of the sublittoral/profundal boundary with the seasons.

The lack of a fixed terminology was indicated by Berg (1938) who discussed the earlier zonation systems, particularly that of Wesenberg-Lund (1917), and it was he who noted the difference between the zoological and botanical usage of the term 'littoral'. In marine and botanical terminology the littoral constitutes the region exposed by means of fluctuations in level and subject to wave action, and while the transition zone in lakes is much less apparent than on the sea shore whenever tides are reasonably extensive, the confusion in terminology seems unnecessary. Berg felt that each group had the right to use its terms in its own way, but consistent use of terminology would seem logical. In Esrom Lake the zones defined by Berg were:
Littoral (0–4 m)—from normal water line to the lower limit of rooted vegetation.

TABLE 3.1. Systems of benthic zonation (from Welch, 1935, after Naumann, 1930)

Zone	Thienemann (German lakes)	Wesenberg-Lund (Furesee, Denmark)	Ekman (Vättern Sweden)	Blomgren, Lundqvist, Naumann; in part, Sernander, Thomasson, Thunmark (Swedish lakes)	Lenz, compromise proposal	Forel Lac Léman Switzerland)	Muttkowski (Lake Mendota, Wisconsin, USA)
I Zone above uppermost part of water-level amplitude; never continuously submerged; never subject to splash of waves	General shore region: beach			epilittoral	epilittoral		
II Zone not continuously submerged but at times subject to splash of waves	General shore region: beach			supralittoral	supralittoral	(drier beach)	
III Zone submerged by high water	General shore region: beach			eulittoral (littoral)	eulittoral (littoral)	(wetter beach)	shore-shoals zone; surf-line zone (rachion) (littoral; eulittoral)
IV Permanently submerged zone: (1) emergent aquatic plants	General shore region: littoral	littoral	littoral	sublittoral (littoral)	(littoral)	littoral	upright plant zone (vegetation zone; eulittoral; littoral)
(2) floating-leaf aquatic plants	General shore region: littoral	littoral	littoral	sublittoral (littoral)	(littoral)	littoral	upright plant zone / recumbent plant zone (vegetation zone; eulittoral; littoral)
(3) submerged aquatic plants	General shore region: littoral	littoral	sublittoral	macroelittoral (eulittoral; littoral)	(littoral)	littoral	recumbent plant zone (vegetation zone; eulittoral; littoral)
(4) transition zone	sublittoral	sublittoral	profundal	macroelittoral (eulittoral; littoral)	euprofundal (profundal)	deep region	sublittoral (littoral)
(5) plantless muddy-bottom deposit: (a) upper part	profundal	sublittoral	profundal	profundal	euprofundal (profundal)	deep region	aphytal
(5) plantless muddy-bottom deposit: (b) under part	profundal	profundal	profundal	profundal	euprofundal (profundal)	deep region	aphytal

Sublittoral (4–14/15 m)—from the lower limit to the lowest point inhabited by molluscs other than *Pisidium*.
Profundal (15–17 m to the lowest)—from the level at which the mixed-fauna sublittoral ends, into a zone poor in species, monotonous—primarily *Chironomus*, *Pisidium*, *Chaoborus*, and tubificids.

These are, therefore, defined by reference to the fauna and flora, as these are held to represent the final expression of the interplay of ecological factors used by many to achieve such a division.

The system employed by Stankovic (1955) in Lake Ochrid is based on plant associations and other factors:

Littoral—0–20 m, the erosion zone; sand-rock substrates, diverse habitats, upper part (0–5 m) wave washed, or with plants, lower part (5–20 m) with *Chara* prairies.
Sublittoral—deposition layer for littorogenic material; with the *Dreissena* shell zone. The thermal regime dampened by being in the metalimnion. *Nostoc* present, but no macrophytes.
Profundal—below the hypolimnion; sediments soft mud, uniform and constant ecological factors, deepest part almost meromictic.

The majority of the profundal forms in this lake are not found in the littoral, and consist of the following forms:

(1) Eurybathyl—dominant in profundal though present in upper regions.
(2) Relict—profundal only or scarcely reaching sublittoral.
(3) Subterranean—entering from groundwater.
(4) Profundal forms of uncertain systematic position.
(5) Highly adapted profundal species derived from littoral forms.

Unlike the situation found in most post-glacial lakes, the eurybathyl forms do not dominate the profundal. Presumably the age of the lake had led to the evolution of a specialised euprofundal fauna, whereas in post-glacial lakes the:

> true profundal fauna is a selection fauna, recruited from the sublittoral and littoral zones and reduced today to a few hardy and highly adaptable species through the medium of the many purges at the hand of seasonal cycles (Eggleton, 1939).

While we may not support this statement in its entirety, it is clear that there is, in fact, a general reduction of diversity with depth (as well as a reduction in numbers, as we shall see). Part of this is undoubtedly due to the prevailing definition of 'littoral', which is spatial rather than functional so that the total invertebrate fauna of the shallow water can be arrayed against the inhabitants of the mud at greater depths without reference to the reduction in the number of available microhabitats.

Having constructed curves to represent the abundance of benthic organisms in relation to depth, Lundbeck (1926) suggested that there were characteristic shapes for these curves according to the types of lakes then known (eutrophic, oligotrophic, humic mud lakes, and later mesotrophic lakes), and he drew up theoretical curves without even indicating values for the coordinates for idealised lakes (figure 3.3A–C).

The eutrophic-lake model shows the distribution of littoral, sublittoral and profundal species as well as a total envelope for all benthos, together with schematised representations of the distributions of plants, oxygen concentration, temperature, and muddy sediments. The curve of vertical distribution of total benthic fauna shows two peaks, one at about 4 m made up of littoral forms, the other of profundal forms at about the 16 m level. The decline in both these groups of species between 4 m and 16 m is not matched by a proportionate increase in the sublittoral elements. The situation is reminiscent of estuaries, where the marine and freshwater elements are scarce in brackish waters and the number of species specially adapted to brackish water is not sufficient to make up the deficit. It would seem to be difficult to become a specialist at survival

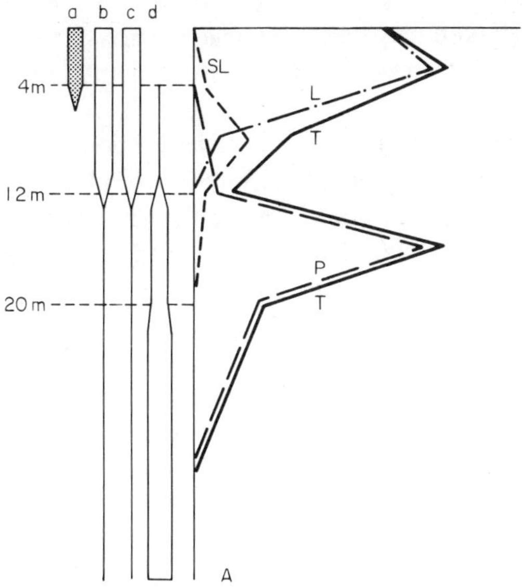

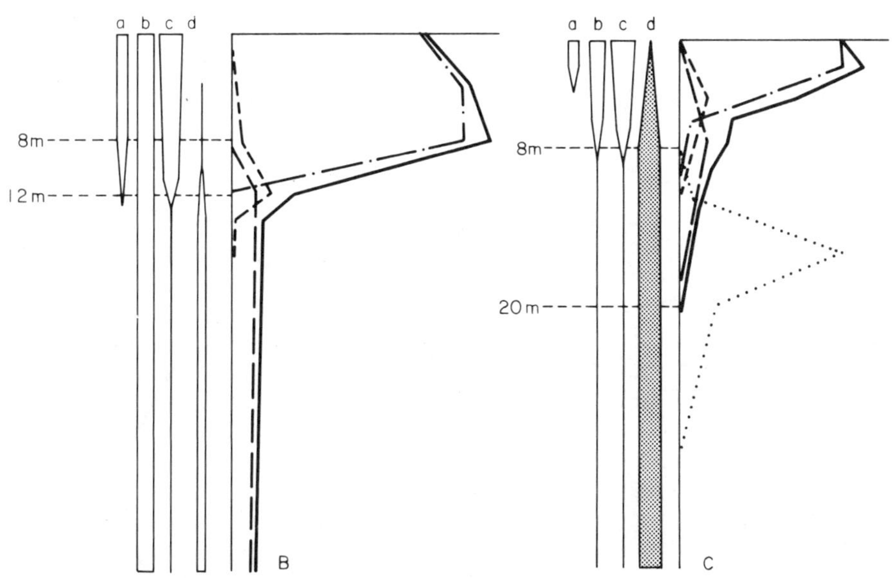

FIGURE 3.3. The ideal curves for depth-distribution of benthos in Eutrophic (A) Oligotrophic (B) and Dystrophic (C) lake types (Lundbeck, 1926). L—littoral, SL—sublittoral, P—profundal components of total fauna (T). a—rooted plants, b—oxygen in the water, c—temperature, d—silt. Dotted line in C refers to *Chaoborus*.

in a widely variable environment such as an estuary. Even most non-tidal brackish water situations are subject to evaporation or inundation by rain, and hence to a wide fluctuation in salinity as well as temperature.

In subsequent discussions this point will be explored further, but it is of value to note here that, while some authors have discussed a sublittoral minimum, others have proposed that active migration creates a concentration zone in the upper profundal, although both may be closely related parts of the same relationship, being no more than two halves of a serpentine distortion of an otherwise smooth curve relating fauna to depth.

While the slight drop in quantity of benthos in the littoral may be due to wave action and the occurrence of sandy shores, Lundbeck also attributed the sublittoral minimum to physical conditions related to the distinct environmental requirements of the 'littoral' and 'profundal', rather than to a shortage of suitable food. There is an indication that predation pressure is supposed to be particularly intense in this region but, as usual, most of these predictions about the cause of observed distribution remains untested by selective field and laboratory experimentation. This explanation was accepted by Rawson (1930) and Miyadi (1932).

The curves for the idealised oligotrophic lake (figure 3B) show a similar slight reduction of benthos in the shallowest littoral zone, but after the large peak of littoral organisms there is no marked increase in either sublittoral or profundal forms, the shortage here being attributed to a lack of food generated by the phytoplankton, which is, by definition, less abundant in oligotrophic lakes.

In the 'humic lake type' the deeper layers are inhabited by *Chaoborus* (which feeds up in the surface layers) despite the shortage of food and oxygen. The 'profundal' element is regarded as present but pressed up into the shallower parts of the lake, and the same fate has befallen the sublittoral forms. Just how this effect is

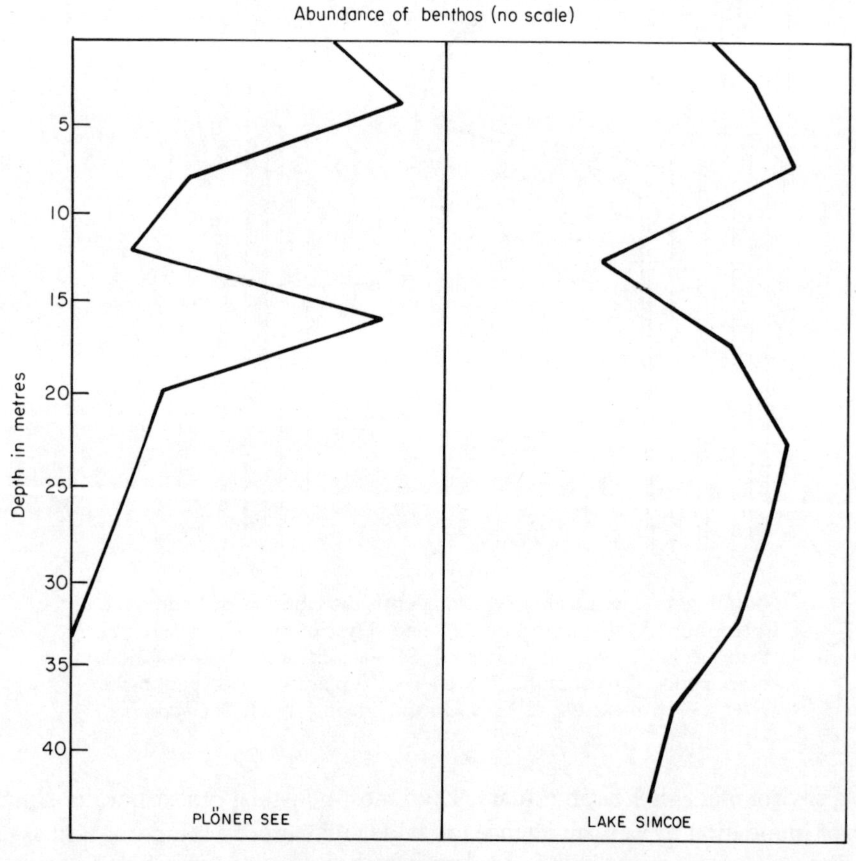

FIGURE 3.4. The depth distribution of total benthos in Lake Simcoe and Plöner See. (See Rawson, 1930.)

detected, when these groups of animals are primarily recognised by their spatial distribution is hard to grasp; presumably one defines them with relation to their zonation in 'real' or eutrophic lakes. Although Lundbeck pointed out that the large shallow water component in all three types of lake is, in the main, comprised of chironomids, he paid little attention to seasonal variation, intra or inter lacustrine variation, or other confounding factors. This is a synthetic, idealised overview similar to that of the lake typology system itself. The observed distributions, of course, depend upon methodology. When two sampling methods are used simultaneously, the bathymetric distributions obtained may not agree. Dr. A. M. Beeton (personal communication) compared the Smith McIntyre with the Petersen when the former was introduced to the St. Lawrence Great Lakes in 1960. Most organisms were caught at 15 fathoms with the Petersen in Lake Michigan, but the peak occurred at 25 fathoms using the new tool, and the representation of taxonomic groups differed in detail.

A number of people compared their own data to those of Lundbeck. Rawson (1930) found a curve like the one for eutrophic lakes could be derived from his Lake Simcoe data (figure 3.4) and attributed shifts in the actual positions of the maxima and minima to the size of this Canadian lake. More significant is the presence of a much more abundant benthic fauna extending right down to the bottom, in contrast to the situation shown by Lundbeck's curves. This was attributed to the presence of an adequate oxygen supply in Lake Simcoe in summertime. The same is true in Danish Esrom Lake (Berg, 1938) as shown in figure 3.5, and in fact the sharp inflection in the curve somewhere in the upper third of the depth-range studied is the really significant similarity to Lundbeck's proposed curve. Reworking some of the Esrom data, adding standard deviations of the means, illustrates that little confidence can be placed in the exceedingly variable data utilised in these speculations (figure 3.6). The maxima are also made up of quite different organisms, even

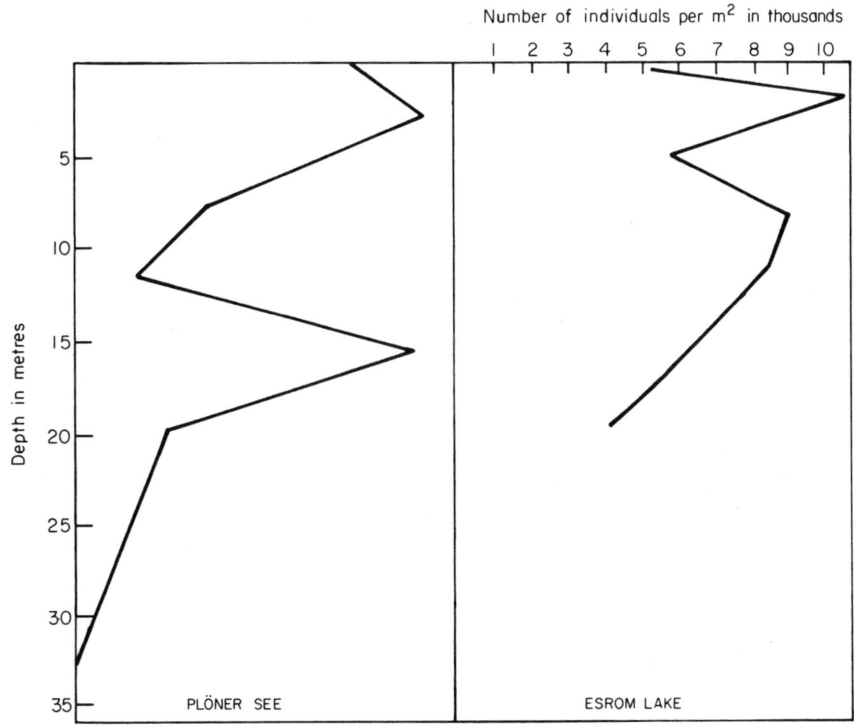

FIGURE 3.5. The depth distribution of total benthos in Esrom Lake and Plöner See. (See Berg, 1938.)

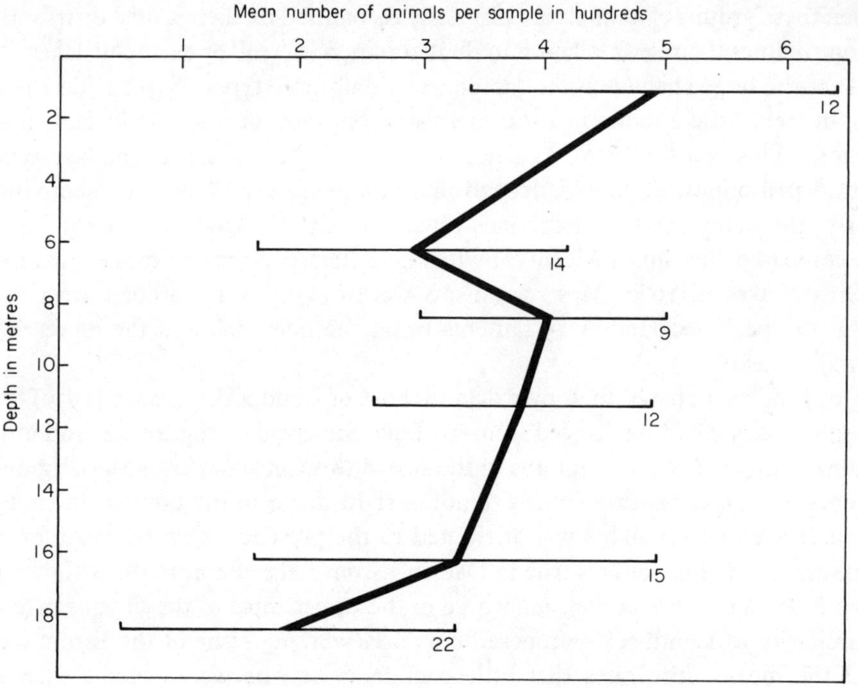

FIGURE 3.6. The average number of animals per sample in Esrom Lake, showing confidence limits. Numbers represent the number of samples taken (calculated from Berg, 1938).

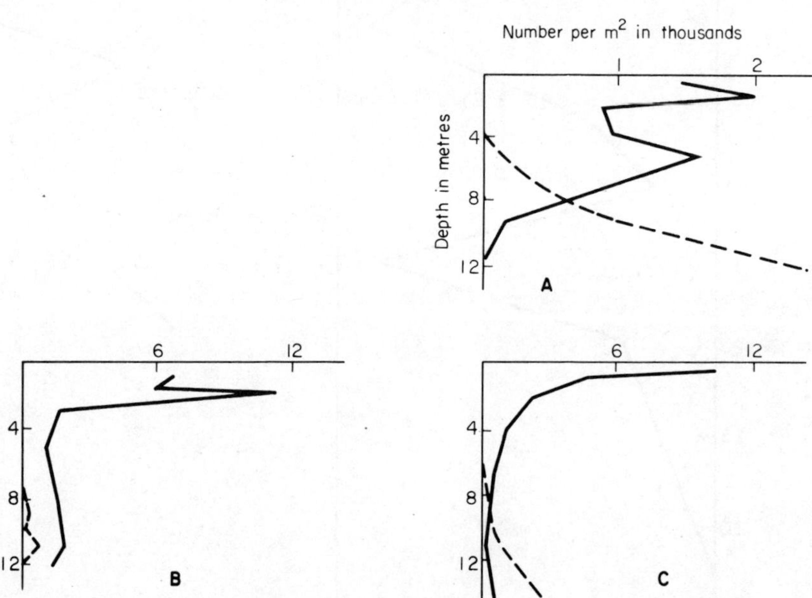

FIGURE 3.7. The depth distribution of benthos in three Scandinavian humic lakes. A—Gribsø (polyhumic), B—Stråken (mesohumic), C—Skärshultsjon (polyhumic). Dotted line—*Chaoborus*. (Berg and Petersen, 1956.)

at the crudest level of identification. Berg (1938) indicated that the maximum at 8–11 m in Esrom could be attributed solely to *Dreissena* whereas it is usually composed of chironomids. The subject was raised again by Berg and Petersen (1956) using their study on another Danish locality, humic Lake Gribsø and information on Sweden's Lakes Straken and Skarshultsjön derived from Brundin (1949). These are summarised in figure 3.7A–C, showing that there is some agreement but that Gribsø shows two maxima in the curve instead of one. While Lang (1931) claimed an increase in population with increasing humic content, Brundin

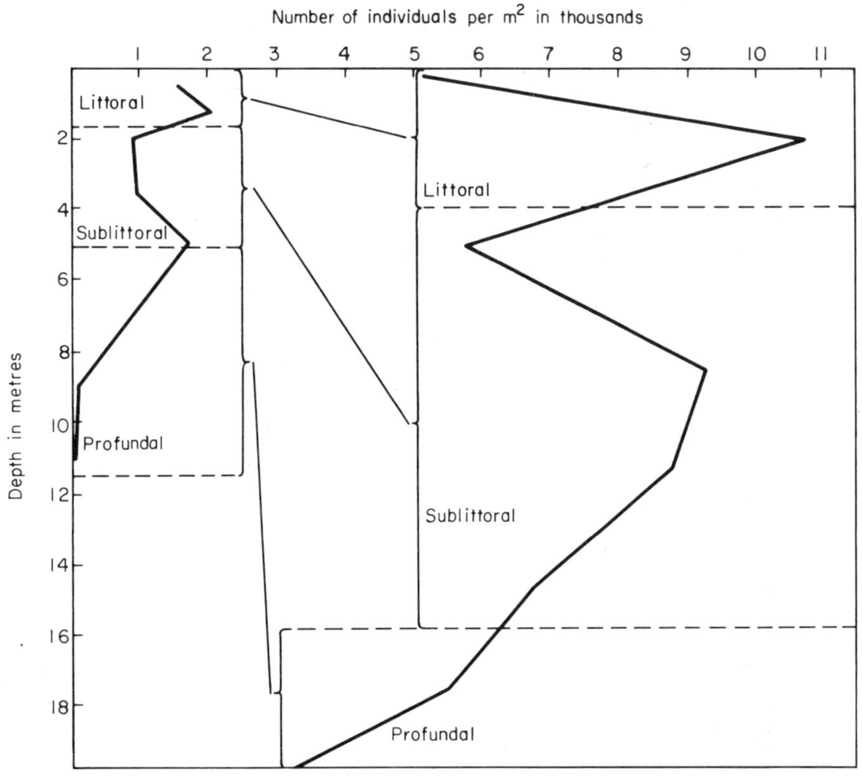

FIGURE 3.8. A comparison of benthic fauna distribution in Eutrophic Esrom Lake and Dystrophic Gribsø, Denmark (Berg and Petersen, 1956).

(1942, 1949) observed the reverse trend. Berg and Petersen (1956) argued for the significance of the actual composition of the humic material involved when predicting populations. It should be noted that the correspondence of the curve for Gribsø with that of the eutrophic Esrom lake type may be affected by the past history of this lake—once eutrophic and subsequently affected by peat drainage by man. However, Berg and Petersen (1956) see great significance in the different 'zones' in which parts of the curve are located (figure 3.8).

By this time, the three basic models had been combined into a single diagram (figure 3.9) by Lundbeck (1936). Deevey (1941) produced curves for the Connecticut lakes (figure 3.10) and drew attention to their overall similarity to Lundbeck's slopes for oligotrophic lakes, and for the mesotrophic and eutrophic lakes apart from the littoral region. He indicated that, though there was some theoretical basis for the existence of curves of types I and III, the lakes conforming to these patterns were heterogeneous in regard to their chironomid typology. The typologically distinct lakes Quassapaug and Linsley Pond both demonstrate

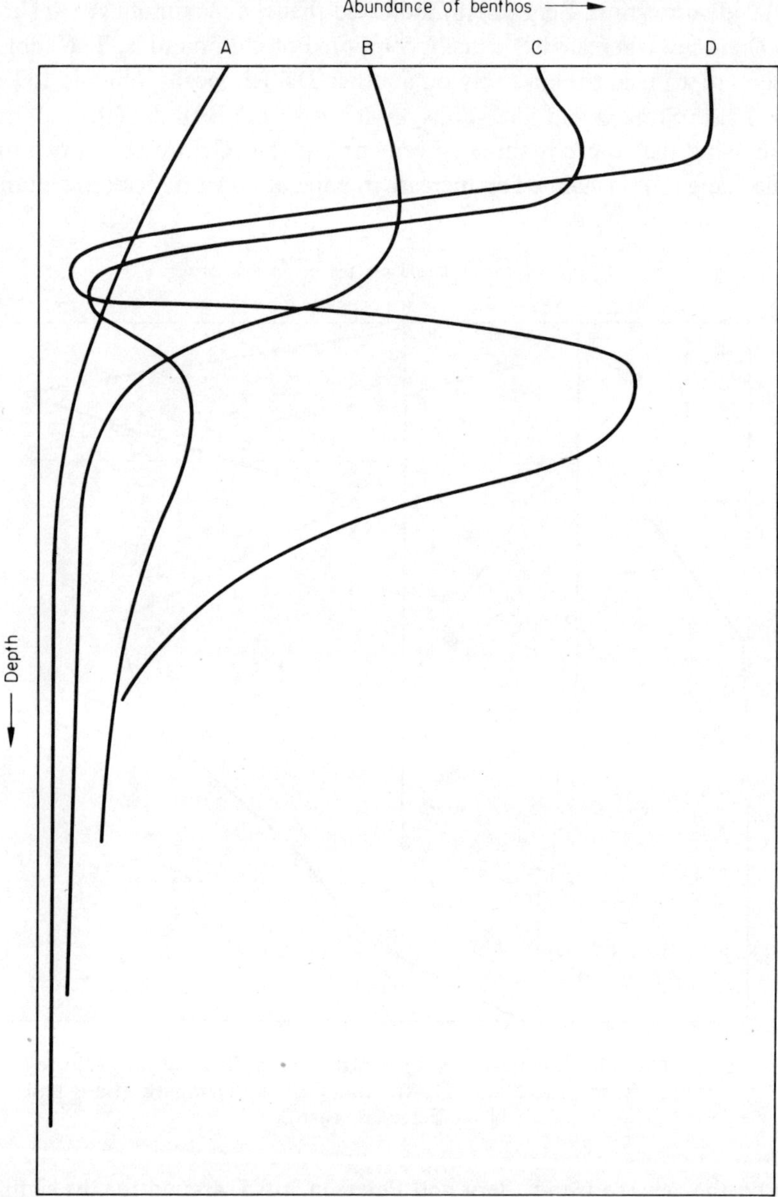

FIGURE 3.9. Idealised depth distribution of benthos in relation to lake typology (Lundbeck, 1936). A—ultraoligotrophic, B—oligotrophic, C—mesotrophic, D—eutrophic.

sublittoral minima, so that Deevey (1941) felt that no single explanation of the curves was tenable, even if there was a pattern to be discerned. Considerable emphasis was placed on factors that vary with the seasons, such as migrations from deep to shallow water in the face of diminishing oxygen supply in summer in productive lakes, or quite marked fluctuations of many shallow water organisms, such as chironomids, particularly where these have many generations each year. Both Deevey and Eggleton (1931) were therefore aware of the fact that the distribution of benthos in relation to depth changes month by month (see p. 121).

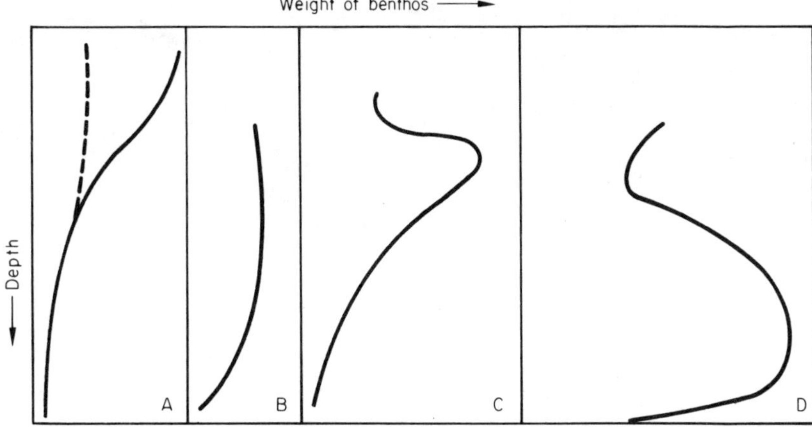

FIGURE 3.10. Schematised benthic weight distribution in Connecticut lakes (Deevey, 1941). A—2 'Chironomus' lakes but mostly 'Trissocladius' lakes, B—(variant of A)—2 mesotrophic 'Chironomus' lakes, C—quantitatively rich lakes (i.e. Linsley Pond) with shallow peak of standing stock, D—relatively productive lakes with deep peak of standing stock.

Dugdale (1955) observed a *maximum* in the abundance of chironomid larvae of *Chironomus plumosus* in the approximate region of the sublittoral zone of Mendota, Wisconsin, USA (±3 m according to the graph) and similar patterns have been found elsewhere (Bardach, Morril and Gambony, 1951, Lake Okoboji, Iowa; Scott, Hile and Speith, 1928, Lake Wawasee, and Turkey Lake, Indiana). According to Dugdale, the results of Bryson and Ragotzkie (1955) indicate that internal waves may bring occasional renewals of O_2 to regions just below the thermocline, and such internal waves have been observed in Mendota. Thus these

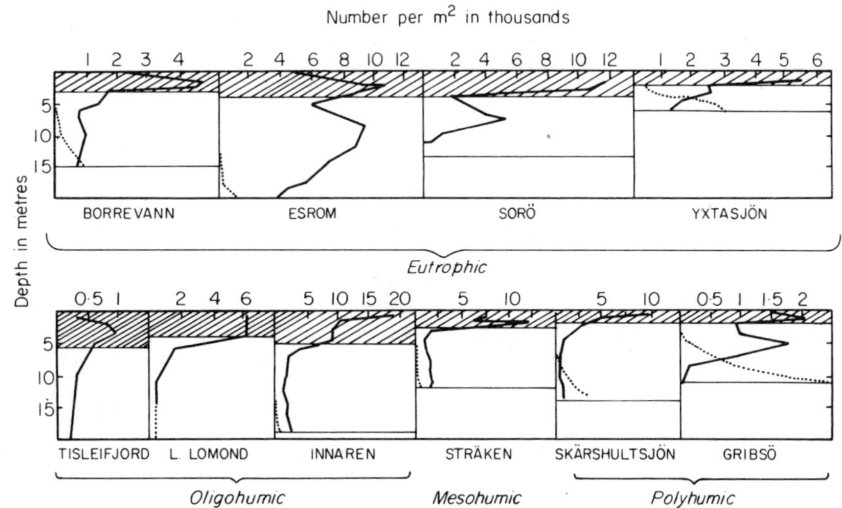

FIGURE 3.11. Vertical distribution of benthos in lakes of various types (Økland, 1964). Shaded area—area occupied by macrophytes, dotted line—distribution of *Chaoborus*, solid line—distribution of the remaining benthos.

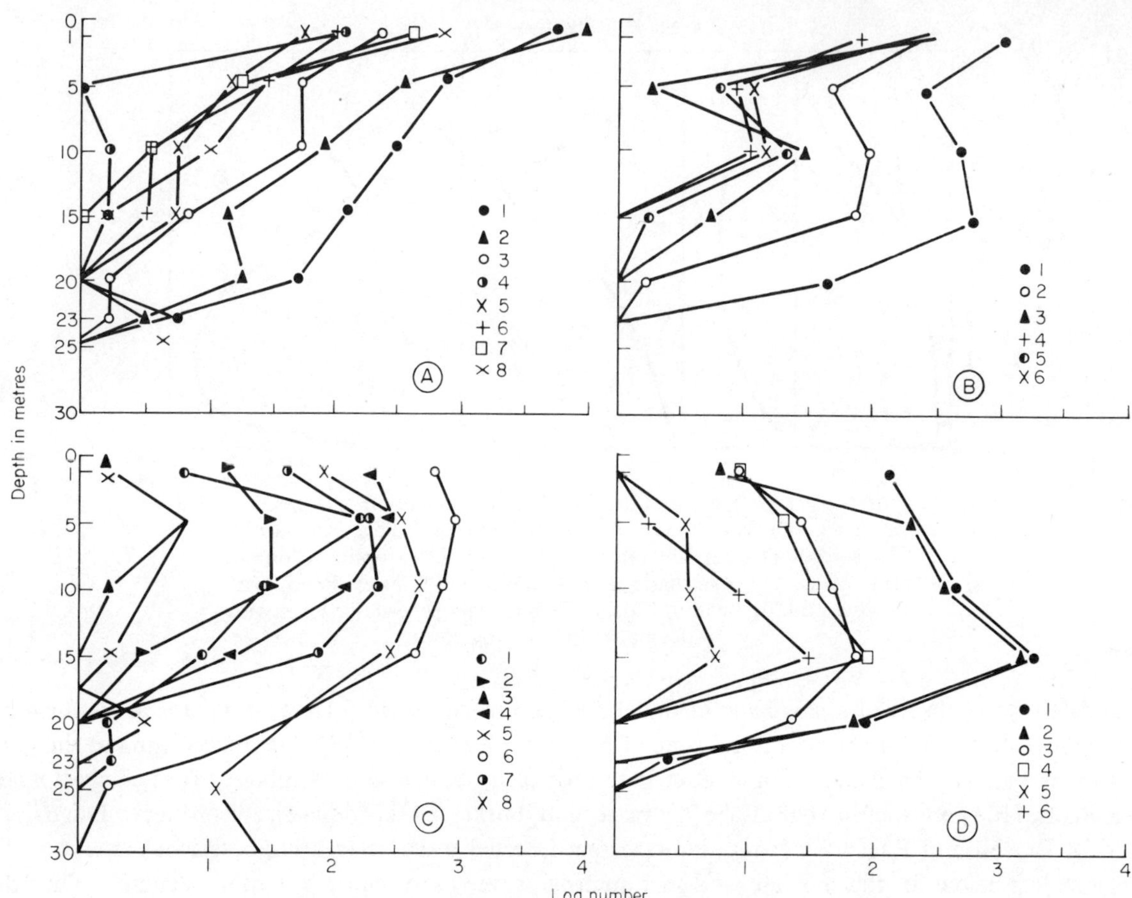

FIGURE 3.12. Distribution of various species with depth, shown as logarithm of the number per metre² at each depth sampled from 1 m to 30 m. A: 1 = *Microspectra fusca*; 2 = *Lundstroemia pseudo-praecox*; 3 = *Valvata piscinalis*; 4 = *Potamopyrgus jenkinsi*; 5 = mites; 6 = *Glyptotendipes paripes*; 7 = *Caenis horaria*: 8 = ostracods. B: 1 = ?*Limnodrilus hoffmeisteri* (immature); 2 = *Limnodrilus hoffmeisteri*; 3 = *Stylodrilus heringianus*; 4 = *Microtendipes* '*diffinis*'; 5 = *Chironomus* (*Dicrotendipes*) *pulsus*; 6 = *Polypedilum* '*nubeculosum*'. C: 1 = *Aulodrilus pluriseta*; 2 = *Helobdella stagnalis*; 3 = *Glossiphonia heteroclita*; 4 = *Pisidium* spp.; 5 = *Sialis lutaria*; 6 = *Procladius choreus*; 7 = *Asellus aquaticus*; 8 = copepods. D: 1 = immature *Tubifex* and *Potamothrix hammoniensis*; 2 = *Chironomus striatus*; 3 = *Potamothrix hammoniensis*; 4 = cocoons of tubificids; 5 = *Ilyodrilus templetoni*; 6 = *Tubifex tubifex*.

boundary effects would extend down to the region where near optimal O_2 and food conditions prevail, according to Lundbeck's theory. However, patchy egg distribution resulting from concentrations of adults or from internal currents may produce the observed patterns.

Treatment of data on vertical distribution in Wyland Lake, Indiana (Gerking, 1962), by analysis of variance failed to demonstrate statistically significant differences in relation to depth, but there was an apparent minimum at 2–4 m, with equivalent densities in the shallows and the region deeper than 6 m, but this is a very shallow body of water. A series of curves were examined by Økland (1964) in relation to data from eutrophic Lake Borrevann in Norway (figure 3.11) but there seems to be no consistent pattern, a conclusion reached by Hayes (1957). Before we dismiss this matter as being of mere historic interest, however, it might be worth contemplating a careful test of the Lundbeck models. Two such tests come to mind. In the first, we might elect to survey a number of moderately deep lakes with a simple bowl shaped profile in which thermal stratification in summer leads to a hypolimnetic oxygen deficit. Using appropriate equipment with adequate replicate samples at each point along a number of transects, establishing the proper taxonomic identity of the true in-faunal elements to be considered in terms of both biomass and abundance, it should be possible to relate the distribution of benthos to depth, and to relate any deviation from a steady decline of these quantities with increasing depth to the frequency and amplitude of seiches. The seiches, or internal waves, should create an 'estuarine' zone in which cold, deoxygenated water alternates with warmer, oxygenated water over the bottom. The demonstration of such a correlation would then lead to a series of laboratory experiments. If there does prove to be a 'kink' in the curve of depth distribution for the benthos of an eutrophic lake, then differences in the shape of the curve in lakes in which oxygen supply is always available would be sought. We have practically all the data available from published surveys in our laboratory, but the attempt to compare the curves so derived is no more promising than similar attempts by others already cited; so the test should be based on a properly designed field programme. Establishing the distributions of the various species present may lead to the identification of groups of species exhibiting similar spatial patterns which, in itself, leads to other testable hypotheses. Although the benthos of Rostherne Mere failed to penetrate the region from 23 m to the bottom at 30 m (apart from dormant copepods and some *Procladius choreus* at 25 m), most species could be found from 1 m to 23 m. Various assemblages showed discrete distribution patterns in terms of relative abundance however (figure 3.12). The identification of such patterns in the spatial distribution of associations of benthic species will be discussed later on in terms of horizontal variability (which is, of course, a further extension of the subject under discussion) but many of the intensive surveys undertaken in the last few years have demonstrated the same thing as was apparent in Rostherne Mere—a few species may have similar distribution patterns but there are very considerable areas of overlap in the patterns, which makes the identification of zones inhabited by communities or associations almost impossible.

4 PRODUCTION AND PRODUCTIVITY

M. G. JOHNSON

The terms 'production' and 'productivity' should be distinguished. Production, as defined for limnologists by Thienemann (1931*b*), is the sum of growth increments of the individuals of a species population, both survivors and non-survivors, through a discrete time period. Generally, production of macroinvertebrates is referable to areal units. Productivity, on the other hand, indicates the trophic nature of a water body or subsystem, often implying the characteristics responsible for low or high productivity (Winberg, 1968). Possibly quantitative assessment of productivity may be achieved most closely with Ohle's (1956) 'bioactivity'. One of the purposes of this chapter is to explore the relationship between macroinvertebrate production and lake productivity.

It seems appropriate to concern ourselves first with studies aimed at measurement of production of lake benthic macroinvertebrates, assuming that reliable estimates of biomass and numbers of species populations of interest can be obtained. What is the state of the science? Are there sufficient data to commence the search for meaningful generalisation? We may assume that the techniques and results are needed, for example, in intensive aquaculture, in understanding and perhaps manipulating the role of macroinvertebrates in the self-purification of polluted waters, and in gaining a broader appreciation of the useful as well as damaging effects of water management in its broadest sense. A second topic, consistent with the recommended use of the term 'productivity', concerns the use of standing stocks to indicate lake productivity, which may be used —often together with other indices—to predict production of fish.

Production

Techniques

Marine biologists spearheaded the development and testing of techniques. Although Petersen (1911) suggested that the growth of marine macroinvertebrates was sufficient to double its biomass annually, Boysen-Jensen (1919) apparently was the first to set down a method, which continues to be used in various forms, and with much refinement, today. He calculated the production of the important benthic species in two bays of the Limfjord of Denmark. Each May between 1910 and 1917 he measured numbers and weights of bivalves and polychaetes. The growth increment of survivors and non-survivors (the decrease in numbers multiplied by the mean average weight) was added to the weight of newborn.

Production of chironomids (*Chironomus* spp.) in the Plöner See was calculated by Lundbeck (1926) as follows:

The estimated biomass of non-survivors between the time of peak numbers and the time of maximum biomass was added subsequently to the maximum biomass plus the weight increase of all larvae (table 4.1). Winberg (1968) indicated two problems, both leading to underestimation of production. First, recruitment of newborn would deflate the estimate of dead larvae and mean weight of survivors. Secondly, the weight of older larvae may have been underestimated through loss of larger larvae in pupation in emergence. Anderson and Hooper (1956) used the Boysen-Jensen technique to calculate production of *Tanytarsus jucundus*

TABLE 4.1. Bottom fauna production and lake typology from Lundbeck (1926)

Type*	*Chironomus*			Remainder			Molluscs			Total		
A I′	6	16	<1	29	124	17	846	1016	43?	881	1034	<100?
A II	(9)			(42)			(400)			(457)		
A II′	72	>200	4	81	142	29	255	988	54	408	1161	141
a)	30	42	4	84	89	73	83	122	54	197	246	145
b)	102	173	<100	83	126	40	176	404	68	301	604	242
c)	52	72	10	60	142	29	385	988	<100	497	1161	141
A III	104	1125	—	57	326	7	134	1000	—	295	1178	7
A′ I′	(11)			(28)			?			?		
A′ III	11	19	1	36	53	23	4	6	1	51	71	35
B′ I′	(7)			(69)			(11)			(87)		
B′ II	4	7	2	46	69	18	12	22	3	62	87	40
B′ II′	(23)			(54)			(29)			(100)		
B′ III	7	17	1	36	46	29	2	>2	—	45	65	30
B II	6	5	3	45	75	12	—			51	84	15
B III	12	15	4	62	91	12	—			74	106	16
a)	(15)			(91)						(106)		
b)	8	12	4	33	>33	12	—			41	>42	16
C′ II?	(—)			(41)			(—)			(41)		

Three columns for mean, maximum, maximum values in kgh/a.
* See table 2.4.

(=*Tribelos jucundus**) in Sugarloaf Lake in Michigan. Borutzky (1939*a*) and Yablonskaya (1947) measured production of the midge *Chironomus plumosus* on the basis of a thorough understanding of its life history and a more intense analysis than that performed by Lundbeck. Emergence traps were tended frequently to estimate numbers of emerging adults and egg depositions. Numbers and weights of larvae, pupating larvae and dead numbers of each cohort were estimated from grab samples taken two to three times monthly at several depths. They obtained estimates of numbers lost to predators as the difference between the maximum number in the cohort and the sum of those found dead, those which emerged and the survivors. To avoid problems due to migrations of larvae the entire population in the lake was calculated. Production was obtained as the sum of weights (calculated from length–weight regressions) of larvae consumed, larvae found dead, and emerged adults plus the difference between initial and final biomass. Also, the difference in weight between pre-pupal larvae and adults was included (perhaps 25 per cent loss in females and 50 per cent in males). However, respiratory expenditure could account for much of this and should not be included in production.

Winberg (1968) compared results from Borutzky's method with that of Boysen-Jensen using Yablonskaya's (1947) data (table 4.2). In the former method the separate treatment of dead, consumed and emerged individuals allowed better definition of animal weights at emergence and elimination (non-predatory and predatory mortalities), compared with the rough averages used by Boysen-Jensen and Lundbeck.

More recently Sokolova (1968) used Borutzky's method on several chironomids in the Russian Uchinsk reservoir with two refinements. She measured the number of egg layings in specially designed collectors and she was able to deal with early larval stages in the microbenthos. The foundation for these field techniques and analytical methods was a good understanding of life histories and distributions.

Nees and Dugdale (1959) used a simple model to calculate production of *Tribelos jucundus* with the data of Anderson and Hooper (1956) (figure 4.1). Curves of this type (numbers versus mean weight) have come to be

* Referred to as *Tribelos* in this chapter (=*Tanytarsus* or *Phaenopsectra*).

called Allen curves, following Allen's (1951) study on Horokiwi Stream of New Zealand, although they are basically the same as Boysen-Jensen's model. Production, which is the area under the curve, may be integrated in a number of ways. Anderson and Hooper used the approximation procedure of Boysen-Jensen. Nees and Dugdale's model, which requires exponential decline in numbers and increase in weight, allows

TABLE 4.2. Calculation of the eliminated biomass of *Chironomus plumosus* in Lake Maloe Medvezh'e (Yablonskaya, 1947, cited from Winberg, 1968)

	Development completed and emerged		Consumed by predators		Died between moults		Total loss (kg dry weight)	
Period of observation	Nos. 10^6	Mean dry weight of 1 larva (mg)*	Nos. 10^6	Mean dry weight of 1 larva (mg)	Nos. 10^6	Mean dry weight of 1 larva (mg)†	Borutski	Boysen-Jensen
5.vi–6.vii	0.3	6.80	75.1	2.03	176.2	0.58	256	511
6.vii–20.ix	10.2	5.70	95.1	4.60	72.0	2.96	709	816
20.ix–16.iv	0.8	6.08	4.2	4.50	35.3	2.77	122	181
16.iv–17.vi	7.4	6.90	2.8	6.80	5.7	7.53	113	108
5.vi–17.vi	—	—	—	—	—	—	1200	1616

* Weight of larva prior to pupation.
† Weight obtained from length measurements of the dead larvae.

direct calculation of the integral. Their estimate of production of *Tribelos jucundus* was 40 per cent greater than that arrived at with Boysen-Jensen's approximation. However, Allen curves can be integrated with graphical methods, as Allen himself did, eliminating the need for simplifying assumptions about the rates of change in numbers or mean animals weight. Obviously periods when mean weight may be declining present no special problems in graphical integration, while mathematical modelling of this not altogether uncommon trait would present difficulties.

Other examples of utilisation of the Boysen-Jensen method are several estimates of production of amphipods by Russian researchers. Markosyan (1948) followed the changes in numbers and individual mean weight in cohorts of *Gammarus lacustris* in Lake Sevan. Annual production was 42.3 g m^{-2}, about twice the mean annual biomass. Greze (1951) did essentially the same for *Pontoporeia affinis* in a lake and in a relatively warmer river. The amphipods reproduced after 1 year in the river and after 2 years in the lake; production was 45.5 g m^{-2} in the river, 13.10 g m^{-2} in the lake. Bekman examined *G. lacustris* (1954) and four amphipods (1959, 1962) in Baikal.

Limited use has been made of instantaneous growth rates and mean biomass to obtain production ($P = B \times G$) of benthic macroinvertebrates, although these have been used widely by fisheries workers (Ricker, 1971; Gerking, 1966). Winberg (1971) explained some of the difficulties inherent in this approach. Individuals of different size and age groups can be expected to differ in rate of growth; therefore the production of each group should be calculated and summed. The problem may, of course, be minimal with recognisable cohorts in which the size range is less than in populations of continuously reproducing animals.

Teal (1957) isolated worms in cores to determine the increase in biomass without predation; he was able to calculate loss through mortality by comparison of increase of biomass in cores with the biomass change in Root Spring.

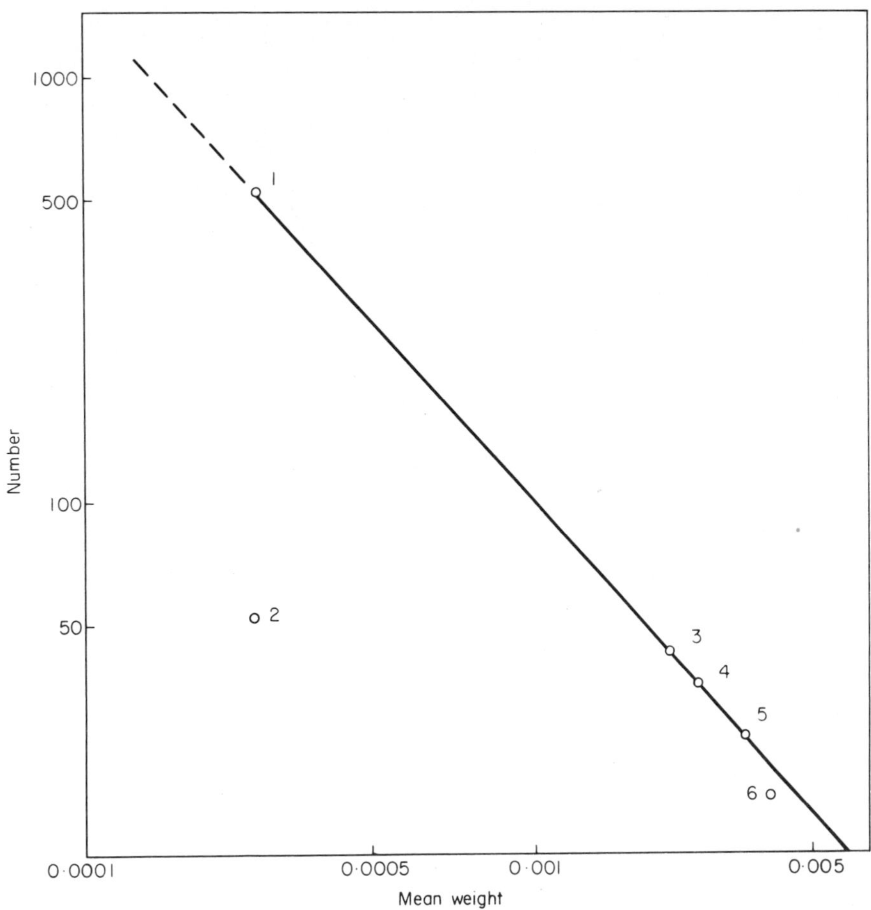

FIGURE 4.1. Relationship between the number and mean individual weight of *Tribelos jucundus* in Sugarloaf Lake (log. scale). [Sample dates: 1 August, 2 September, 3 December, 4 January, 5 March, 6 April (Nees and Dugdale, 1959).]

Johnson and Brinkhurst (1971*b*) used the mean biomass-instantaneous growth rate model to determine production of several dominant species of the sediments of the Bay of Quinte and nearby Lake Ontario. Cohorts of chironomids were followed with field sampling at 1-month and sometimes 2-week intervals. Values of *G* (instantaneous growth rate) were more closely related to temperature than to mean weight. Cohorts of oligochaetes and sphaeriids of average size were set up in the laboratory in native muds to permit calculation of instantaneous growth rates. Temperature appeared to have the greatest effect on *G* (figure 4.2). Differences among stations were detected in oligochaetes which could have been differences in part due to species composition. However, values of *G* in *Pontoporeia affinis* and *Asellus racovitzai* were influenced less by temperature and more by age and size of the animals, possibly in combination with environmental factors. In fact, the changes in *G* through the life cycle of these two species in the Bay of Quinte and Lake Ontario illustrate the sort of complexity inimical to broad application of *G* values calculated for one or even a few sizes (figure 4.3). The main advantage of this method is to permit calculation of production of populations of animals such as oligochaetes and sphaeriids with protracted periods of reproduction. Although laboratory experiments are required which may introduce some unknown factors into results, oligochaetes

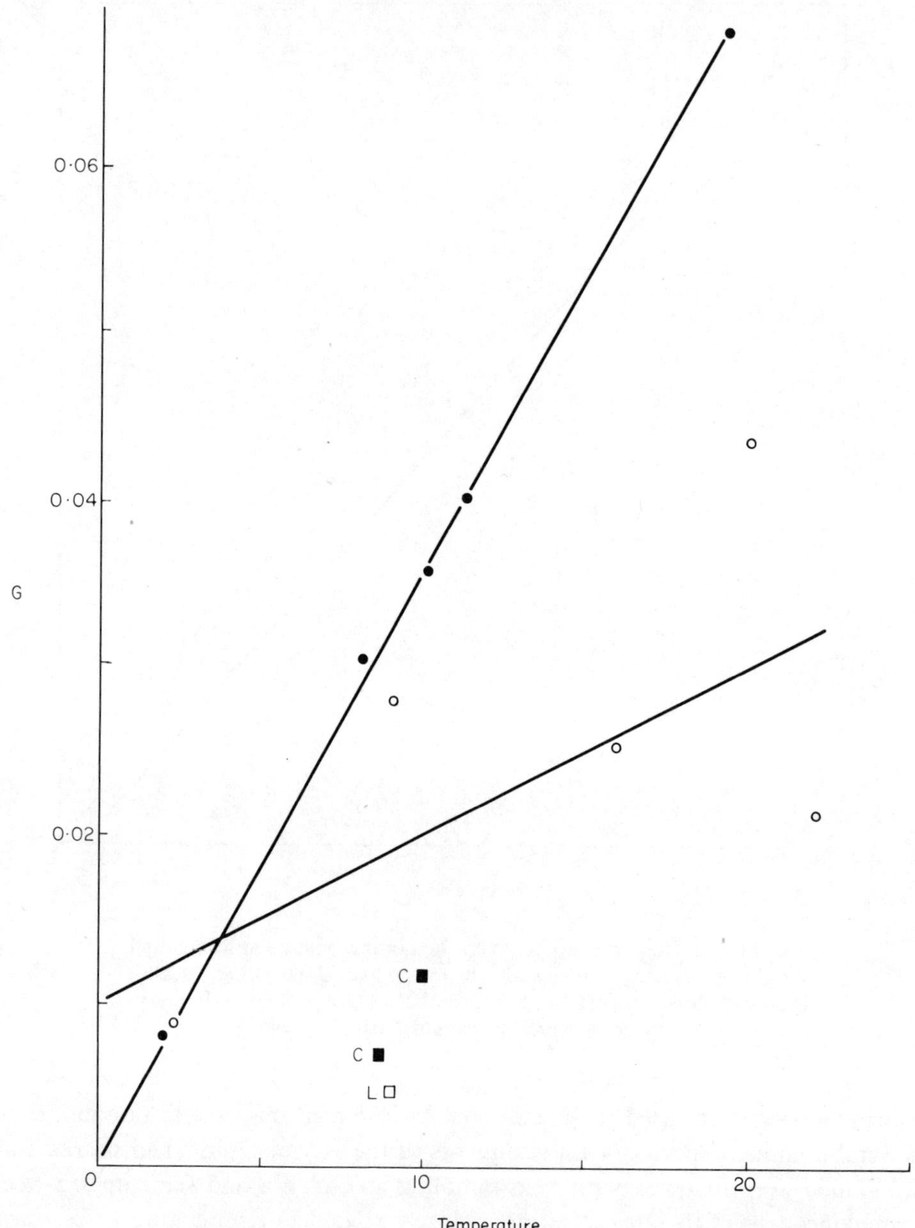

FIGURE 4.2. Instantaneous growth rates in relation to temperature for Oligochaetes (Johnson and Brinkhurst, 1971*b*). Lines represent equations calculated with least squares method. Open and closed circles and squares represent data from four stations in the Bay of Quinte-Lake Ontario trophic gradient.

and sphaeriids (at least the pisidia) are infaunal feeders which may be expected to perform similarly in the mud in the lake and that brought into the laboratory.

Cooper (1965) used a method, often employed on planktonic crustaceans, to estimate production of *Hyalella azteca* in Sugarloaf Lake, Michigan. Measurements of antennal segment numbers and head lengths

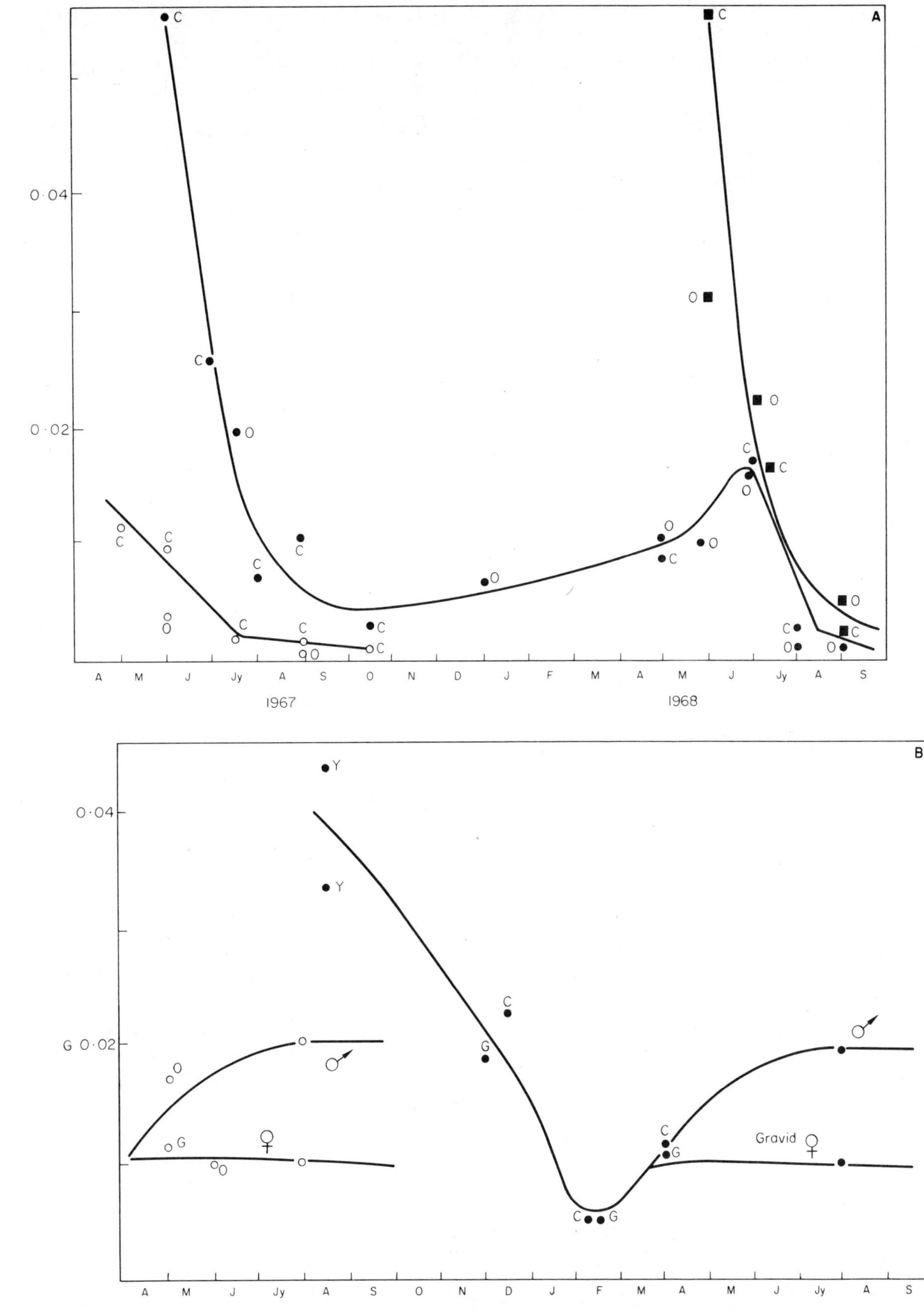

FIGURE 4.3. Instantaneous growth rates (A) *Pontoporeia affinis* (B) *Asellus racovitzai* (Johnson and Brinkhurst, 1971*b*). Open circles at left—1966 year class in 1967 (age 1); closed circles—1967 year class; squares on right—1968 year class.

provided the means to separate the amphipods into six instars and the adult stage. Laboratory experiments at various temperatures provided data on temperature-specific moulting rates. The technique consisted of

> . . . extrapolation of the instar frequency distribution from one sample period to the next using the number of eggs present in the females, the number of amphipods in each instar, laboratory estimates of temperature = specific moulting rates, observed ambient temperatures and time intervals between sampling dates. Thus for every sample after the first, there exists an observed and an expected instar frequency distribution. The difference between the expected and the observed numbers of animals is the estimated number of animals removed from the population during the interval between samples.

With this mortality expressed as a fraction of the biomass, Cooper calculated production as the product of mortality and mean biomass. Average daily production was 0.129 kg ha^{-1} and mean biomass was 4.07 kg ha^{-1}. The population was relatively stable in size and structure due to a size-specific mortality factor operating on the mature amphipods—a predilection by yellow perch (*Perca flavescens*) for that size.

Production may also be calculated from data on respiration rates and growth efficiencies of animals, because the latter is defined in terms of production or growth (P) and respiration (R) ($E_g = P/(P+R)$), where E_g, the growth efficiency, is the 'energy coefficient of growth of the second order' of Ivlev (1945), 'tissue growth efficiency' of Odum (1957) and 'net efficiency of growth' of Richman (1958). An oxycalorific quotient of 0.00338 cal per mg O_2 has been used to convert respiration data to energy units (Ivlev, 1934; Teal, 1957; Johnson and Brinkhurst, 1971*b*). The caloric equivalent of oxygen consumption varies by only 5 per cent over the RQ range 0.71–1.00 (Slobodkin, 1962). One advantage of the method, which Winberg (1968) termed the 'physiological approach', is that an estimate of production is available from weight-frequency data, provided that respiration rates and growth efficiencies have been established. Therefore, the approach may be useful for species with continuous reproduction. In fact, its primary use to date has been on zooplankters (Winberg, 1968), although Johnson (1970) used the method on benthic macroinvertebrates of the Bay of Quinte and Lake Ontario. His estimates were approximately the same as those obtained using the instantaneous growth rate–mean biomass technique (Johnson and Brinkhurst, 1971*b*). It should be pointed out, however, that some common data were applied to both estimates. The limitations of this technique due to positive interspecific interaction were discovered in working with three tubificid species that dominate the benthos of Toronto Harbour, Lake Ontario (Brinkhurst, 1970) (see p. 105).

Techniques which involve estimation of benthic macroinvertebrate production as the ration of fish populations appear to have limited potential in lakes of any size, except perhaps those with very simple communities of well studied fishes. Furthermore, macroinvertebrate production in emergent insects and that directed to the decomposer cycle, and to macroinvertebrate predators, would not be included in such estimates.

A variety of techniques has been described here in general terms. Discussions of these in detail, replete with mathematical treatments, are now available (Kakaj, 1967, 1968; Winberg, 1968; Edmondson and Winberg, 1971). Although many of the methods appear powerful, the need for sound interpretations of life histories, distributions and responses of species to environmental factors needs re-emphasising. Jonasson's (1965) studies on *Chironomus anthracinus* in Esrom is an excellent example of the kind of understanding required before reliable estimates of production and their interpretation can be made.

Turnover ratio

Measurements of benthic macroinvertebrate production are so scarce that only generalisations about annual turnover ratios (P/B values) will be made here. Insufficient data exist for any meaningful review of seasonal, annual and successional variations in production rates. However, evidence is mounting which points to some uniformity in turnover ratios, at least when compared with water temperature and taxonomic variations.

The amphipod, *Gammarus lacustris*, had a mean biomass of 20.6 g m^{-2} in the *Chara* zone of Lake Sevan (USSR); Markosyan (1948) estimated its production to be 42.3 g m^{-2}, indicating a turnover ratio (P/B coefficient) of 2. Bekman (1954) reported an annual turnover ratio of 3 in another population of this species. Two populations of *Pontoporeia affinis* had turnover ratios of 1.9 and 3.4 (Greze, 1951). Johnson and Brinkhurst (1971*b*) estimated turnover ratios in *Pontoporeia affinis* at three stations in Lake Ontario and Bay of Quinte. These ratios were 2.3 at a mean bottom water temperature of 7°C, about 2 at 6°C and close to 1 at 3°–4°C. Bekman (1959, 1962) calculated production of three amphipods of Lake Baikal and adjoining waters (Posol'ski Sor). The annual production of *Micruropus kluki* on nearshore sandy sediments was 2.5 times its average biomass. Two other species with annual life cycles, *M. possolskii* and *Gammarus fasciatus*, had respective turnover ratios of 3.6 and 2.9 in Posol'ski Sor. However, the former had a 2-year cycle and the turnover ratio was 1.6 on open Baikal coasts. Cooper's *Hyalella azteca* in Sugarloaf Lake had a turnover ratio of 3.8–4.8 (depending on whether the daily production calculated by Cooper was maintained for 4 or for 5 months).

More production estimates of chironomids have been made than for other comparable taxa (table 4.3). Higher turnover ratios are characteristic of littoral chironomid associations, and lower rates are observed in profundal chironomids. Unfortunately the average temperatures corresponding to these ratios are generally unavailable. However, they are available from the Lake Ontario studies (Johnson and Brinkhurst,

TABLE 4.3. Annual number of generations and turnover ratios for groups of chironomids and some individual species

Organism	Water	Number of generations in year	Annual TR	Author
Chironomidae	Uchinsk Res., profundal	1	4.5	Sokolova, 1968
	Uchinsk Res., sublittoral	1–2	8.0	
	Uchinsk Res., littoral	2 & more	18.5	
Chironomidae	Masurian lakes, sublittoral	2 & more	15.0	Kajak and Rybak, 1966
	Masurian lakes, profundal	1	3.8	
Chironomidae	Costello L. littoral	1–2	8–9	Miller, 1941
	Costello L. profundal	0.5–1	2–3	
Chironomidae	Inner Bay of Quinte (sublittoral)	1–2	14.7	Johnson and Brinkhurst, 1971
	Middle Bay of Quinte (profundal)	1	8.3	
	Outer Bay of Quinte (profundal)	1	5.2	
	Lake Ontario (profundal)	1 & less	3.1	
Tribelos jucundus	Sugarloaf L.	1	3.4	Anderson and Hooper, 1956
Calopsectra dives	Root Spring (10 C)	1	3.5	
Anatopynia dyari	Root Spring (10 C)	1	2.7	
Chironomus plumosus	Lake Beloie, 2–13 m	2	2.4	Borutski, 1939
Chironomus plumosus	Bol'shoe Medvezh'e	2	3.0	Yablonskaya, 1947
	Maloe Medvezh'e	2	2.6	
Chironomus	Plensk Lake	?	3.4	Lundbeck, 1926

1971*b*). Turnover ratios averaged 14.7 at 11°C in the inner Bay of Quinte, 8.3 at 8°C in the middle Bay, 5.2 at 7°C in the outer Bay and 3.1 at 6°C in Lake Ontario at a depth of 40 m. Maximum temperatures were 22°C, 20°C, 18°C, and 17°C at these four locations. Turnover ratios of other groups and species are provided in this study, together with temperature data. Brinkhurst (1972) suggested a turnover rate of 15 for tubificids in Toronto Harbour, based on constant standing stock of 20.6 g dry wt m^{-2} (18.3 g ash free dry wt) with a production of 1550 kcal m^{-2} $year^{-1}$, assimilation of 1743 kcal at an average temperature of just over 10°C.

Standing stock sometimes has been used as an index of productivity, although the danger is generally recognised. However, Johnson and Brinkhurst indicated (shown here in figure 4.4) that 'standing stock values, together with data on mean temperature may be useful in making inferences about benthic macroinvertebrate production in the [St. Lawrence] Great Lakes'.

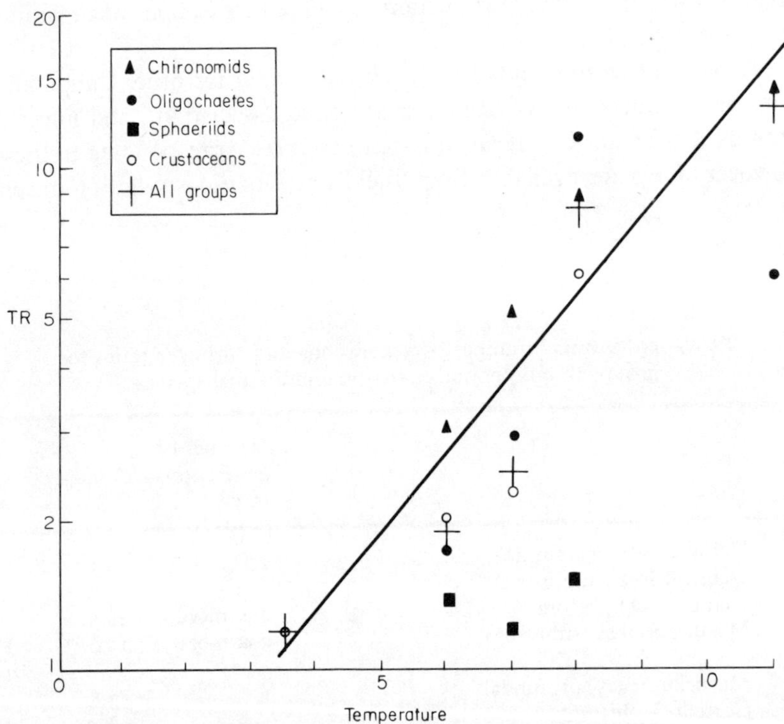

Figure 4.4. Relation between annual mean temperature (C) and turnover ratio (TR) of the macroinvertebrate community and of broad taxonomic groups at five stations in the Bay of Quinte and Lake Ontario (Johnson and Brinkhurst, 1971*b*).

Waters (1969) pointed to the similarities in turnover ratios *per generation* from both published accounts and theoretical calculations in which the shape of Allen curves, growth pattern, ratio of initial and final weights and numbers were modified within realistic limits. The turnover ratio of freshwater benthic invertebrates *per generation* was relatively constant, about 2.5 to 5 with a mode near 3.5. Waters' turnover ratios multiplied by the number of generations (1 or less in cold, deep waters, often near 1 in deep waters of moderately cool temperature and 2 or more in the warmed, shallow zone of lakes) yield turnover ratios *per year* similar to those given in this account.

If further investigations substantiate this fundamental relationship of turnover ratio with temperature, more importance may be placed on standing stock values. Also, such data may be interpreted differently as indices of lake productivity. What it does suggest, however, is that temperature may have a controlling influence on the turnover ratio of the whole macroinvertebrate community as it affects the ingestion, respiration and growth of individuals within the community. That is, biomass of the animals may be adjusted to the utilisable energy supply consistent with a turnover ratio set by temperature.

Benthic community metabolism

The growing interest in functional aspects of benthic macroinvertebrate communities—for example, production of biomass, use of energy and geochemical cycling—requires a useful conceptual basis. In a general way this has been provided through the studies of Odum (1957), Golley (1968), Engelmann (1966, 1968), Darnell (1968), Slobodkin (1962), Mann (1969) and others.

In these studies, we attempt to delineate the flows of energy, or sometimes materials, through an entire system. Inputs are measurable in terms of sunlight energy trapped by photosynthesis in primary production, but in benthic terms the rain of sediment from the illuminated shallow water zone (autochthonous supply) may be augmented by river or windborne flows from terrestrial sources (allochthonous material) much of which is nowadays introduced by man *via* erosion or more directly from the sewer pipe and the factory outfall. The sedimented material is the energy and materials (food) source for the microbiota of bacteria, protozoa and other minute denizens of the mud! These probably form the primary food of all so-called detritus feeders (detritus being the original term for any otherwise unidentifiable trash in the sediment, now known to be largely bacteria) including the oligochaetes. Chironomids may depend more directly on the rain of material from above but more of that later. It is clear that an analysis of import, respiratory losses, assimilation, and decomposition can be used to build functional pictures of energy utilisation and efficiency of biological communities in the same way as metabolic parameters can be established for individuals. Brinkhurst and Johnson (1971*c*) attempted to apply these concepts specifically to benthic community metabolism and a summary account of their work is given here.

Imported energy was measured by catching sedimented detritus while benthic community respiration was measured in cored samples of bottom muds. Assimilation of energy by macroinvertebrates was estimated as the sum of growth and respiration, with detritivores and invertebrate carnivores treated separately. The energy passed on to and used by fish was estimated to be, at most, 90 per cent of available macroinvertebrate production. Two estimates of community metabolism, one including and the other excluding predicted respiration by fish, were not widely different.

The first value of interest was the proportion of energy reaching the sediment that was utilised by the benthic community. This value was low (0.23) in the inner Bay of Quinte and increased to near 1 in the outer bay and Lake Ontario. Proportionately more poorly utilised allochthonous import occurred in the inner bay, which was substantiated by the relatively high organic content in bottom mud there. Clearly, data on the organic content of bottom muds are not indicative of benthic productivity, rather, high organic content indicates inefficiencies in energy transfer, perhaps partly explaining why others have found inverse relationships between macroinvertebrate standing stocks and organic content of sediments (for example, Rawson, 1930, figure 11). The second measurement of interest was the proportion of total energy utilised (and exported) that was attributable to macroinvertebrates. The difference between total benthic respiration and oxygen consumption by macroinvertebrates may be regarded as the 'cost' to the macroinvertebrate community of mediation (and competition?) by the microbiota. This value was lower in the inner bay (0.1) and higher (0.3) at lakeward stations. The third proportion of interest was the growth efficiency (growth/assimilation) of the macroinvertebrate assemblage, which varied from 0.68 in the inner bay to 0.34 at a Lake Ontario station. The chironomid-dominated association had the greatest, and the amphipod-dominated association the lowest, growth efficiency.

These three proportions were combined in a simple model of benthic invertebrate production, $P = c(a \cdot b \cdot IM)$, where c is the proportion of growth to respired and exported energy and is derived from the average growth efficiency of macroinvertebrates, a is the proportion of imported energy used by the total benthic community and b is the proportion of the latter used by macroinvertebrates. The relationship between production and energy import was deduced. All of the parameters a, b and c probably decrease with increasing import, although c may be low initially at low import and sparse food supply, and should decrease at higher levels of import at which the environment is substantially altered through the use of that import. More time and energy must be devoted by the animal to respiratory and other activities (Alsterberg, 1922; Brundin, 1951). Finally, at extremely high levels of import, c may become critically low and production by certain species may cease altogether. Critically low growth efficiencies are speculative but they may exist in relation to prolonged development time of an animal, prolonged exposure to predators, and other factors. Changes in the species composition to more 'tolerant' species would tend to counteract the tendency for relative production to decline in an increasingly severe environment. Also, species able to maximise the value of b; that is, to minimise 'loss' to mediating microflora, could have a competitive advantage. At any rate, this would be a useful rationale in the study of succession of macroinvertebrates in eutrophication, in that it provides testable hypotheses.

In summary, the graphical relation of production of macroinvertebrates to energy import, in view of the probable changes in the parameters, is an inverted 'U' intersecting the abscissa (import) at the origin and again at extremely high energy import levels. The maximum macroinvertebrate production (which may or may not be an optimum, for example, for fish production) or any other level of production, eventually should be predictable at a given site from import data. Import of energy by bottom sediments is related, in part, to primary productivity and the latter, in turn, is related to nutrient loadings and, finally, to the influence of man. In time it should be possible to develop, and test, models that would include nutrient loadings, primary production, energy import to the benthos (with modification of the benthic environment; for example, oxygen deficits) and production and diversity in benthic macroinvertebrates, as well as other consumers.

Standing Stocks and Lake Productivity

The benthic macroinvertebrate community, particularly standing stocks of benthos, has appealed to many biologists as a valuable index of lake productivity. The relative stability of this community, compared for example with that of the plankton, and its physical location in the lake system where near-surface events tend to be integrated, are in part responsible for the popularity of the benthos as an indicator in many inquiries. Of course, many studies have dealt with a wide variety of lake characteristics, biotic and abiotic, but in general benthic macroinvertebrates have been included. A large number of these surveys have been done by fisheries biologists searching for a reasonable degree of prediction of sustained fish yields. Others have carried the work farther into the field of regional limnology. Alm (1922) introduced this field of quantitative comparison of benthic fauna and fish yield (as seen in table 2.3) and it was also employed by Lundbeck

(1926) who estimated production (table 4.4) of chironomids, the rest of the benthos, and mollusc flesh (excluding the heavy, non-living shells) for the various lake types defined in table 2.4. Humic lakes were seen to support a slightly lower biomass than harmonic lakes, and oligotrophic lakes have slightly less benthos than eutrophic lakes (characterised as various *Chironomus* lake types), so long as molluscs are not included, but this is more than compensated for by the quantity of molluscan benthos found in oligotrophic lakes, especially along the shallow margins. This was confirmed by a later study of alpine lakes (Lundbeck, 1936, table 4.4) where benthic production of a series of lakes was quite uniform apart from fluctuations in mollusca. Several critics of the Lake Typology system, including Valle (1927) and Brundin (1949, 1951) suggested that quantitative as well as qualitative criteria should be used in determining lake typology.

TABLE 4.4. Biomass of benthos in relation to typology after Lundbeck (1936)

Type*	Molluscs	Remainder	Total
A Ia	15 (6–20)	38 (24–59)	53 (30–75)
A Ib	326 (10–1932)	59 (28–85)	355 (50–1986)
A I/IIa	26 (9–34)	40 (25–55)	66 (39–109)
A I/IIb	115 (1–404)	52 (41–67)	167 (68–445)
A IIa	22 (5–44)	90 (81–98)	112 (87–142)
A IIb	8 (?–15)	82 (30–154)	90 (30–154)
A′ IIa	27 (19–36)	25 (19–31)	52 (38–66)
B′ I/IIb	11	27	38
B′ IIc	1 (?–1)	49 (47–52)	50 (47–53)
B IIc	1424 (1–5645)	76 (54–95)	1500 (65–5738)

Values are mean (minimum–maximum) in kg/ha for so-called 'normal' lakes i.e. excluding those affected by man, or by rivers. The original table also separates data by depth zones.

* See Table 2.10.

The importance of geologic characteristics of lake watersheds and nutrient supplies to lake productivity were emphasised by Naumann (1932), Deevey (1940, 1941), Moyle (1946) and others. The importance of lake morphometry was stressed by Thienemann (1927) and Rawson (1930), while the modifying effect of lake dimensions on basic edaphic factors was well understood and stated by Rawson some time ago (1939).

Rawson (1930) demonstrated a relationship between standing stocks of benthic macroinvertebrates and the product of lake area and depth in seven North American lakes (figure 4.5). He suggested '40 square miles (10 360 ha) as a tentative limit at which area ceases . . . to have importance in this connection', and decided that 'depths greater than 100 ft (30 m) have no dominant effect'. The product of area × depth was not referred to as 'volume' since Rawson felt that the two factors should be considered as separate influences. Chief factors which may result in a deviation from this relationship were, according to Rawson, 'the configuration of the shoreline, the nature of the watershed and the climate of the country'.

Deevey (1941) compared standing stocks of lake groups in Germany, Russia, Sweden, Norway, Finland and Connecticut, USA; he concluded that 'the quantity of bottom fauna in a lake evidently does not reflect the real, or primary typology (edaphic factors and climate)'. This rather hasty conclusion apparently was based on two facts: first, according to Deevey, eutrophic lakes in northern Germany had standing stocks no greater than his Connecticut lakes which were 'oligotypic for phosphorus and mesotrophic from the standpoint of the increment in the hypolimnetic oxygen deficit' and, secondly, Green Lake, Lake Mendota and

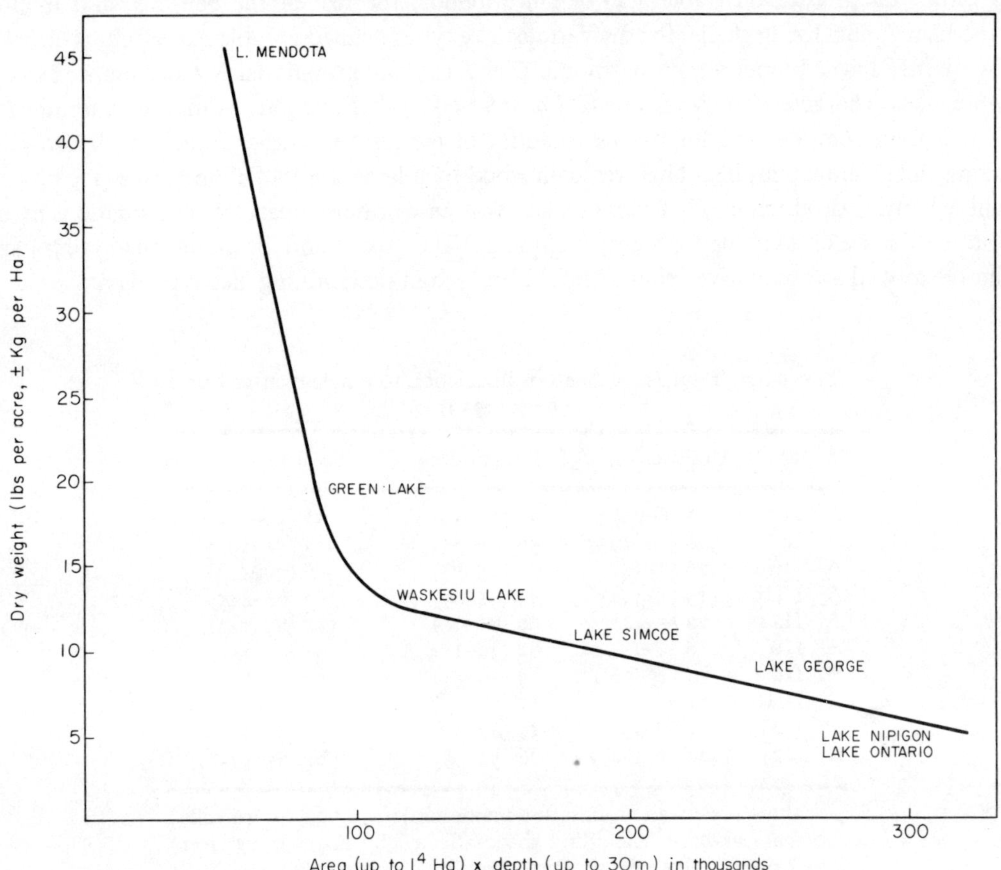

FIGURE 4.5. The relation between benthos and the product of depth and area (within limits) of lakes (Rawson, 1930).

Linsley Pond did not rank in terms of bottom fauna as they did in mean plankton crops. Deevey appreciated that 'morphometric typology' may have obscured patterns, so he continued his analysis by comparing standing stocks to area—which produced a 'shotgun plot'—and standing stocks to mean depth. In the latter 'the resulting plot resembles an hyperbola, with the North German lakes ranged along one axis, the Alpenrandseen and other deep lakes along the other, and the remaining lakes in the corner' (figure 4.6). Rather strangely, this plot shows that the northern German lakes had much greater standing stocks than did his Connecticut lakes. His final conclusion was that, 'since benthic productivity is correlated neither with primary nor secondary (morphometric) typology, one may conclude that both classes of factors, perhaps together with others, are responsible, and that in all probability no simple relationship exists between the quantity of bottom fauna and the lake type'.

Rawson appreciated the real complexity of these interactions and his interpretations of lake characteristics and their basic productivities (1942, 1952, 1953*a*, 1953*b*, 1957, 1959) added to a growing understanding of Canadian lakes. Among these, his analysis of large alpine lakes (1942) showed the influence and interaction of the major factors, edaphic, climatic and morphometric. Bottom fauna standing stocks were positively related to plankton stocks, while the latter, in turn, was related to the concentration of salts dissolved in the water. Extremes in climate and morphometry were found in certain cases to prevent the expression of fav-

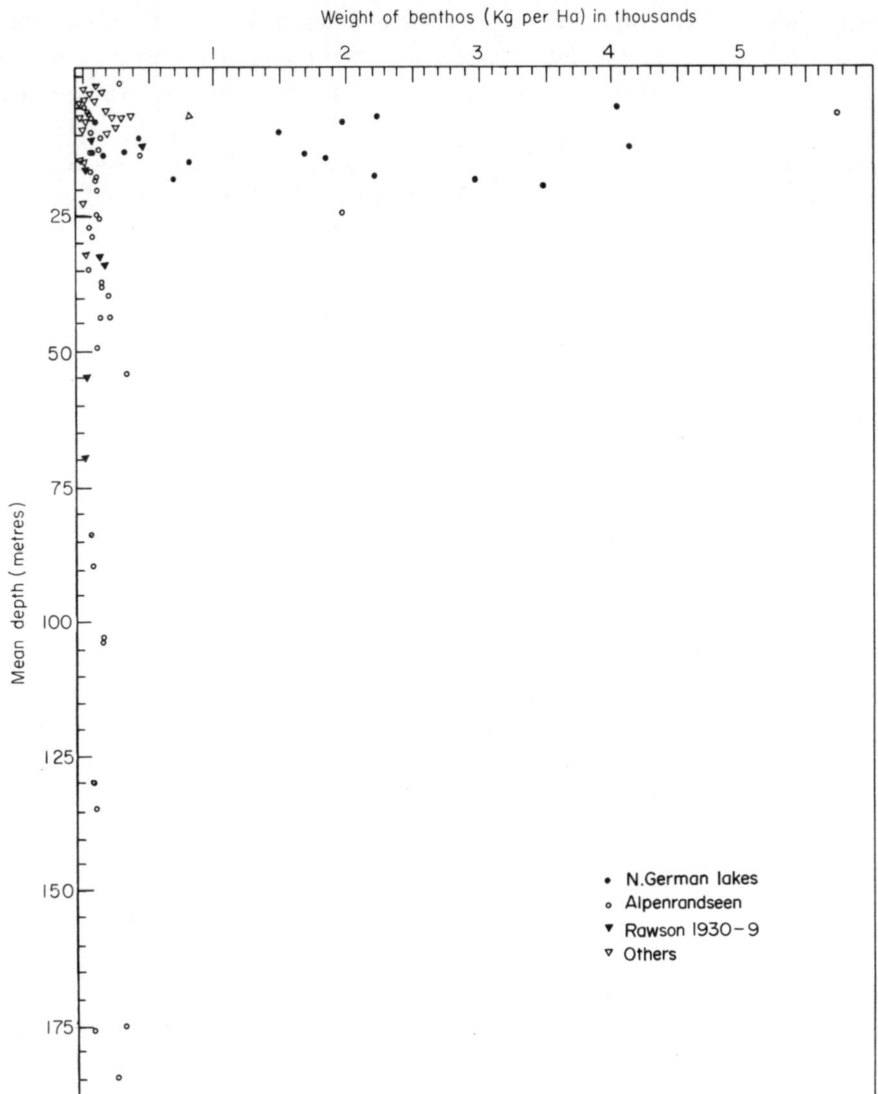

FIGURE 4.6. Relation between bottom fauna and mean depth for 116 lakes of temperate latitudes (Deevey, 1941).

ourable edaphic situations in these alpine lakes. Lakes of the western plains, especially those Saskatchewan lakes occurring on glacial drift and on the Precambrian Shield, or straddling both zones, may have been responsible for Rawson's unflagging interest in the field of regional limnology. In the Saskatchewan waters, he almost always found consistent agreement among physical and biological indices of lake productivity (Rawson, 1960).

Bio-indices of lake productivity were obtained by Northcote and Larkin (1956) for a large number of lakes in British Columbia, representing ten limnological regions with a wide range of climate and altitude. The clearest positive correlations were between dissolved solids concentrations and crops of plankton, and between benthic macroinvertebrates and fish. Sparse bottom faunas were confined to waters with less than

180 ppm dissolved solids and were most often recorded in lakes with more than 120 ppm. Lakes with moderate standing stocks varied widely in dissolved solids concentration. The only generalisation on bottom fauna and lake depth was 'that fauna from lakes of great mean depth were never as high as those found in *some* lakes of low mean depth'.

A subsequent study in British Columbia included the examination of nine lakes, selected to minimise variation in climate and lake morphometry, to evaluate the importance of total dissolved solids in determining standing stocks of plankton, bottom fauna and fish (Sparrow, 1966). Ranking by physical and chemical 'indices' of productivity, including mean depth and dissolved solids, did not agree with ranking based on standing stocks. Possible complicating factors were seasonal water level fluctuations, basin shape, presence or absence of macrophytes and cyprinids, faunal deficiencies (*Gammarus* sp. was absent in some lakes) and perimeter to area ratios.

Reimers *et al.* (1955) found that rankings based on chemical, physical and invertebrate abundance were in almost total disagreement in ten California mountain lakes. Yet growth in trout (*Salvelinus fontinalis*, *Salmo gairdneri* and *S. trutta*) was positively correlated to total dissolved solids.

Hayes (1957) drew on Deevey's and additional lake survey data and found no systematic trends in bottom fauna stocks in relation to mean depth (figure 4.7). Hayes stated that 'the conclusions then, which were drawn by Deevey are confirmed. Perhaps they are also strengthened by the inclusion of additional lakes and a somewhat different treatment of the data'.

In pursuing the question further we can examine, first, some operational difficulties in conducting analyses of this type, and secondly, some major conceptual difficulties. Most readers will appreciate the problem encountered in comparing the work of numerous authors: type of grab and grade of sieve; frequency and

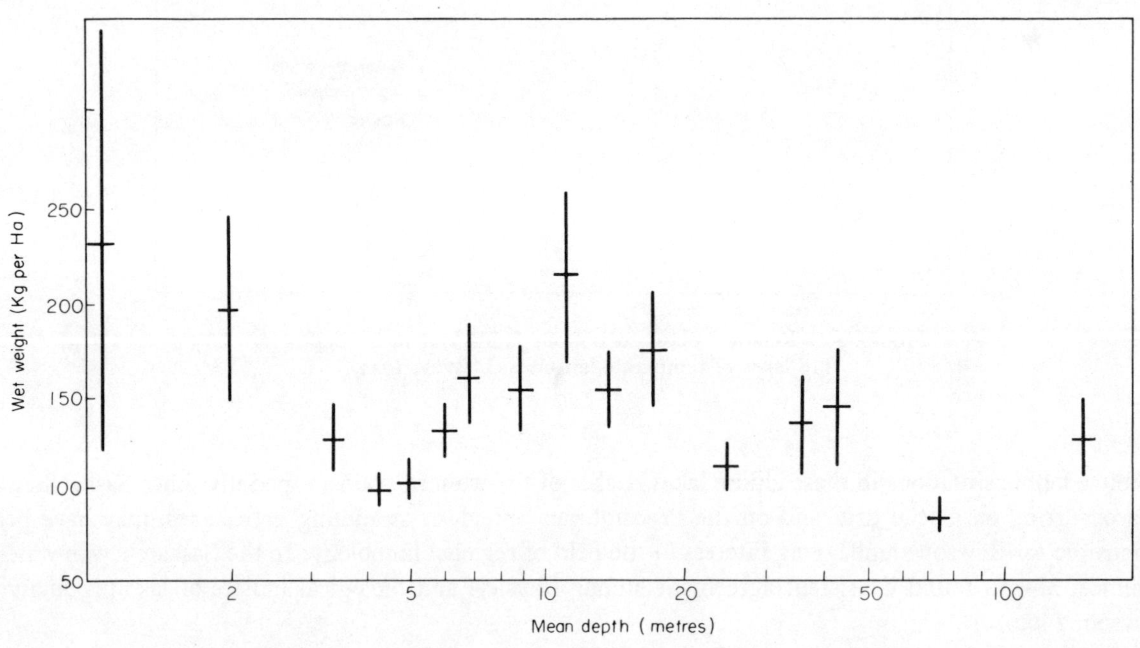

FIGURE 4.7. The relationship between depth and weight of benthos (excluding molluscs) in 158 lakes from the Alps, N. Germany, N. Canada, USA. Each point mean for 6–16 lakes, vertical line equals standard error (Hayes, 1957).

time of sampling; depths of sampling; method of derivation of dry weight (weights of alcohol preserved animals may be much too low); whether mollusc shell weights were deducted; whether the mean standing stock for a lake was appropriately weighed in relation to areas of depth zones; and so on. Some errors will undoubtedly cancel one another, others will be additive, and, in general, there is bound to be some difficulty in recognising the strengths of various authors' data (see chapter 6).

Conceptual problems are more difficult and, unfortunately, have been given less attention than obvious methodology problems. The fact that standing stocks are, in themselves, only an index of benthic macroinvertebrate production, and that actual production rates, with probably high year-to-year variation, are affected by many variables, is generally recognised. The degree to which benthic macroinvertebrate production reflects production of fish is another complicating problem, which will not be examined here, in the application of lake productivity indices to fisheries management.

Benthic macroinvertebrate production may be related to the rate of supply of energy to bottom sediments, although the efficiency of use of this energy by macroinvertebrates can be expected to vary over a wide range (Johnson and Brinkhurst, 1971*c*). However, there may be good correlation between benthic and limnetic production (usually plus marginal production also). Standing stocks of benthic macroinvertebrates often have been correlated directly with standing stocks of net plankton (Rawson, 1942; Deevey, 1941). Total dissolved solids also may reflect additions of specific nutrients (Moyle, 1946) and, hence, may correlate well with primary production. Therefore the relationship between production of benthic macroinvertebrates and total dissolved solids—albeit remote and tenuous—is, and has been, useful as the 'edaphic' component in lake productivity models. Climate, on the other hand, has not been quantified in a way that would be of much value with respect to benthic production, in the way that mean epilimnetic temperatures and standing stocks of plankton have been directly related (Rawson, 1942). Mean temperature in the deep water zone as well as in the marginal areas, would be required. Temperature may be less important as a primary limiting factor than as a controlling factor in the previously discussed turnover ratio. To illustrate further, two lakes may have the same rate of production of benthic macroinvertebrates, one under colder conditions, on the average over the lake bottom, than the other. Very likely the latter lake would be shallower. However, if turnover ratio is determined by temperature, the standing stock of the warmer, shallower basin would be the lesser of the two. To carry this argument to a set of lakes, representing a series in mean bottom temperature and depth, it is clear that a *positive* relationship between standing stocks and mean depth must be shown. Deevey (1941) found a positive relationship, as did Hayes (1957) through mean lake depths of 4–12 m (figure 4.7). Hayes' data showed an inverse relationship at mean depths greater than 12 m, and perhaps these lakes have similarly cold temperatures (4°–6°C) over long periods, so that the expected inverse relationship to depth is not obscured. In spite of this confusion, mean depth is a key component which should be related to production of benthic macroinvertebrates. Energy in sedimenting detritus is used in vertical transit and less energy would remain with increasing depth. Temperature effects may be complex, with the two major ones opposed; that is, increased temperature would encourage more rapid energy use but would permit a more rapid rate of sedimentation. In deeper lakes the effect of temperature would be more consistent and a decrease in production of macroinvertebrates with increased lake depth is to be expected. The problem comes in assuming that standing stocks are proportional to production. There are two courses open to the investigator: first to convert standing stocks to estimated production rates, assuming the values of turnover ratios; while the second is to stratify the data on the basis of arbitrary intervals in mean bottom temperature (cold, intermediate temperature, warm and so on). The first course of action may be premature, although there seems little doubt that even these crude data on production would be better than standing stock estimates alone. The second course may weaken the analysis, even though edaphic influences may be revealed more clearly in the process, because subdivision of data on the basis of temperature would also divide data with respect to depth.

In summary then, the traditional use of total dissolved solids and mean depth seems appropriate. Ryder's morphoedaphic index (1965), total dissolved solids divided by mean depth, proved to be reasonably successful in the prediction of fish yields (probably a much better index of fish production than standing stocks) but it has not been related to bottom fauna. Area may have additional value in the attempt to incorporate the effect of diminishing enrichment of the profundal zone of a lake from the littoral zone, and allochthonous import which would be expected with increasing lake area.

Four sets of North American lakes—Rawson's central Canadian lakes; alpine lakes from British Columbia, California and Colorado; lakes of the St. Lawrence basin; Atlantic region lakes in Nova Scotia, Maine and Connecticut—have been examined statistically, first separately and then as a unit. Pertinent data were readily available on 116 lakes in all (Adamstone, 1924; Bajkov, 1930; Colborn, 1966; Cooper, 1939, 1940, 1941, 1942; Cooper and Fuller, 1945; Cronk, 1932; Deevey, 1940, 1941; Henson, 1954; Johnson and Brinkhurst, 1971*b*; Juday, 1921, 1924, 1942; Larkin, 1964; Mendis, 1956; Miller, 1937; Rawson, 1930, 1934, 1942, 1953*a*, 1953*b*, 1957, 1959, 1960*a*, 1960*b*; Rawson and Atton, 1953; Rawson and Moore, 1944; Reimers *et al.* 1955; Scott *et al.* 1928; Smith, 1952, 1961; Tebo, 1955; Wood, 1963). Stepwise multiple regression was performed, first with standing stocks as the dependent variable, then with mean depth, area and total dissolved solids as the three independent variables. Logarithms of all variables were taken to reflect the expected curvilinear relationships. In all but one instance (the St. Lawrence basin set of lakes) between 42 and 64 per cent of the total variability in standing stocks could be accounted by these factors (table 4.5). Standing stocks were consistently related inversely to mean depth and area, and directly to total

TABLE 4.5. Summary of stepwise multiple regression analysis of standing stocks and production index of benthic macroinvertebrates in North American lakes in relation to three independent variables, mean lake depth, lake area and total dissolved solids concentration. In stepwise multiple regression the effect of the independent variable which accounts for most of the variability in the dependent variable is assessed first, then the additional effect of the 'next most important' independent variable is assessed, and so on. For example, variation in total dissolved solids accounted for 21.6% of the variability in standing stocks of 'all lakes', area accounted for an additional 16.4% and depth accounted for 4.3% more variability, but these three figures do not represent the relative effects of the three factors. However, the rank may indicate their relative importance in each set

Lake group	Number of lakes	Percentage of variability accounted for	All variables stepwise with three factors
A standing stocks			
(1) Alpine	18	56.4	Area (54.5) TDS (1.9), Depth (0.0)
(2) Prairies	31	63.5	Depth (47.9) TDS (13.3), Area (2.3)
(3) St. Lawrence	17	39.9	TDS (35.3), Area (4.5), Depth (0.1)
(4) Atlantic	50	48.6	TDS (37.7), Depth (10.6), Area (0.3)
All lakes	116	42.3	TDS (21.6), Area (16.4), Depth (4.3)
B production index			
(1) Alpine	18	56.8	Area (53.2), TDS (2.3), Depth (1.3)
(2) Prairies	31	77.7	Depth (65.5), TDS (8.5), Area (3.6)
(3) St. Lawrence	17	56.3	TDS (31.3), Depth (24.1), Area (0.9)
(4) Atlantic	50	62.5	Depth (49.0), TDS (13.2), Area (0.3)
All lakes	116	58.7	TDS (30.0), Depth (28.1), Area (0.6)

TABLE 4.6. Regression coefficients obtained in correlating standing stocks and the production index with Ryder's morphoedaphic index. Logarithmic transformations were made on all data

Set	Number of lakes	Standing stocks	Production index
Alpine	18	0.203	0.290
Prairie	31	0.782**	0.856**
St. Lawrence	17	0.488*	0.725**
Atlantic	50	0.690**	0.773**

Significant (P < 0.05*; P < 0.01**).

dissolved solids. Area apparently was the most important factor in the alpine set and mean depth accounted for most variability in standing stocks in the prairies set. In the St. Lawrence and Atlantic lake groups and the 'all lakes' group dissolved solids concentration was most important. However, in single-factor analysis, dissolved solids and mean depth generally appeared to be of major importance in influencing size of standing stocks.

When the production index was calculated (standing stocks multiplied by estimated turnover rate defined before analysis on the basis of lake temperature data) and related to the three independent variables, percentage of the variability accounted for in regression increased substantially, with the exception of the alpine set of lakes where little difference was noted. In this group of colder lakes the estimated turnover rates were 1, 2 or 3, while there was a greater range in turnover rate in all of the other groups. From 56 to 78 per cent of the variability in the production index was attributed to variations in depth, area and dissolved solids

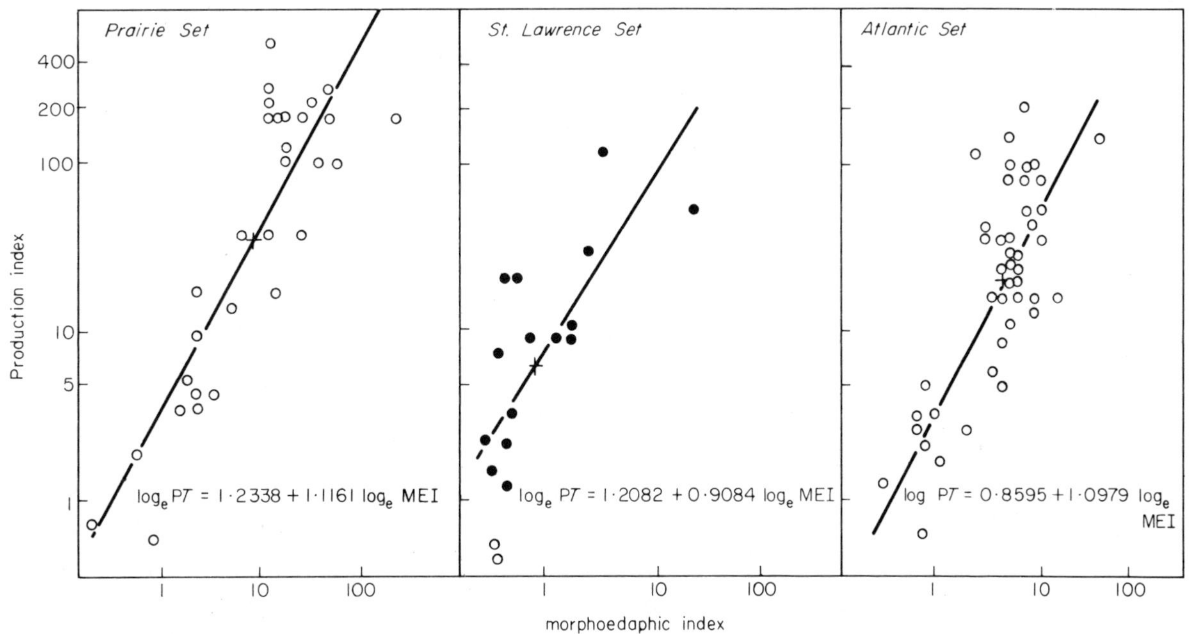

FIGURE 4.8. Relationship between Morphoedaphic Index (TDS/ mean depth) and Production Index (SS × TR) for three sets of lakes where highly significant correlations occurred.

in the four sets while, for all lakes, close to 60 per cent of the variability was accounted for. Again, depth and dissolved solids appeared to be the most influential factors. The prairies group conformed most closely to this regression model, although the other sets and the total of lakes conformed well considering the limitations of the model.

It is not expected that the overall model has any great value for predictive purposes, particularly in view of its broad basis and general nature. This, however, was not the main objective of the analysis. Sufficient evidence is presented to support the fundamental relationship between macroinvertebrate production and the combined effects of lake depth, area and dissolved solids. Even though the model developed here is relatively simple and needs refinement, it serves to indicate the inadequacy of earlier published analyses of these and similar data.

Finally, Ryder's morphoedaphic index was calculated for each lake and was related to, first, standing stocks and second, the production index (table 4.6). Ryder obtained coefficients of correlation with the index and fish production of 0.856 for twenty-three moderately to intensively fished lakes and 0.740 in the case of eleven lakes with restricted fisheries or incomplete records. Similarly high correlation coefficients were obtained with data of three sets but not for the alpine set, as expected from the results of multiple factor analysis. The use of the production index provided higher correlation coefficients. The relationship between Ryder's index and our estimates of production (figure 4.8) may be of some use in predicting macroinvertebrate production. However, the main purpose here is to affirm the conceptual relationship among production and prominent environmental factors.

5 COMMUNITY ANALYSIS

A. V. TYLER

The aim of this chapter is not to review the special properties of lake benthos in a community context, but to pull together study techniques and concepts that can be applied in work on the benthos. These approaches have seen accelerated development over the last 20 years through research on a variety of terrestrial and aquatic communities. Since the field is again as broad as the subject matter in the rest of this volume, the chapter will be a compendium of methods and ideas rather than a detailed review of all subjects dealt with.

We can start from the position that the community idea itself has been well written about already (Whittaker, 1970; Odum, 1971), and adopt the definition of Mills (1969) that 'community means a group of organisms occurring in a particular environment, presumably interacting with each other and with the environment, and separable by means of ecological survey from other groups'. This working conceptualisation is purposely flexible so that different ecological situations can be treated without mind twisting agonies about whether a group of organisms living together should be called an assemblage, community, formation, or continuum segment. The emphasis is on cohabitation, in a relatively homogeneous habitat and on the premise that many of the cohabitants are linked in their effects on one another.

Finding the Elusive Centre of the Community

A certain community ecologist investigating interactions between four or five species that are often found together, desires to go to a site where the species that he has selected are invariably present in good abundance, and where they do not come into serious contact with other assemblages that are to the north or south, deeper or shallower. He would like to go where his assemblage show its strongest, most straightforward, uninterfered with development. In a sense, he would like to look at his species group in the centre of their community. There he can set up a station and study details of feeding relationships, use of space, effects of predation, and so forth. He wonders whether it is possible to find such a site.

Non-randomness is the rule in small scale distributions of benthic species. Contagious distributions are brought about by selection and exclusion actions of both physical and biotic factors of the environment. The fact of non-randomness leads to questions of whether some species tend to occur together more often than they are apart, and whether there are objective ways of testing this cohabitation.

A host of association coefficients have been invented to test whether pairs of species occur together at frequencies greater than randomness. Reviews have been written by Cole (1949) and Hurlbert (1969). The chi-square statistic for presence–absence data continues to be useful, and may be modified as an index (Lie and Kelley, 1970), or used directly as a test of frequencies (figure 5.1). In cases where there are many combinations of species pairs, significance tests will cause acceptance of many pairs of species as being associates when they are not (α error, Dixon and Massey, 1957). Repeated surveys help to avoid these errors.

Fager's method of species grouping has been widely applied, and gives results that make intuitive sense (Fager, 1956; Fager and McGowan, 1963; Fager and Longhurst, 1968). Species that are together in at least half of the samples are considered associated (affinity index $\geqslant 0.50$). Following calculation of the affinity index (figure 5.1) on all species pairs, groups are formed so that each species pair in the group is associated. In cases where a species can belong to more than one group, the largest group to which it can belong is

Chi-square test of association in 500 Samples ($T = 500$)

	Species B present	absent
Species A present	$a = 319$	$b = 62$
absent	$c = 81$	$d = 38$

$$\chi^2 = \frac{[(ad - bc) - 0.5T]^2 \times T}{(a+b)(a+c)(b+d)(c+d)} = 12.9 \; (P \ll 0.01)$$

Fager's coefficient

$$t = [J/(N_A N_B)^{1/2}] - \tfrac{1}{2}(N_B)^{1/2}$$

J = Number joint occurrences
N_A = Number occurrences of species A
N_B = Number occurrences of species B

Euclidean distance coefficient

$$d^2_{1,2} = \sum_{i=1}^{n} (X_{i1} - X_{i2})^2.$$

1, 2 refer to two samples
X = density for species i

FIGURE 5.1. Some useful measures of association. The chi-square test and Fager's coefficient are applied to presence–absence data. They test for significant association between each species pair. The euclidean distance coefficient is applied to density data. As shown, it is used to determine similarity between pairs of samples. It can be used to compare pairs of species when 1, 2 refer to species and X = density of the species in sample i.

accepted. Since some species of a group will be linked to some species of another group, groups themselves are joined by different degrees of association. The groups are amenable to further study because the members are frequently part of one another's environment. The method is simple and understandable, the

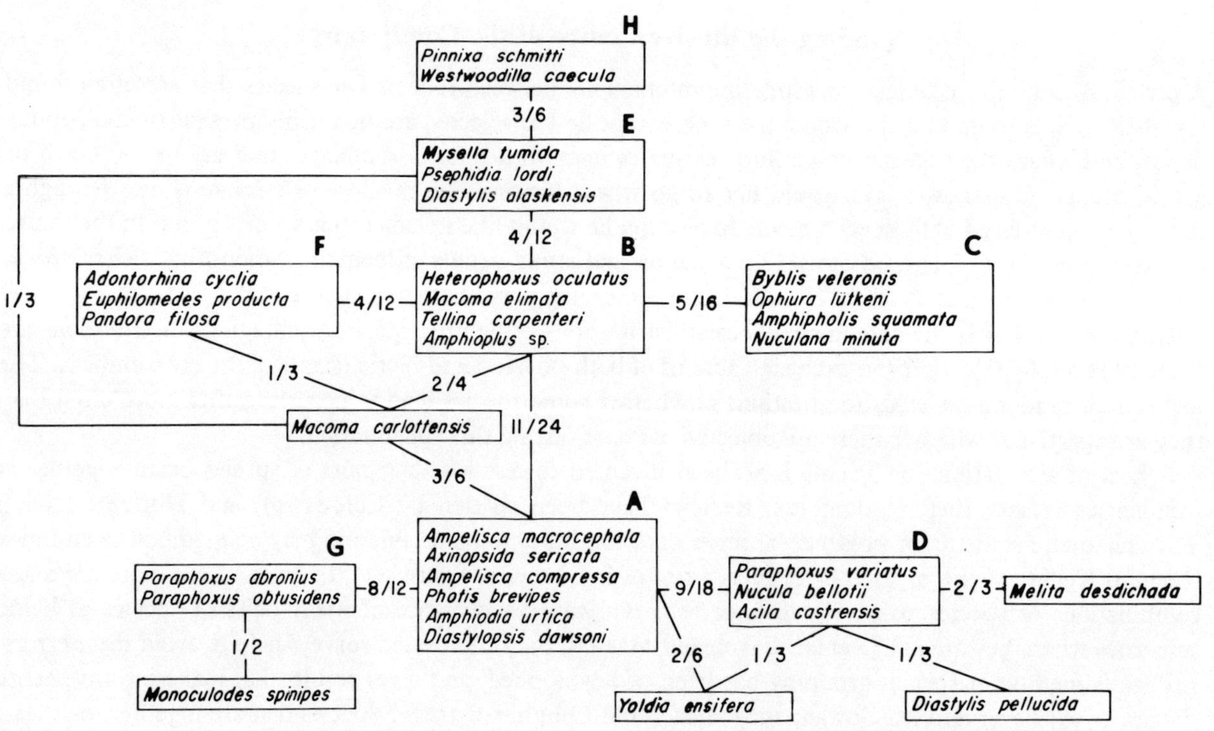

FIGURE 5.2. Recurrent groups and intergroup affinities of infauna assemblages off the coast of the State of Washington (from Lie and Kelley, 1970).

results are easily interpreted, and compare well with results from methods in which biological intuition fails (Lie and Kelley, 1970). It should be noted that pairs of species that are significantly associated by the chi-square test could also be grouped by Fager's scheme (no one yet has done so). Weaknesses of Fager's method are that species must belong to one group only, and that uncommon species must be ignored. Analysis of benthic communities off the coast of Washington (Lie and Kelley, 1970) are shown in figure 5.2.

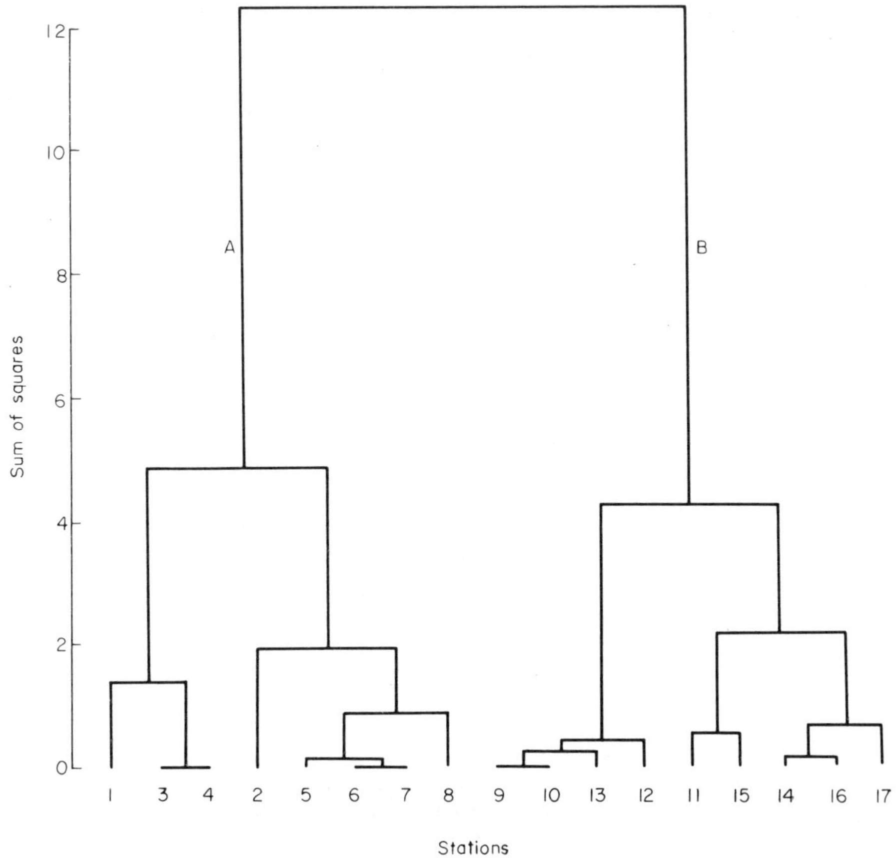

FIGURE 5.3. Dendrogram for hierarchical classification of stations on the Fred England Bed transect (Prince Edward Island, Canada) from mean high tide level (station 1) to a depth of 3 m (from Hughes and Thomas, 1971).

An effective method of cluster analysis that is based on species density measurements instead of presence–absence data has been adapted from numerical taxonomy. Distance coefficients (Sokal, 1961) can be calculated on the densities of all species for all possible sample pairs (figure 5.1). The agglomerative procedure is as follows: the sample pair with the lowest distance coefficient is considered linked. The densities within this sample pair are averaged as one sample. Distances are calculated between this new (second order) group and all other samples. Again the sample that gives the smallest increase in distance is considered linked, and a third order group is formed. Any sample pairs with distance coefficients less than the third order group are considered linked as second order groups of two samples. The linkage is made with the sample that gives the lowest distance coefficient. The procedure iterates until all groups are linked (Orloci, 1967). The linkages are displayed as a dendrogram (as in figure 5.3), where an analysis of Hughes and Thomas (1971) from a shallow water transect in an estuary is interpreted as two communities and four subcommunities. The transect data that this analysis was based on are given in figure 5.4.

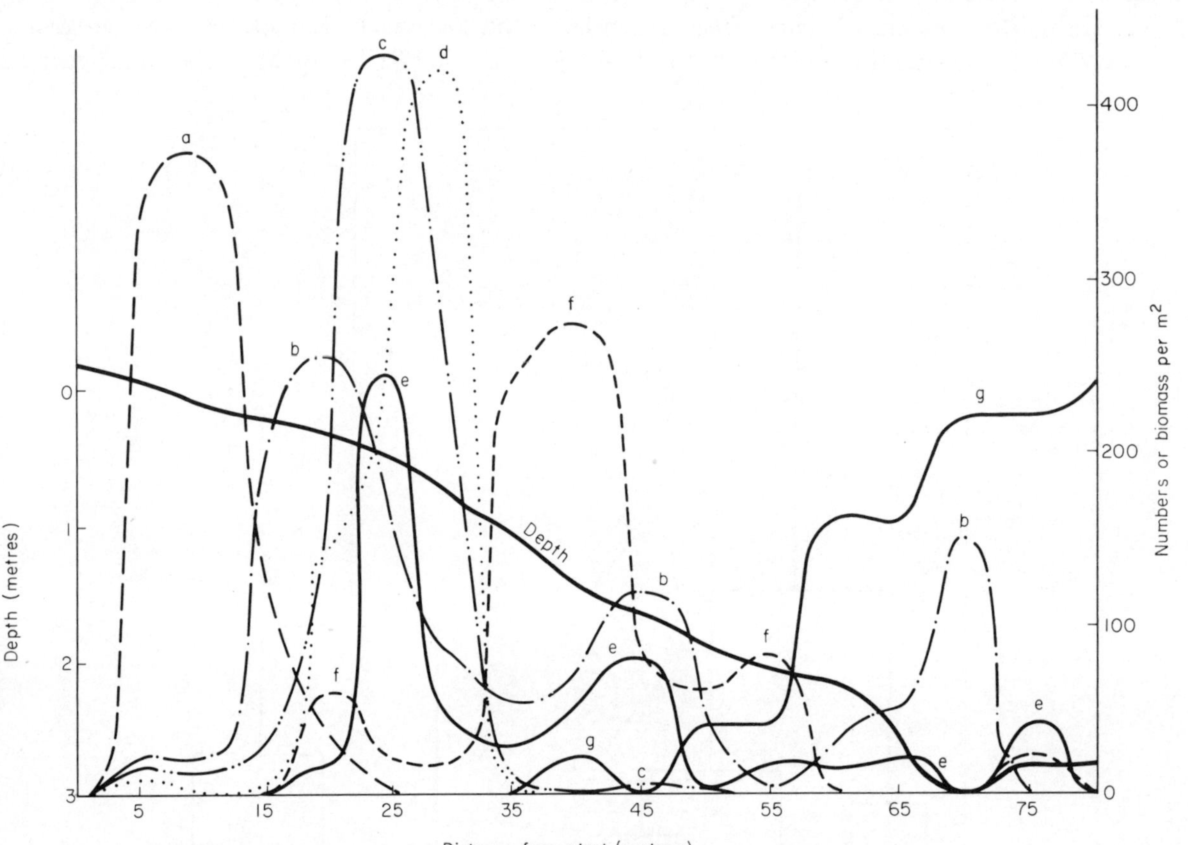

FIGURE 5.4. Depth, numbers/m² of fauna and biomass (g/m²) of flora for common species on Fred England Bed transect: a, *Mya arenaria* (×2); b, *Nereis virens* (×10); c, *Nassarius obsoletus*; d, *Zostera marina* (×10); e, *Mytilus edulis* (×2); f, *Neopanope texana* (×20); g, *Yoldia limatula* (×20) (from Hughes and Thomas, 1971).

Community classifications provide comprehensible description of outstanding features of organism distributions, but they tend to override some of the subtleties of the data. The concept of communities as parts of continua is attractive to many ecologists. The subject of the distribution of organisms and communities along environmental gradients is most strongly developed for terrestrial plants. The manner in which species densities change along single and double factor gradients, the placement of abundance modes, the nature of distributional overlap, have been reviewed by Whittaker (1967). On the premise of competitive interaction, Whittaker (1970) lists four possibilities of species arrangement along single factor gradients:

(1) Competing species, including dominant plants, exclude one another along sharp boundaries. Other species evolve toward close association with the dominants and toward adaptation for living with one another. There thus develop distinct zones along the gradient, each zone having its own assemblage of species adapted to one another, and giving way at a sharp boundary to another assemblage of species adapted to one another.

(2) Competing species exclude one another along sharp boundaries, but do not become organised into groups with parallel distributions.

(3) Competition does not, for the most part, result in sharp boundaries between species populations. Evolution of species toward adaptation to one another will, however, result in the appearance of groups of species with similar distributions.

(4) Competition does not usually produce sharp boundaries between species populations, and evolution of species in relation to one another does not produce well-defined groups of species with similar distributions. Centres and boundaries of species populations are scattered along the environmental gradient.

Similar hypotheses have been published by Terborgh (1971). Whittaker studied gradients in mountain ranges in the United States—the Siskiyou Mountains (Oregon), Santa Catalina Mountains (Arizona), and

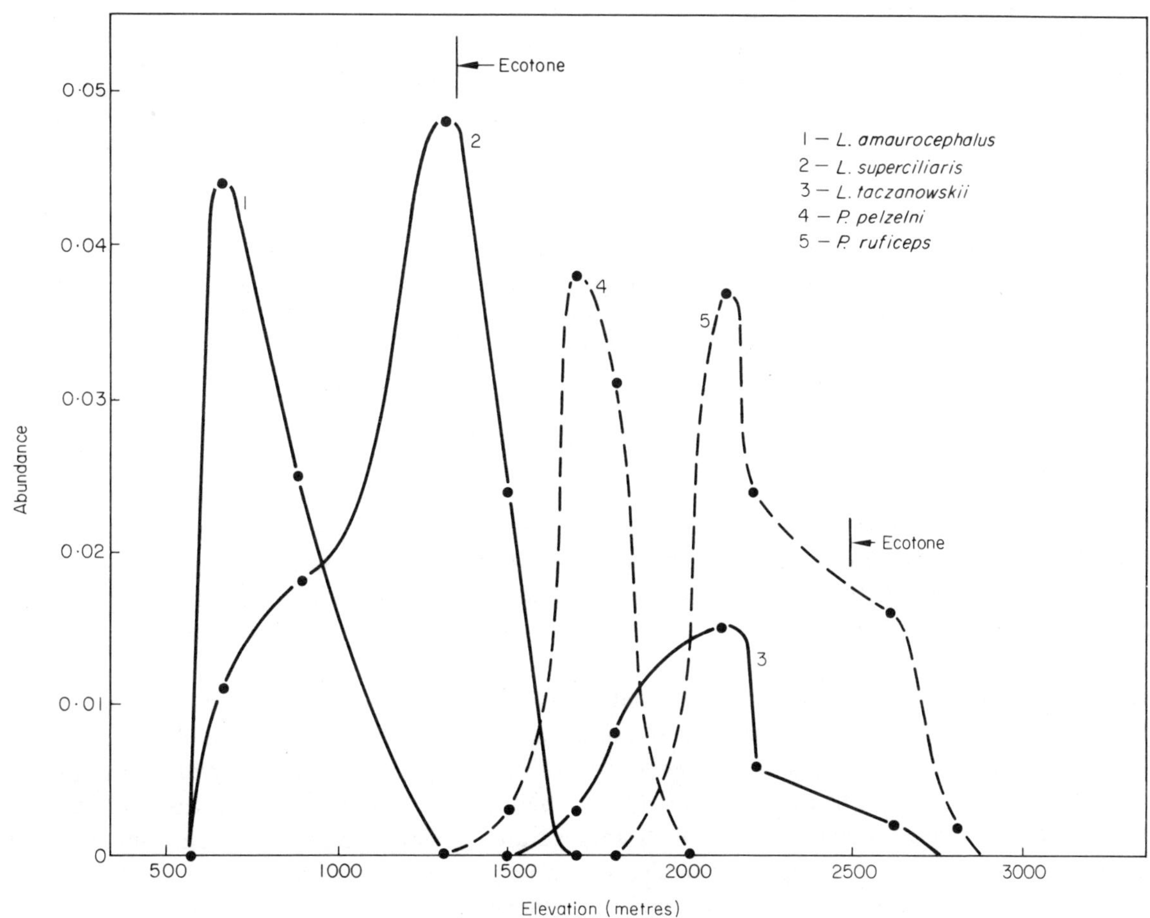

FIGURE 5.5. Population density curves for species in family Tyrannidae (Flycatchers) on a Peruvian mountain. Species 1 and 2 overlap broadly, but 2 reaches maximum abundance in the absence of 1. Both 1 and 2 appear abruptly above the lowland–montane rainforest ecotone. Truncation of the curves (repulsion interaction) is apparent in the zones of replacement of species 2 and 3 and of species 4 and 5. The genera are *Leptopogon* and *Pseudotriccus* (from Terborgh, 1971).

Great Smoky Mountains (Tennessee)—and concluded that situation 4 prevailed: 'The broad overlap and scattered centers of species populations along a gradient imply that most communities intergrade continuously along environmental gradients rather than forming clearly-separated zones'. He admits clear separation can be caused by abrupt environmental discontinuity, or disturbance (fire, man), and points out that vegetation zones that have been described are based on dominant forms only. Most other species do not follow the same zonations. Terborgh (1971) examined bird distributions on a 3000 m altitude gradient in the Cordillera Vilcabamba range in central Peru. His conclusions, in part, were similar to Whittaker's: that total species assemblages show gradual change with distance away from collection site, not sudden changes of many species. He found, however, that when attention is given to congeneric species, additional insight is gained. Congeners tend to replace one another along the gradient (figure 5.5). He found evidence that these species groups tended to suppress one another's density, and concluded that congener displacement should be interpreted as evidence of interspecific competition. He observed that bird species shifts sometimes corresponded to vegetation ecotones, and felt that modal placement along the gradient was brought about by interplay of competitive exclusion and ecotone location. This trend in analysis is rather amenable to research on benthos in relation to gradients of particle size, dissolved oxygen, water depth pollutants.

At this point the writer might be expected to mention *alpha* and *beta* diversity in relation to gradient steepness, niche occupation, the course of evolution, and pollution studies. However, it is the author's contention that the calculation of diversity indices will add little to community description or to the understanding of what goes on in communities. Conclusions based on these indices are often evident before the calculations are made. This is not to say that questions about the diversity of species are trivial, since questions about diversity ask why are there so many species, and why are they in the abundances that we see? But the time for excitement over calculations of diversity indices is over. There are better ways to investigate communities now. In a sense, that is what this chapter is about. It is a pity that some pollution biologists studying benthos are now caught up with this algebra. For some recent, mature thinking about diversity questions, the reader is referred to Margalef (1969).

Not unexpectedly, workers investigating the distribution of organisms along gradients have taken to multivariate analysis. One does not always have the good fortune to work with single factor gradients wherein, after cluster analysis, sample similarity is ranked in the linear sequence of a transect, for example, in figure 5.3 samples remained ordered according to distance from shore. In larger bodies of water, factors strongly related to distance from shore have a chance to become intermingled with other factors, and multivariate approaches such as principal component analysis, factor analysis, multiple regression will be useful in assessing the interplay on the communities.

Reviews of these techniques have been written by Lawley and Maxwell, 1963 and Cattell, 1965*a*, *b*. Full use of multivariate methods require intensive sampling. Multifactor gradients should be sampled with either randomly placed stations or grids rather than transects. Since the methods are particularly useful in relating groups of species simultaneously to several variables, it does not make sense to carry out these analyses unless two or more environmental variables are measured at sample time. Factor analyses are utilised best when small areas are sampled thoroughly, and where most species encountered have continuous distributions within the area. The analyses are difficult to grasp unless one has a fair understanding of matrix algebra, or the help of a patient statistician. In factor analysis, data are transformed into 'factor loadings' which cannot be interpreted in terms of the environmental variables originally measured. Stations that have similar species composition may tend to cluster themselves in the factor loading plot. Lie and Kelley (1970) found station similarities by this means, and noted that the stations grouped on Factor I seemed to represent a deep water, soft bottom community, since the habitat feature that they all had in common was silt and clay sediment (figure 5.6). These authors found that communities outlined by chi-square affinity index, Fager's recurrent group analysis, and factor analysis had fair correspondence.

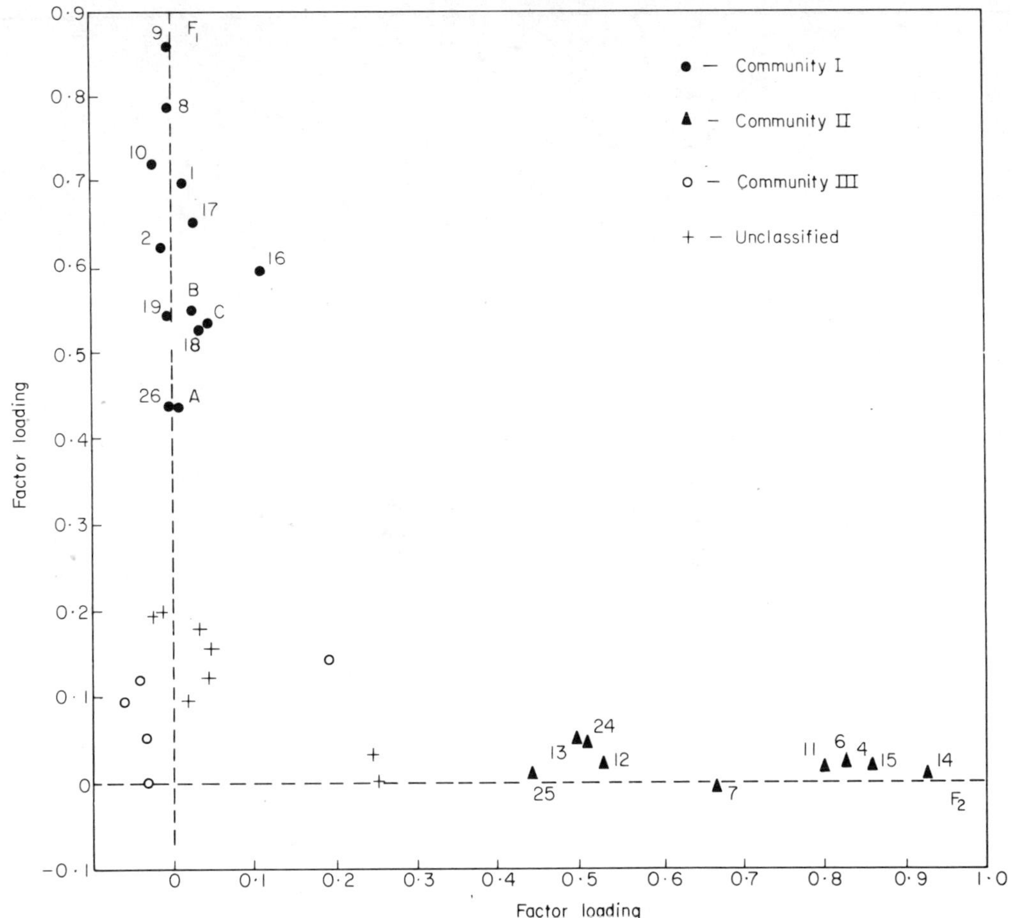

FIGURE 5.6. Factor analysis of infauna assemblages off the coast of the State of Washington. Two factor plot for stations with factors I and II rotated. Station numbers are shown within plot. Resulting clusters are classified as communities (from Lie and Kelley, 1970).

Cassie and Michael (1968) analysed station species compositions in relation to sediment grain size, and sediment carbon content by multiple regression and principal component techniques. Similar coarse and fine sediment communities were identified by both methods. The authors felt that the principal component analysis was better because it allowed isopleth mapping of community similarities (figure 5.7).

It would appear that multivariate analysis could be pushed much further in research on benthic communities if more physical factor data were put into the analysis. Cassie and Michael (1971) were able to put carbon content and particle size into their multivariate regression by using arc sine and square root transformations of raw data to gain multivariate normal distributions. Cassie justifies these transformations in an appendix of the paper. He suggests that the techniques should be more extensively applied. If only one or two factors are entered in an analysis, a cluster technique such as Euclidian distance seems preferable to multivariate methods because the concept of distance is simpler than the concepts of factor loading, relative changes in eigenvalues, and axis rotation. Further, in developing multifactor research, one must be wise enough not to get into a 'measure everything' study. Habitat properties selected for measurement should not be mere

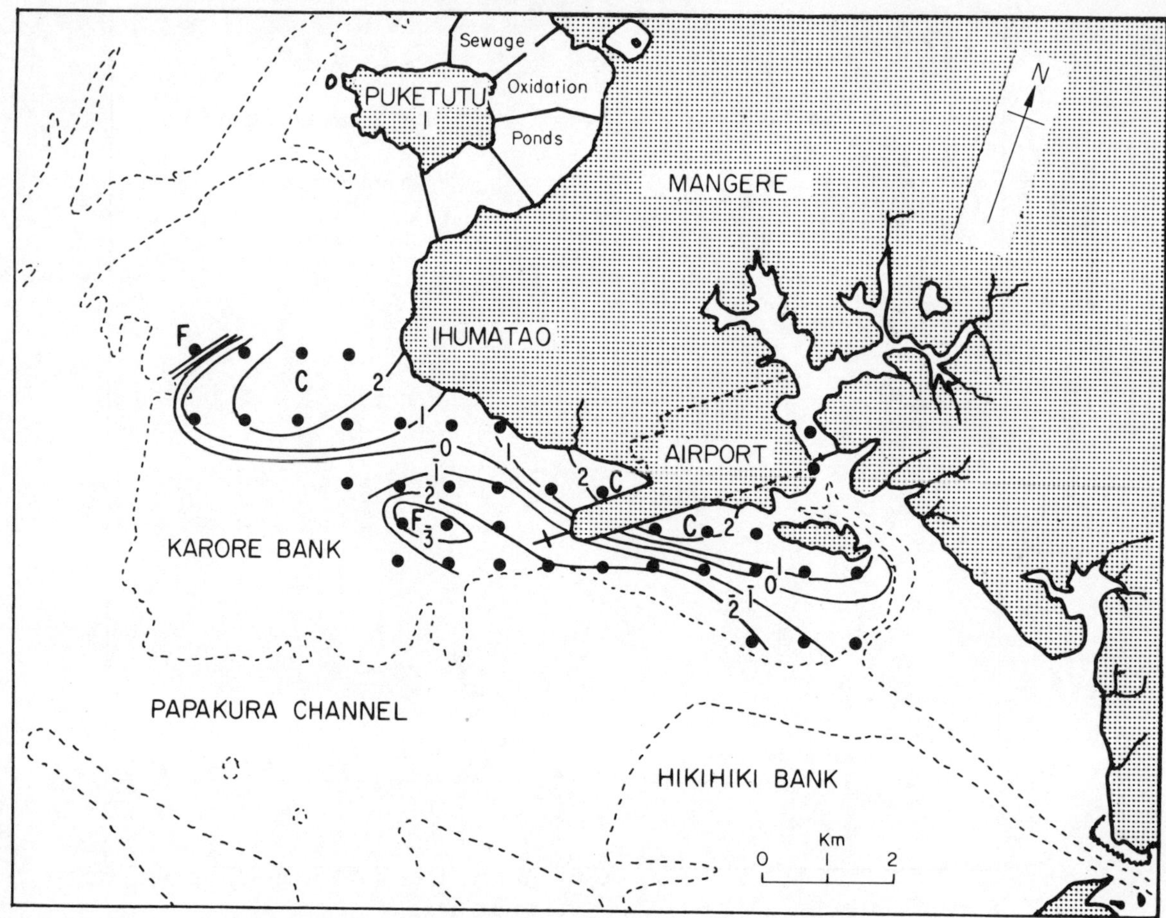

FIGURE 5.7. Isopleths of benthic faunal similarity derived from principal component analysis for a New Zealand mudflat. Stations are indicated as circles (from Cassie and Michael, 1968).

correlates of one another, and there should be some hypothetical reasoning behind their selection. (See also Knight and Tyler, 1973.)

What is Community Structure Made of?

Structure generally means organisation and, for non-human communities, structure must at least imply departure from randomness. But, in addition, the term must imply that the departures are directed by processes of evolution. The concept of structure is related to the concept of niche: structure is to niche what phenotype is to genotype, with the constraint that structure involves only those aspects of the niche that are interspecific, interindividual functions. Structures of communities are the functional relationships within and among species that bring about species population changes.

All structural adaptations can be thought of as respondents to two distinct but interconnected realms: opportunities to use energy and opportunities to use materials; energy flow and biogeochemical cycling. Relationships of predation; competition for food and space; parasitism; within and between species parasite picking and cleaning behaviour; saprobic digestion; fungi–algae, algae–coral symbiosis; nitrification nodules;

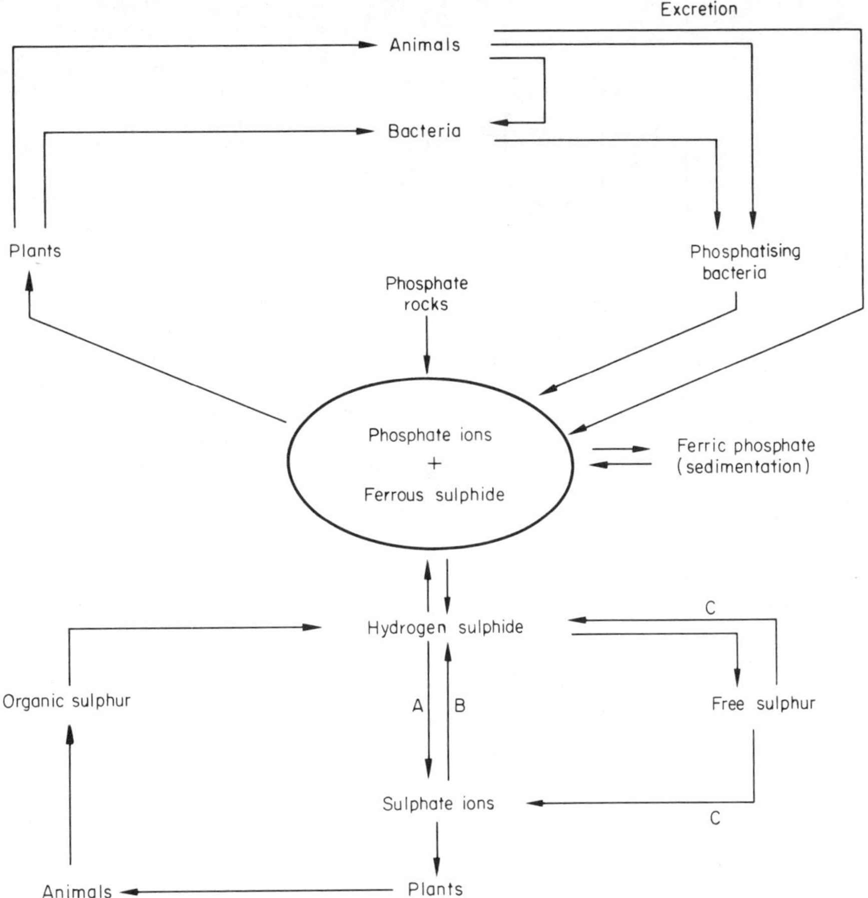

FIGURE 5.8. Intersection of phosphate, sulphur, and iron cycles in lakes. A—Aerobic sulphide bacteria, B—anaerobic sulphate reducing bacteria, C—colourless chemautotrophic bacteria, and also green or purple sulphur bacteria. (Redrawn from Odum, 1971.)

and so on; are structural functions that are linked into the community system as operators on energy flow or substance cycling. Materials and chemical energy move together, of course, but certain species are particularly important in a community for their unique roles in biogeochemical cycling.

The phosphate, sulphur, and iron cycles are interconnected in lake sediments (figure 5.8). When waters are oxygenated, phosphate ions and ferrous sulphide precipitate as ferric phosphate. 'An oxidised mud surface not merely holds phosphate but prevents diffusion of phosphate and ferrous ions from deeper layers in the mud' (Hutchinson 1957). Under reducing conditions, phosphate ions are liberated and, where much H_2S is formed, phosphate will be more mobile. The operation of these elemental cycles depends upon the good health of several species of bacteria that in no way act as plant or animal food-energy sources within the cycle, but function more like catalysts.

Energy flow, compartmental models that have been developed over a period of years have advanced the conceptualisation of trophic structure. It has emerged that there are two major energy transfer pathways in aquatic systems: one based on primary production within the system, and another based on detritus originating either from aquatic or terrestrial primary production, the latter often being the more important of the two.

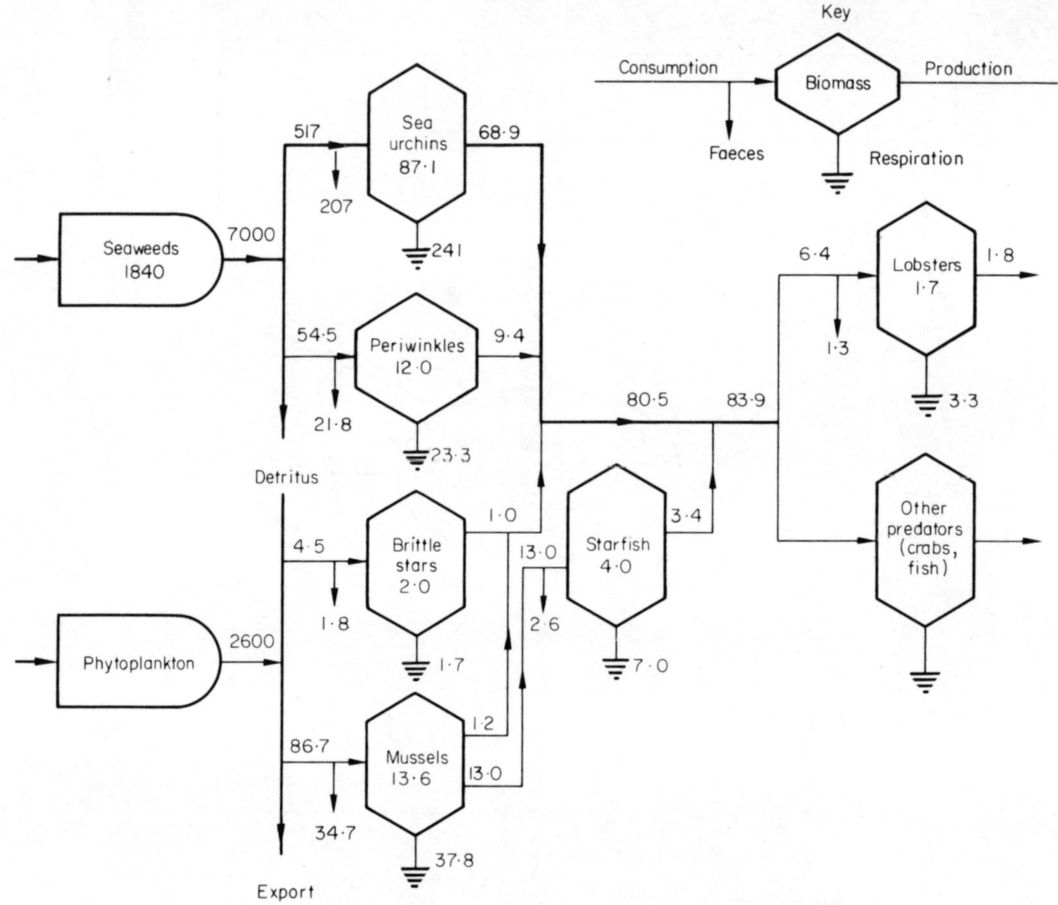

FIGURE 5.9. Energy flow through the bottom community in the seaweed zone of St. Margaret's Bay, Nova Scotia. Units are kcal/m^2 per year, except for biomass, which is in kcal/m^2 (from Miller, Mann and Scarratt, 1971).

A structural outline of community energy flow with production based on aquatic photosynthesis from within the community is given in figure 5.9. There are three trophic levels supported mainly by production from large plants (*Laminaria*). Phytoplankton production entered the system but was not quite so important. There is also evidence that a large portion of seaweed production is released as dissolved organic matter (Mann, 1972), and is transported out of the bay, presumably forming part of the base of a production system elsewhere.

A large sector of heterotroph production in lakes is based on terrestrial primary production that is transferred to the water. An extreme example, and one of the most complete studies of energy flow for freshwater benthic communities, was carried out on Root Spring by Teal (1957). Seventy-eight per cent of the food-energy available to primary consumers was from falling leaves, apples, and other terrestrially produced debris. The spring was only 2 m in diameter, with mud bottom, but contained over forty species of animals. Only a few of these species were sufficiently abundant to account for large portions of the energy usage. These were species that fed on detritus (the isopod *Asellus militaris*, the bivalve *Pisidium virginicum*, the amphipod *Crangonyx gracilis*), or algae and detritus (gastropod *Physa* sp.), larger pieces of vegetational debris (caddisfly larvae *Frenesia difficilis*, *F. missa*, *Limnophilus* sp.), or mud swallowers (the oligochaete *Limnodrilus hoffmeisteri*, the chironomid *Calopsectra dives*). Of the food-energy that either entered or was produced within the community, only 24 per cent was not taken up by the primary consumers, an indication of impressive adaptation of aquatic animals to spin-off from terrestrial production. The important carnivores (trophic level III) were few: two planarians and also a chironomid that could eat plant as well as animal material. The relative lack of diversity at the third trophic level was likely due to constraints of physical space rather than energy flow rates *per se*, since flow to the herbivores was substantial (2300 kcal/m^2/year compared with 3368 at Silver Springs, Florida. Odum (1957).

LAKE OPINICON August	*Labidesthes* 61–81 mm	*Pomoxis* 75–115 mm	*Notropis* 40–70 mm	*Ambloplites* 45–70 mm	*Ambloplites* 75–115 mm	*Lepomis* 60–85 mm	*Lepomis* 86–115 mm	*Lepomis* 130–170 mm	*Fundulus* 65–85 mm	*Perca* 60–110 mm	*Pimephales* 50–75 mm	*Micropterus* 80–120 mm
Chydorus	+	+	+	+	+	+			+	+	+	
Polyphenus	+											
Daphnia	+											
Diptera adults	+		+	+								
Chaoborus larvae	+	+										
Chaoborus pupae	+	+										
Copepoda		+										
Bosmina	+	+	+									
Chironomid pupae				+								
Hymenoptera				+	+	+	+	+				
Trichoptera					+							
Ephemeroptera nymphs					+							
Chironomid larvae						+	+	+	+	+		
Fish							+					+
Odonata nymphs							+	+				
Plant seeds								+	+			
Pleuroxis									+			
Sida										+		
Ostracoda										+		
Acroperus											+	
Bottom ooze											+	
Higher plants												+

FIGURE 5.10. Partition plot of predacious fish (across top) and their food items (along side) in an oligotrophic Canadian lake. Plus sign indicates that the food was a principal item in the stomach contents, i.e., greater than 10 per cent of the volume. (Constructed from data by Keast, 1965.)

The importance of detritus based production systems for major aquatic ecosystems has been recognised. Teal (1962) summarised the energy flow structure of a coastal plain saltmarsh and showed the dependence of the system on a few abundant algae–detritus feeders: crabs *Uca* and *Sesarnia;* annelids *Capitella, Streblospio, Manayunkia;* molluscs *Littorina, Modiolus,* and nematodes. The source of the detritus was the marsh grass, *Spartina.*

Odum and Heald (1970) studied energy flow in a Florida mangrove swamp and found that production in the detritus based community was again dependent on relatively few, abundant users of decaying mangrove leaves: a xanthid crab; four mysids; four amphipods; one penaeid shrimp; two caridean shrimp; one snapping shrimp; three small fishes (*Mugil, Cyprinodon, Poecilia*); harpacticoid copepods; isopods; and chironomids. Production within the detritus usage groups was the main source of food for the young of a large group of man-exploited fish. Because of the extent of the mangrove swamps, these areas must be significant nursery grounds.

The identification of energy usage groups from among sympatric species may not seem at all obvious at times. Consider the lake community investigated by Keast (1965) in Ontario (Canada) where, in August, twelve species of fish and their feeding stanzas (species subdivided by size according to feeding habit) had twenty-two items as principal foods (figure 5.10). Principal foods are considered, for purposes of this chapter, as those items that each made up at least 10 per cent of the volume of a predator's diet. All predators, except large centrarchids, took the cladoceran *Chydorus,* but most of the predators did not get most of the other food items. Of the 242 possible re-occurrences of food items among predators only twenty-five showed up (twenty-two food items multiplied by eleven possible re-occurrences for each food item among twelve predators). Most items occurred as principal foods in only one or two predators (seventeen of twenty-two

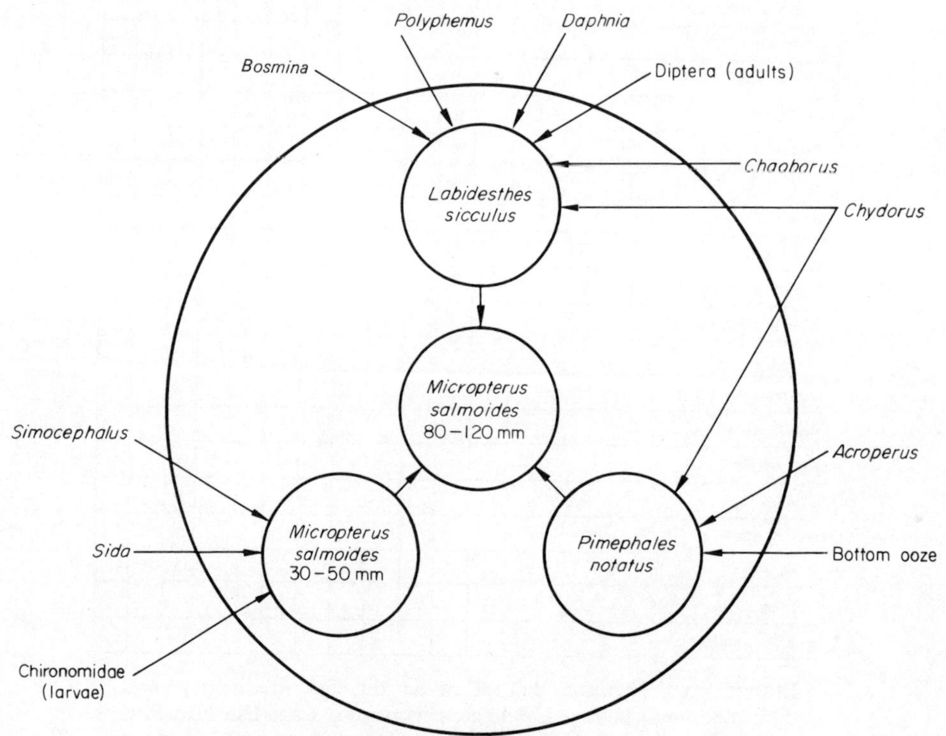

FIGURE 5.11. Energy-flow in a usage group extracted from Figure 5.10 and other data by Keast, 1965.

food items). An impressive degree of specialisation is exhibited by the predators. The flow of food-energy is highly structured.

What about energy usage groups within this community? From the point of view of bass production (*Micropterus*) the usage group to be extracted is shown in figure 5.11. The cannibalistic relationship within *M. salmoides* was added from Keast's June data. The production of large *M. salmoides* is dependent upon cladocerans, dipterans, and whatever is in bottom ooze.

In attempting rational fishery exploitation, governments become enthusiastic about population studies of the species caught by the fishermen. To estimate how many fish to take, biologists rightly investigate recruitment rates, growth rates and mortality rates. Application of this kind of information is optimistically termed 'resource management'. Clearly when people exploit fish populations they are also exploiting the benthos, and in fact a system that is sensitive to alterations in energy flow and balance in biogeochemical cycles. In order to manage resources, governments have to know how to protect the benthos and other parts of the production structure. The structure can easily be altered qualitatively by either depleting or adding chemicals or biologically useful energy, whether the additives are naturally occurring or alien to nature. Failure in part of the system will cause synergistic reactions that are likely to bring about collapse of utilisable species. For management of these species, linked usage groups must be identified and properties of selected species must be known. Studies of conditions of survival of water fleas cannot be scoffed at as far out if people want fish in the waters for their children. Resource management research must not only come to grips with the dynamics of populations that are exploited, but must find equal urgency in systems research of community relations and environmental quality reactions.

Tinkering with the Keys

In many communities there are key species that have a disproportionate influence on the kinds of plants and animals that live together. These species exert their influence mainly through competitive mechanisms, or through predation. Some are not particularly abundant, and they often are those not exploited by humans. As a consequence they have not been given the attention that their position in the community warrants, and probably many exist without anyone being aware of the sensitivity of the community system to them. Sometimes a good way to detect their influence is by experimental manipulation of community structure, that is, field experiments that alter the numbers and kinds of organisms that live together. Action categories of key species could be considered as follows:

(1) Species that add to the physical structure of the habitat such as dominant plant species and coral. Decreased heterogeneity in physical structure due to removal of one of these species could eliminate several others that require the structure for refuge or attachment.
(2) Some species alter or disturb the substrate surface by digging or burrowing, such as do carp or tube dwelling polychaetes (Fager, 1964; Young and Rhoads, 1971). The activities of one such species can greatly alter faunal composition.
(3) Species that occupy the substrate in a contiguous manner and by their presence physically force out many other species. Intertidal mussels and barnacles fit into this category. One wonders whether dense beds of unionid bivalves act in this category or in category (2).
(4) Single herbivore species that have the capacity to decimate stands of vegetation.
(5) Carnivores that act to prevent domination of the community by species in categories (2) to (4).

Paine (1966) has developed the concept of key carnivores in studies of intertidal communities. With enclosures, he kept carnivorous starfish (*Pisaster*) from an intertidal area, and found that, in their absence, acorn barnacles (*Balanus*) filled in much of the substrate space. Later, mussels (*Mytilus*) and goose-necked barnacles (*Mitella*) began to crowd over the acorn barnacles. Other species displaced were large, attached algae, chitons, limpets, and members of the sponge-nudibranch food chain. Altogether, exclusion of *Pisaster* brought a fifteen species system to an eight species system. Paine termed *Pisaster* the 'keystone species', which seems appropriate since Webster's defines the keystone as the one holding the others in place.

Mann and Breen (1972) give evidence that lobsters (*Homarus americanus*) are key carnivores in kelp forests (figure 5.9), and that in the absence of lobsters, kelp forests and associated fauna would disappear. Lobsters prey heavily upon sea urchins which are major consumers of kelp. Perhaps it is more accurate to say that sea urchins are destroyers of kelp since they eat through the stipes, often leaving the blades to drift away. Similarly, sea otters are key carnivores in California, their predation being critical for maintenance of the kelp forests there (McLean, 1962; North, 1965).

If lobsters and sea otters are key carnivores, then sea urchins, of course, must be key herbivores. Different species of sea urchins have been singled out by various workers on both coasts of North America and Europe as being capable of devastating seaweed beds (Mann and Breen, 1972). The grazing of sea urchins apparently also prevents the build-up of dense mats of filamentous algae in some shallow marine areas. While diving in Passamaquoddy Bay (New Brunswick, Canada) during July, the author has seen algal mats fringed by *S. droebachiensis*. The mats are usually gone before summer's end.

While Paine (1966, 1969) put forward the concept of key carnivores, his work also suggests that there are key crowders—action category (3). When *Pisaster* predation was eliminated, most space was eventually occupied by mussels which displaced even the seaweed.

The alternative to key species is that an action category in a community could be filled by a group of species. One might wonder whether the activities of key species in northern or alpine systems are carried out in parallel by species flocks in some tropical systems. Somewhat to the contrary, Paine (1966) found key carnivores present in temperate and complex subtropical intertidal communities, but not in an apparently comparable tropical habitat in Costa Rica. There, neither a key carnivore nor parallel species flock was present.

On Hawaiian reefs, standing crops of attached algae are kept low by several species of surgeon fishes and parrot fishes (Randall, 1961). Cages attached to the substrate excluded only these moderate sized fishes. After 2 months of protection some species of algae were as high as 30 mm as compared to a slight stubble outside the cages. A similar experiment was performed in the Virgin Islands of the Caribbean. After a period of about 2 months one species of red algae had reached a height of 185 mm. This was in spite of the fact that several herbivorous sea urchins (*Diadema antillarum*) were included in the enclosure. Not only algae grazing, but also grazing on sea grasses (spermatophytes: *Thalassia testudinum* and *Cymodocea manatorum*) is carried out by a species flock in the Caribbean. Randall (1965) showed that the characteristic fringing band of exposed, light sand around reefs is due to the overgrazing of several species of parrot fish and other herbivores. To demonstrate this he planted sea grasses (*Thalassia*) within the barren area bordering a reef in a strip from the reef edge to the grass bed—a distance of 20 feet. After 12 days the grasses had been cropped by several species of parrot fish to a distance of 7 feet from the reef. By 25 days after planting, the blades had been eaten all the way to the grass bed. Though this experiment did not prove that *Thalassia* would grow in the denuded band, it did show which species were *Thalassia* eaters.

For the next experiment, a corridor of concrete blocks was laid to the grass bed, and a pile of blocks was built within the bed. After 8 months there was a broad area of denuded sand around the end of the new artificial reef.

The aim of this section is not to classify as many species as possible into action categories, but to draw attention to the existence of key species, and to the possibility of their involvement in several types of activity. Key species and their effects seem to be best elucidated by field experiments in which either the habitat or the numbers and kinds of species living together are altered. Induced differences in species composition are kept from outside interference by an enclosure. The more selective the enclosure is to the particular species being altered, the better the experiment. Most experiments published to date have dealt with species exclusions, (see Kajak, 1972, Straskraba, 1965), but experiments should also adopt strategies in which densities are increased. The widespread use of SCUBA and the relative ease with which many benthic species can be manipulated should make *in situ* experimentation on benthos attractive.

Putting the Links Together

How does one go about associating energy flow with change in animal numbers? The flow of energy and materials brings on structure, but by what arrangement will there be a decent marriage between ecological energetics and population dynamics considering questions of feedback, density dependence, stability, natality and mortality?

Is it possible to put together, in a meaningful way, information on the interconnections of key species and usage groups in terms of how numbers and biomass change in time? What about questions of how sensitive one part of a production system is to changes in another part? How does one relate known population functions or responses so that the unknown areas of the system are more clearly identified? In short, how does one work towards community dynamics modelling?

The first thing must be to look for rather basic and general connections among species populations that would influence the population sizes. Certainly static energy flow models, as in figure 5.9, help one to understand some of the relationships between components of the community. Changing from statics to dynamics means incorporating rules of change as functions of time. Populations, in the form of biomass or numbers, operate on energy flow through growth functions, natality functions, and so on. Population models for single species are usually built around the effects of species density on these functions, that is to say, natality is made a function of population density. But since energy flow provides a linkage among species populations it would be better, where possible, to consider population functions as ration-dependent. Population density and acquired rations clearly must often be related to one another. As density increases, food becomes divided among progressively more individuals, and individual rations must decrease unless food is in unlimited supply.

One advantage of making population functions ration-dependent is that the effects of rations on population change can be inferred from experimentation with individuals, whereas experimentation with changes in population density is often not possible. Finding how population functions—such as birth rate—respond to changes in population density, may take years of data gathering from large scale surveys. However, since good correlations between density and brood strength are considered first class evidence for density dependence, it should be pointed out that similar data for correlations could be attained for ration estimates and brood strength. Correlations could be attempted between brood rations and brood strength, and also spawning-adult rations and brood strength. A number of methods for estimating rations have been developed recently, particular techniques depending on the type of animal involved (Davis and Warren, 1968; Edmondson and Winberg, 1971).

Some population functions, on the other hand, are strictly dependent on the density of the species, and not acting through rations. The number of juveniles settling on a square metre of substrate depends on the amount of space not already occupied by the previous broods. The rate at which a species is killed by predation depends on its density. There is sometimes a prey-density threshold below which a predator no longer actively searches.

Suppose the trophic yield from a three species food resource is divided among three carnivorous, benthic species, each species more or less specialising on one of the prey but at the same time including all three

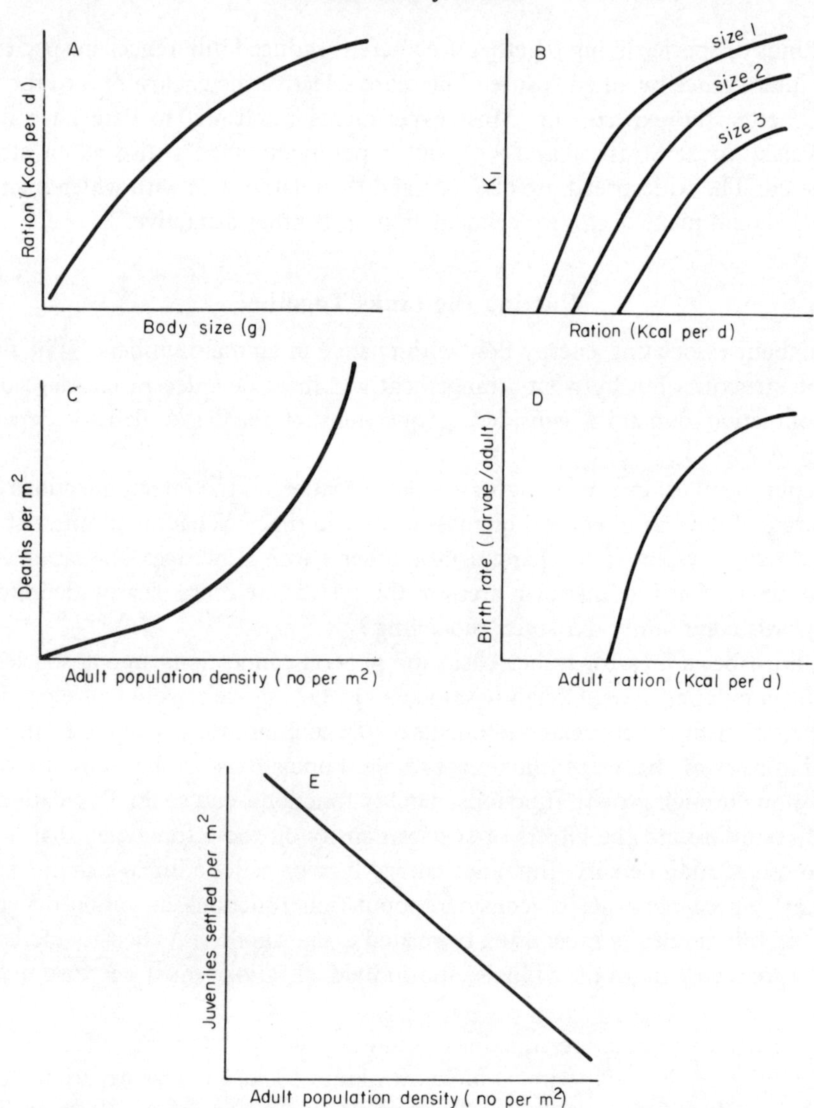

FIGURE 5.12. Functional relationships for a population simulation of benthic carnivores.

prey in their diets. The population dynamics of one of the predator species might be simulated as follows. The density of the population will be set initially at a value N. All individuals are at first one season old, with a measurable average individual size called size 1. If each individual is allowed to eat as much as it wants, the resulting ration will be found from consulting graph A, figure 5.12, which relates maximum selected ration to body weight. The graphs in this figure are called the functional relationships of the simulation. A specific growth efficiency (K_1) is attributed to the individual according to graph B, and in the model (figure 5.13) we move from the ration box to the mean individual growth increment box. Growth increment is measured in calories or biomass. Its addition produces a new mean individual size: size 2. The product of the growth increment and population density gives gross production (move to the next box). Part of the gross production is eaten by carnivores of the trophic level above, and becomes trophic yield. The mortality rate can be found by consulting graph C, which relates deaths per square metre to the popu-

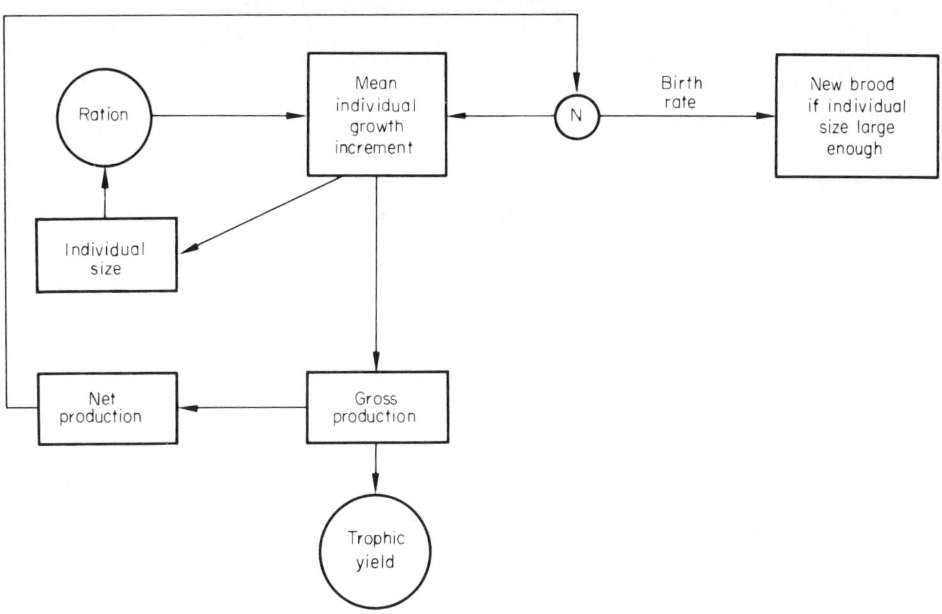

FIGURE 5.13. Flow chart for a population simulation of benthic carnivores.

lation density, which has already been set at *N* for this season. Number of deaths can be converted to calories of trophic yield, and the number of deaths multiplied by the mean individual increment gives the production removed by predation. Net production (move to the next box) is the difference between gross production and that removed by predation, assuming no other mortality. *N* minus the number of deaths gives the new population size at the start of season 2. The cycle is now completed. The brood will recycle in the model until all individuals are gone. Sometime before this depletion when individual size reaches size of maturity, say size 2 in season 2, a new brood is hatched. The size of the new brood is determined by graphs D and E. Graph D gives larvae hatched per adult as a function of ration. Graph E gives the rule about how many larvae can find settling space in the substrate, which is a function of the adult population density. The new brood will proceed through the same cycling model as the first brood. Eventually three or four broods will be cycling simultaneously and, of course, a computer will be necessary to keep track of the population sizes, rations, production increments, and so on.

Each of the three benthic carnivores, species I, II and III, is modelled in similar fashion, with parameters of functional relationships in graphs A to E altered to suit the species, and any other peculiarity of the species added to its cycle.

Species I, II and III are interconnected through rations. Their dynamics models allowed unlimited rations, an unrealistic state that can now be modified. It would be possible to simulate the population changes in prey species 1, 2 and 3 in the same way as were the changes in benthic carnivores I, II and III. Then, presumably, we would have to simulate changes in the food of the prey species, and proceed in this manner through progressively lower trophic levels until we reached primary production. The resulting model would be a cumbersome simulation of a food web with overwhelming information requirements. It is unlikely that we could find enough research time to understand the necessary functional relationships (the kind outlined in figure 5.12), much less determine reasonable values for the constants of equations describing those relationships. It would be better to set out a framework that can be empirically tested, and

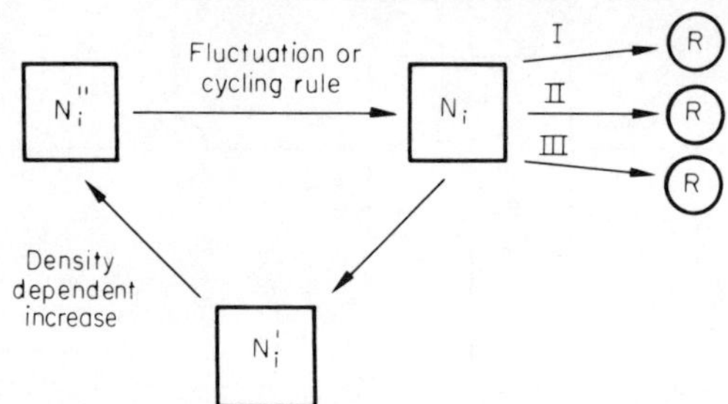

FIGURE 5.14. Flow chart for a population simulation of food species.

then modified by research findings. In this way, the model might eventually be capable of predictions under a given set of circumstances.

As an alternative to generating food density changes by elaborations of the trophic structure of the model, we could generate them by imposing strictly random fluctuations on food species densities and set limits to the amplitudes of those fluctuations. Also, we could impose regular cycles of various forms and frequencies on the food species. We could then learn how the system responded to these 'driving' trophic factors. Benthic communities are in fact ultimately driven by solar factors such as radiation, season, and weather that occur in cycles, or else give the appearance of occurring at random. Fluctuations in the sizes of species populations are usually indistinguishable from random changes, some arctic species being exceptional. Predators, such as the three species in this model, must be able to cope with these unexpected variations in prey populations. If the model that we have put them in will not allow them to cope, then something must be wrong with our understanding of how they react to their environment.

Although we can build driving functions into the food species submodels, we can also make the productivity of each food species respond to biomass removal (predation). If standing stock is decreased, productivity might increase in a compensatory way.

Suppose each of the three benthic carnivores takes a ration from food resource species 1, that has an initial population density of N_1 (figure 5.14). We will let each predator have a different capturing efficiency for N_1, that is, each takes a different proportion of N_1. The population density is then reduced to N_1'. Let the rate of increase of N_1' vary along a hump-shaped curve as N_1' changes. By selecting the rate that corresponds to N_1', we can calculate the new population size after reproduction: N_1''. We can now inflict random or cyclic function alteration on N_1'' to get a new N_1 (figure 5.14), from which the three benthic predators again take a ration. The total ration taken by each predator must not exceed the value given in graph A, figure 5.12. If it does, we will give the predator a smaller take from the food species that he is least efficient at capturing.

The model is conceptually complete at this point, though it certainly must be somewhat naïve. The benthic carnivores are barely distinguishable from one another, being different only in the parameters of their functional relationships. In reality species I might be edged off the rock if species II reached a high density, only to return when species II was reduced to some much lower density. This sort of structure can be added to a model only with good information on the particular species being studied. When all available information is put into a model, one can then study the concurrent changes in net production, population age structure, population density, trophic yield, and other 'system state variables' that were built into the model. If these concurrent changes do not match with empirical information on how these variables actually change, then one can try to deduce from the discrepancies what new studies must be carried out so that the model can be altered. By a combination of modelling, observation, and experimentation, a researcher should be able to increase his understanding of complex interactions with greater facility.

Behavioural studies will doubtless have to be carried out to find the rules of change of predation in relation to change in prey density, and also in relation to variations in contagious distributions. Are there a finite number of different predation strategies, and does a single species use only one or two of these? What would cause switching from one strategy to another? Are there different energy-budget requirements for each strategy? If the energetic cost of predation varies in some systematic manner there may be a feed-back loop between ration acquired and strategy usage.

Community dynamics is an extension of population dynamics with roots in ecological energetics and behavioural science. No single person could hope to supply the information for a community systems model, nor would one person hope to have enough research time to acquire the information that would allow the model to mimic nature. A group of people would have to work together within a project organisation that itself mimics the structure of the production system.

PART II

SOURCES OF VARIABILITY

6 SPATIAL AND TEMPORAL COMPLEXITY

In the first section we examined some of the mainly holistic studies of lake benthos that have been undertaken. Opponents of this approach would suggest that no two lakes are, in reality, alike and that the complexity of nature prevents the holistic view from achieving its goal of developing general statements about the nature of lakes. In this section we will examine some of the underlying causes of the bewildering complexity of factors that interact to produce the diversity of even benthic associations.

The holistic approach is adopted for one or two fundamentally different reasons. The first, quite legitimate, reason is that generality may be derived faster from the broad overview than from amassing quantities of detailed but unrelated information, so that the acknowledged complexity of lakes is ignored for the purpose of modelling. If the modelling leads to testable predictions which stimulate disciplined field and laboratory study, then the feedback system between observation and predictive theory should lead to a refining of the model so that its predictive ability increases. If the modelling leads only to intra-mural debates on modelling techniques, to the exclusion of the testing process, it will rapidly lose touch with reality and follow the path to extinction taken by so many scientific fads.

The second reason for the holistic approach is probably reflected more in the writings of the earliest limnologists than in more recent work, but the concept of the lake bottom as uniform, unchanging environment still persists as a dangerous tradition—one which is not justified by what little we do know about conditions in the sediment of lakes. While fluctuations of temperature, light and concentration of dissolved gases as well as other materials are readily apparent at the water surface, in the deep water zone of a lake they may seem to vary little. The sediments of the shallow waters of a lake may vary from rock to sand, clay to silt, whereas in the deepest parts an accumulation of apparently uniform fine silt usually coats the bottom. The apparent uniformity is, however, a little misleading as some of the more extensive studies of the benthos of lakes have revealed. The complexity of benthic ecology may be demonstrable even within a single lake, but the cause of some of this variation is hard to detect. The complex chemistry of the sediment-water interface has been the subject of only a few detailed studies, and a systematic investigation of the microbiology of the decomposition cycle has scarcely begun. The systematics, distribution, relative abundance and life histories of most benthic organisms have seldom been accurately determined, and their interaction with each other and with the fish and the plankton have rarely been investigated. Hence, any attempt to correlate benthic events with simple physicochemical parameters established in the water column should be regarded, at least, as somewhat optimistic.

This review of some of the complicating factors in lakes in relation to benthic studies is meant, therefore, to temper the optimism of some of the current group of model builders, and also to attempt to set out some of the variables that our future syntheses should encompass. While the list is formidable, it is not intended to deter completely all future study in this area, but rather to suggest those factors that should be considered or which might be eliminated by a careful selection of study site, equipment, and sampling programme, once a set of samples is required to test an hypothesis arrived at *before* the sampling begins.

The first and most obvious complicating factor to be considered is the morphometry of the lake basin. Few lakes are as felicitously basin like as L. Esrom (Berg, 1938), Lake Tiberias, Israel (Gitay, 1968, figure 6.1), or Bala Lake, Wales (Dunn, 1961, figure 6.2). Some are as complex as Canada's Lake Nipigon (Adam-

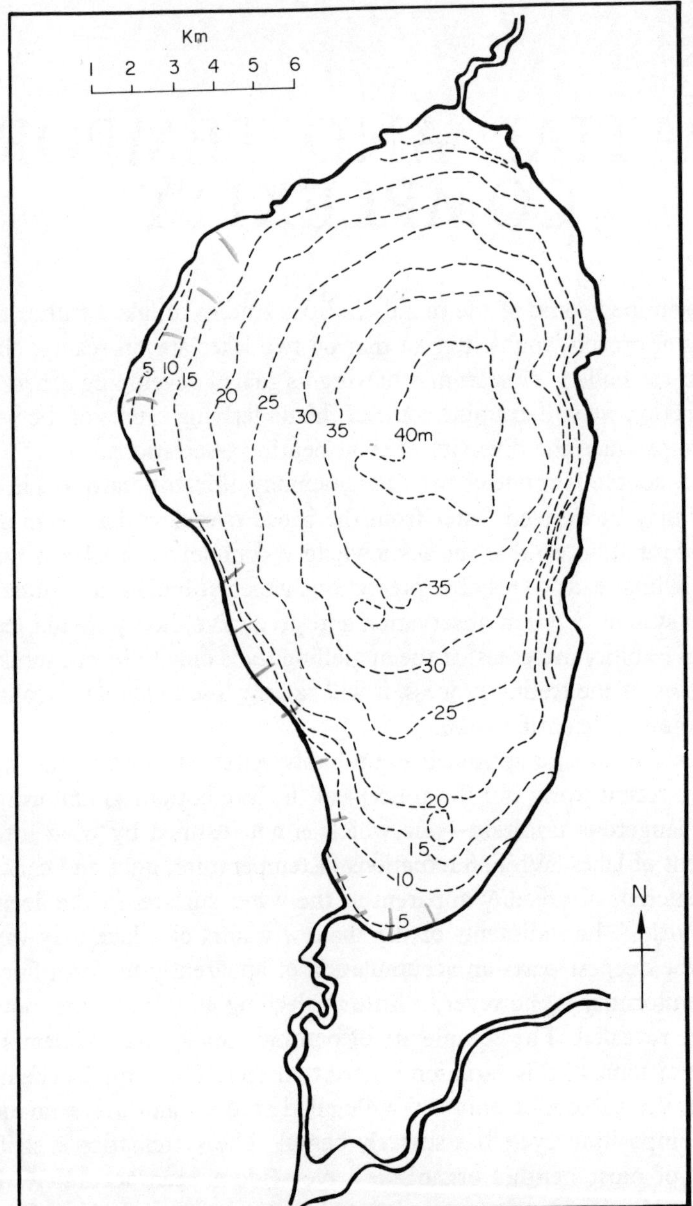

FIGURE 6.1. Contour map of Lake Tiberias, Israel (Gitay, 1968).

stone, 1924), Great Slave Lake (Rawson, 1953*b*), Lac la Ronge (Oliver 1960, figure 6.3) or Scottish Loch Lomond (Slack, 1965, figure 6.4). This complexity is usually reflected in the nature of the benthos, as demonstrated by the aforementioned as well as by Mikulski and Gisinski (1961) and Johnson and Brinkhurst (1971*a–c*). In other lakes, less obvious variations in morphometry delimit a number of basins. Windermere is clearly divisible into a northern and southern basin, Lac Léman consists of the main basin 'le Grand Lac' and the more westerly Lac Léman 'le Petit Lac' (Dussart, 1963). Lake Erie is divisible into a shallow western and a deeper central basin at about the level of the series of large islands and the prominent Point Pelee, but a further division can be made at about Long Point in the eastern end (figure 6.5). Ahren

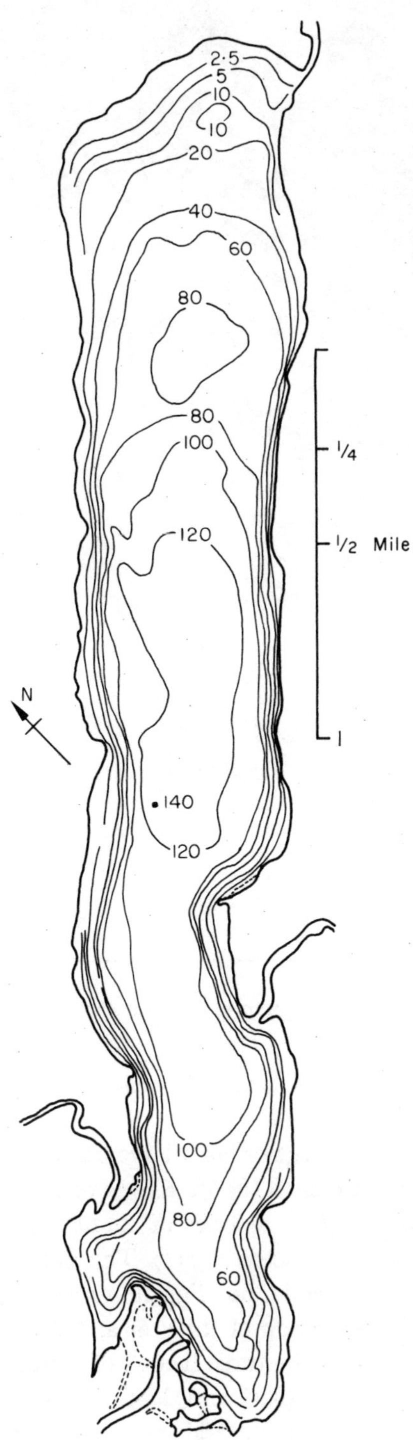

FIGURE 6.2. Contour map of Bala Lake (Llyn Tegid), Wales (Dunn, 1961).

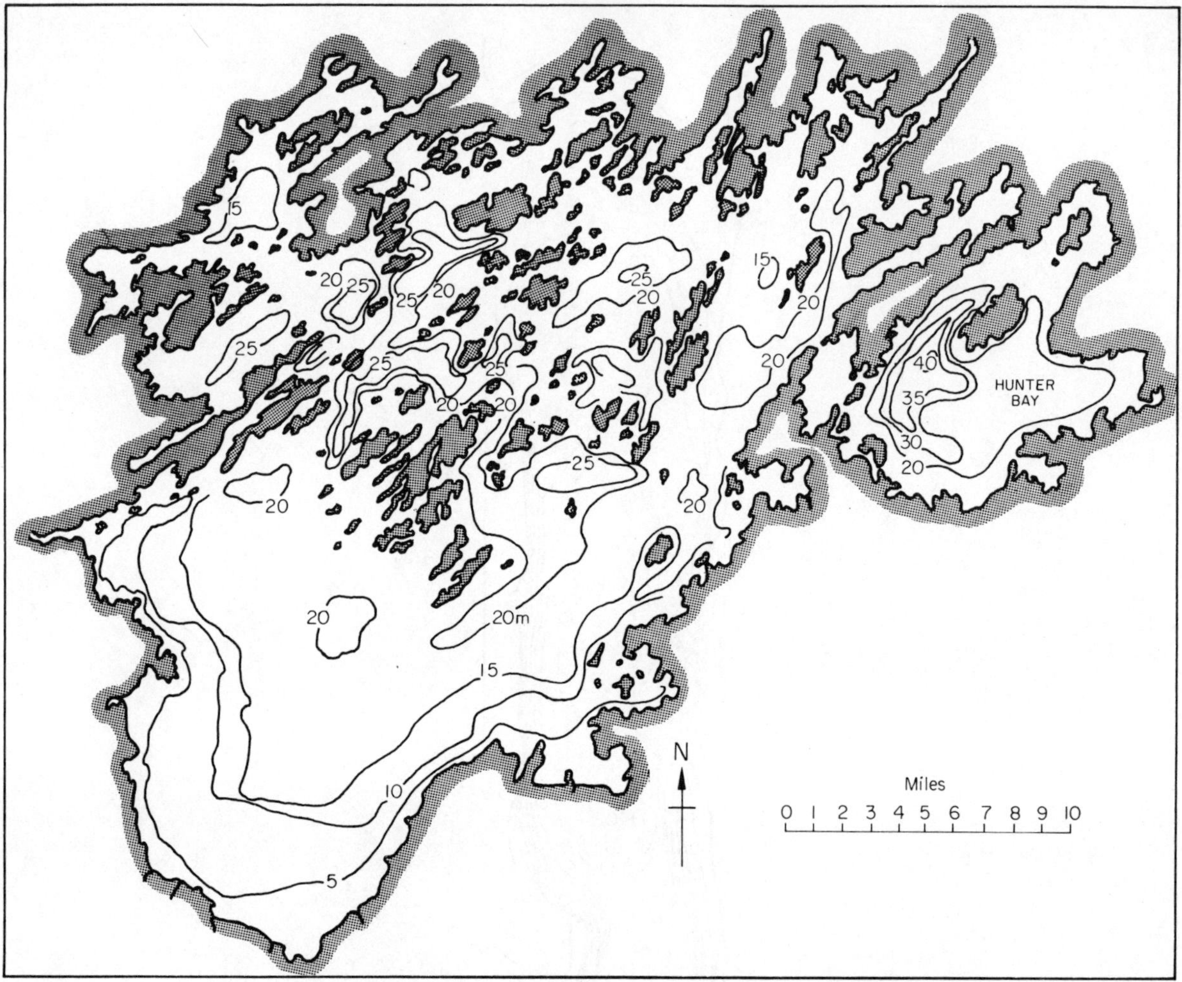

FIGURE 6.3. Contour map of Lac La Ronge (Oliver, 1960).

and Grimas (1965) demonstrated that Lake Mälaren in Sweden consisted of two independent lakes, largely because of human activity.

While these are very obvious divisions of large or fairly large lakes, even the smallest lakes may be divisible into several sub-units. Douglas Lake, Michigan (figure 6.6) is one of the better known examples of what came to be called 'depression individuality' in a series of studies. The chief among these investigations, from the benthic standpoint, was that of Eggleton (1931). The individuality of the depression fauna was qualitatively as well as quantitatively noticeable, but Eggleton referred to this variability as only part of a more general variability, dependent upon season of the year and depth. The number of species and individuals both were seen to vary according to the three factors of depth, time and location, but the seasonal variability followed a different course at each place and depth. These other variables will be considered in more detail below, but we should note here the general statement by Eggleton (1935) that, contrary to his expectation, a study of the literature revealed that 'typically the benthic fauna was not evenly distributed in any lake yet studied'. He noted that no two species had the same distribution pattern, one species could be differently distributed (in relation, say, to depth) in different lakes, and that depth distribution varied seasonally, so that one set of data along a single transect could not be considered typical of anything. Eggle-

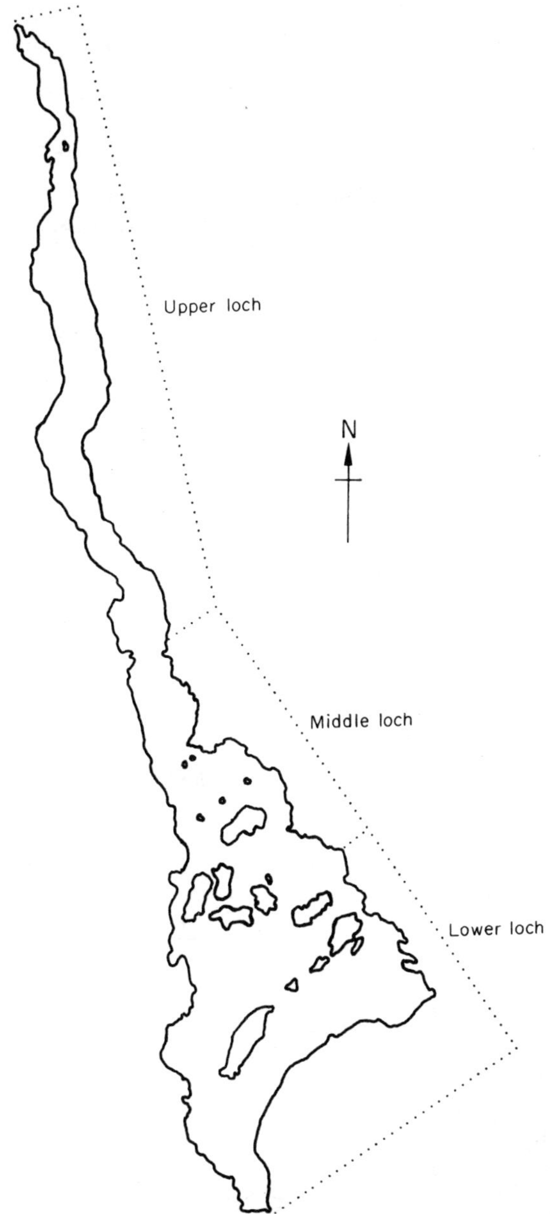

FIGURE 6.4. The three zones of Loch Lomond, Scotland (Slack, 1965).

ton indicated that he had set out to investigate the degree of uniformity of the bottom fauna of quite small lakes, but his initial emphasis on uniformity was quickly abandoned in favour of an emphasis on dynamic change of a variable pattern produced by a series of interacting environmental factors.

Others had shown differences between separate transects in a single lake, of course. Bardach *et al.* (1951) demonstrated the variability between the east and west shores of L. Okoboji, Iowa (figure 6.7) in terms of total benthos, and detailed studies such as that by Neave (1932) on *Hexagenia* in Lake Winnipeg, Manitoba,

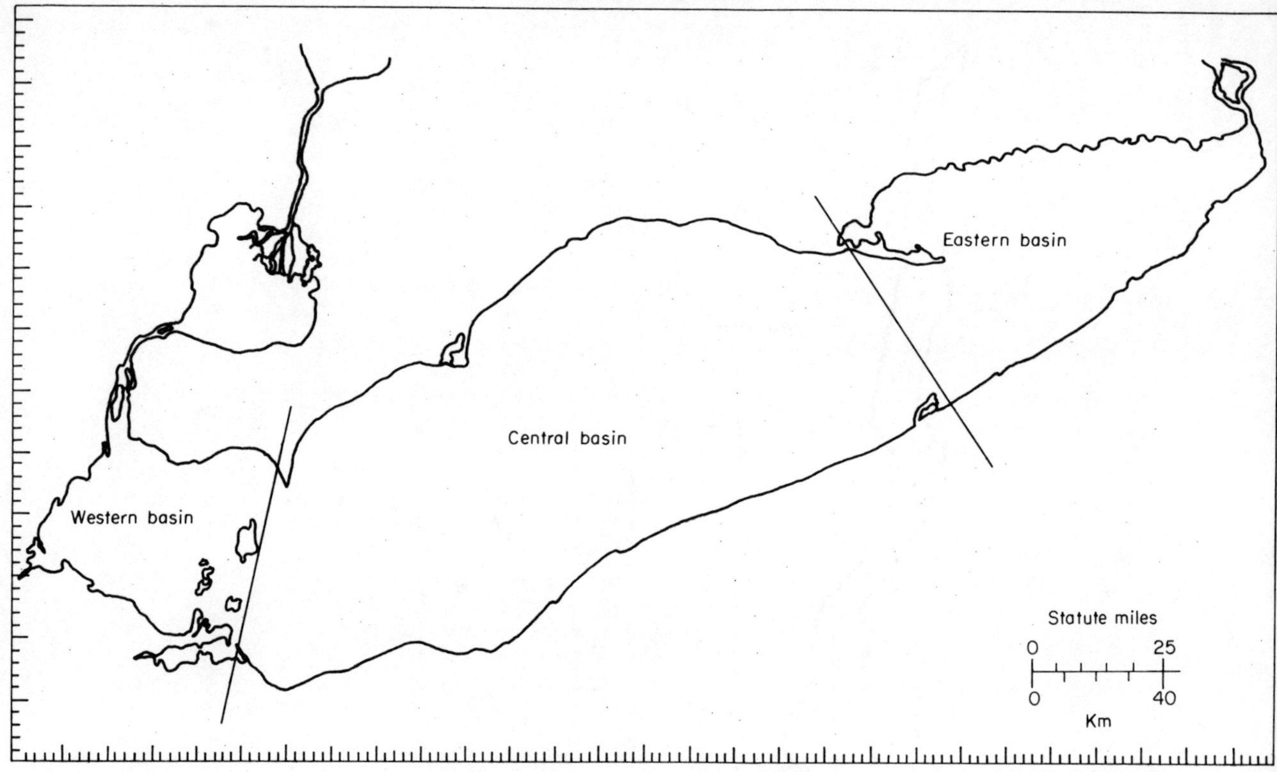

FIGURE 6.5. The three basins of Lake Erie.

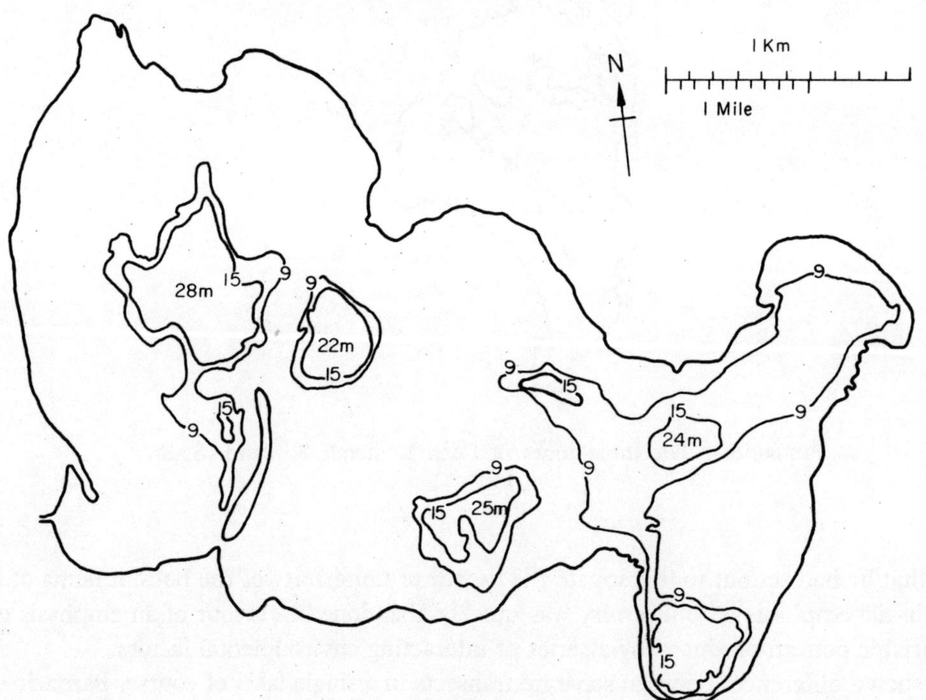

FIGURE 6.6. Contour map of Douglas Lake, Michigan (Eggleton, 1931).

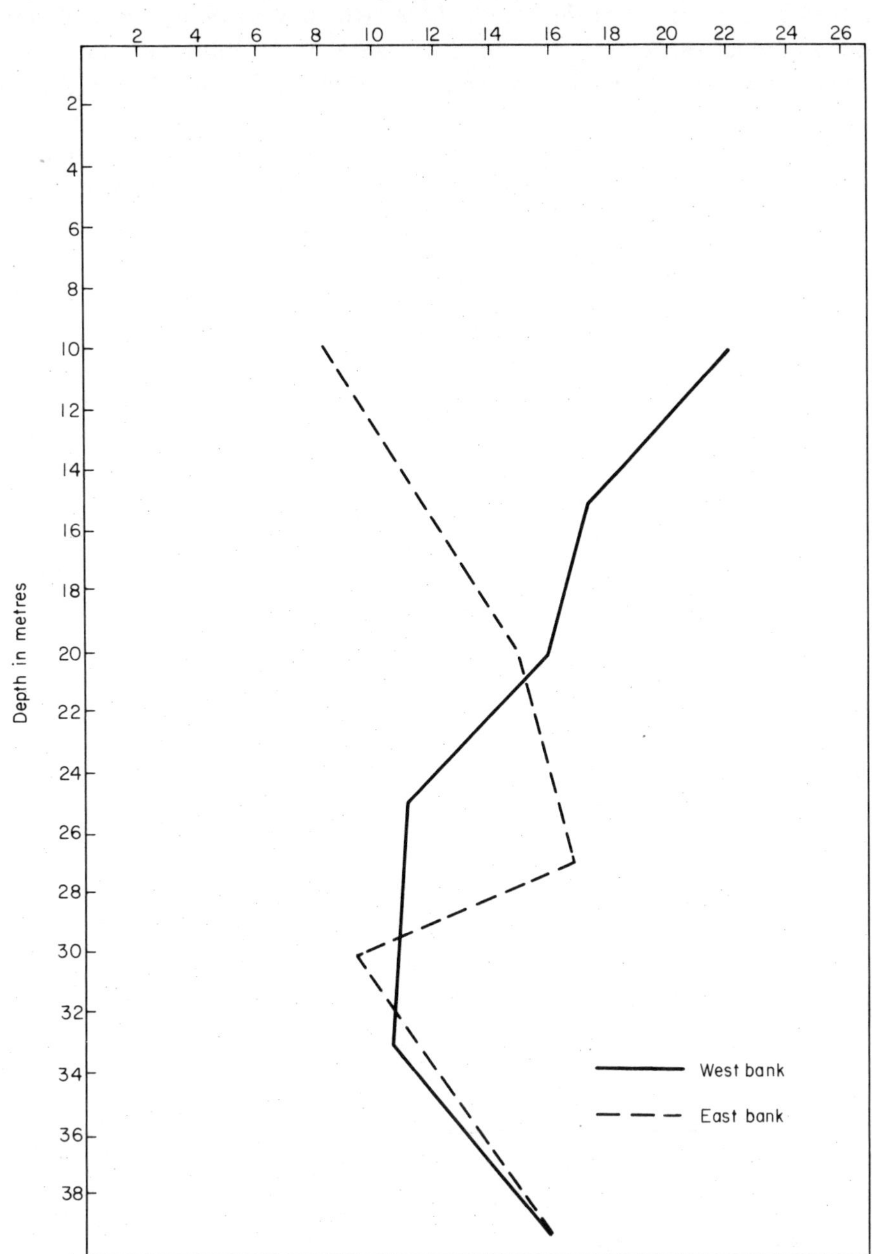

FIGURE 6.7. The vertical distribution of benthos in Lake Okoboji, Iowa (data from Bardach *et al.*, 1951).

commonly demonstrate markedly uneven distributions of benthic animals. Dugdale (1955) made a pilot study of Lake Mendota, and found that the lake had to be considered as consisting of at least three areas, the bays in particular differing from the main lake where depth differences were apparent. Despite this, the view persists that the profundal is a fairly uniform biological system. Schneider (1965) extended the earlier work by Beatty and Hooper (1958) on the littoral of Sugarloaf Lake, Michigan, and suggested that littoral had received little attention because it lacked 'the uniformity of the profundal region'. This suggests that we are still influenced by the concept of the seemingly monotonous milieu of the lake bottom despite the fact that when studies are made they invariably demonstrate that the apparently uniform habitat may be divisible into discrete zones, regions, or plant and animal associations, a state of affairs demonstrated by the study of Sugarloaf Lake itself.

One of the more obvious causes of horizontal variations in the occurrence of benthic organisms is the nature of the sediment. The difficulty in establishing causal relationships between sediments and their faunas is probably a methodological one. How does one characterise a sediment? No detailed attempt will be made to answer this difficult question here—let it suffice to say that analyses of grain size, total organic content or nitrogen content and the like, *cannot be expected to explain inadequately described distributions of partially identified organisms*. Only a detailed description of factors such as the type and extent of nutrient content of the sediment, its microbiota and other potential nutritional resources, as well as an analysis of the food requirements of benthic species, is likely to clarify the reasons behind some of the suggested associations between organisms and sediments. As Northcote (1952) suggested, to recognise boundaries of sediment types implies a workable classification of sediments—and we have none. Northcote demonstrated the relationship between the number of individuals present in four sediment types, as illustrated in table 6.1, derived from his data. Ever since the pioneering studies of Ekman (1915, 1917), Borner (1917), and others, various authors have published accounts of fauna and their relationship to various substrate types. Sand, particularly on wave washed beaches, is known to be a physically difficult habitat for macroinvertebrates and one that few forms are specially adapted to exploit. Even this generalisation may be challenged. For example, Berg (1938) found an abundant fauna in sand in contrast to examples cited earlier, and attributed this to the partial decomposition of organic material present, as opposed to its more decayed state in other regions of the lake, where there may actually be a greater total mass of organic material present. Hence Berg suggested that wave action on littoral sand is a dominating factor in the limitation of the fauna of such beaches. Many accounts stress the importance of a weed cover over sand or mud—but this would seem to involve an invalid comparison as the weed (no matter what kind) must surely support a host of organisms not truly associated with the sediment and the decomposition cycle.

TABLE 6.1. A comparison of sediment characteristics and mean numbers of benthic organisms in Hatzik lake (modified after Northcote, 1952)

	Sampling area			
	A	B	C	D
No. of organisms	53	42	12	65
Organic matter retained on screens (cc)	360	720	20	141
Inorganic matter retained on screens (cc)	54	8	12	34
Ratio of organic/inorganic	6.2	85.0	1.5	4.0

While wave action, relative exposure of a shore, and local geology, will produce a diversity of littoral habitats that differ macroscopically in substrate type from rock through stones, sand, and mud, to weed choked bays, we are concerned here with substrate variation within the soft sediment range. Much of the unevenness of benthic distributions in a lake might, at a guess, be attributed to the dynamics of the water column from which freshly sedimenting autochthonous and allochthonous material is derived. Studies like that of Gould and Buddinger (1958) on Lake Washington suggest an active sorting and shifting of sediments

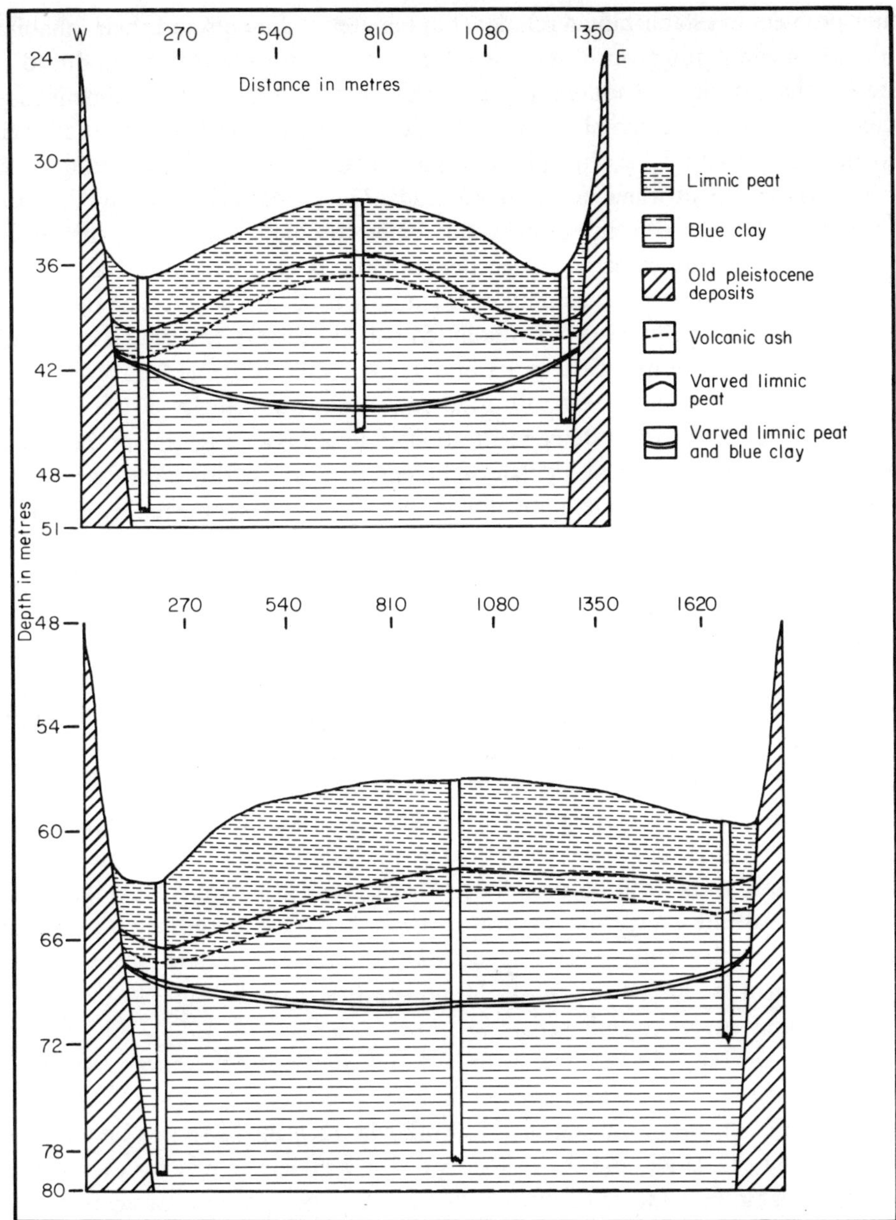

FIGURE 6.8. Cross-sections of Lake Washington showing stratigraphic sequence of trough fill (not to scale). (Gould and Budinger, 1958).

in relation to the thermal regime which, in this case, has resulted in a W-shaped instead of a U-shaped profile of the lake in section (figure 6.8). The measurement of sedimentation rate has always been bedevilled by the problem of resuspension of material, and collection devices have seldom been evaluated by parallel trials. Johnson and Brinkhurst (1971*c*) presented data on a number of devices, and suggested that a funnel trap (20 cm diameter) was the most suitable.

Another major problem in establishing a relationship between sediments and their inhabitants is that one might regard the sediment at any given instant as the accumulated waste matter produced by the fauna or rejected by it rather than as the food source. Hence a high organic content of a sediment may indicate relatively low bacterial activity and minimal benthic production potential rather than the reverse. Refractory materials build up high organic levels in sediment, particularly where peat formation is the result! The cycling of glucose at the sediment/water interface was studied in Toronto Harbour by Wood and Chua, 1973. By studying natural substrate concentrations and heterotrophic uptake by the microbiota, these authors were able to estimate rates of exchange between the pools of dissolved and particulate organic matter, the microbial and non-microbial communities, in both mud and water. The same general pattern of events was discernable in both polluted and less polluted parts of the system, which may suggest some uniformity in the general result in terms of the types of organic matter available for study. The most polluted site had the highest pool size of glucose in both mud and water, but velocity of uptake and turnover time showed no relationship to either substrate concentration or total organic matter in the sediments. Activity in the sediment must be supported by particulate sedimentation plus hydrolysis of large organic molecules aided by the microflora, whereas water column activity can largely be supported by export of substrate by turbulent diffusion or irrigation by the worms (discussed later in this chapter). Pollution may alter the catabolism of the glucose, which ranged from 22–44 per cent in the water and sediments in the polluted zone, to 9–23 per cent in the cleaner area. The observed substrate concentrations in both mud and water may actually reflect minimal or residual concentrations below which the microbial community has difficulty in assimilating the substrate.

So long as the material is physically habitable in terms of supporting a temporary or permanent burrow, leaving appendages and gills free enough to function and being within a tolerable range for unselective particle feeders (if there be any such thing), the key factors are more likely to be the nature and rate of descent of fresh food particles for those that feed on settling material, and the nature and recolonisation rate of the microflora of faeces that are continually recycled by the sediment ingesters. Fine balances between the precise biochemical nature of the food base, its rate of settlement, the nature and vigour of the microflora and the differing abilities of the competing species to utilise these, are more likely to determine the quality and relative quantity of benthos than precise adaptation to inorganic granule size. Granulometry may be highly relevant to studies of the interstitial fauna of sand beaches or the so-called psammon, but may matter much less in complex underwater organic soils.

As an example of the outcome of analysing sediments and correlating them to the distribution of organisms, a study of oligochaetes in Lake Maggiore (Italy) can be cited. This is chosen because of the attempt to restrict the study to one small part of the lake, and to work with identified species. The sediment was separated into four fractions by elutriation and the loss on ignition was determined for each dried sample. Della Croce (1955) claimed that granulometry had made it possible to explain how 'in many cases an irregularity of distribution of Oligochaeta at the same depth and position is to be attributed to an inhomogeneity of structure of sediments within the same depth'. Unfortunately, despite the much greater than usual degree of care and the use of statistical analyses, this study can be criticised by applying a number of statistical tests to the data. When this was done (Brinkhurst, 1965) it seemed possible that some extraneous factors (such as predators or changes with time) were responsible for a large degree of the observed variability.

Most statements of the preference of an organism (or usually a whole group of organisms) for a particular substrate are based on qualitative studies, or are essentially parochial and non-comparable to other statements about the same species. Until both substrate and organism can be adequately classified, or until more specific components of the sediments are analysed as continuous variables in a research programme which is designed so that most other variables are minimised (say by taking a set of core samples with adequate replicates in a short space of time along a single submarine contour that passes over various soft substrates),

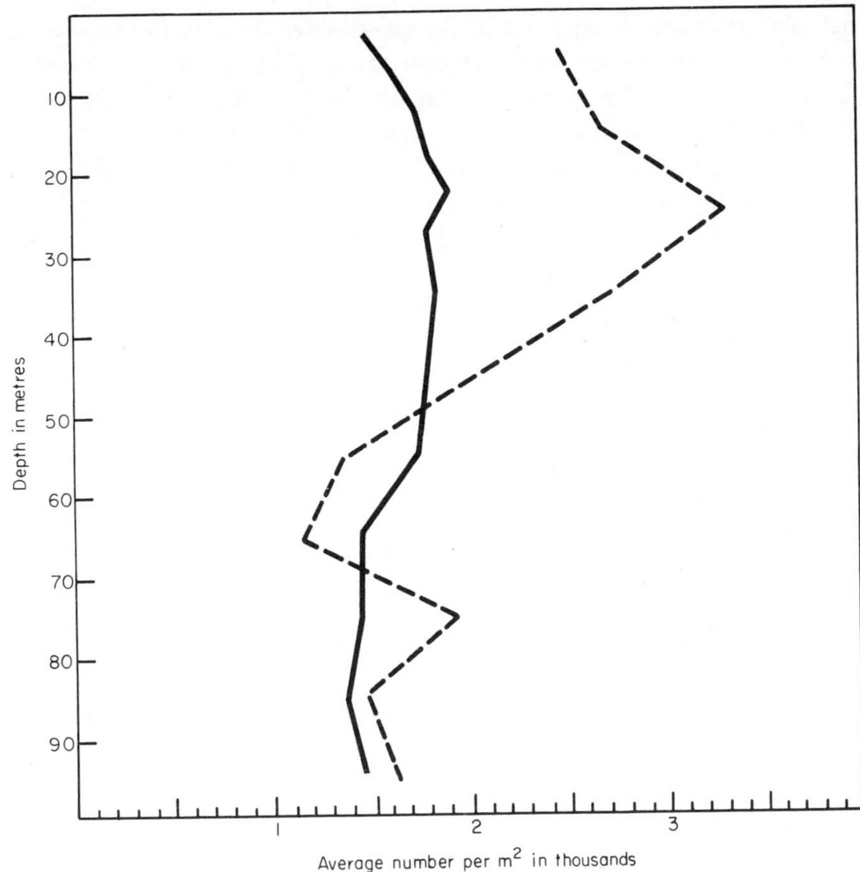

FIGURE 6.9. Comparison of the average number of bottom organisms in the delta region and in the main part of Great Slave Lake (Rawson, 1953).

descriptive notes on the substrates occupied by organisms will tend to differ from each other and produce more and more imprecise data. Careful studies of the relationship between identified species and substrate characteristics such as that by Cook (1971) for marine oligochaetes are more impressive but scarce.

A precise identification of the food preferences of organisms dependent upon the decomposition cycle would appear to provide a method with potentially far greater precision in determining the causal basis of observed distribution patterns, than analyses of sediment for grain size or total organic matter and similar non-specific variables. That this has seldom been accomplished is due to the lack of study of the microflora and fauna and the specific components of sediments, and the identification of benthic forms as 'detritivores' —with the implication that such a diet would not be subject to further subdivision into specific constituents by specialists with narrow food preferences.

In one sense, the whole Saprobien System used since the beginning of the century in river pollution biology (see p. 8) reflects not only variations in ability to withstand oxygen deprivation by the various components of the fauna but also their dependency on certain food sources. The system was applied to lakes soon after its initiation, an early example being the identification by Borner (1917) of zones in St. Moritz Lake constituting a mesosaprobic north shore affected by human settlement and an oligosaprobic south shore. The deep water in the middle was termed polysaprobic by virtue of the oxygen depletion caused by allochthonous material. This terminology, updated by the quantitative identification of associations of species rather than by reliance upon the presence of 'indicator species', might have been fruitfully applied to lake studies, but was supplanted by the trophic system terminology discussed earlier. Monard (1919) identified the effect of the nutrient load of allochthonous material in the Areuse delta fans on Lake Neuchâtel. He also noted that the fauna of a submerged bank (La Motte) was poorer than that of the equivalent

TABLE 6.2. Comparisons of average numbers and wet weights of organisms per m^2 at depths of 0–100 m in the delta region and in the main part of Great Slave Lake (Rawson, 1953)

Organism	Main lake	Delta	% difference
Amphipoda	1132	1416	+25
Sphaeriidae	73	46	−37
Oligochaeta	162	726	+350
Chironomidae	74	92	+24
Ostracoda	65	21	−68
Gastropoda	11	0	−100
Nematoda	5	19	+270
Miscellaneous	17	8	−53
Total organisms	1539	2328	+51
Total weight (grams)	2.5	3.29	+32

depth zone along the margin, a factor also noted by Weerekoon (1956) in his study of McDougal Bank in Loch Lomond. The effects of waves, predation and supply of detritus were suggested as causal factors but studies were not, to our knowledge, undertaken to test these hypotheses. Monard (1919) had also identified local 'cities' of dense benthic populations in Lake Neuchâtel at about the 'sublittoral level', and noted that these were found at deeper levels in the delta fan—hence local conditions might override the normal vertical physicochemical gradient. The effect of delta fans on the benthos of Great Slave Lake was reported by Rawson (1953*b*) where 50 per cent more organisms were found in the delta as opposed to regions of similar depth in the main basin (figure 6.9). The weight of benthos differed by 30 per cent in the upper 50 m but below 50 m there was little difference in standing stocks in the two zones. The effect was also dependent upon the particular groups concerned, with some increases of up to 350 per cent, and others a 100 per cent decrease in the delta as opposed to the main lake (table 6.2).

Raverra (1966) reported the effect of canal and river systems on the fauna at a depth of 20 m in Lunzer Untersee. According to Lundbeck (1926) the 'sublittoral minimum' (p. 36) could be attributed to nutritional conditions locally rather than to other factors commonly involved, but Humphries (1936) observed that the supply of organic matter was the same all over the parts of Windermere examined and hence it could not be considered a limiting factor—perhaps another indication that if the claim is, in fact, reliable, then *quality* of organic matter is significant. A clear demonstration of this is provided by Johnson and Brinkhurst (1971*c*) who made an analysis of the utilisation of energy reaching the benthos *via* the sediments. In the fjord-like system referred to as the Bay of Quinte on Lake Ontario, the upper end of the system receives inputs with considerable amounts of domestic and industrial waste. In this region a large amount of inert fibrous material is locked away, unused, in the sediment, so that a measure of the standing stock of benthos, in proportion to the organic content of the mud, would be a spurious value to use in comparative studies. The diversity and production rates of benthos are, in fact, greater at a point further down the system where maximal *useable* food exists in reasonably well-tolerated physical-chemical conditions. Further out in the system, in open Lake Ontario, the benthos may well be limited by food supply as much as by prevailing climate.

Food supply may determine the species distribution as well as the actual biomass of benthos. Predatory benthic organisms clearly depend upon the presence of prey species whose size and activity make them available to the predator. Those forms dependent on macroscopic plants, or the aufwuchs developed thereon, are excluded from the benthos as defined here, but are an obvious example of food-limited invertebrates in lacustrine systems. Others in the true benthos may depend on macroscopic plant debris that is settled out below a bank of vegetation, or may require those micro-organisms that accomplish the decomposition of such material. Slack (1965) suggested that the availability of food might explain the otherwise anomalous appearance of *Sergentia coracina* in the oligotrophic north end of Loch Lomond (Scotland) and the presence of *Tanytarsus signatus* in the eutrophic south (though, in fact, the problem only exists as a deviation from a simplistic 'type species' concept).

Traditionally, it is felt that the vertical gradient in benthic forms, both qualitative and quantitative (p. 30) may depend in large part upon the food supply. The food source may be allochthonous material, especially near shore and below rivers, or it may be autochthonous. In either instance, the decomposition of this material—dead algal cells, animal faeces or their dead bodies—begins as soon as it starts its downward progress to the bottom. The longer this journey is, the more completely mineralised the material should be upon reaching the bottom, and hence there should exist a gradient in terms of food supply with depth. Wave action along the margin may denude a beach, eventually producing a sandy desert inhabited only by the psammon or interstitial forms. This process may lead to the build-up of food in a band below the lake margin, which may be reflected in a concentration of benthic organisms. However, bottom topography is seldom simple, and resuspension of sediments may well be a very active process in many lakes (Gorham, 1958). The transport of sediments as described by Gould and Buddinger (1958) may disturb this simplified picture and, together with deep water currents related to wind circulation and through flow of discrete bodies of river water, may achieve a good deal of regional disparity in food distribution. The fauna itself affects the sediment by virtue of burrowing, as our studies on irrigation of sediments by worms suggest. Values for faecal production of between 1.2 and 12.7 mg dry faeces mg^{-1} dry worm day^{-1} are quite impressive when one notes field densities of worms in excess of 40 g m^{-2} dry weight (worms minus gut contents). Initial estimates of water flows of 1.5 μl $worm^{-1}$ hr^{-1} become significant where worm densities can exceed 200 000 m^{-2} on average in a polluted harbour zone. Work on the African Lake Sibayi by Allanson and Hart *et al.* (unpublished) suggests that plankton densities over the deeper parts of the lake (35–40 m) may exceed those over the shallow regions by a considerable amount, that submerged valleys seemed to be less disturbed than other parts of the bottom, and that apparently fresh accumulations of plankton could be transported to some of the deepest parts of the lake on certain occasions. The same kind of capricious combination of circumstances that would put a quantity of a certain algal association into a certain depression at one point at one time could well produce the sort of depression individuality described for Douglas Lake by Eggleton (1931). Studies on fish ponds have often involved experimental manipulations denied those working on larger systems. The experiments by Lellak (1965) suggested that the quantity of organic matter in sediment bore little relationship to the quanity of benthos present or to the fish stocks supported. Food manufactured in the water column was thought to be the prime factor in determining benthic production. In an earlier paper (Lellak, 1957) the effect of fish on benthos production was determined, not only from the point of view of predation (see below), but by virtue of the activity of the fish in the whole system. It was suggested that fish might adversely affect the zooplankton population and thus allow more phytoplankton to settle on the bottom in situations where a large fish population confined in a cage allowed the development of a larger benthic population than when the fish were absent. In addition, the faeces of the crowded fish might make organic matter available in a particularly effective form. The fish stock therefore affects the benthos in important ways (Lellak, 1966)—first by preying upon them, and secondly by affecting the relative abundance of zooplankton species which would control production of nannoplankton. When fish density is high, predation rates may increase but so may the amount of settled food, and the opposite may be true of a situation where diminished fish stocks are found.

The whole question of benthos production has already been described, particularly in relation to the production of fish (p. 46), but one piece of the relevant literature requires special mention here. After studying the nitrogen concentration of Lake Simcoe sediments, Rawson (1930) suggested that some factor other than food determined population levels for benthic organisms, but that the resulting benthic population determined the organic content of the sediment (as assessed by the nitrogen concentration) by virtue of its feeding activity. Observing an inverse relationship between nitrogen and standing stock at one time of the year (May–June, 1927 and 1928), Rawson suggested that a heavy standing stock more effectively depleted the resources of the sediment than a sparse fauna. Other suggested relationships between standing stock of benthos, and various parameters are discussed in later papers by Rawson referred to above (p. 58), but it is of interest to note here the suggestion of an impact of the benthos on its food supply. Kajak *et al.* (1968) suggested that benthic standing stocks depend upon the interaction between species and food supply, and in general it seems better to visualise the system as part of a cyclic arrangement of interdependent factors than as a simple one-sided view of a series of factors controlling benthic production or standing stock in some sort of vacuum. There is, essentially, a cycle of materials and a cascade of energy through a maze of interconnecting 'pools' that must be interdependent so that, while benthic production may depend upon food supply (especially in the sense of a benthos dependent upon the decomposition cycle), it will, of course, affect that food supply in turn. Situations in which food supply is limiting may be found where geography and climate and a host of intralacustrine factors supply a diverse, efficient benthic fauna capable of exploiting a greater input of material than can reach the lake bottom. The reverse may also be true of other situations in which alterations of fish stocks, regulation of lakes, or an excessive input of decomposable organic matter and/or toxins may adversely affect the benthos to such an extent as to render complete utilisation of the food supply impossible. One has only to consider meromictic lakes or situations such as Rostherne Mere (a lake in which the benthos was missing from the deepest zone during the years it was investigated—Brinkhurst and Walsh, 1967) to see that such situations exist. Despite this, a study of food requirements and food resources of benthic associations might clarify many qualitative and quantitative observations and suggest more immediate causal relationships between sediment and organism.

While it is possible that the benthos may determine the available nutrients in the sediment at a given moment as well as being dependent upon it, the same is true for the upward interaction between benthos and fish. Fishery biologists commonly assume that the abundance of summer standing stock of benthos indicates its potential for supporting fish stocks, and the most casual of these mistaken conclusions ignore fundamentally important assumptions about methodology, variation of benthos in time and space, relationship between standing stock and productivity, selective feeding by fish and a host of other significant factors. It may be that it would be better to regard the benthos at any instant as the residue that has survived fish predation to date rather than the future supply—or better still to regard the situation once again as a dynamic interaction of two forces, both subject to still other similar and/or independent constraints. While much of this interaction is discussed above under the heading of production biology, the effect of fish predation, spatial distribution of benthic organisms and their relative abundance should be noted, though there is little detailed information available.

Lundbeck (1926) suggested that fish predation was a major cause of the sublittoral minimum observed in studies of vertical distribution of the benthos. Such a concentration of feeding activity by fish related, in the main, to the presence of physical/chemical gradients, has often been postulated. Dugdale (1955) suggested that non-random grazing by fish affected benthos distribution, and Verbeke (1957) suggested this as the explanation for the decrease in chironomid larvae at depths of between 7 m and 14 m in African Lake Edward where chaoborid larvae showed no such decline. Studies of fish gut showed that few chaoborids were eaten, and the same observation has been made by others (Welch, 1967). Studies on *Chironomus anthracinus* in Esrom Lake (Jonasson, 1965) suggest that, when fish are excluded from the hypolimnion because of oxygen deficits, there was less mortality among the larvae than in the period between overturn and the onset of cold weather that inhibited fish feeding.

Many insect species are preyed upon during the emergence period, when they leave their relatively protected larval environment and begin that journey to the surface in order to become aerial adults. Emergence of aquatic insects is well known to be a strictly seasonal affair, with various species succeeding one another in time of emergence. A typical study of this pattern was made by Morgan and Waddell (1961) on a small trout lake (or loch) in Scotland. The numbers and weights of various insect groups described, and a number of studies on fish feeding are discussed. From these it is clear that a single species of fish may depend on different food sources at various times or in various lakes or parts of lakes. Despite some criticism of the methods of obtaining fish for stomach analyses, particularly with diurnal fluctuations in food preferences taken into account, the study tends to support the concept of individual fish continuing to feed on a preferred species or perhaps the one that was most accessible when it began feeding—so that individual stomachs may hold a high proportion of an individual food source. Otherwise, availability seems to be the chief determining factor in fish feeding—there seems to be little evidence of natural selection favouring narrow, highly specialised feeding habits in most freshwater fish, undoubtedly because of the lack of consistency of supply of any one item in the diet. However, this may be justifiably regarded as an overstatement, and the reader is referred to the more comprehensive review by Nilsson (1967).

The subject of availability and utilisation of bottom animals is often overlooked by those regarding the benthos as a resource to be exploited by fish regardless of the form in which the biomass or calories exist. The importance of the make-up of the benthic community in relation to fish production cannot be over-

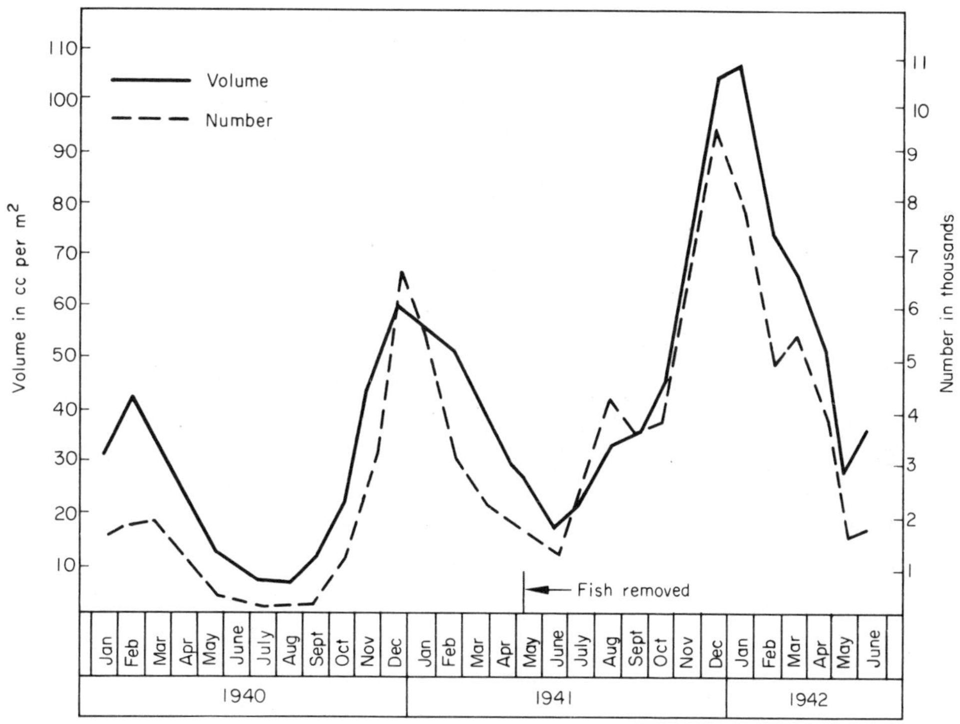

FIGURE 6.10. Seasonal fluctuations in volume and number per m² in Third Sister Lake, Michigan (Ball and Hayne, 1952).

emphasised. Not all situations would be as extreme as that in the River Thames at Reading, England, where Mann (1964) demonstrated that, although large clams made up only about 10 per cent of the numbers of benthic animals, they accounted for 90 per cent of the energy content and an even larger proportion of the biomass. They are not, however, available as food for the two common fish species present. Grimas (1963) summarised a number of factors in considering benthic fauna in relation to fish predation, particularly in impoundment studies that may be regarded as large scale field experiments. It is clear again that a high standing stock of benthos does not ensure good fish production, that a decrease in epibenthic or emerging forms or other preferred fish-food species in favour of, say, oligochaetes, would have a deleterious effect on fish yield. Conversely, the benthos must be affected by such selective feeding activity by the fish.

Most of the detailed work on the relationship between benthos and fish has been done in small ponds in which fish populations can be regulated, or in enclosures in such small water bodies. While such studies may not relate to conditions in larger lakes they should be considered briefly in the absence of other information. Removal of the fish in Third Sister Lake, Michigan, led to a general increase in standing stock of benthos (both volume and number) without disturbing the normal seasonal pattern (figure 6.10). The average increase was about 2.6 times the original standing stock (Ball and Hayne, 1952). In a more detailed experiment (Hayne and Ball, 1956) fish populations were moved from one set of ponds to another so that the comparison of benthic faunas in ponds with and without fish could be made alternately in each set. A distinction was made between organisms used by fish and those not used, although this may simply be regarded as those which leave traces in fish guts by virtue of external skeletons and those that do not (leeches, oligochaetes, large snails), with the exception of the mayfly *Hexagenia*, classified as a non fish-food item despite the fact that it has at least some heavily sclerotised cuticle. The effect of feeding by fish is clearly demonstrated (figure 6.11) and whereas the changes in 'non-utilised' forms show a similar reversal in standing stocks in ponds 4 and 5, this may be due to a degree of overlooked predation. The standing stocks of benthos were not reflected in the relative production of fish in the ponds, however, emphasising that standing stock estimates cannot be used directly to demonstrate productive capacity of lakes for fisheries.

A similar lack of correspondence between gut contents of fish and the proportions of benthic organisms in the lake was demonstrated by Gerking (1962) in another small water body—Wyland Lake, Indiana. Few

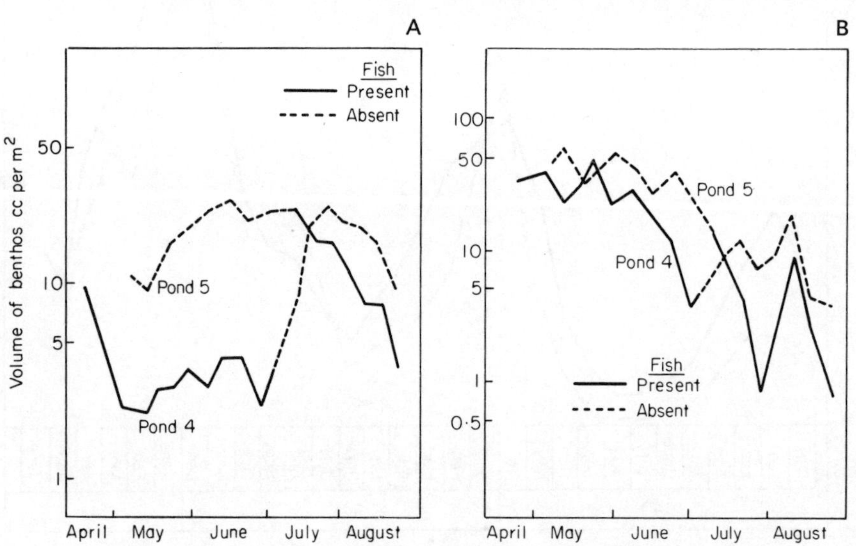

FIGURE 6.11. Fluctuations in volume of standing stock of benthos utilised (A) and not utilised (B) by fish (according to Hayne and Ball, 1956).

molluscs were utilised but culicids and ceratopogonids were used heavily in regard to their relative abundance. The determination of difference between total and available fish food was regarded as impossible owing to the changes in distribution with time both in fish and invertebrates. Much feeding was concentrated on pupating dipterans rising through the water column, and Gerking supports the contention of Borutzky, Berg and Lundbeck that *Chironomus* larvae migrate horizontally toward the shallow water in summer and away from it in the fall (hence bringing them into contact with feeding fish during the period of minimal food supply and at a time when oxygen depletion excludes fish from the hypolimnion in such lakes). This contradicts the view of Jonasson (1955) that the effect is due to inadequate sampling of the smallest larvae, and Gerking supports his argument by pointing out that Borutzky used sieves with meshes as fine as 0.25 mm. Further consideration of migration will be found in the section called Temporal Factors (page 115).

According to Gerking (1962) the well-known midsummer minimum in benthic standing stock is caused by—or accentuated by—fish predation, and he describes the benthos as having a substantial production rate constantly eroded by fish predation during summer in a 'keep-up' phase, followed by a period of winter 'catch-up' when standing stocks are restored. The difficulty in accepting this view is illustrated in the arguments put forward by Ball and Hayne (1952). The summer minimum is produced in the marginal fauna of Third Sister Lake by a decline that is initiated at the time of maximum standing stock—just as the ice cover is established. According to their data oxygen remains available, and the phenomenon occurs in the absence of fish as well as in their presence (figure 6.10). It is also true for the shallow water forms as well as for the deep water species normally considered in this context, hence the explanations may not be so clear as had been thought. Predation was not seen as a major cause of mortality for most taxa at the time of sampling Marion Lake, British Columbia (Hamilton, 1965), the most heavily preyed upon being nymphs of the Odonata, larval Trichoptera, and *Helisoma*—three of the larger forms present. *Crangonyx* was preyed upon more heavily than the smaller *Hyalella* and the chironomids that were utilised were either large, or frequently planktonic, or were in the pupal or imaginal stage. The usual discrepancy between abundance in nature and in fish stomachs is clearly demonstrable from the data. The importance of predation by invertebrates rather than fish was also noted—in fact it was suggested that *most* of the predation in benthic communities is due to this, and the predation by fish was clearly linked to the migratory behaviour of organisms such as *Sergentia* and *Psectrocladius* which made up 67 per cent of all chironomid larvae found in fish guts.

Another study of the effect of removing fish from a pond and subsequently re-introducing them has been reported by Macan (1966, *et seq.*). The influence of predators in this situation was to reduce the diversity of the fauna by excluding 'casual' species, whereas the effect on scarce species varied from no change (*Haliplus confinis*), slight increase (*Nemoura cinerea*), to a decrease or to absence (three water beetles). Abundant species were often reduced drastically in numbers once fish were re-introduced, and these included tadpoles, *Deronectes assimilis*, *Cloëon dipterum* and perhaps *Leptocerus aterrius*. It is significant to note that other species of *Deronectes* and *Cloëon* were not so affected, further emphasising the need to work initially at the specific level taxonomically. *Notonecta* nymphs were also severely depleted by fish, and it is clear that those forms that swim in open water or hang from the surface film are accessible to fish and utilised by them. The effect of fish on the marginal fauna in this weedy pond was to reduce the number of species and the abundance of many, but no species seemed to benefit in terms of increased abundance or range. Some of the larger, more important trout-food organisms (*Leptophlebia marginata*, *L. vespertina*, *Pyrrhosoma nymphula*, *Limnaea pereger*) were abundant both before and after the fish were introduced, suggesting that predation allowed for growth and survival of specimens that would otherwise have perished, perhaps through the operation of territoriality or other modes of intraspecific competition for limited resources. Unfortunately, there is no evidence of the effects of these changes on the fauna of the sediments in the deeper parts of the lake.

Experimental studies with enclosures or exclosures for fish have been made by Lellak (1957), Hruska (1961) and others, but the effect of the enclosure itself often obscures the results. The mere provision of a substrate for benthic aufwuchs plays a role here, together with problems related to the inherent variability of the bottom. Kajak and Pieczynski (1966) attempted short term field experiments using cylinders to which invertebrate predators were added. Predation of tubificid oligochaetes was estimated by Kajak and Wisniewski (1966) from evidence of regeneration of the tail ends cropped off by fish, as noted by Poddubnaja (1962). Kennedy (1969) attempted to use the degree of parasitic infection of tubificids and fish to relate predation on the former by the latter. In other experiments, Kajak *et al.* (1968) demonstrated selection of food by non-predatory chironomid larvae which normally utilise algae growing on the mud surface but which may, on occasion, include much more 'detritus' in their food. The life cycle may be completed on a variety of diets.

TABLE 6.3. The effect of crowding on the feeding behaviour of *Procladius choreus* (Kajak *et al.* 1968)

Situation	% *P. choreus* with *Chironomus* in gut	No. *Chironomus* in gut of *P. choreus*	% *P. choreus* with crustacea in gut
In lake	58	1	86
In laboratory after 8 days:			
(1) control	67	1	33
(2) increased population of *P. choreus*	100	6.2	11

The food of predatory chironomids is also variable, shifting from the more normal ostracods to a diet of *Chironomus* when this is available, or when the predator (*Procladius choreus*) is crowded. The following (table 6.3) indicates one such result. Lellak (1966) has demonstrated that interactions between plankton and fish are at least as important as 'climate' in determining the quality and quantity of the benthos assemblage. If feeding by invertebrate and vertebrate predators is selective and responsive to changes in the availability of the food, it is clearly affecting the proportional changes in the representation of benthic species, and this effect will vary with time. Hence the pattern of distribution and abundance observed during a benthic study is a single frozen frame from a continuous motion picture rather than a definitive portrait of lake type. The removal of fish species can affect the plankton composition (Novotna and Korinek, 1966) which, in turn, alters the flow of material to the benthos, and the reaction to this by the benthos will be dependent upon life style (that is to say, chironomids can exploit the situation rapidly if reproducing adults are available).

There are other biotic interactions between species, some of which may be referred to as competition and which may involve replacement of an indigenous species by an exotic introduction or by gradual expansion of the range of one species at the expense of another. *Asellus aquaticus* seems able to exclude *A. meridianus* from its original European and British habitats, and laboratory experiments confirmed the ability of the former to exclude the latter by some form of violent interaction (Hynes and Williams, 1965). A similar but perhaps more complex story involves the two amphipod species *Gammarus pulex* and *G. duebeni*. According to Hynes (1954) *G. duebeni* is potentially able to colonise certain types of freshwater streams but is unable to do so in the face of competition from *G. pulex*. The former is found in brackish water all around Britain, but is found in only a few western and northern freshwater streams there, and in a few in western France (Hynes, 1959). The dependence of *G. duebeni* on sodium ions was reported by Sutcliffe (1967*a*), who showed that all of the freshwater localities for this species had sodium concentrations in excess of 1 mM l^{-1} as opposed to the normal levels of 0.1–0.5 mM l^{-1}. Two exceptions are freshwater localities in Ireland and the Kintyre peninsula in Scotland. In the latter instance, the population was thought to be maintained by selection for individuals with a supra-normal ability to take up sodium. In Ireland

G. duebeni occurs widely in freshwater localities, but here it appears to constitute a different physiological race to that found in brackish water (Sutcliffe and Shaw, 1968; Sutcliffe, 1967*b*, 1970).

Both intra and interspecific competition in flatworms have been studied by T. B. Reynoldson and his co-workers in some detail, two recent publications being specifically concerned with this theme (Reynoldson and Bellamy, 1970, 1971). Laboratory studies on size, structure, population numbers and biomass revealed changes related to breeding (such as shrinkage of adults, mortality of small individuals and curtailment of egg production) the same as those observed in field populations. The effect of ranging population density on food uptake when the food supply is constant suggests that the major changes in population structure were due to intraspecific competition for food, which may occur even where food remains unused owing to the feeding behaviour of the worms.

Competition between *Polycelis nigra* and *P. tenuis* was examined in relation to five criteria (distribution and/or relative abundance; use of a common resource; natural shifts in fecundity, survival, and so on; field experimentation in which both common resource and population were manipulated; effects of introduction or removal) the conclusion being that there was an 'almost irresistible case' for events in a Welsh lake to be explained by interspecific competition.

Variations in abundance of one species may affect the abundance of others as demonstrated by Kajak (1963*a*). Here, reduction in numbers of *Chironomus plumosus* promoted an increase in several other benthic species (*C. anthracinus*, *Microtendipes chloris*, *Valvata piscinalis*) but an increase in *C. plumosus* caused the reverse. As noted above, these cage experiments are confounded by changes produced by the presence of the cage itself, which makes it difficult to assess the results of experiments (Kajak, 1964). Many benthic studies have demonstrated the spatial co-existence of species closely associated systematically, or by virtue of their apparent feeding habits and other ecological requirements. Two or more *Chaoborus* species co-existed in forty-five of fifty-nine lakes for which data were assembled by Stahl (1966) and it was suggested here that competitive exclusion did not occur because populations remained at a level below which a shortage of common resources occurs. While one may suppose that niche separation is minimal in this group, the same might seem to be true of tubificid oligochaetes. However, careful study of their feeding shows that they are selective (Brinkhurst, Chua and Kaushik, 1972) and that different bacteria survive in the gut of starved worms of different species (Wavre and Brinkhurst, 1971). Furthermore, mixed cultures of three tubificid species respire less and grow more, utilising more energy overall, than they do when maintained in isolation (Brinkhurst, Chua and Kaushik, 1972). This discovery was made during an attempt to assess worm production by solving the balanced energy formula, which can be expressed simply as Ingestion = Production + Respiration + Egestion. The fluid excreta and secretions such as mucus are often overlooked in such studies, though they may constitute a significant proportion of the energy budget. One of the parameters noted above is also obtained by back calculation in most studies, and this became true of the work with tubificids once we learned that the whole mud presented as food contained less nitrogen, calories, and organic matter in general, than the faeces of the worms feeding upon it; this showed that they had selected nutritious components of the mud, mostly bacteria, as food. As Brinkhurst and Kennedy (1965) had demonstrated interspecific interactions in laboratory culture, this work was carried out on both mixed and pure cultures of the same species. In the respiration studies the same individuals were used—first isolated, then combined, or vice versa. Respiration of mixed species complexes (any pair or all three species, namely, *T. tubifex*, *L. hoffmeisteri* and *P. multisetosus*) was about 30 per cent less than that of the same organisms in pure culture, so that the annual budget would be 9.4 kcal g^{-1} mixed and 13.3 kcal g^{-1} pure. The equivalent values of growth, when *P. multisetosus* appears to stimulate growth of the other two species more pronouncedly than they affect it or each other, the annual values would be 75.2 kcal g^{-1} in mixed culture but 22.5 kcal g^{-1} in pure culture. The respiratory effect can be produced by placing one worm species in water formerly occupied by another (Chua and Brinkhurst, 1973) and the effect persists until the culture water is heated, indicating that it might be proteinaceous. These results suggest that worms in pure culture are active, not feeding so much as in mixed culture, as they may be searching for their preferred food, the faeces of other worm species (which are known to be distinctive—Wavre and Brinkhurst, 1971). This is confirmed by finding that feeding (as measured by faecal output) increases 24 per cent in mixed culture, that assimilation efficiency increases 6 per cent (Ingestion/Assimilation), and worms of one species actually move towards captive worms of another species rather than others of their own kind. This work suggests a selective advantage, in energy terms, for the tightly clumped distribution of worms in multiple-species assemblages in the field, and proves the existence of positive interactions rather than those commonly thought of as competitive.

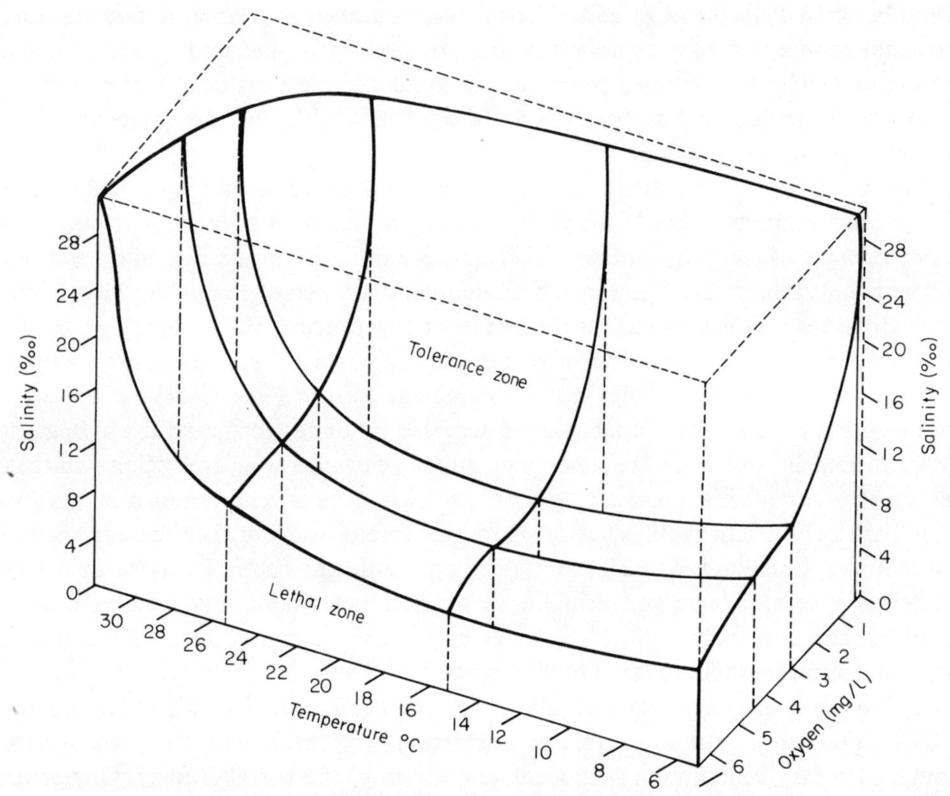

FIGURE 6.12. The boundary of lethal conditions for the American lobster for combinations of temperature, salinity, and oxygen (McLesse, 1956).

Such biotic interactions of the sort described in these few examples may be more significant than the ability to tolerate variations in simple chemical/physical parameters.

While it is clear from successional studies in estuaries and in polluted situations that organisms differ widely in their ability to tolerate physiological stresses, the establishment of precise tolerance levels for specific variables seems likely to prove impossible. A simple example of the interaction of factors involved may be derived from an examination of two experiments involving only three variables—temperature, oxygen and either salinity or cyanide concentration (figures 6.12 and 6.13). In lakes such as Rostherne Mere (Brinkhurst and Walsh, 1967) conditions conspire to make the deepest parts of the lake uninhabitable by

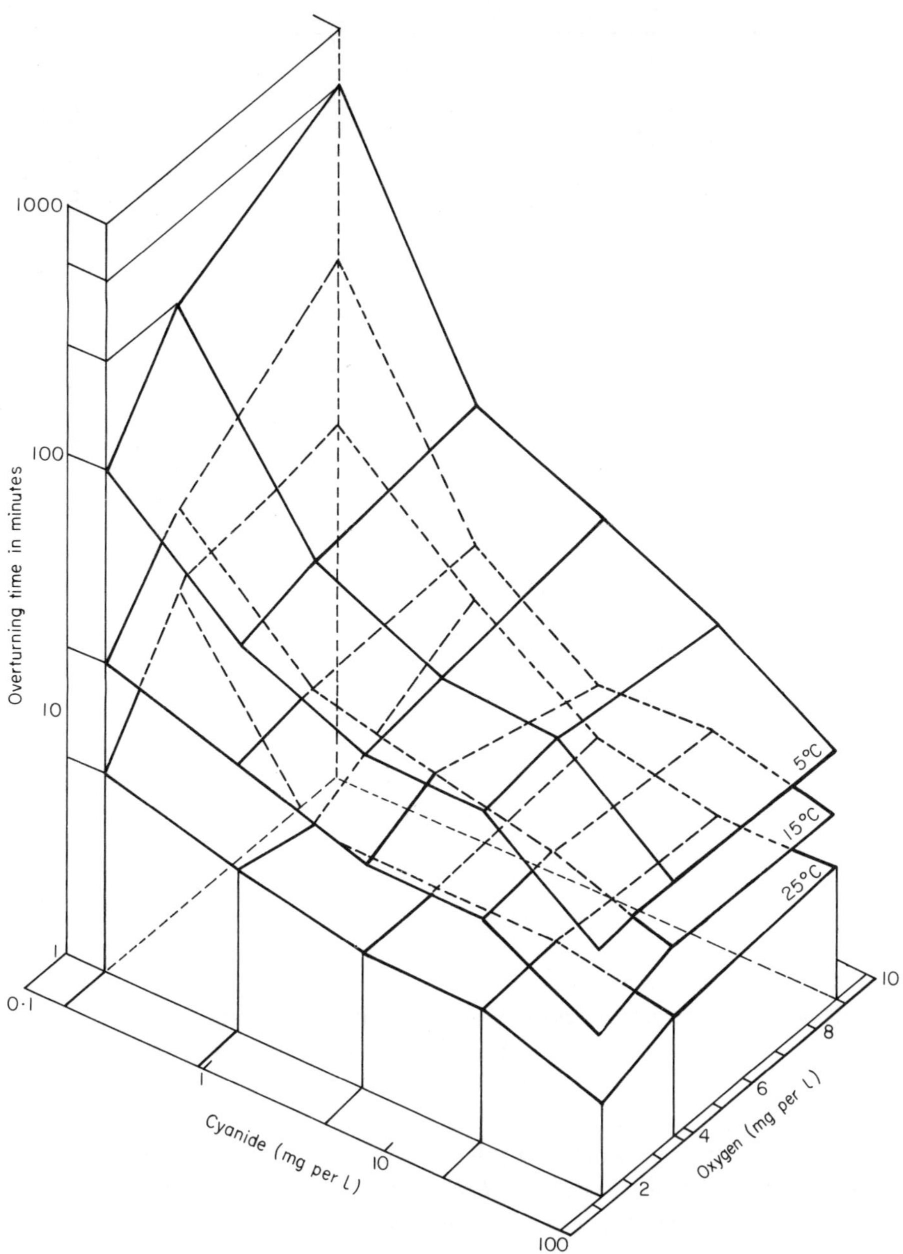

FIGURE 6.13. Survival time of minnows (*Phoxinus laevis*) plotted against cyanide and oxygen concentrations at three temperatures (Wuhrmann and Woker, 1955).

benthic organisms. The same is true for some meromictic lakes and, especially, hypersaline lakes. Some species, such as the nematode *Eudorylaimus andrassyi* and the tubificid *Potamothrix heuscheri* may survive anoxic conditions for more than 8 months in the field and for 6 months in sediment under water devoid of oxygen in sealed bottles at 15°C (Por and Massy, 1968). On the other hand, temperature tolerance of four crustaceans (*Asellus intermedius, Hyalella azteca, Gammarus fasciatus, G. pseudolimnaeus*) seemed to exceed what was necessary for survival in the field (Sprague, 1963) but response to oxygen shortage varied with the

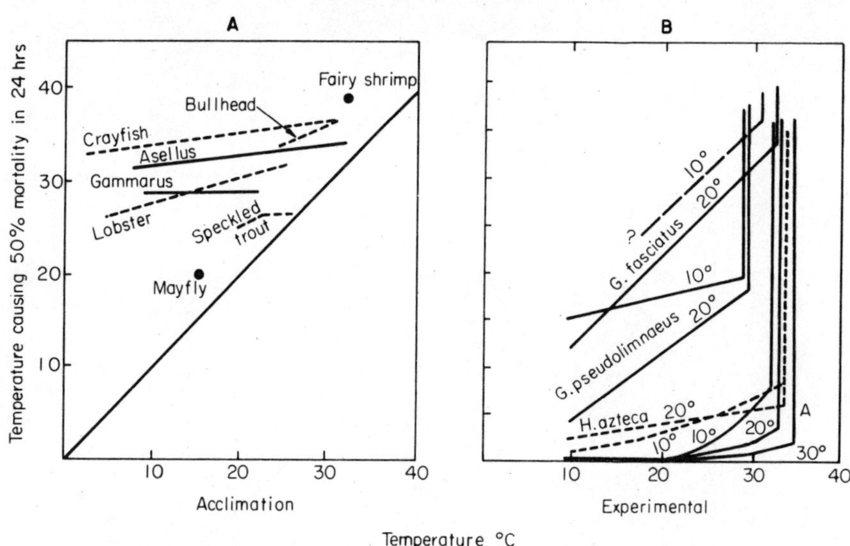

FIGURE 6.14A–B. Temperature and oxygen tolerance of various animals (Sprague, 1963). A, Temperatures resisted for 24 hours; B, Relation between temperature and oxygen conditions causing 50 per cent mortality in four species of crustaceans in 24 hours. In A, *Asellus* = *A. intermedius*, *Gammarus* = *G. pseudolimnaeus*.

species in a way seemingly related to their ability to withstand organic pollution (figure 6.14) and hence their physiological tolerance may be exceeded in normal circumstances.

The measurement of the oxygen requirements of individual species is thoroughly confused by factors such as acclimation (Berg, 1953), substrate preferences (Eriksen, 1963; Chua and Brinkhurst, 1973), activity (Walshe, 1950; Edwards and Learner, 1960), body size (Edwards, 1958), as well as temperature and food supply, although ambient oxygen concentration may have little effect on respiratory adjustors such as those found in deep water in lakes that have summer oxygen deficits (Berg *et al.* 1959, 1962, 1965). Seasonal variation of some of the respiratory values obtained for individuals of one size class are noted in some of these studies, such as that on *Erpobdella testacea* (Mann, 1956) which seem to go some way toward explaining the tolerance of certain species to situations of oxygen stress. Little tolerance work has been done on species that may be intolerant of oxygen stress as inferred by their natural distribution. Few of the tolerant species are, however, excluded from situations where less tolerant species can thrive. One example, not yet substantiated by experiment, is seen in the distribution of *Tubifex tubifex*, which may prefer situations in which other species find it difficult to survive, either because there is too little active decomposition or too much (Brinkhurst, 1970).

Despite the numerous, though often sketchy, studies of tolerance of this and that chemical and physical factor, there have been few instances of clearly demonstrated limitation of distribution of benthic animals by these factors alone. Perhaps if there were more laboratory tests of the predictions supplied by successional studies in water pollution biology there would be a greater appreciation of the forensic role of benthic studies in the field. An apparent threshold for the survival of many species may exist at 40 per cent saturation with oxygen or more, as indicated originally by Thienemann for *Tanytarsus* and suggested by personal experience in pollution surveys, but this remains an untested hypothesis.

The onset of summer stratification may cause benthic forms to migrate (see section headed Temporal Factors) or may result in their death as oxygen in the hypolimnion is utilised. Borutzky (1939*b*) reported dead larvae 10 cm below the mud/water interface in Lake Beloie, USSR, and Ohle (1960) (using photography and television equipment) found dead chironomids in Grosser Plöner See. The progressive change in Lake Erie, or more precisely in Erie's western basin, was dramatically demonstrated in 1953. Unusually low wind velocities in August and September allowed that shallow basin to stratify long enough for the oxygen to be depleted by the intensive oxygen demand of the sediments, and dead larvae of the burrowing mayfly *Hexagenia* were found in large numbers on September 5, none being found 9 days later (Britt, 1955*a*). The population apparently recovered in 1954 (Britt 1955*b*), but the mayfly larva is no longer a major component of the benthos in the area.

Temperature refugia have been suggested as the basis for the observed distribution of so-called glacial relicts. As the ice sheets retreated from the northern hemisphere, certain cold-adapted species are said to have survived in cold places—springs, the deepest parts of large lakes, high mountain lakes and so on. These cold water forms or stenotherms have not been systematically studied to determine their temperature tolerance. More interest has been shown in attempting to trace the historic distribution routes of relicts which survived glaciation in the old lakes (Baikal, the Jugoslav lake series around Ochrid) and the causes of endemicity in these lakes (Segerstrale, 1957). The age of the lakes may well provide an answer for much of the endemicity, providing as they do not only a refuge for relicts, but a continuous habitat that has permitted speciation to occur in a manner usually prevented by the relatively ephemeral nature of most lakes (Brooks, 1950).

As with respiration studies, the interpretation of distribution patterns in relation to temperature tolerances displayed in terms of lethal effects in laboratory tests is unlikely to succeed without taking into account the ability of species to compete with others at temperature ranges well within the outer limits of tolerance.

One recent dramatic demonstration of the effect of destroying summer stratification and oxygen deficit in a lake was carried out on El Capitan Reservoir, California (Fast, 1968, Inland Fisheries Branch, 1970). By blowing air into the hypolimnion, the temperature of the deeper water raised as the lake circulated, bringing oxygen into the hypolimnion. The chironomid species *C. attenuatus*, *Procladius bellus*, *P. denticu-*

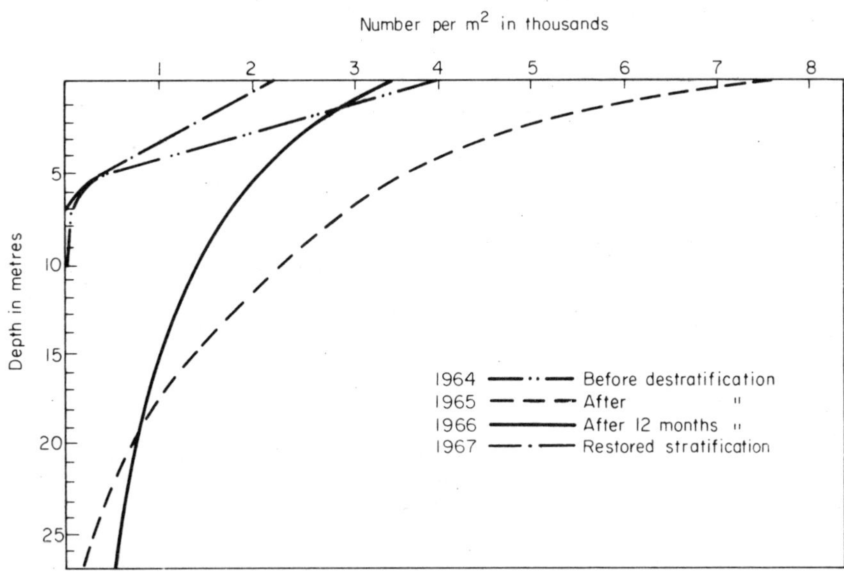

FIGURE 6.15. Summer distributions of chironomid larvae before, during and after artificial destratification of El Capitan reservoir, California (Inland Fisheries Branch, 1970).

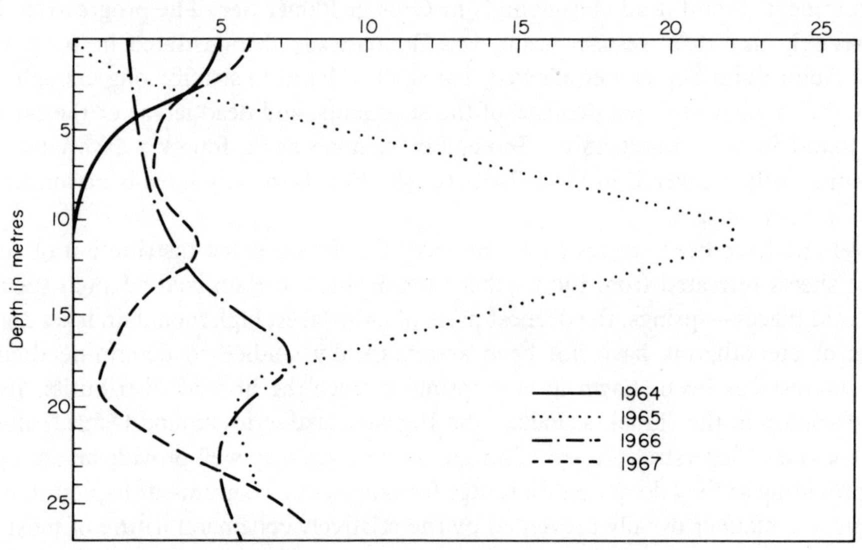

FIGURE 6.16. Summer distribution of oligochaetes before, during and after artificial destratification of El Capitan reservoir, California (Inland Fisheries Branch, 1970).

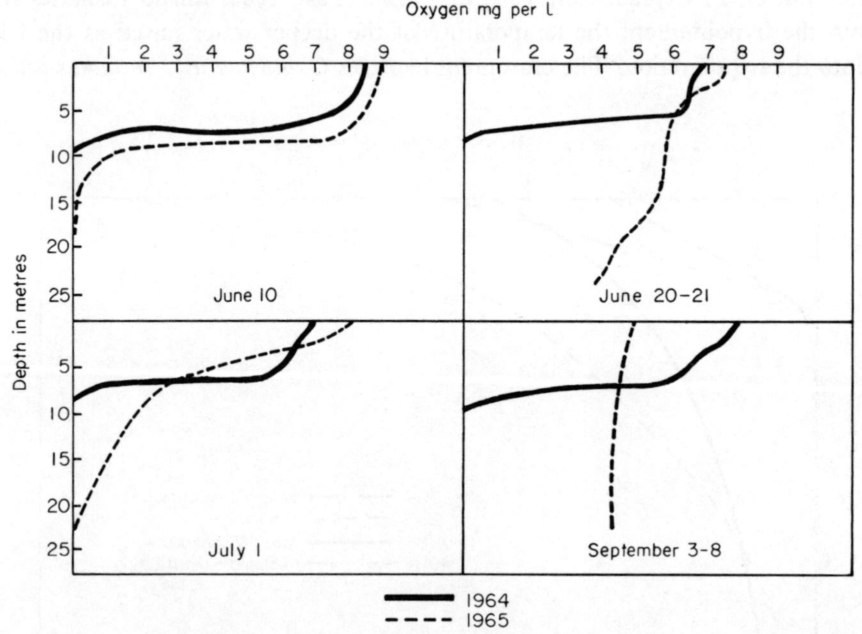

FIGURE 6.17. Oxygen concentrations during comparable periods of 1964 and 1965 in El Capitan Reservoir, aerated from June 10 to 21 and July 1 to Oct. 4 1965 to destroy stratification (Inland Fisheries Branch, 1970).

latus and *Tanytarsus* spp. were treated as a group in this study. They tended to disappear from the zone below 10 m in a normal summer but were found at all depths after destratification. There was an increase in the number of chironomids during the winter following destratification, but this was markedly greater than the usual increase in abundance in the deeper zones following normal destratification. The distribution is summed up in figure 6.15, where it can be seen that in 1965 and 1966, when stratification was prevented, midges were found at all depths and in large numbers relative to their abundance in stratified conditions (1964, 1967). Oligochaetes responded in the same general way. Worms were usually excluded from the sub 10 m zone in summer, were increased in abundance in the winter following destratification, and generally were more abundant and penetrated more deeply into the lake after destratification than before (1965 and 1966 in contrast to 1964—figure 6.16). In 1966, however, the distribution pattern had changed drastically from that observed previously, and even in 1967 many survived in the sub 20 m zone despite the return of stratified conditions, an almost complete oxygen deficiency on the bottom after April 1967, and a total absence of O_2 from the whole zone below 10 m by September (figure 6.17). A variety of species was present, including *Limnodrilus hoffmeisteri*, *Bothrioneurum vejdovskyanum*, *Potamothrix bavaricus*, *P. hammoniensis*, and *Tubifex tubifex*, the former being much the commonest species present. The same story can also be told for the nematode population (figure 6.18), and it is clear that low temperature, low oxygen, accumulation of toxic chemicals and other factors related to stratification were limiting the distribution and abundance of many species in 1964 as opposed to 1965 and 1966, but that by 1967 the original pattern was apparently re-developing. That the populations of oligochaetes and nematodes did not instantly return to their previous

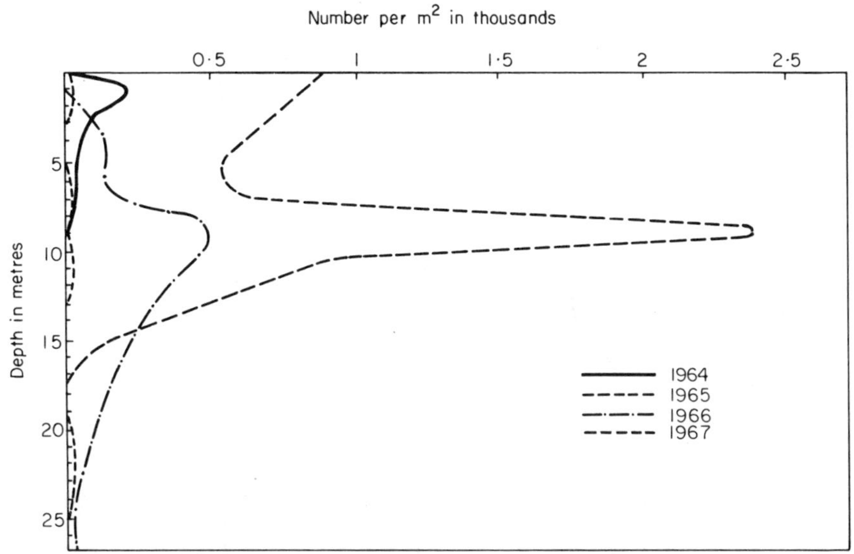

FIGURE 6.18. Distribution of nematodes before, during and after artificial destratification in El Capitan reservoir California (Inland Fisheries Branch, 1970).

distribution patterns once stratification resumed shows that this was not a simple response to narrow temperature and oxygen conditions, but that other factors play a role in setting these limits. Hydrogen sulphide built up rapidly in 1967 as in 1964, but other toxic substances may take longer to accumulate after two summers of destratification.

In general, the contribution of laboratory studies of physiology to ecological problems may be hampered by a number of factors, including:

(1) Physiological responses which generally depend on a multivariate set of parameters interacting simultaneously (McLeese, 1956; Wuhrmann and Woker, 1955). Their evolution depends on maintaining paranormal conditions in the laboratory (Eriksen, 1963).

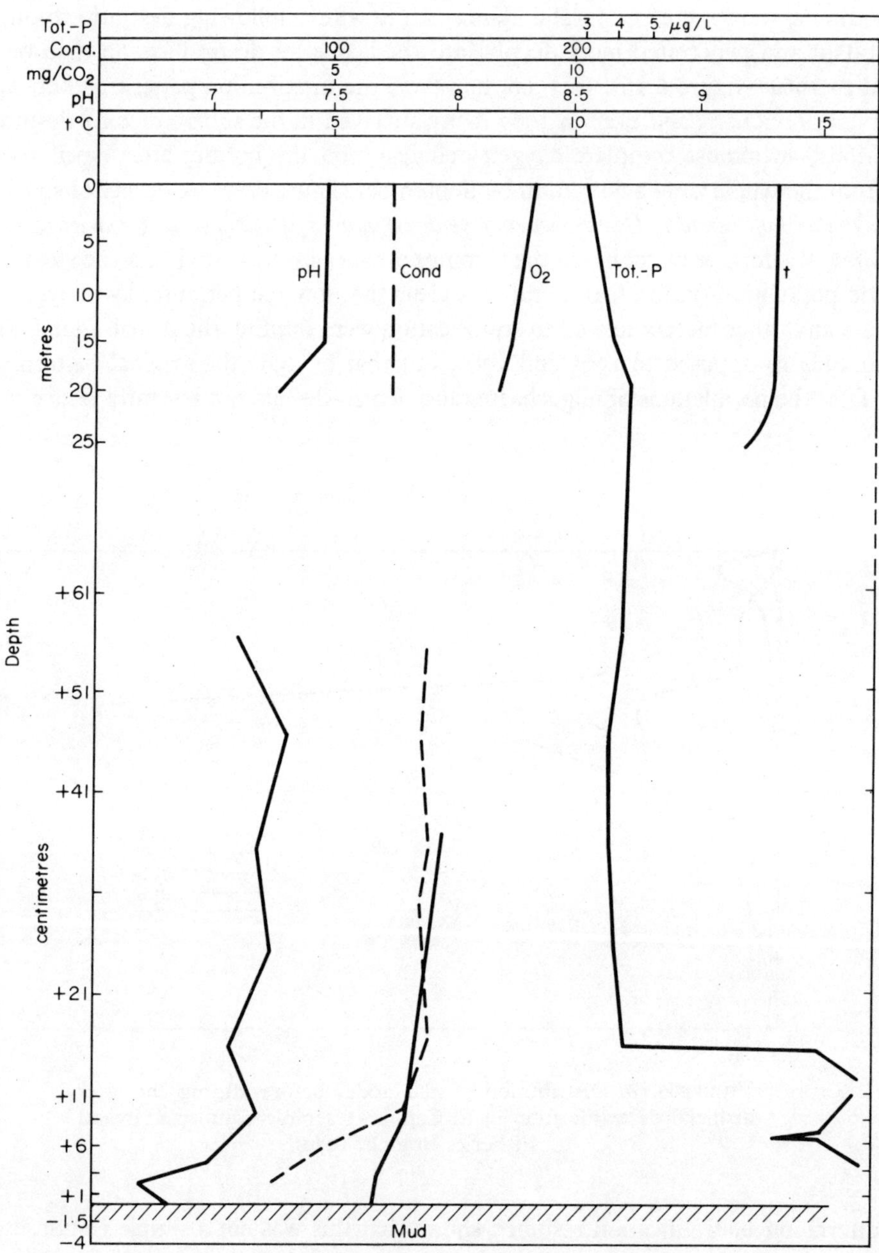

FIGURE 6.19. Microstratification of pH, conductivity, total phosphorus and oxygen at the mud/water interface (Millbrink, 1969).

(2) Species that adapt to local circumstances such that their feeding and behaviour may differ radically from site to site (*Mysis relicta*—Lasenby, 1971) or that may even constitute physiological races (*Gammarus duebeni*—Sutcliffe and Shaw, 1968).
(3) Species may interact in such a way that their growth and respiration in pure culture is unlike that in mixed species associations (tubificids—Brinkhurst *et al.* 1972).

While the destratification of El Capitan indicates physiological responses to changed benthic conditions and hence suggests the possibility of establishing tolerance limits for species that might be used as a quantitative basis for the qualitative successions described by the pollution biologist and lake typologist, the establishment of such criteria in the laboratory is no simple matter.

The correlation of physical–chemical conditions in the water column with the distribution and abundance of benthic organisms is obscured by the existence of microstratifications, particularly in oxygen concentration, close to the mud–water interface. These were discussed by Alsterberg (1922), who showed that the detection of the environmental conditions occupied by benthic forms involved sampling a layer a few millimetres thick, close to the mud surface. These microstratifications were not limited to productive lakes but occur in many lake types. Mortimer (1971) reviewed his earlier studies on the redox potential of the interface region. In this work the depth of the oxidised layer of sediment was shown to vary in relation to shifts in the redox potential dependent on the access of atmospheric oxygen to the deeper water. Thermal stratification or ice cover are well-known causes of exclusion of oxygen supplies, and the effects of this on the solubility of various ions are reasonably well understood.

Two recent demonstrations of microstratifications at the mud–water interface were presented by Milbrink (1969) using data from Lake Mälaren, Sweden (figure 6.19) and Boltt (1969) on Lake Sibayi, S. Africa. The latter study (table 6.4) demonstrated that microstratification can be a transient event in this monomictic lake, presumably because of variation in diffusion currents in lakes (discussed by Mortimer).

Changes in the behaviour pattern of invertebrates in relation to gradual changes in oxygen, carbon dioxide or other parameters at the interface may well be responsible for some of the distribution patterns observed in lakes. Promising evidence of this is being accumulated for *Grandidierella* in Lake Sibayi by Boltt (unpublished data). Thus a direct relationship between chemical conditions and distribution might be hard to establish without a long sequence of observations being made.

TABLE 6.4. Data from the sediment water interface of Lake Sibayi from Boltt (1969). The pH meter was calibrated against buffers prior to each determination

Date	Depth	Surface pH	pH at shown distances above the substrate 9.0 cm	5.0 cm	0.5 cm
25/9/69	19.0 m	8.40	8.43	—	8.37
31/10/69	19.0 m	8.36	8.26	8.21	8.37
30/10/69	20.0 m	8.53	8.46	8.44	8.47
25/9/69	30.6 m	8.50	8.05	7.91	8.01
23/10/69	31.5 m	8.38	8.19	7.72	7.29
24/10/69	31.5 m	8.53	8.43	8.35	7.93
26/9/69	31.6 m	8.50	8.38	8.40	8.32

The activity of the organisms themselves may help to overcome the effects of these microscopic layers. Many forms may irrigate their burrows actively, drawing water down through the deoxygenated water layer or down into the deoxygenated mud layer. A worsening of conditions will usually provoke active irrigation at first, but this behaviour may be replaced by emigration or quiescence if the losses due to increased activity outweigh the benefits in the form of oxygen supply and carbon dioxide or metabolite removal. Alsterberg (1922, 1924) described the activity of tubificid worms and their effect on sediments. Although Schumacher (1963) detected a correlation between the abundance of worms and the depth of the oxidised layer of the sediment (figure 6.20), cause and effect may be looked at two ways in the absence of experimental

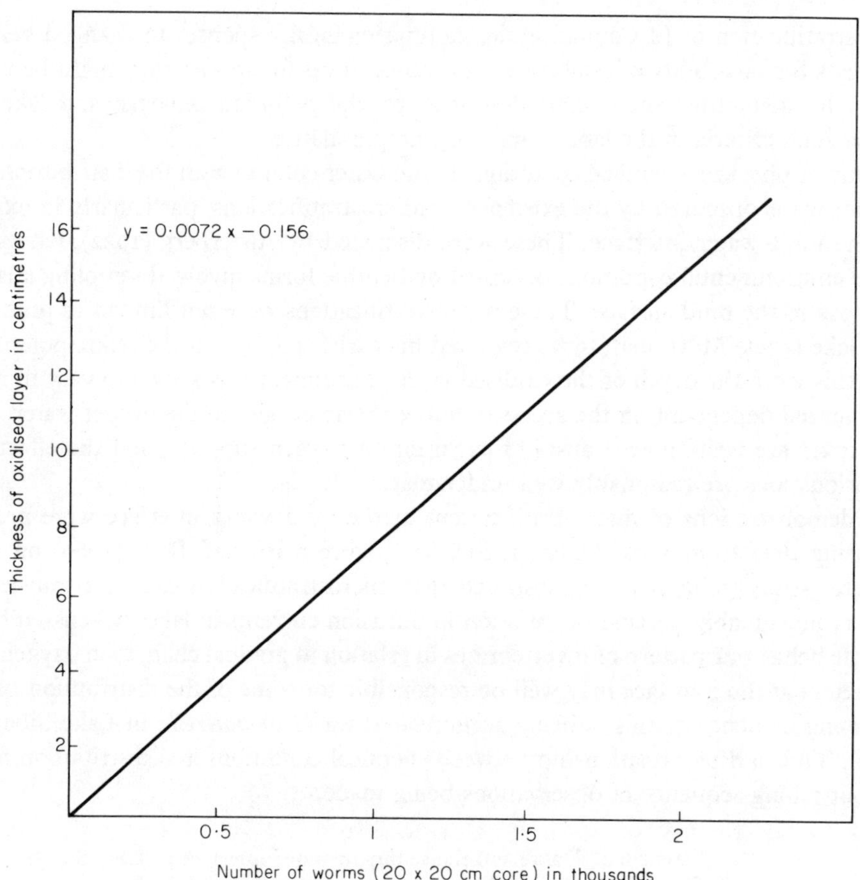

FIGURE 6.20. Relationship between the thickness of the oxidised sediment layer and the number of tubificids present (Schumacher, 1963).

work. The somewhat greater interest in chironomids and their ability to withstand oxygen deficiency was discussed by Brundin (1951), who considered size to be a factor of some importance in relation to the ability to pump water. The longer tubificids are known to be able to vary the degree of extension of the body into the water during respiratory pumping activity, but this is not possible for chironomids.

While some attention has been focused on seasonal changes in oxygen concentrations in deep water in eutrophic lakes, one special area of the lake bottom should be considered in respect to rapidly fluctuating conditions which may determine the bathymetric distribution of species. In a lake in which a sharp thermocline develops, seiches will result in the exposure of the bottom just above and below thermocline level to a tidal flow of water of very different thermal and chemical characteristics (see p. 43). As the season progresses, this zone itself may shift downward, become broader and hence the transitions may be damped out. The situation will vary from year to year, but there may be a zone that resembles an estuary in that the fauna is adapted to withstand fluctuating conditions rather than one specialised set of conditions. The scarcity of such forms may produce a situation in which minimal diversity is to be found in the unstable zone, much as it does in estuaries. There does not, however, seem to be a truly 'estuarine' or thermoclinal element in the fauna. Presumably the condition is too variable in position and extent, and too transient in geological time, to permit such a development to occur generally.

Temporal Factors

There is a series of temporal causes of variability in the observed distribution and abundance of benthic species which must be taken into account in designing sampling programmes, and these vary from diurnal through seasonal to progressive changes.

Vertical migration is known to occur in zooplankton populations, and the active migration of some predators that specialise in utilising the night time concentration of plankton has been recognised for many years. The phantom-larvae of the genus *Chaoborus* provide perhaps the best examples of this activity. During the day, the larvae may be found on the bottom or at mid water. The mid water and some of the bottom dwelling forms migrate to the surface at night, but others move only from the mud to mid water, the migratory pattern being constant in any given lake but varying from lake to lake depending upon the transparency of the water (Malueg and Hasler, 1966). These migrations involved mixed species flocks of *Chaoborus* species, and the movement seems to be clearly related to light intensity, but is also affected by temperature in one instance. Oxygen concentration seems to have no effect. A recent review discusses the relationship between migration and age, season and food supply, confirming that there is a complex relationship to light but that migrations are not made for feeding purposes alone (Goldspink and Scott, 1971). The authors suggest that the migration has some of the attributes of epideictic behaviour.

Similar feeding migrations are well documented in the opossum shrimp, *Mysis relicta*, but the story has been shown to depend on geographic location by Lasenby (1971). In the small arctic Char Lake the shrimp feeds, for the most part, on benthic diatoms and bacteria though they will attack chironomid larvae in test situations. The shrimp do not migrate there, but in Stoney Lake in Southern Ontario they migrate and feed on zooplankton in summer. During the day, however, they feed on detrital material, rising to attack live *Daphnia* during the night. Their horizontal, seasonal migration is noted below. Age may be a factor here, too, according to an unpublished Ph.D thesis by M. Teraguchi (University of Wisconsin, 1969).

The migration of *Mysis* as well as of *Pontoporeia affinis* is also determined by light intensity (Beeton, 1960; Marzolf, 1965) but is modified by temperature to the extent that migration through the discontinuity layer is limited. *Pontoporeia* may always be found in the benthos, with little more than 7 per cent of the population in the water column at any one time, the distribution of adults apparently being well correlated with the abundance of bacteria in the sediment. The value of such vertical movements as these that involve only a small proportion of (presumably) non-feeding organisms, may be related to genetic exchange in aquatic species (Marzolf, 1965) or may merely ensure the widest possible distribution of the species in relation to localised food depletion or predation by fish.

Vertical movement may lead to passive dispersal owing to the wind driven circulation of the epilimnion or to the pumping action of seiches. As such standing waves pile up epilimnetic water, first on one side of the lake and then the other, an animal entering the epilimnion may be transported horizontally before returning to the hypolimnion. Even those migrants that fail to penetrate the thermocline may well become redistributed within the lake by virtue of both passive and active movement horizontally.

Whatever the significance, such migrations may well be the rule rather than the exception, as demonstrated by Mundie (1959) in Lac La Ronge, where chironomids, mayflies, caddisflies, water mites, corixids, leeches, ceratopogonids as well as *Hyalella*, *Pontoporeia* and *Mysis* were found in surface water at night.

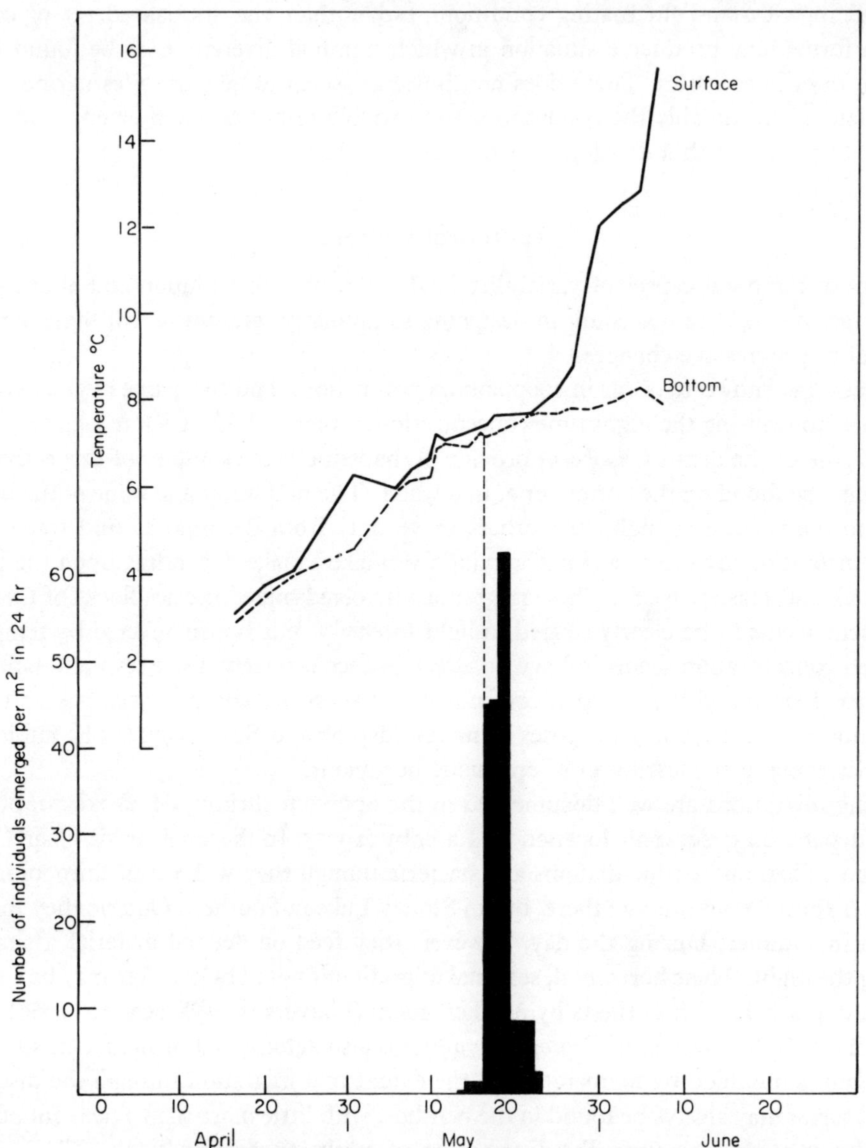

FIGURE 6.21. The relationship between temperature and emergence in *Chironomus anthracinus* in Esrom Lake, Denmark (Jonasson, 1965).

This behaviour varies in relation to maturity in the chironomid population at Marion Lake, where *Polypedilum tritum*, *Chironomus modestus*, and *Sergentia* species migrate as mature larvae, whereas only immature larvae of *P. nubeculosum* are found in surface water (Hamilton, 1965). The diurnal migration of the *Sergentia* species could be described in this lake, and it would seem that vertical migration may be a widespread phenomenon, probably by both active and passive (*via* currents or seiche activity) horizontal redistribution. *Chironomus plumosus* larvae of all instars are found in the water column of shallow Lake Suwa (Japan) at all times of the day and night (Yamagishi and Fukuhara, 1971*a*).

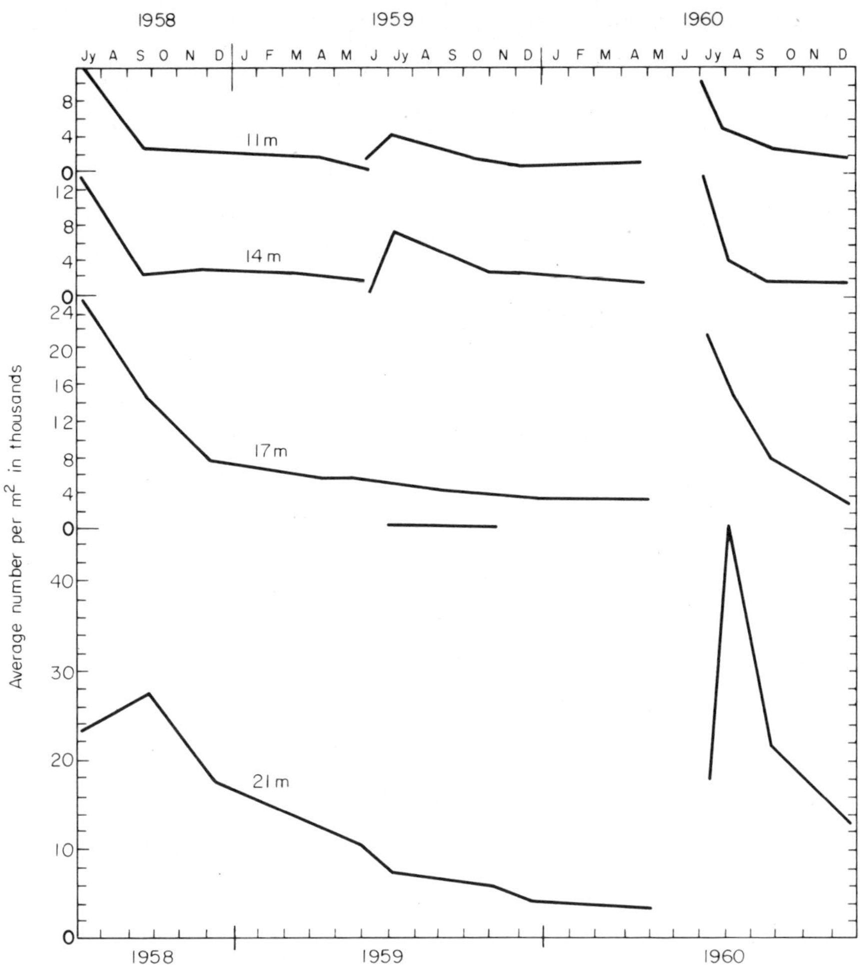

FIGURE 6.22. Seasonal fluctuation in abundance of *C. anthracinus* at different depths, 1958–62 in Esrom Lake, Denmark (Jonasson, 1965).

Most studies on lakes, especially by academics, are made in midsummer, but nonetheless we should be aware of the extent of seasonal variations in distribution and abundance. Insect species with aerial adult stages in their life histories may even be absent or in egg form for part of the year, and some of the data on this is reviewed by Corbet (1964).

One of the clearest accounts of changes in populations throughout the year is for the *Chironomus anthracinus* populations of the Lake Esrom benthos by Jonasson (1961, 1964, 1965). It is as well to start with this work rather than earlier work since the account is simplified by considering only a single species, and covers a period of 11 years. Jonasson (1961) showed that in Lake Esrom *C. anthracinus* emerged in great numbers over a period of a few days in May, the peak emergence taking place over about 3 days (figure 6.21). The time of emergence was limited to quiet periods in the lake from 1900 hours to 1000 hours, little taking place at other times. An account of the probable factors that dictate emergence was focused on the food available for rapid maturation of the larvae from first through to fourth stage larvae. With abundant food and the right temperatures, fourth stage larvae were obtained before the onset of winter, and this generally occurred

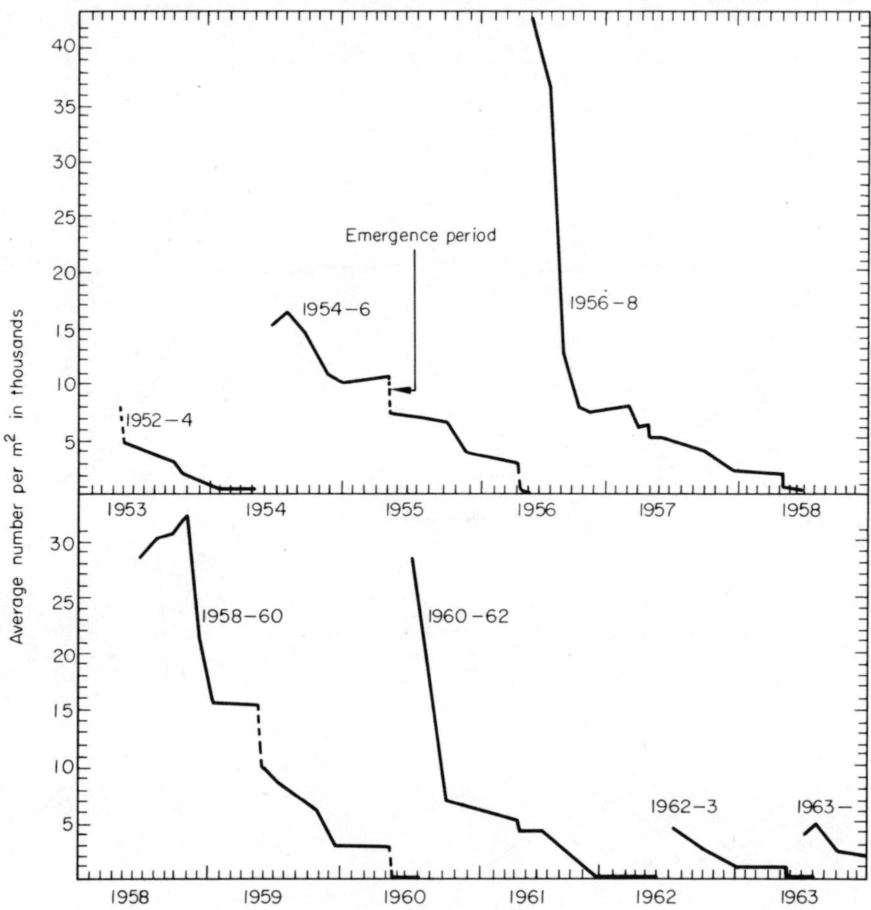

FIGURE 6.23. Seasonal fluctuation in abundance of *C. anthracinus* 1956–64, Esrom Lake, Denmark (Jonasson, 1965). Two-year life cycles begin in even numbered years (52, 54–60). A one-year cycle appears in 1962–3.

in populations above 17 m, but apparently not, to any great extent, at 17 m and below (figure 6.22—Jonasson, 1965). Below 17 m in the profundal in most years, the larvae required a 2-year life cycle (figure 6.23). The question as to why there should be a gap in the population between the 2 years (although a small emergence was seen in the odd years) was answered by Jonasson with the suggestion that the existing chironomid population still present in the fourth instar demolished the eggs laid by the emergents of that year. The suggestion is that the new larvae could only come into the population at a time when there was an extremely low number of the later fourth instar larvae.

An indication of the events that take place is given in a figure by Jonasson (figure 6.24) where emergence takes place just prior to the beginning of summer stagnation. Between summer stagnation and the autumnal overturn, predation at the bottom below the hypolimnion is at its lowest ebb, since the fish cannot get there. Between the autumnal overturn and the date at which temperatures become so low that fish no longer feed, there is a loss to the population by the activities of the fish. After this date the population stabilises and only losses due to natural mortality occur. In May of the following year, emergence takes place and repopulation of the deep layers begins afresh.

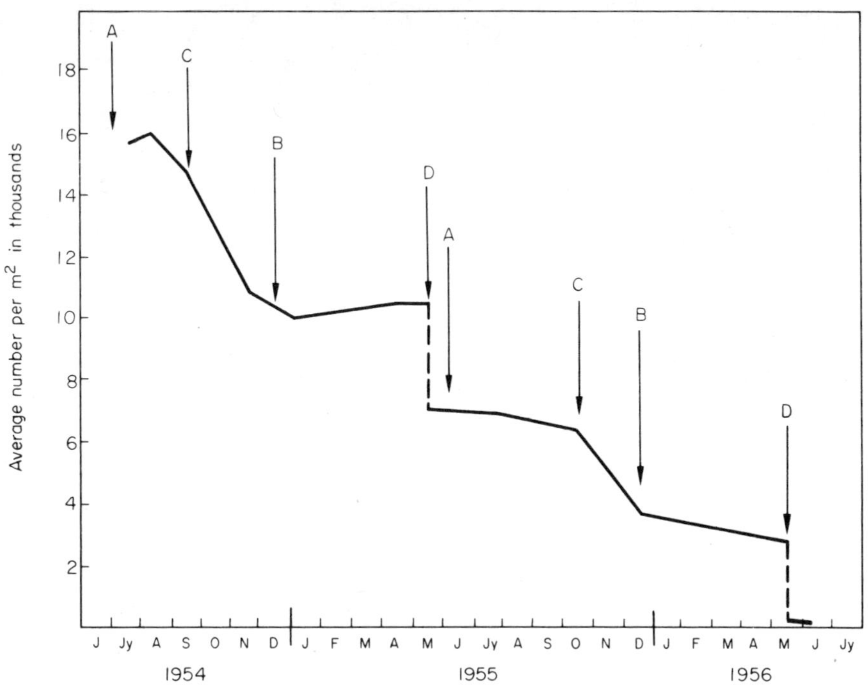

FIGURE 6.24. Seasonal fluctuation in abundance of *C. anthracinus* during a two-year life cycle in Esrom lake (Jonasson, 1965). A—beginning of summer stagnation; B—end of fish predation because of low temperature; C—autumn overturn; D—emergence.

From this study it is clear that the populations of animals in different depth zones of the lake behave differently. As far as the voltine chironomid species are concerned the marginal forms, at least in Esrom, pass through their life cycle each year. The deep water forms, on the other hand, appear to take 2 years in the majority of cases. This means that the pattern of numbers through the year is going to be differed in relation to depth. Predation in the epilimnion is likely to be consistent throughout the summer, at least in the shallow areas, whereas it is cut off in the hypolimnion in the summer by the onset of deoxygenation, and by the cool temperatures of the winter.

The possibility of seasonal changes in population occurring in other groups of animals which do not have an aerial phase in their life history, as do the chironomids, must also be examined. Evidence for changes in the oligochaete populations can be seen from the Eggleton (1931) study on Third Sister Lake where changes ranging from about 1000 to 16 000 worms per square metre have been noted over a period of months. Similarly, studies by Henson (1954) show that the populations of both oligochaetes and also of amphipods in Cayuga Lake (New York State) fluctuate in much the same way.

Seasonal fluctuations below the lake margin have also been reported by Oliver (1960) using data from Lac La Ronge, Saskatchewan. Variations at three stations were followed through 2 years from May to September. Greatest fluctuations were shown by the chironomid fauna, which in this case was dominated by *Chironomus anthracinus*, but rather different patterns were shown by the chironomid fauna at the two open water stations (figures 6.25 and 6.26). In the shallower station between 15 and 20 m there were two peaks of chironomids during the study period, the May peak and the August peak, possibly indicating a double life cycle per year or perhaps two overlapping life cycles. In the deeper water station below 25 m there appears at the most one peak a year, which may indicate a simple annual life cycle there. The shapes of the curves may be compared

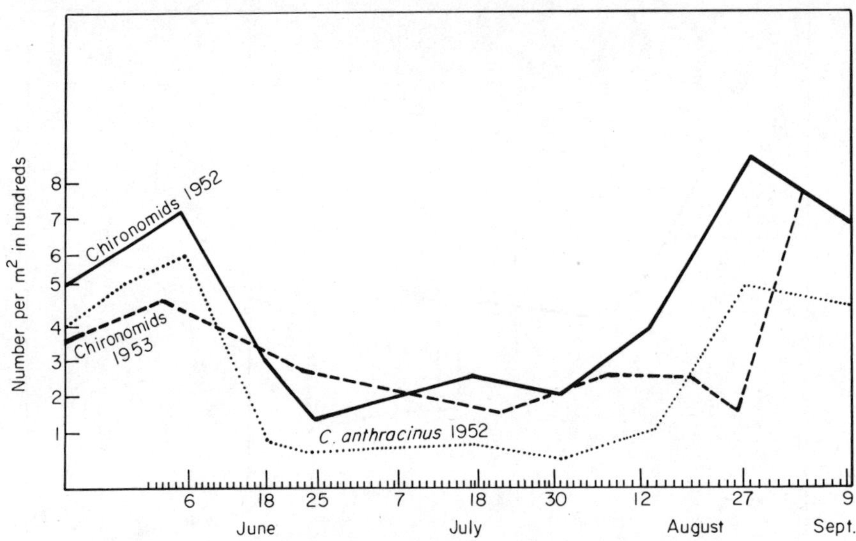

FIGURE 6.25. Variation in abundance of chironomids at 15–20 m in Lac la Ronge, Canada in two successive years. The commonest species is *C. anthracinus* (data from Oliver, 1960).

with those shown by Jonasson for Esrom where he also showed that the deep water population behaved somewhat differently to that in shallower water.

The frequency of summer emergence may be the cause of the familiar summer minimum in standing stock of benthos, noted by many authors including Northcote (1952), but Gerking (1962) emphasised summer predation by bluegill sunfish as the dominant factor in cropping the shallow water fauna, developing his concept of 'catch-up' and 'keep-up'. As fish production in Wyland Lake, Indiana, was limited to the 5 summer months but fish food was produced throughout the year, the benthos was visualised as 'catching-up' on summer depletion during the winter, and merely 'keeping-up' if not actually losing ground to predation in summer. The summer decline in standing stock of benthos (a 274 per cent fluctuation according to Ball, 1948) was attributed to emergence by Ball and Hayne (1952) because it was initiated immediately

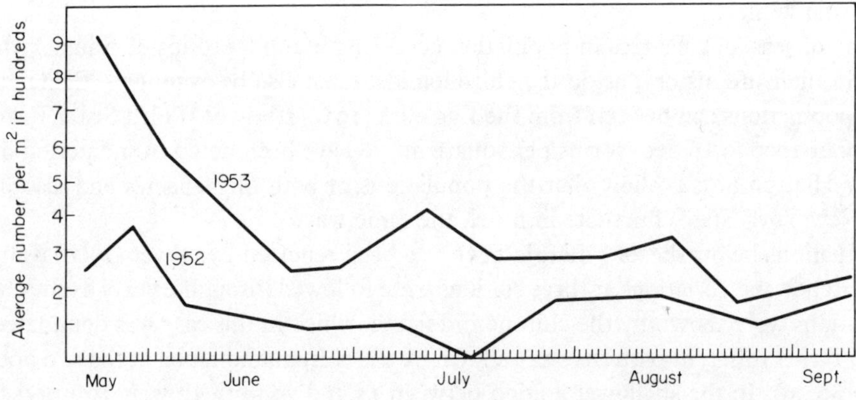

FIGURE 6.26. Variation in abundance of chironomids at depths below 25 m in Lac la Ronge, Canada in two successive years (data from Oliver, 1960).

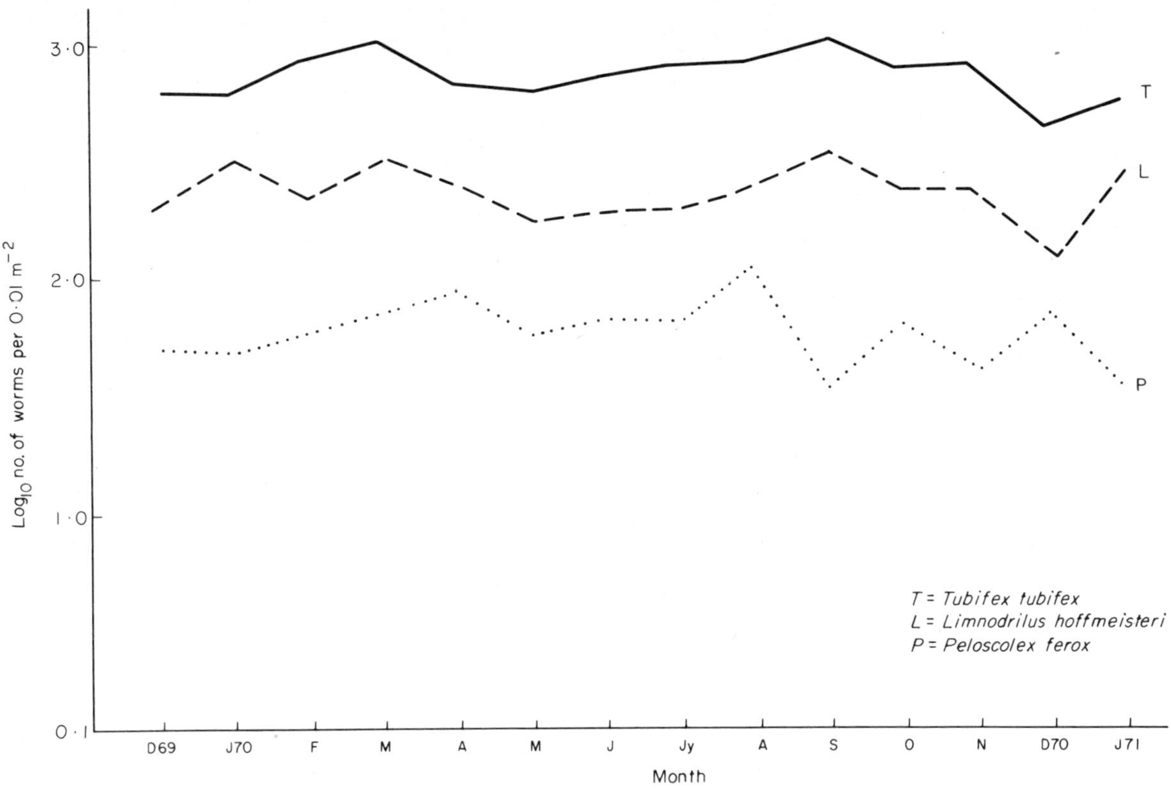

FIGURE 6.27. Abundance of three tubificids, Toronto Harbour, 1970.

after the maximum density period which was correlated with the presence of an ice cover in a series of experimental ponds whether fish were present or not! We are considering shallow water organisms in these studies, however, and events in the deep water benthos may differ. Where the benthos is comprised entirely of tubificid oligochaetes, such as in the non-stratifying Toronto Harbour, numbers and biomass fluctuate throughout the year, but it is difficult to handle the required number of samples (at least six per site per visit) required to obtain reliable monthly estimates. The variability in this data (figures 6.27 and 6.28) is so great that no statistically significant trends could be detected (hence the use of the logarithmic transformation employed!).

Studies on Douglas and Third Sister Lakes in Michigan (Eggleton, 1931) generated curves for total numbers of benthos at various depths on a series of dates (November, 1926; September–December, 1927; February, April, June, October and November, 1928; and February, 1929) and from these Eggleton defined the concentration zone as the peak in abundance found in the lower sublittoral–upper profundal zone. This is clearly an extension of the 'sublittoral minimum' concept (discussed on p. 42) as both are merely deviations from a simple curve, such as that proposed by Lundbeck (1936) for oligotrophic lakes, but attention is focused on the lower maximum rather than the preceding minimum. The concentration zone is supposedly produced by the upward migration of profundal species associated with a reversal of the bathymetric distribution of *Chaoborus* together with the reproduction of chironomids (and *Chironomus* in particular) in the shallow parts of the lake. Hence it is a summer phenomenon, so that the 'typical' curves for lakes (assuming for the moment that methodology and sampling programmes are adequate) may be affected by the seasons. The difficulty here lies in the interpretation placed on the data by Eggleton, as there seem to be some

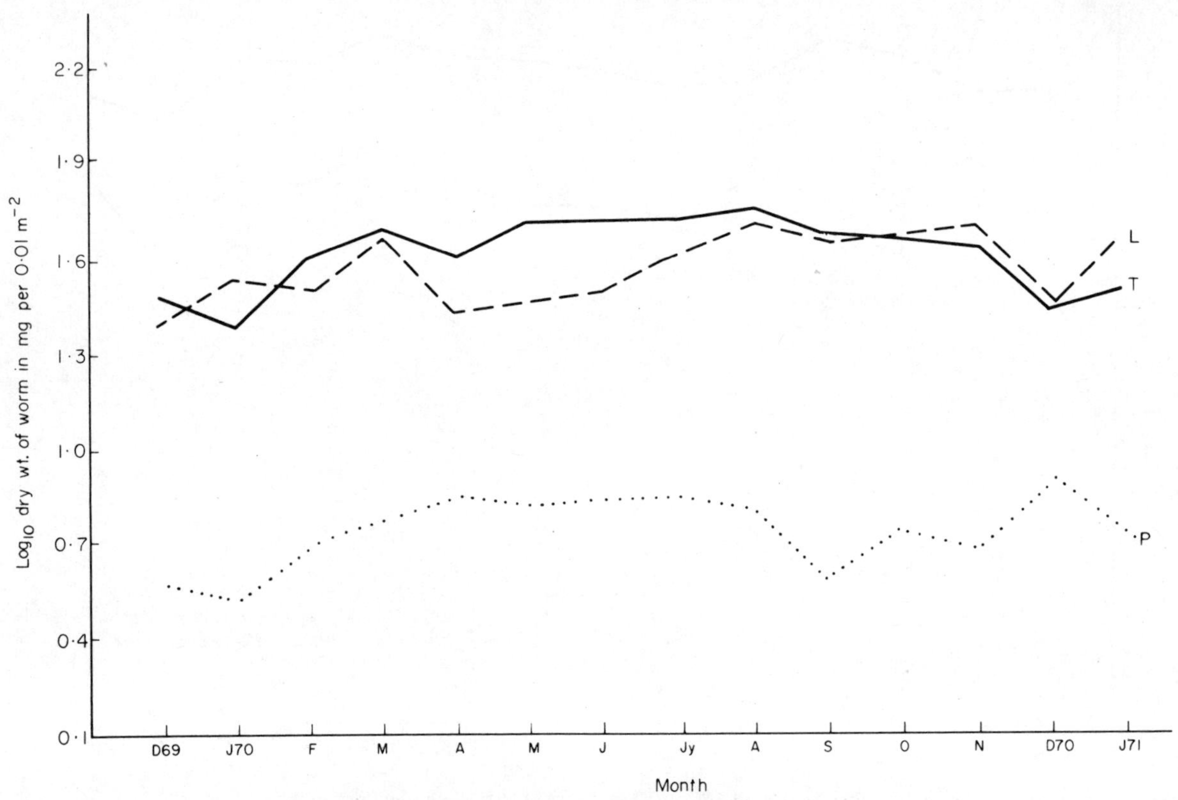

FIGURE 6.28. Biomass of three tubificids, Toronto Harbour, 1970.

critical points, on some occasions, at which samples were not taken. Despite this, there are a series of curves that are (presumably) derived from samples taken while Third Sister Lake was isothermal, in which the largest number of benthic organisms is reported from the greatest depths, whereas curves for June, September, October and part of November show maxima at intermediate depths. In one good sequence from September to December, 1927 (figure 6.29) the curve is shown to change from one form to another. Hence, there is a change in distribution of fauna in response to hypolimnetic conditions. One of the problems of interpretation is clearly revealed here. There is an estimate of the abundance of benthos at 12 m on October 11, and a good deal of discussion about the change at this level that has occurred since the previous

TABLE 6.5. A list of changes in populations of three groups of benthic organisms at three different depths in Third Sister Lake between summer and late fall 1927. Date from Eggleton, 1931.

Depth	Organisms		
	chaoborids	oligochaetes	chironomids
7 m	nearly disappeared	increased equivalent to loss in chaoborids	reduced by half
9 m	remain scarce	increased	increased
12 m	huge increase	increased	remained low

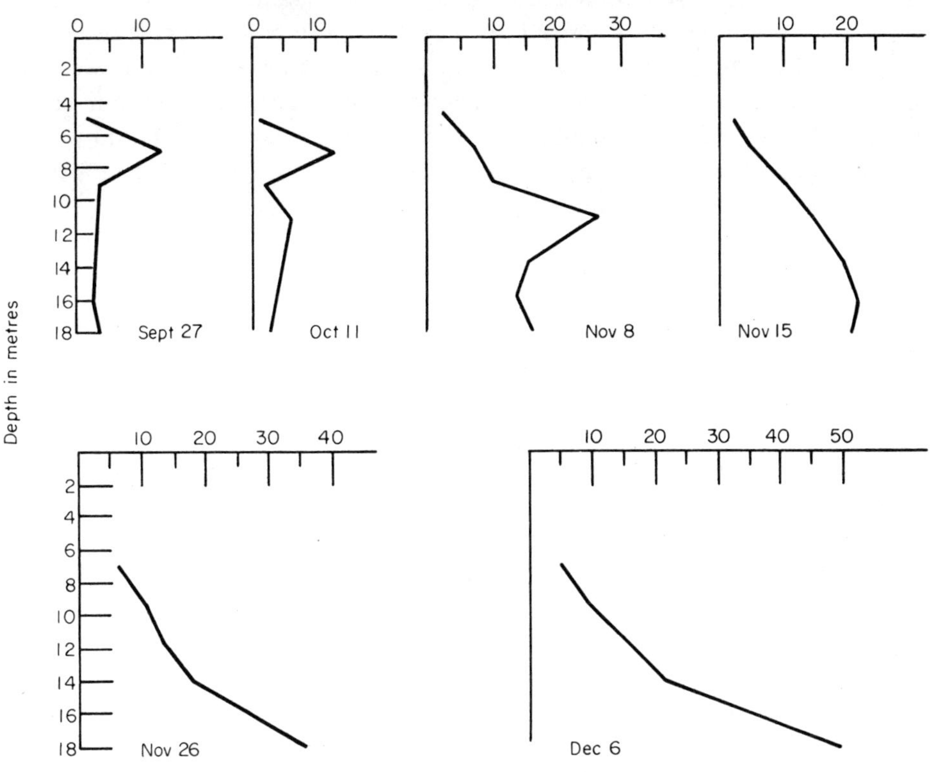

FIGURE 6.29. Depth distribution of bottom fauna in Third Sister Lake, Michigan, 1927 (Eggleton, 1931).

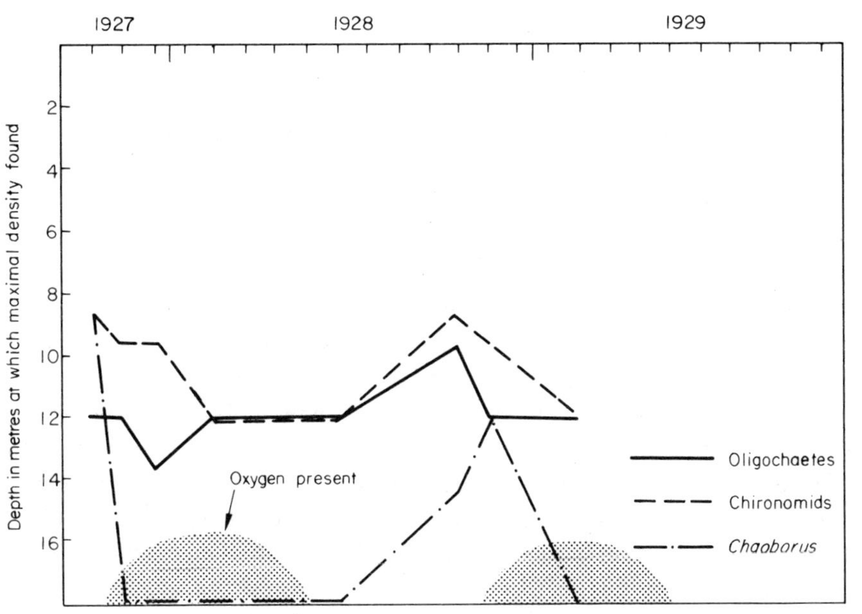

FIGURE 6.30. Depths at which peak populations of chironomids, chaoborids and oligochaetes are found in Third Sister Lake, Michigan (data from Eggleton, 1931).

date (September 27) although there does not appear to be any datum for 12 m on that date. An analysis of information from different groups of organisms is revealing. By November, changes had occurred from distributions observed in September–October, when chironomids and chaoborids were equally abundant but oligochaetes were scarce at the level of the population maximum (7 m), as shown in table 6.5.

The net result is that the curve representing the entire fauna is unduly influenced by the migration of the chaoborids. Changes in other groups may well be related simply to emergence and recruitment as part of the ordinary life histories rather than to any actual migrations.

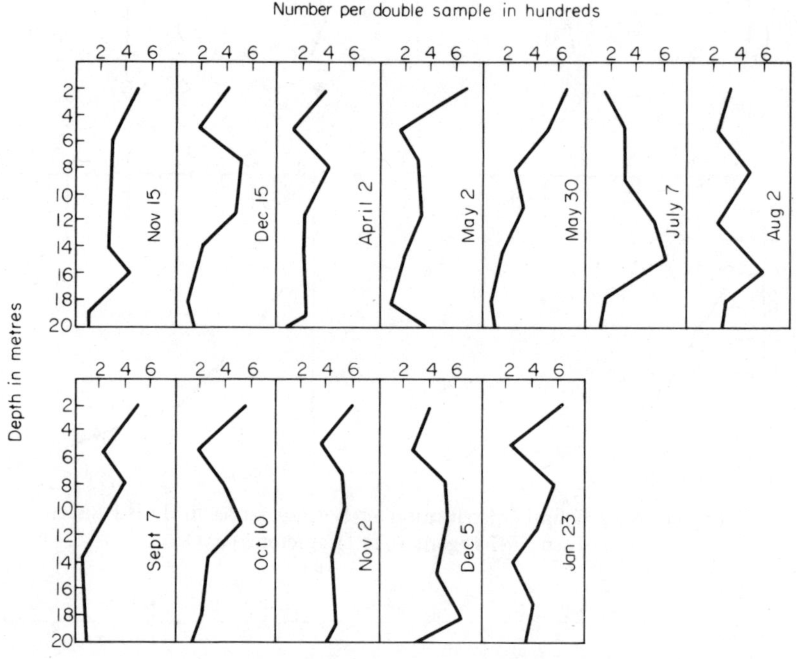

FIGURE 6.31. Depth distribution of benthos in Esrom Lake, Denmark for various months (data from Berg, 1938).

The levels at which peak populations of chironomids, chaoborids and oligochaetes are recorded and are plotted in figure 6.30 are calculated from Eggleton's data, and this makes the migration of chaoborids quite plain. Replotting data from Esrom Lake tabulated by Berg (1938) shows apparent changes in the slope of the curve (figure 6.31), but they are not as pronounced as those from Third Sister or Linsley Pond (figure 6.32A) as demonstrated by Deevey (1941) again heavily dependent upon *Chaoborus* migration (figure 6.32B). Another way of demonstrating migrations or changes due to emergence and recruitment is to plot the number of organisms present at each depth from month to month. This was done for Rostherne Mere by Brinkhurst and Walsh (1967) as shown in figure 6.33, and this process has been applied to Berg's data from Esrom Lake (figure 6.34). If the concept of a characteristic curve of numbers in relation to depths has any validity, one would expect to see relative constancy of numbers at any given depth over a given period of time, but this is far from the situation in these two lakes at least. The changes with time at the various depths are not even synchronous, and so the distribution of benthos with depth must vary with time. Sometimes these changes will depend upon the life cycles of species such as *Chaoborus*, as already noted, or other organisms that dominate the benthos in a given lake, such as chironomids in Lake Simcoe (figure 6.35) or *Pontoporeia affinis* in Great Slave Lake (figure 6.36—Rawson, 1930, 1953*b*).

Horizontal movement of *Chironomus* larvae and all other benthic organisms except oligochaetes may occur in summer, according to Gerking (1962) who noted that evidence of such movement had been cited

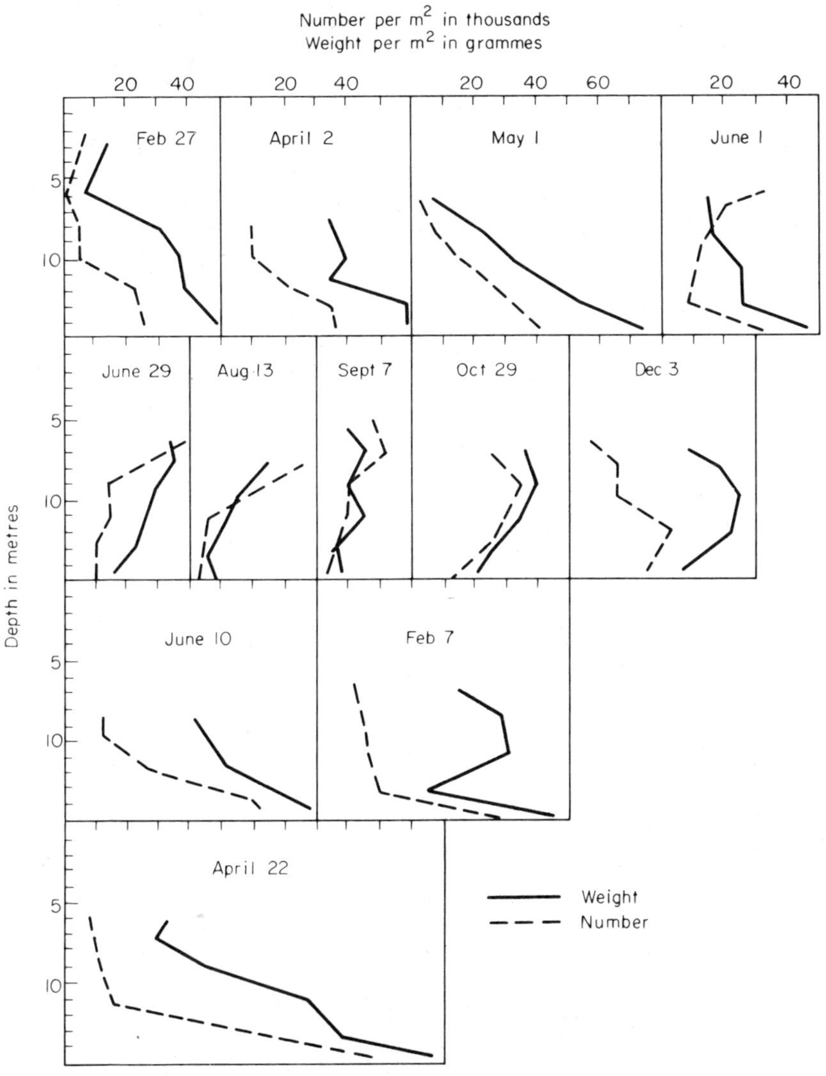

FIGURE 6.32A. Distribution of benthos in Linsley Pond, USA for various months (Deevey, 1941). Solid lines—weight, dotted lines—number.

by many earlier authors. As well as movements of chironomids, Lundbeck (1926) had cited migration in relation to temperature to account for the discrepancy of distribution between dead shells and live specimens of *Dreissensia*, and similar migrations of this and thirteen other species were noted by Berg (1938). Gerking dismissed the contention of Jonasson (1955) that the earlier data represented an artifact caused by the use of

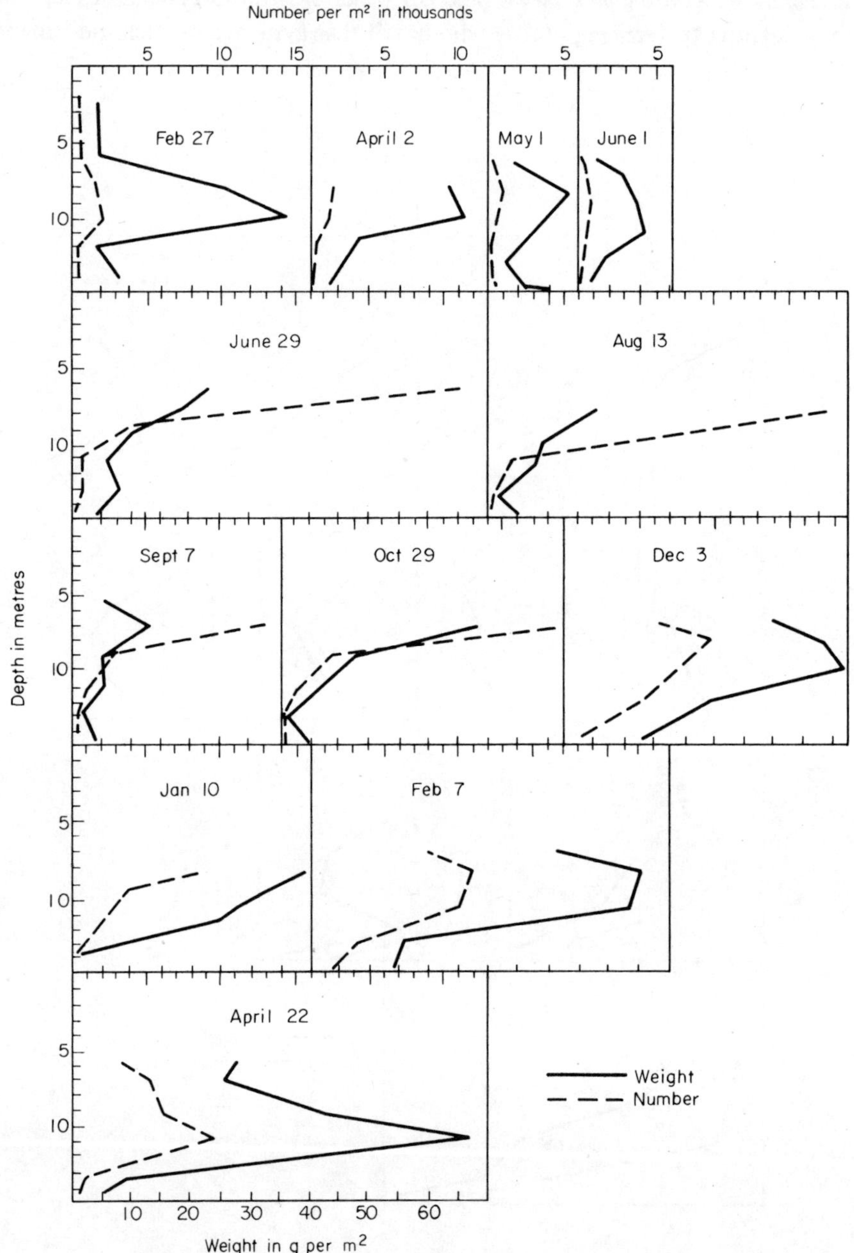

FIGURE 6.32B. Vertical distribution of *Chironomus* in Linsley Pond, 1937–8 (Deevey, 1941). Solid line—weight; dotted line—number.

coarse screens in sorting samples, noting that Borutzky used sieves of the recommended sizes (0.25 and 0.5 mm aperture). Dugdale (1955), who doubted the veracity of these theories of shoreward migration, preferred to believe in the effect of differential development rates such as those already discussed, but recent knowledge of the presence of benthic forms (other than oligochaetes) in the water column at night suggests the possibility of horizontal migration, especially in the face of oxygen deprivation.

The occupation of the deep water of Lake Tiberias for the short 3-month aerobic season was described by Por (1968). Two mechanisms were proposed, development *in situ* from resting eggs and active migration While the *Pelmatohydra* sp., some red rhabdocoels, and the two cladocerans of the genus *Leydigia* may use the former mechanism, the cladocerans *Alona* and *Ilyocryptus* appear to migrate, as do three copepods.

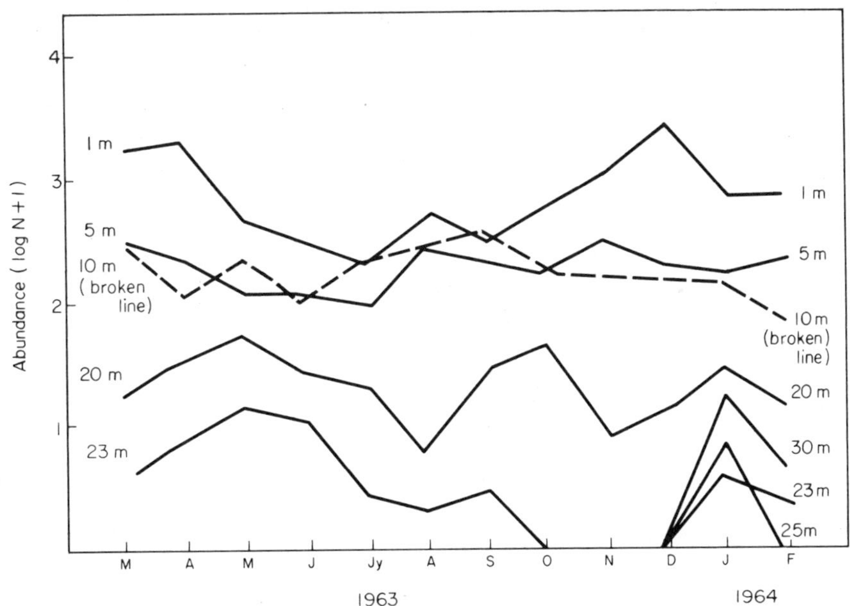

FIGURE 6.33. Abundance of benthos at each of seven depths on 12 successive months in Rosthern Mere, Great Britain (Brinkhurst and Walsh, 1967).

Three chironomids occupy the deeper water while it is aerobic (*Tanypus punctipennis*, *Procladius choreus* and *Cryptocladopelma virescens*) but little is said about their migratory ability beyond noting that they are scarce and may survive for several months during the depletion of oxygen beneath the thermocline.

In a recent study of *Mysis relicta*, Lasenby (1971) demonstrated that, in Stoney Lake, Southern Ontario, this crustacean was scattered throughout the deep zone in November to May, whereas it was confined to the deepest point in June to August. However, in the period late August to September the population migrated into relatively shallow water close to an inlet stream and proceeded to make diurnal migrations. It was therefore excluded from the region in which the oxygen deficit was marked in late summer.

The chironomid *Spaniotoma akamusi* burrows into the mud during May to September in Lake Suwa, Japan, being found between 20 and 70 cm deep but not often in shallower sediments. Pupation and emergence follows in October in this species, and the lake is ice covered during January and February. Growth is completed between October and March, with no further increase in body length of larvae during the burrowing period, as one might expect (Yamagishi and Fukuhara, 1971*b*).

Climatic differences between years may affect the intensity and duration of oxygen deficit periods due to ice cover or thermal stratification. The effect of these on the chironomid fauna of West Lake Okoboji (Iowa) was clearly demonstrated by Bardach (1955) who recognised years in which the thermocline was established early on, and those in which its appearance was delayed. In late thermocline years, the chironomid population was large (table 6.6, figure 6.37).

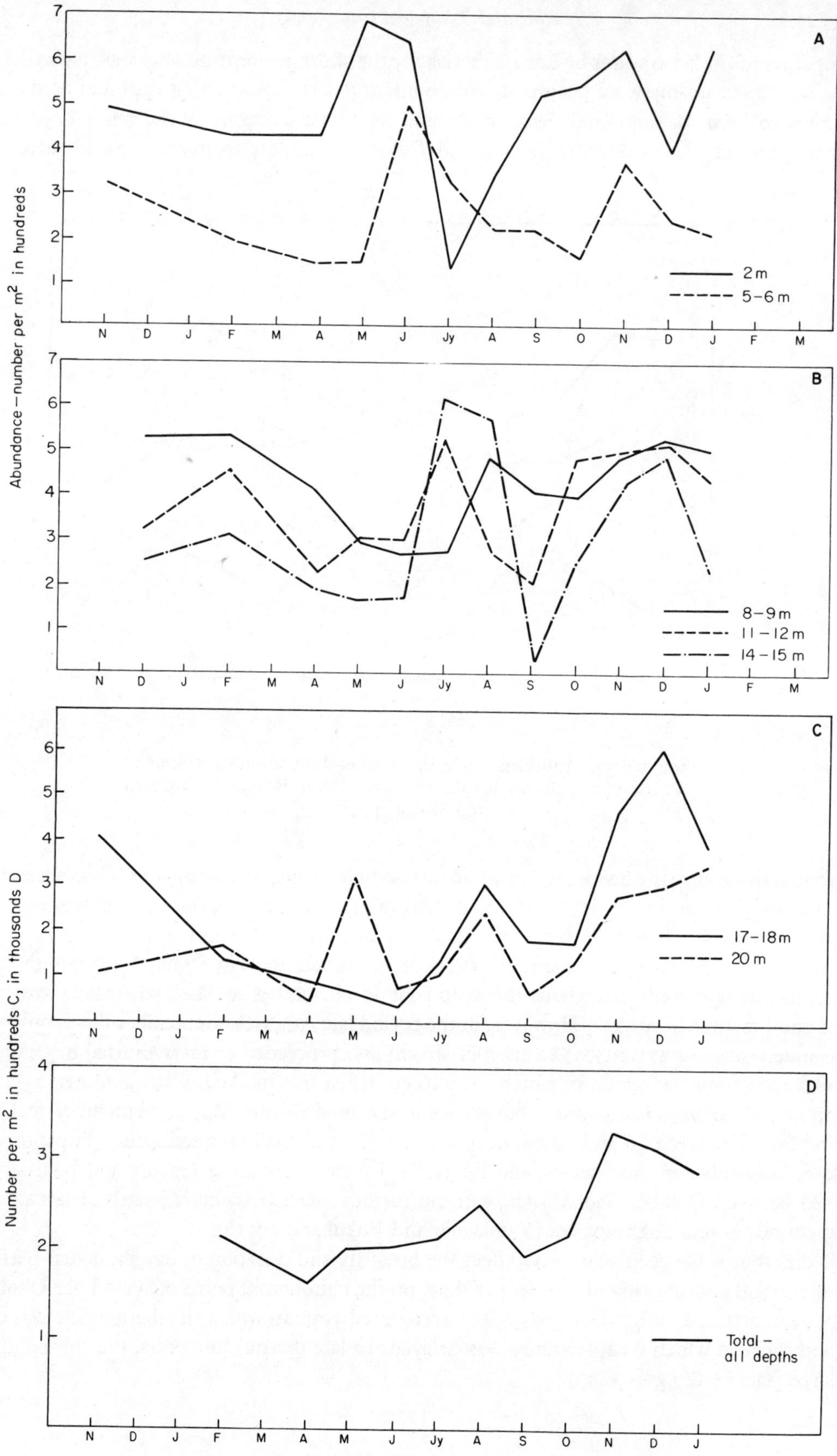

FIGURE 6.34. Abundance of benthos at various depths for 12 successive months in Esrom Lake (data from Berg, 1938).

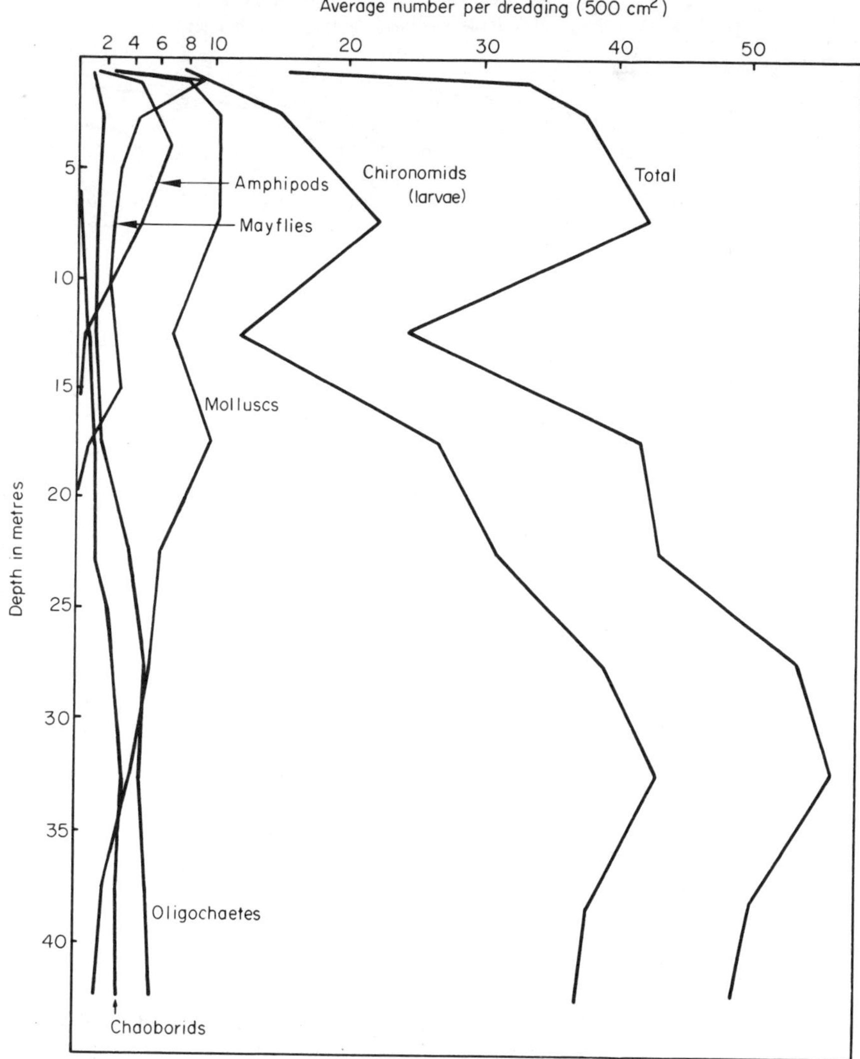

FIGURE 6.35. Average distribution of the major benthic groups in Lake Simcoe, Canada (Rawson, 1930).

The demonstration of 2-year life cycles in *Chironomus anthracinus* by Jonasson (1965) indicated another source of year-to-year variation in benthic fauna (figure 6.23).

The concept of annual variation is not new. Alm (1922) and Lundbeck (1926) recorded halving or doubling of standing stocks in successive years, and Eggleton (1931, 1935, 1937, 1952) emphasised the need to continue studies over several years in order to obtain a true picture of events. While some of his studies refer to data from different places or different months in the 2 years, such annual variability would not be surprising, especially in terms of numbers rather than the biomass usually recorded. Morgan and Waddell (1961) indicate that such variations may involve sixfold changes in standing stocks. In a 2-year study of Cayuga Lake (New York) in 1952–3, Henson (1954) recorded differences in standing stocks as well as in seasonal trends in various components of the benthos. Eggleton (1937) has suggested that there were pronounced seasonal differences between the years 1931 and 1932 in Lake Michigan, but data were taken

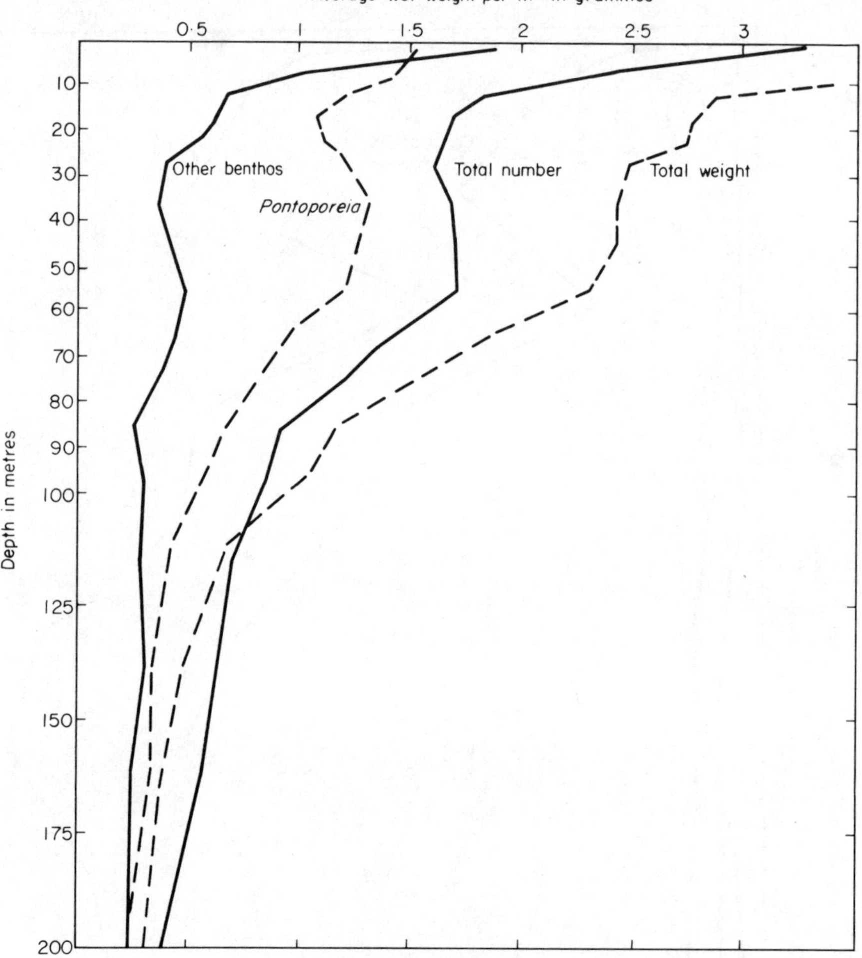

FIGURE 6.36. Distribution of benthos down to 200 m in Great Slave Lake, Canada (Rawson, 1963).

TABLE 6.6. Mid-summer density of *Chironomus* larvae at various depths in West Okoboji Lake, Iowa. Wet volume in cm³ per litre (Bardach, 1955)

Depth in m	Early thermocline years 1953	1951	Late thermocline year 1950
5	—	—	—
7	2.0		1.6
10	4	7.5	11.4
13	13.8	—	—
15	10.3	7.5	22.1
17	6.4	11.7	—
20	5.2	—	35.8
24	6.0	6.1	12.4
25	3.0	4.0	10.0
30	0.5	0.7	6.1

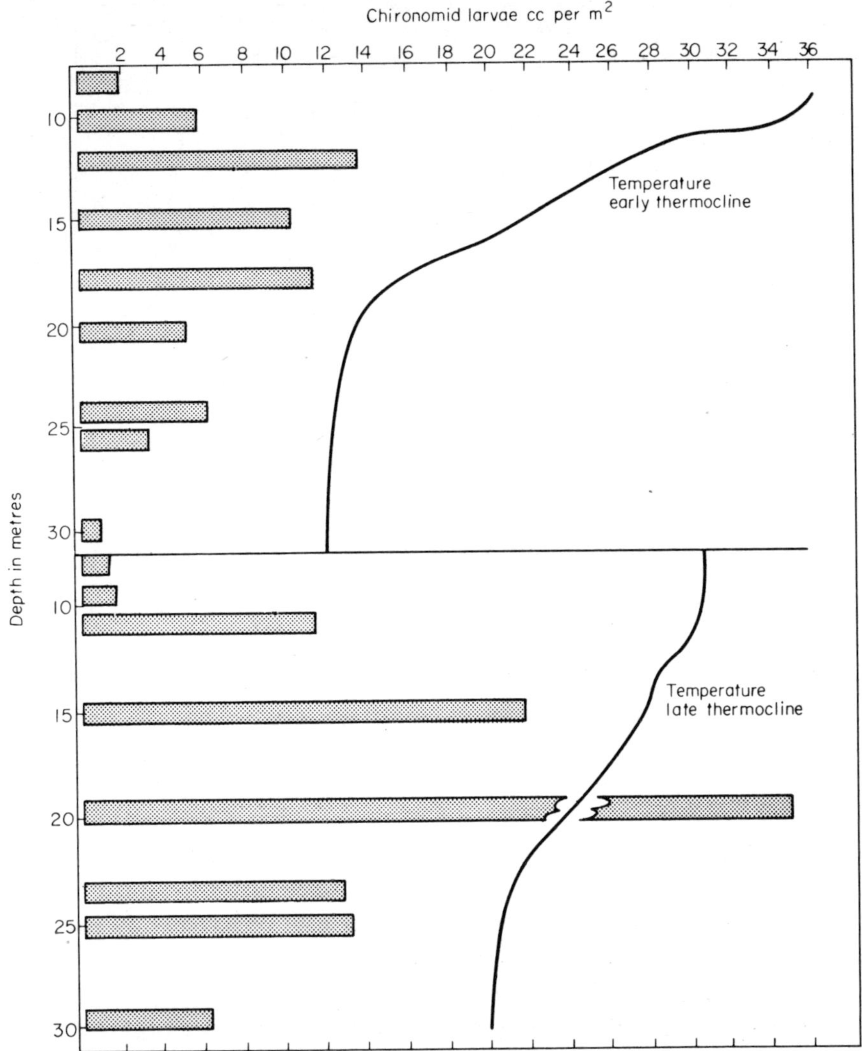

FIGURE 6.37. Mid-summer density of *Chironomus* larvae in West Okoboji Lake, Iowa in summers with early and late thermoclines (Bardach, 1955).

from the south-central portions of the lake in one year and in Green Bay, Michigan in the other (figure 6.38).

In Cayuga Lake the data for the second year is somewhat scant (figure 6.39). The number and weight of oligochaetes about doubled in the second year, whereas the number of *Pontoporeia* was halved, largely due to a lack of young specimens.

In Lac La Ronge, Saskatchewan, the variation over 4 years (1948, 1949, 1952, 1953) for a total of from 175 to 215 samples was 39.6, 43.6, 27.1 and 29.7 animals per dredge, and subsequent analyses suggested that there were significant differences in numbers recorded in the two sets of consecutive years (Oliver, 1960). Again, however, the samples in the later years were taken from a more restricted part of the lake than those in the earlier years. Using data from locations sampled in both periods plus some from 1950 supported

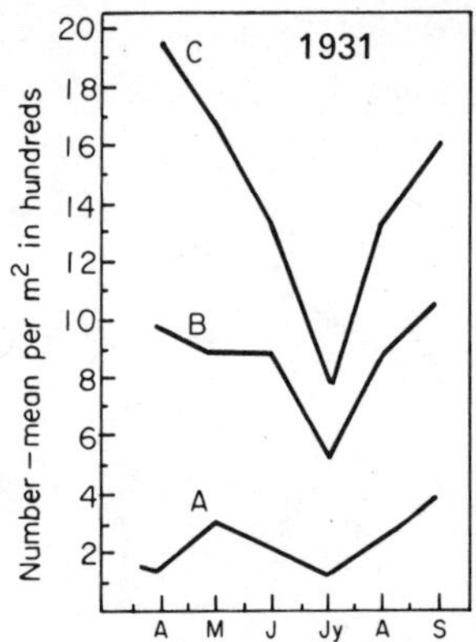

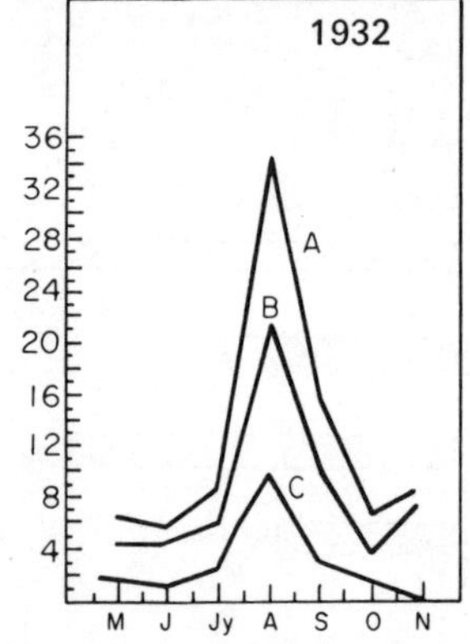

FIGURE 6.38. Seasonal changes in bottom fauna in Lake Michigan, USA 1931–2 (Eggleton, 1937). A—Tubificidae; B—*Pontoporeia*; C—total.

the conclusion reached above, and showed that 1950 samples contained more animals than in any previous year—54.5 per dredge.

While depth-distribution patterns for numbers remained similar in the two periods, the distributions of weight of benthos did not (figure 6.40). Weight data from the main lake as a whole were not only lower in 1952–3 than in the earlier years, but were distributed very differently in relation to depth, whereas the analysis of numerical distribution of the various groups of organisms demonstrated close agreement in the pattern from year to year except at the shallowest zone.

In Hunter Bay (figure 6.3) the numbers and weights do not differ from year to year. Here the amphipod *Pontoporeia affinis* makes up 60 per cent of the benthos as opposed to less than 25 per cent in the main lake, and *Chironomus anthracinus* plus other less abundant chironomids make up 4 per cent of the Hunter Bay fauna, 52 per cent in the main lake. Once again, the suggestion is that insects with aerial stages in their life histories fluctuate seasonally because of that emergence, but may be affected by year-to-year changes to a greater extent than fully aquatic forms.

Although it deals with the littoral fauna, the study of Sugarloaf Lake, Michigan, by Schneider (1965) deals with year-to-year variation on the basis of samples taken in November 1955 and January 1958. Because of the difference in sampling data within the years concerned, some adjustment of the data had to be made based on an earlier publication relating to the 1955 collections. There was no significant difference in mean benthic biomass, and the stations with the most benthos in 1955 were the same in 1958, but the rank-order

TABLE 6.7. Annual variation in the mean numbers of benthic organisms collected in Great Slave Lake (Northcote, 1952)

Years		Depth (m) 0–5	6–10	11–20	21–40	41–60	61–140
1944	Number of dredgings	8	9	15	9	8	7
	Mean number of organisms	74.50	72.44	76.40	101.44	82.37	75.14
1945	Number of dredgings	17	9	9	13	6	12
	Mean number of organisms	89.29	79.11	39.44	51.92	69.00	48.25
1946	Number of dredgings	13	15	25	16	10	12
	Mean number of organisms	73.61	100.60	71.56	98.81	89.60	76.58

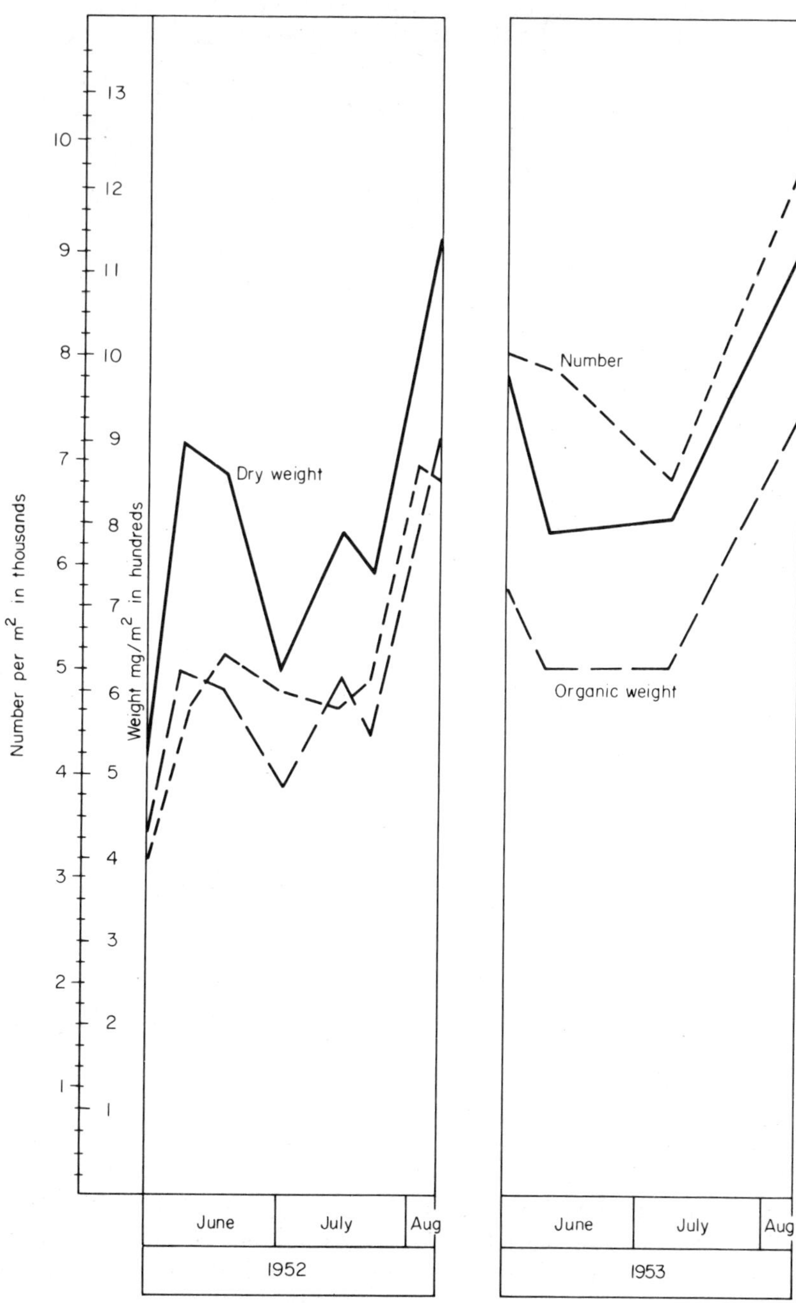

FIGURE 6.39. Changes in bottom fauna of Cayuga Lake, 1952–3. Samples from 98–105 m (Henson, 1954).

of stations according to numbers of organisms differed from year to year. While some species increased in abundance, others decreased over the elapsed time, and a third group changed little, if at all. In a careful investigation of changes in the Austrian Lunzer Untersee, Raverra (1966) demonstrated an overall lowering in the benthic standing stock in 1964 as opposed to the same season in 1955. While the chironomids increased in number in the later year, reductions occurred in either oligochaetes or *Pisidium* (in which changes were

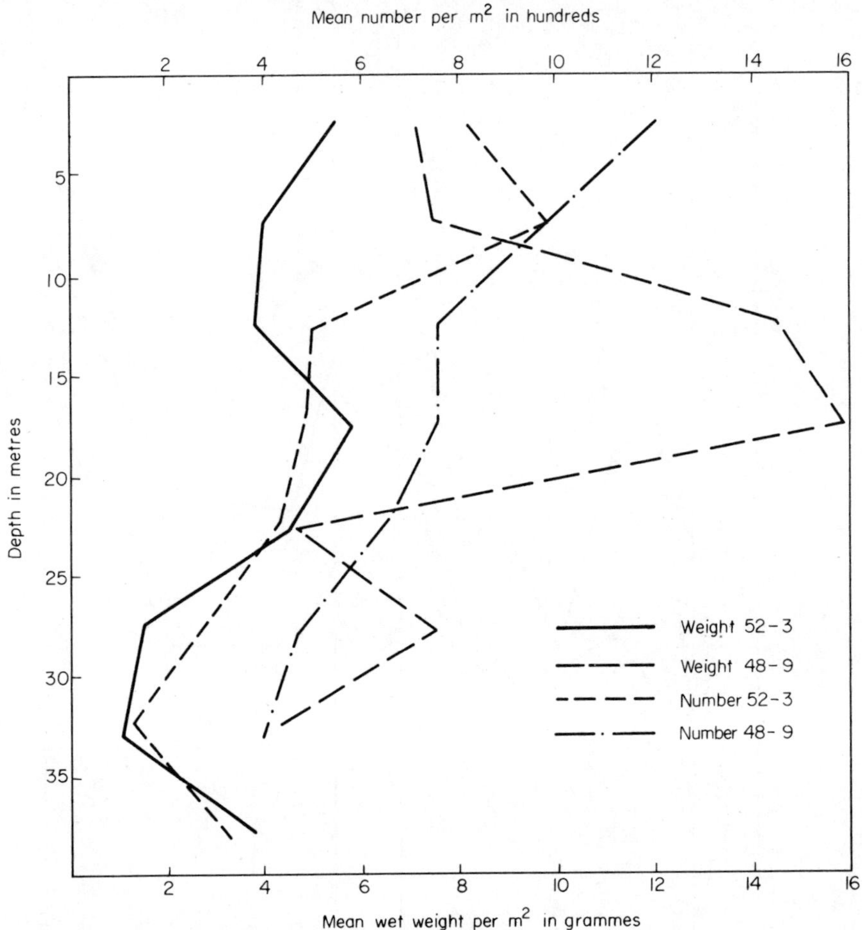

FIGURE 6.40. Depth distribution of benthos in Lac la Ronge, Canada 1948–9 and 1952–3 (Oliver, 1960).

not consistent), the overall decline being attributed to a low average temperature in 1964–5. The proportional representation of the various groups changed little at the three stations sampled.

While Northcote (1952) found the benthos of Great Slave Lake (Canada) to be stable over a 3-year period (table 6.7) many studies reveal quite significant year-to-year variations which may be related to life history patterns, climatic variations that affect the success of breeding stocks of aerial insects and the establishment of thermocline within the lake, and a host of other variables. Climatic disasters, such as unusual freezing over in lakes not normally subject to ice cover, or extreme flood conditions, may introduce instability into the observable patterns of distribution and abundance, so that, at any given point in time, the benthos may reflect a transitional phase in the re-establishment of a stable pattern (if such a pattern truly exists). Some trends are of long term duration, however, if our interpretation of certain studies can be regarded as accurate. As the impact of man on watersheds and lakes themselves continually expands, the ecosystem responds. The best examples are probably those changes that we infer from regional studies that suggest a correlation between the type of faunal association and the degree of organic pollution and/or enrichment with nutrients that has come to be termed cultural eutrophication.

Before considering the changes in benthic associations that can be related to different degrees of eutrophy, it is worth considering briefly the concept of succession commonly associated with the use of this term. In many popular accounts of environmental degradation, eutrophication has been held to represent the natural process of ageing of a lake and this is also true of some of the scientific literature. As we have seen in the earlier chapter on lake typology, it is not possible to define an oligotrophic or eutrophic lake by any consistent set of characteristics. A number of spectra may be observed in chemical, physical and biological properties of lakes, but the points at which one might be tempted to draw lines across what are, in reality, continuous variables do not coincide. There are those who would insist that this means we should abandon the search for a lake typology, and deal with the situation by means of recent mathematical tools which enable us to analyse multivariate systems of this sort, but unfortunately there is a need to simplify diversity and label things in dealing with a lay audience. We suspect that, for practical purposes, adjectives like eutrophic and oligotrophic have been useful to limnologists despite our inability to define them, unless we are mentally caged by such thinking. Granting, for a moment, that some will wish to continue using the terms, we should remind the users of some of the shortcomings discussed in more detail on p. 7. The trophic system excludes those lakes that do not have a proper balance of chemical conditions and is concerned only with 'harmonic' lakes. The much debated dystrophic lake type (Hansen, 1962), exists in a different dimension to that of the trophic series, according to many authors. Again, changes with time may lead toward oligo-

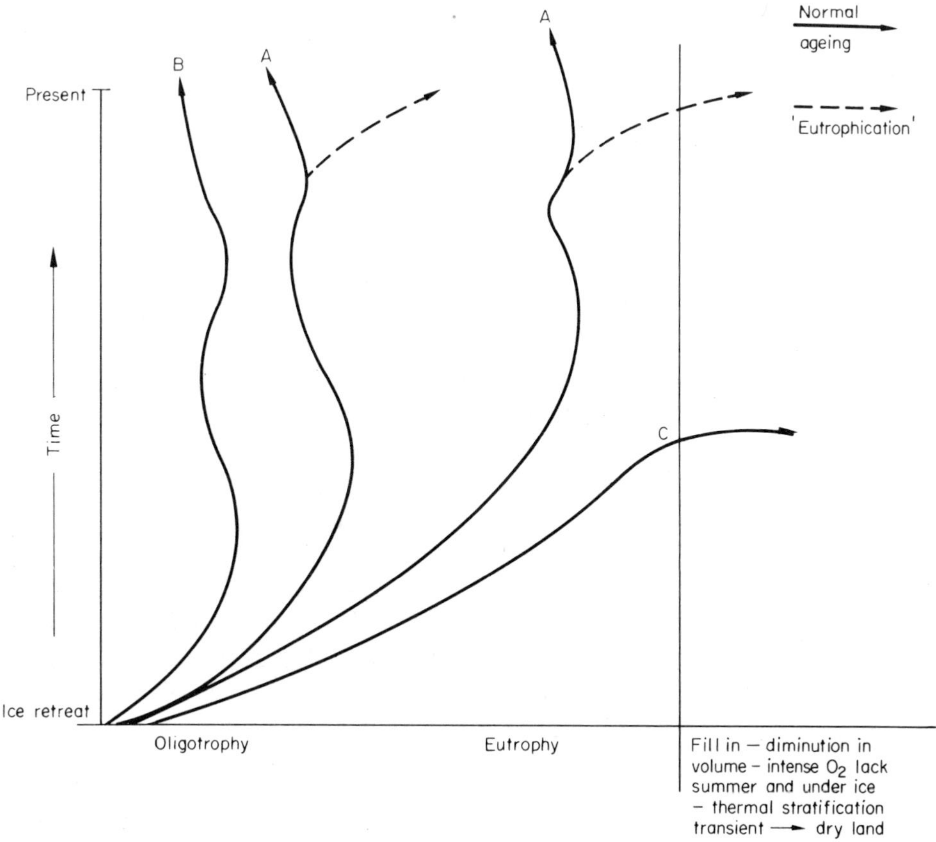

FIGURE 6.41. Theoretical pattern of changes in productivity with time since the retreat of the last glaciation in a temperate zone (Brinkhurst, 1969).

trophy rather than eutrophy in an undisturbed watershed as indicated by Welch (1935) and by studies of lakes such as Lake Washington. Supposing we consider a valley emerging from a glacial period. Soon after water fills the basin, the drainage of mineral nutrients to the lake should lead to the rapid development of intense primary production. With time, these nutrients, to a large extent, will be exported from the lake or laid down in the sediments. The input will decrease as the soils are leached and as nutrients get locked up in climax vegetation. Though some nutrients still reach the lake from the watershed, and some are recycled from the sediment, there must be a long period of declining production or at least of fluctuating conditions dependent upon the vagaries of climate. Such a life history would be represented by curve A of figure 6.41. In a lake such as Superior where rainfall is the main water source and great depth mitigates against active filling of the basin as well, one would expect to see oligotrophy as virtually indestructible (curve B). In situations where bottom sediments can be actively stirred and brought up to the photic zone, the rapid build-up of rooted vegetation will speed up the process of self-destruction leading to fill-in and extinction of the lake (curve C). Here a new succession has taken over, and movement toward this state can be accelerated by altering the input of nutrients by a number of activities (deforestation, farming, urbanisation) which affect soil erosion, leaching, rainfall, or runoff, and by the importation of nutrients into the watershed as food or fertilisers. The addition of organic matter to the lake *via* food processing and human wastes stimulates algae, particularly *Cladophora* and helps to generate hypolimnetic oxygen deficits—which in turn releases nutrients from the sediment where it is retained when the surface layers of sediment are oxidised. Ironically, while much of the world finds increasing aquatic productivity a desirable goal in order to raise fish for human consumption, the urbanised western world prefers recreational facilities, clean industrial processing water, cheap supplies of potable water and ecologically expensive salmonids to the profitable carp. Time will tell whether we can afford the luxury of oligotrophic lakes for long, but we should note that, if eutrophication is more nearly akin to rejuvenation than to senescence, recovery should follow rapidly on the heels of appropriate control of nutrients as, indeed, it does. The literature concerned with the deliberate fertilisation of lakes suggests that single applications have a transient effect—the additional input is not added to a circulating pool of nutrients but is rapidly accumulated by the sediment. In fact, it is quite probable that lakes live largely upon income, with some of the material that is temporarily lost to the sediment being recovered seasonally in lakes that have sufficient income in relation to hypolimnetic volume to exceed their oxygen credit in late summer.

Whatever the causal effects and the direction of the process under various conditions, it is clear that certain species or species associations have been correlated with degrees of intensity of the decomposition processes in sediment since the beginning of the century when the Saprobien System was developed. Thienemann's lake typology system is essentially an extension of this concept, but it was hampered by an inadequate taxonomy of chironomid larvae and a lack of statistical evaluation. While the basic distinction between *Chironomus* and *Tanytarsus* lakes can still be made, the premature attempt to refine the system and to relate it to primary production (as estimated by standing stock) detracted from its value. One of these criticisms was removed in working with tubificid oligochaetes once the taxonomy was clarified (Brinkhurst and Jamieson, 1971). As explained earlier, the first attempt to relate tubificid species to lake types was a failure although there was evidence that certain tubificids were related to the degree of organic pollution in running water systems. But, once the relative abundance of species was taken into account, it proved possible to relate the same or similar species found in rivers to the degree of organic pollution or eutrophy of lake systems, although no precise measurements of key environmental variables such as oxygen were attempted. The reason for this lack of data on environmental factors was the awareness that diurnal or longer term variations in temperature/oxygen values are such that continuous monitoring of an environment might well be required in order to determine those concentrations or variations in rate of concentration; changes that actually determine field distribution and abundance. The more profitable approach seemed to be to use

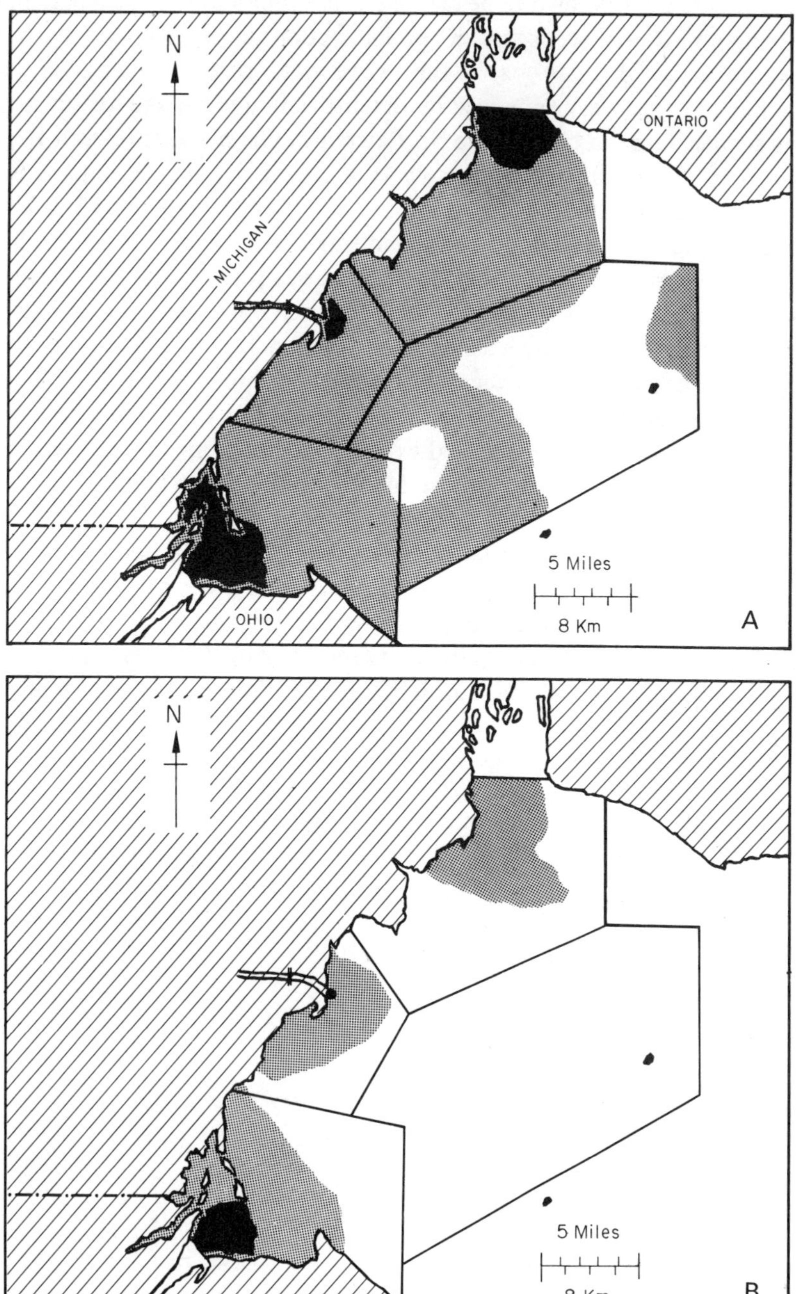

FIGURE 6.42. Distribution of Oligochaeta in Western Lake Erie, 1930 and 1961 (Carr and Hiltunen, 1965). A—1–5 thousand/m^2, B—more than 5 thousand/m^2 (Black, 1930; Stipple, 1961).

extensive collections to document the changing patterns of tubificid populations in time or, more often, in space, where organic pollution was known to be taking place. While studies on changes in species associations usually take a long time to materialise, except in special circumstances such as those in Western Lake Erie when the mayflies disappeared (Britt, 1955*a*, *b*), the recovery of a river by what is termed 'self-purification' downstream of an effluent, or recovery enhanced by the installation of sewage treatment, or the development of trophic gradients such as those in bays of the St. Lawrence, Great Lakes (Green Bay, Saginaw Bay, Bay of Quinte, Hamilton Bay, Toronto Bay) or in the whole of Lake Erie, provide situations where comparative studies suggest changes in the biota in the face of nutrient addition (Johnson and Brinkhurst, 1971*a*). Crude samples enable a sketchy picture of the dominant organisms associated with each trophic stage to be developed, and later refinement further demonstrates the need to quantify relative abundance of the species. The study of the near shore fauna of Lake Erie by Veal and Osmond (1969) demonstrates that adequate sampling produces species lists for Lake Erie in which all seven of the oligochaetes named are found in each basin with the exception of one absentee from the western basin, and one from the eastern. The dominant species, however, are the ones which showed up in the earlier superficial study: *L. hoffmeisteri* in the west, *Peloscolex ferox* and *Potamothrix moldaviensis* in addition in the centre and east. One further step involves the statistical identification of species associations such as those found in the Bay of Quinte (Johnson and Brinkhurst, 1971*a*).

Such changes in benthic associations in relation to pollution have been documented for years, one of the earlier examples being the study by Borner (1917) of St. Moritzer See (Switzerland), in which different zones of the lake were identified in relation to pollution. The large Swedish lakes have been described by Grimas (1967, 1969) and the Italian lakes by Bonomi (1967, 1969). Johnsen, Mathiesen and Røen (1962) documented what are euphemistically called 'cultural influences' on several Danish lakes.

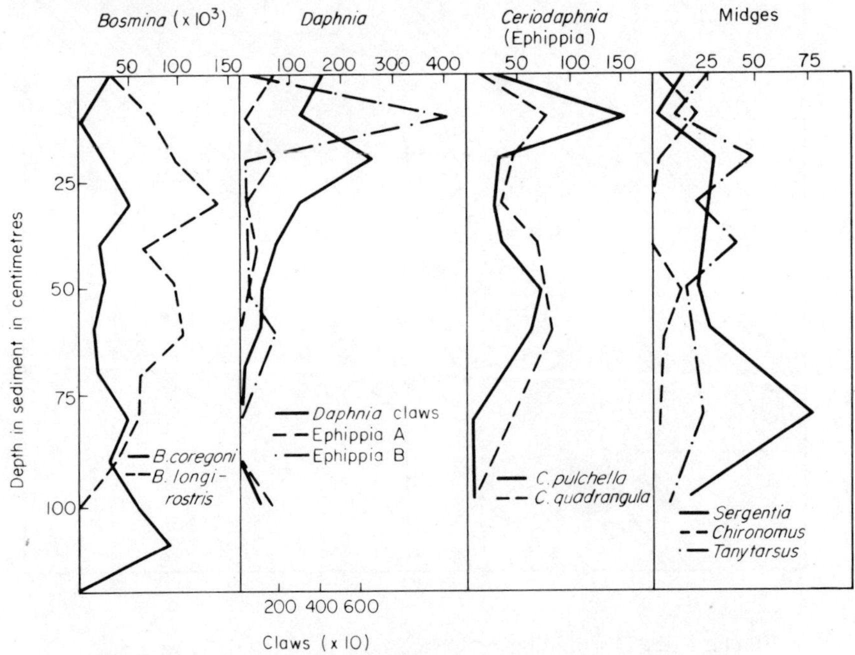

FIGURE 6.43. Changes in abundance of *Bosmina, Daphnia, Ceriodaphnia* and midge remains in the upper 120 cm of Esthwaite Water sediments (Britain) (Goulden, 1964). Numbers—remains/gm ash wt. sediment.

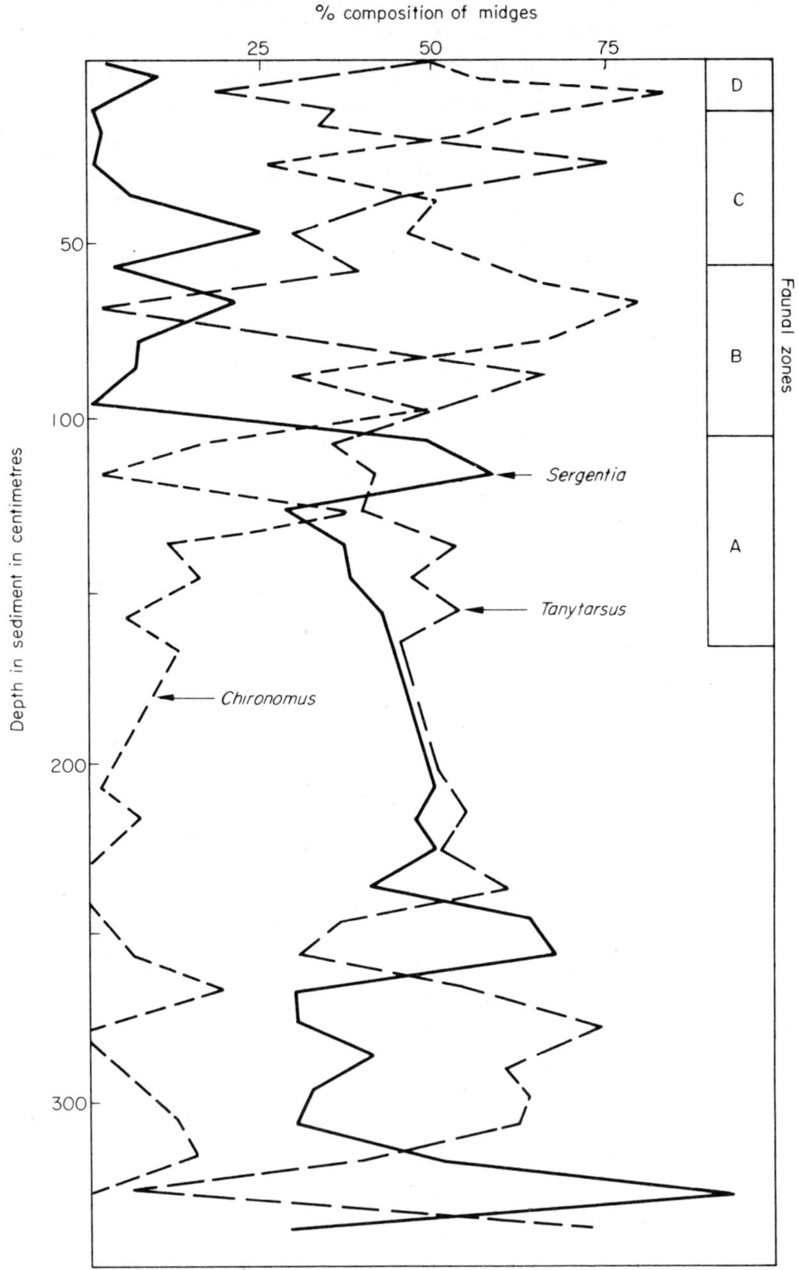

FIGURE 6.44. Percent composition of midge remains in Blelham Tarn, Great Britain (Harmsworth, 1968).

There is, perhaps, little need to document this further here, save to note that progressive changes occur over long periods of time. The best example is undoubtedly that of Western Lake Erie, where a 1930 survey was repeated in 1961 by Carr and Hiltunen (1965) using similar methods and sampling locations. The changes, illustrated in figure 6.42, speak for themselves.

Another, as yet imperfectly used, source of data on the evolution of lakes through time is the study of what are termed microfossils. The larval chironomid head capsules may be preserved for long periods of time in the sediment, and some use of these has been made in attempts to test the Thienemann system of classification and suggested evolutionary development of lakes. Goulden (1964) noted that *Tanytarsus* and *Sergentia* dominated the profundal fauna of Esthwaite Water (Great Britain) until AD 900. Some *Chironomus* head capsules are found at a depth of 130–140 cm below the surface of the sediment, but are then missing until 80 cm. From this point up to the surface (recent time) the genus fluctuates in abundance (figure 6.43) but the other two genera decline. The trend appears to be reversed in the most superficial layers, suggesting that two periods of anoxic summer conditions have now been replaced by the second of two ameliorations in oxygen stress, but other data on the lake does not fully accord with this view. Macan (1970), commenting on this study, suggests that the chemical evidence obtained by Mortimer and the extensive studies by Mackereth on lake cores is the more reliable, and that Goulden is too hasty in assuming that anaerobic conditions are irregular in occurrence in recent time (the hypolimnion has been deoxygenated every summer for at least 20 years) and that the lake was not anaerobic in early post-glacial times as suggested by the chemical evidence. Harmsworth (1968) indicated that some authors, including Goulden as cited above, had verified the transition from dominance of *Tanytarsus* to *Chironomus*-dominance, while others (notably Stahl, 1959, working on Myers Lake, Indiana) concluded that their lakes did not originate as oligotrophic systems. Indeed, Bryce (1962) obtained the reverse trend in Tarn Moss, Yorkshire, England, supposedly because of marl deposition. In the study of Blelham Tarn, closely adjacent to Esthwaite in the English Lake District, despite a good deal of fluctuation from level to level (figure 6.44) 'the most outstanding event in the stratigraphy of the midges is the change from *Tanytarsus–Sergentia* community to a *Chironomus* community'. The existence of a long phase of trophic equilibrium in lakes following an initial burst of production is terminated once morphometric fill-in has proceeded far enough for anoxic conditions to occur, hence liberating trapped nutrients and initiating a second, more productive, trophic equilibrium. This last stage Harmsworth sees as lasting until senescence, by which he presumably means the stage at which rooted plants invade the sediment or a bog forms across the water. While erosion accelerates fill-in, eroded materials import mineral nutrients locked up in chemical complexes, but the erosion of old leached soils may lead to the development of new nutrient resources once the erosion ceases. Refinement of the analyses of cores for biological remains as well as for chemical constituents (such as in the studies outlined above in concert with those of Mackereth, 1965, 1966, in the English Lake District) may clarify even further the difficult questions of rates and direction of successions.

7 THE SAMPLING PROBLEM

The earliest work on benthos consisted of collecting samples for systematic and regional distribution studies, and seems to have been influenced by the belief that the bottom of lakes constituted one of the few homogeneous environments. The physical characteristics of the habitat were apparently so consistent in the cool, dark, still depths of the lake that the animals were thought to be evenly distributed around the lake with, perhaps, some consistent change of fauna with depth.

The final conclusion to be derived from the material already presented is that *this uniformity is not clearly demonstrable in the field*. The effect of bays and rivers, variations in the substrate, seasonal patterns in growth and development, and the reaction of individuals to other individuals of both the same and of other species, all conspire to produce a patchwork of species distribution patterns. These can be classified in terms of statistics as contagious (or clumped), spaced (or uniform), and random, depending on the relationship between the variance between samples, and the sample mean.

The introduction of the dynamic concepts of production have demanded more precise estimates of standing stock than anything required of comparative studies. Hence, the behaviour of the sampling tools and the suitability of the sampling programme should be determined with great precision before any detailed study is undertaken. This may sound so obvious as to be taken for granted, but a study of the literature soon reveals that the student of benthos all too often plunges into a project without appreciating these problems fully, and quits the field before the results have been shown to be truly representative of the particular study area.

For all the thousands of hours that have been spent sampling, sorting, identifying, counting and (sometimes) weighing bottom organisms, a critical survey of the literature reveals the depressing fact that we can make *reliable* estimates of the average standing stock of macrobenthos of only a few of that tiny number of lakes that have been studied in any detail. Despite the demand for sound management of ecosystems, the sobering truth is that the descriptive bases from which modern dynamic studies should stem are woefully inadequate. We rely, for the most part, on models that are largely the intuitive product of a few men. Their work is, to a surprising extent, unsubstantiated by careful field studies, and the coupling of laboratory with field experimentation on lake benthos has seldom been attempted.

Before setting forth a brief account of the sampling devices now in use and the sampling programmes that have been employed, it may be as well to detail the basic characteristics of an ideal quantitative sampling device.

(1) The sampler must penetrate sufficiently deeply into the sediment to trap *all* of the animals inhabiting the mud column beneath the surface area sampled.
(2) The sampler should enclose the same surface area with each bite, and the entire depth should be sampled equally.
(3) During descent the sampler should not disturb the sediment or the enclosed fauna so as to reduce the number of organisms present before the sampler is closed.
(4) The closure of the sampler should be such as to preclude any loss of sediment or sample during retrieval. The closing mechanism, if using jaws, should be strong enough to shear through twigs or other obstructions.

Sampling devices required for comparative studies need not necessarily conform to these rigid requirements, but strictly (absolute) quantitative samples, truly representative of the total benthos are required for production studies. Despite the faith placed in the efficacy of many of the samplers currently used, few appear to conform to these requirements. None conform to anything like these requirements for more than one type of substrate or for part of the macrobenthos. Differences in size, spatial distribution and behaviour make it impossible to sample large, relatively scarce but active epibenthic animals with the same tool required for accurate estimation of, for example, oligochaete populations. Despite this, it might be supposed that every effort has been made to evaluate each sampler as it is designed, but even today papers are submitted to journals justifying new methods on the basis of the satisfactorily large number of creatures caught rather than the efficacy of the device when compared with other standard tools.

Even when a suitable tool has been selected, the problem is far from being solved. The number, spacing and timing of sample sets should be carefully determined in relation to the aim of the study and the pre-

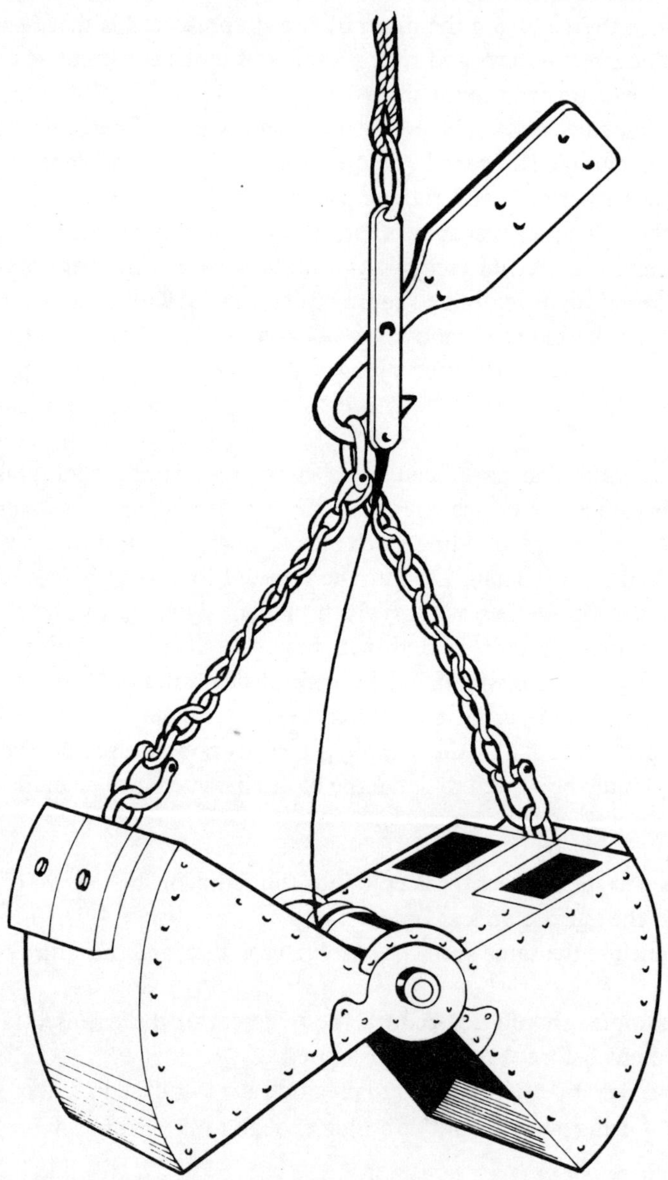

FIGURE 7.1. The Petersen grab open (Welch, 1948).

determined variability between samples taken from established zones of the lake. All too often a mass of data is assembled for no greater reason than to maximise the use of a vessel, and many publications clearly post-rationalise a series of aims and objectives. Most studies are abandoned at just that point at which the requisite pilot investigation has been completed, and there is no attempt to build on this basis by careful field investigation or laboratory testing of the hypotheses advanced.

Despite the seemingly endless variety of sampling devices that have been described, some pattern in the array can be discerned. There are two basic types of grab, the Petersen type which usually depends upon its own weight to effect closure of the more or less half-cylinder shaped jaws, and the Ekman or Birge–Ekman that consists of a box with jaws which retain the sample within the box. A third set may be described as coring devices, usually cylindrical in shape and often utilising a closing device at the upper end that prevents the sample from falling out of the tube. Finally, there are a series of sledges, trawls, burrowing tools, artificial substrates and traps for emerging winged insects that must be noted.

The Petersen is the simplest and oldest of the samplers. In design it resembles the large dockyard grabs used for unloading coal, rocks and other bulk cargoes from barges, with two jaws of about a quarter cylinder in shape, hinged where they join at the central point of the half-circle formed in section by the closed jaws

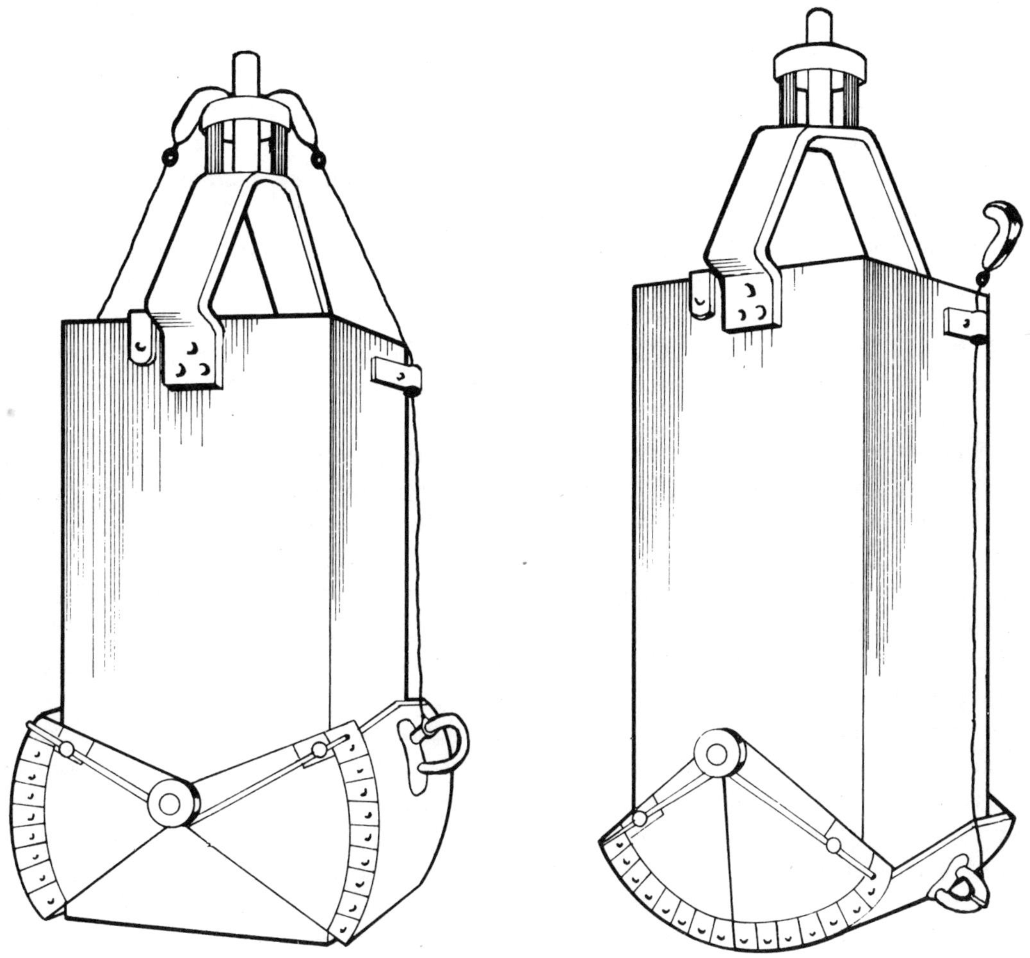

FIGURE 7.2. The tall version of the Ekman grab open and closed (Pavlovski and Zadin, 1956).

(figure 7.1). The device closes automatically by a simple arrangement of the rope or cable used to raise and lower the device. The basic design has been modified in many ways, most of them reviewed and illustrated by Holme (1964) and Holme and McIntyre (1971). The Van Veen version uses two long arms to exert a greater leverage in closing the device, and these are added to strong springs and a stabilising frame in the Smith–Mackintyre or Aberdeen grab.

In an attempt to increase the speed of descent or to avoid the build-up of water pressure, screens or doors have been added to the two jaws. The screened device, known as the Ponar (Powers and Robertson, 1967) was designed for freshwater work, primarily on the St. Lawrence Great Lakes, where oceanographic methods have to be employed. The version with doors was described by Lisitsin and Udincev (1955), but an early illustration of one is reproduced in Deacon (1962). The Franklin–Anderson (Franklin and Anderson, 1961; Kop, 1968) is also used on the Great Lakes, as are the Dietz la Fonde and Shipek (Holme, 1964).

The Ekman grab (figure 7.2) consists of a box with a pair of spring operated jaws that resemble a Petersen grab with the top removed. The jaws are hinged just as in the Petersen, and the hinge is attached at the lower end of the box. The device is commonly operated by a messenger, but a self-closing device is easily designed such as the one which also incorporates a stabilising frame described by Rawson (1947). The basic design was described by Welch (1948) but there have been many modifications made since. Lenz (1931) and Borutzky (1935) used a taller than normal box, and had slits made in one side so that metal sheets could be inserted to divide the sample into horizontal layers. Illustrations of this also appear in Sapkarev (1965). In fairly shallow situations a pole can be attached instead of a rope or cable (Økland, 1962; Mothes, 1966) and in other versions the spring action of the jaws has been replaced with a hand operated lever or threaded closure (Zabolocki, 1936; Allan, 1952; Ford and Hall, 1958). Auerbach (1953) gives an example of a modification to add weight to the Ekman, which is often manufactured from much lighter materials than the Petersen and hence fails to penetrate stiff sediments adequately.

The Szczepanski method (1953) and the sampler described by Hargrave (1969) utilise a single jaw closing device. The latter has the normal box extended by a triangular or wedge-shaped extension of one side, and it is closed by pulling a metal sheet across the lower opening by a rope and allowing a single hinged door to fall across the upper opening (figure 7.3). Designed for use in shallow situations where it can be inserted using a pole, it could nonetheless be adapted for use at greater depth. It has already been used with horizontal dividers.

One of the most interesting devices has not, to our knowledge, been used to any extent in freshwater situations, but it appears to be a very good compromise between the Ekman and the coring devices to be described. This is the sampler described by Enequist (1941) and Nyholm (1952). The sampler is astonishingly simple in design—a tall, rectangular box without top or bottom has a streamlined weight package attached to the sides. The bottom is closed by a pair of inner down-falling doors operated and held shut by the weight of the sampler during retrieval (figure 7.4) and it should be possible to arrange for the doors to be held in the open position without depending on the pressure of water during descent, a factor which will be discussed below.

Milbrink (1968) designed a sampler that appears to be an automated version of the Enequist, in that a tall, open rectangular box is allowed to penetrate the surface but, instead of having a single pair of closing doors at the base and provision for introducing flat sheets horizontally, the horizontal dividers are all *in situ* and are released by pulling a rod upwards a very short distance. The spring loaded dividers then snap into place within the sampler. Moving picture studies revealed that undisturbed samples could be obtained so far as the appearance of the sediment was concerned, but the series of plates attached to the side of the sample box clearly disturbed the adjacent sediment. The effect on the animal population of the sediment sampled needs to be established, and it would seem that the Ekman, as commonly modified to allow for the insertion of horizontal dividers after retrieval, should do just as well.

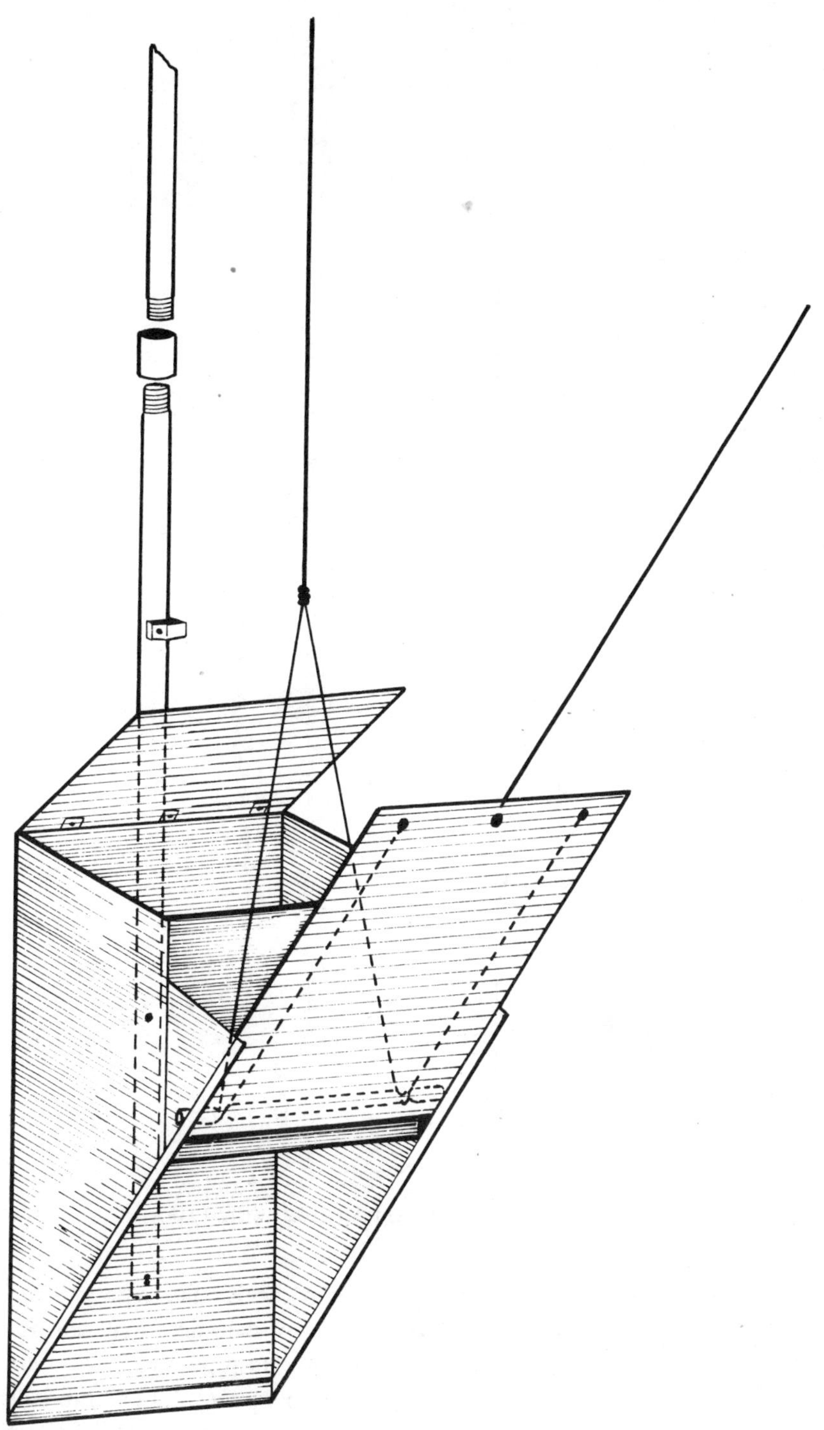

FIGURE 7.3. Sediment sampler (Hargrave, 1969).

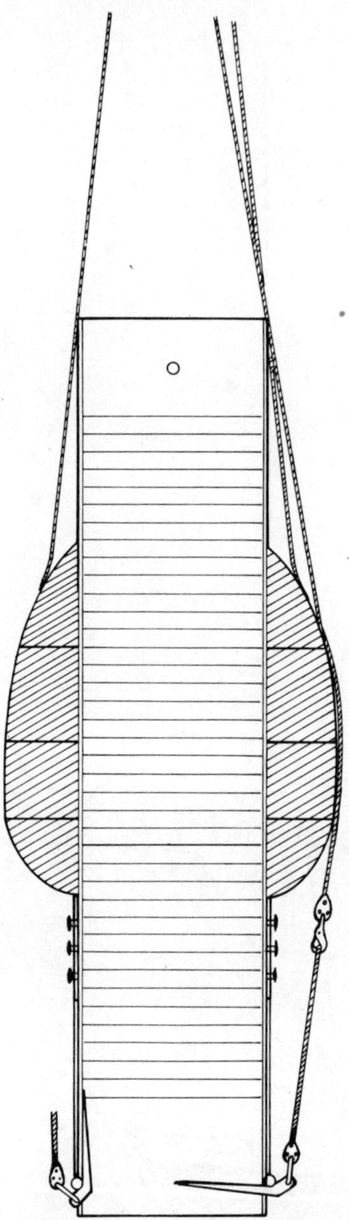

FIGURE 7.4. Enequist sampler (Enequist, 1941).

Two more samplers which almost bridge the gap between the Ekman type and the core samplers are Knudsen (1927) and the Dendy (1944). Both of these consist of cylinders that can be made to enter stiff sediment by the use of a rod or (in the former) a reciprocating pump powered by the unwinding cable that was wrapped around a drum on the top of the sampler, prior to descent. The pump is used to evacuate the space above the sediment within the (closed) sample cylinder, thus forcing the device into the mud. When full, both of these devices are inverted for retrieval. In the case of the Dendy the top of the sampler (in the descent attitude) is a narrow mesh screen which may reduce some of the pressure build-up that must occur in the Knudsen, but when inverted this mesh becomes the retaining bucket base and allows the content to be

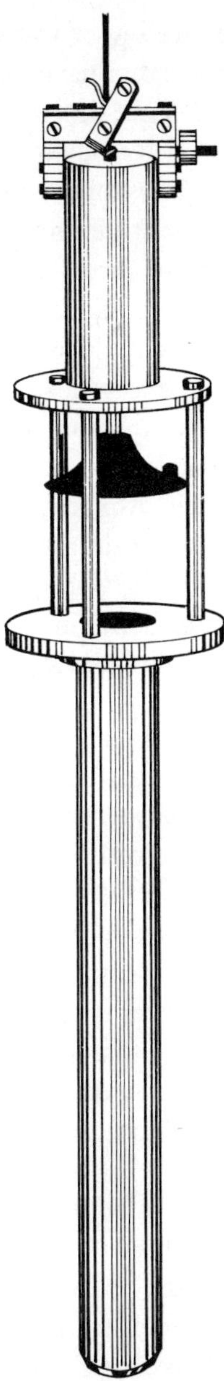

FIGURE 7.5. Kajak–Brinkhurst corer, single version.

partially screened during retrieval unless plugged with stiff clay. The retrieval operation in the Knudsen has been known to fail because of the fine anchoring action it develops.

An unusual sampler that does not conform to the classification used here is the mud burrower designed by Tonolli but modified by Bonomi (1969) which is used to collect large volumes of sediment in order to obtain numbers of specimens and to discover rare species, particularly where animals are relatively scarce.

Coring devices are gaining in popularity, largely because they seem to offer the nearest approximation to the theoretical requirements outlined earlier. Several studies have been made with simple plastic or metal pipes which are inserted by hand into a sediment and then stoppered at the top (Lang, 1931; Lenz, 1931; Rzoska, 1931; Brinkhurst and Kennedy, 1965). Some tubes have been used which are closed at the top even during descent or in which a complete through-flow of water is impeded (Ferencz, 1968; Moore, 1939). Open tubes with simple flap valves and lead weights have been used quite often, but even better are the tubes which are closed by a descending lid of some description that do not even need water pressure to hold open the valve. These have been described by Rawson (1930), Ulomski (1952), Kajak *et al.* (1965), Brinkhurst (1967) (figure 7.5). Mordukhai-Boltovskoi (1958) described a corer that looks particularly useful for hard sediments under shallow water, but perhaps the lid should be further from the top of the core tube when open. At great depths the simple corers with added weights can be supported in simple frames to prevent them from falling over while entering the sediment. Some loss of samples and the limitation of the cross sectional area sampled (owing to sample loss from wide tubes) has led to attempts to make a closing device which blocks the bottom of the tube as well as the top. The earliest and still probably the best is the Jenkin sampler described by Mortimer (1942). The sole problem with this is the complexity and hence relative expense of the apparatus. A simplified version worked by elastic bands was described by Drzycimski (1967). Another version, closed by a ball which displaces water which in turn has replaced sand at the lower end of the corer during the initial phase of withdrawal, was described by Craib (1965). This device can obtain cores in sand, unlike the KB (described by Kajak and modified by Brinkhurst) or the Jenkin. Elgmork (1962) used a modified Friedinger water bottle in the mud/water interface, and of course very thin ooze can be sampled quite easily with water sampling devices. Burke (1969) designed an ingenious sphincter for retaining cores.

Another difficulty with corers is the relatively small sample obtained. This becomes a problem where organisms are scarce. To overcome this, as well as to save time by obtaining several cores at the same time where size is no problem, multiple corers have been proposed. A successful one has been built and described by Hamilton *et al.* (1970). This version returns to the top closing method, employing a rubber ball as used in a number of water samplers of recent design.

Pneumatic devices (apart from the Knudsen already mentioned), include the sampler designed by Hunt (1926) which is simply a method of obtaining a quantity of sand from depth, and the beach-sand corers such as that described by Coffee (1968) in which water is used to assist penetration and the sample is sheathed in plastic and allowed to enter a tube of wider bore than the coring end so as to reduce the friction encountered when trying to get continuous cores in sand. Walker (1967) described a diver operated version of the Mackereth corer, which again is a pneumatic version of a piston corer of the type described by Schneider (1969).

Some of the so-called corers used by divers are really just containers that can be inserted into the sediment by hand, and which can be closed by cleaning sediment away from the lower end (Fager *et al.*, 1966). Such tubes, jars, boxes or whatever should probably still be completely open at both ends when inserted. Where turbidity sediment, and depth (and preferably temperature) permit, sampling by divers is probably the most reliable procedure, particularly in view of the visual observations that can be made.

While it may be possible to slice cores horizontally by pushing the samples up through the tube with a piston inserted at the bottom, or even to obtain such slices by introducing thin sheets as in the Ekman, many feel that animals may migrate rapidly enough to destroy any vertical distribution pattern in the natural sediment. Some have sought to remedy this by freezing the core *in situ* (Shapiro, 1958; Efford, 1960; Gleason and Ohlmacher, 1965), but it would seem likely that any animal capable of really active withdrawal into sediment, such as an oligochaete, may well have reacted to the entry of the core tube before the release of the freezing mixture. Freezing cores, however, may well aid the retention of the sample in the core tube.

Under certain circumstances special collecting methods may have to be employed. These may not be absolutely quantitative but may well be of use in comparative work, so some are mentioned here. Many of the methods used in streams may be applicable to very shallow lakes or to the littoral, and these have been reviewed by Macan (1958) and by the Finnish IBP group (1969). Sampling in weed often presents special problems, and samplers to deal with these have been described by Macan (1970), Økland (1962), Gerking (1957), Gillespie and Brown (1966) and others. Most of these devices aim at cropping the weed from a known area of shallow water, the infauna being sampled separately. In the Russian literature such a sampler was described by But (1938). Over hard substrate, artificial substrates are sometimes used in order to catch animals that will occupy unsampleable crevices. Such methods have been used by Moon (1935), Mundie (1956*a*), Hester and Dendy (1962), Besch, Hoffman and Ellenberger (1967) and others, several of whom have been working with rivers. Some of these methods expose natural rocks on a tray or in a wire box, others present a flat artificial surface for colonisation, and others use a series of artificial plates fixed a short distance apart so as to provide surfaces and crevices.

Emergence traps have been used to study populations of insects with aerial stages in their life history, as described by Jonasson (1954), Mundie (1956*b*) and Sublette and Dendy (1959). Sandberg (1969) described a detailed study using this methodology.

The mobile fraction of the benthos which may inhabit the mud/water interface for all or part of the time may be sufficiently active to avoid corers and grabs. Special methods of study are required for these organisms. These include epibenthic trawls, such as that described by Mortensen (1925) and Thorsen (1957), and modified by Ockelmann (1964). Muus (1964) described a meiobenthos sampler which consists of a self-closing door that scrapes a superficial sample into a bag. The motility of benthic animals while temporarily in the water column has been investigated by Mundie (1959) and Pieczynski and Kajak (1965).

This review has been—of necessity—brief, partly because there are several good descriptions of grabs of various types in surveys such as Welch (1948), Zadin (1960), Southwood (1966), Holme (1964), Holme and McIntyre (1971), and Edmondson and Winberg (1971), but primarily because so few of these samplers conform to anything like the ideal specifications already outlined. Even those reviews of methodology mentioned are usually confined to descriptions of how the sampler obtains a quantity of substrate and how reliably it does so without any consideration of the efficiency with which they perform the actual role for which they were designed, that is, to give a reliable quantitative sample of the benthic organisms.

Before entering into a discussion of the relative efficacy of the samplers that have been carefully evaluated by parallel trials, the fate of the sample—once obtained—should be discussed. Most students of the benthos automatically reach for a sieve or screen to separate the animals from the finer, organic sediments collected. It should be obvious that there is a continuous spectrum in the size of living organisms inhabiting the mud, and that there is no discrete separation into micro- and macrobenthos. While the student of the macrobenthos is prepared to throw away the bacteria and protistans with the sediment he does not wish to reject the smallest chironomid larvae, nematodes, ostracods and the like that are small enough to wash through his screens. Many of these small organisms are quite delicate and can be destroyed by rough sieving or washing by water under pressure. Jonasson (1955) showed that the commonly used screen with a 0.6 mm mesh gauge was inefficient, failing to retain many chironomid larvae up to 10 mm long. The use of smaller mesh sizes may increase the catch of chironomids by as much as 600 per cent, but there may be a considerable increase in the time taken to sieve a sample through screens with, for instance, a 0.2 mm opening. In really strictly quantitative sampling the whole sample should be sorted unscreened under a stereo-microscope, but the time and labour to undertake such a study are beyond the resources of most limnologists. Samples may be sorted alive where the study site is adjacent to stable benches and a good light in a shelter of some sort. Picking over samples on the lakeshore by kneeling on the gravel in a windstorm reduces one's efficiency to the point where the same samples are best preserved, usually accomplished by placing the sample in a plastic bottle with a little formalin (40 per cent) added to the jar. It should be possible to enclose the samples in pre-numbered bolting silk bags which can be swung to and fro to dispose of some of the water in the sediment, then steeped in 90 per cent alcohol. The samples thus preserved would be much pleasanter to sort than those preserved in formalin.

If preserved samples are used, they may be screened prior to sorting, but this process still leaves a time consuming task for the sorters. Several methods have been proposed for overcoming this. Samples may be placed in automatic screening systems like that described by Löffler (1961) and Lauff *et al.* (1961), but personal experience with this sort of device revealed that the machine 'consumed' as much as 20 per cent of a known sample that had been remixed with sediment. Anderson (1959) and Kajak *et al.* (1968) and Edmondson and Winberg (1971) have discussed the merits of separating part of the benthos from the substrate by flotation, using saturated salt solutions or sugar. These techniques that depend on density work well enough when there is a distinct density difference between most of the animals and most of the sediment and detritus, but when—for instance—large quantities of plant matter are present, they cannot always be separated from the animals using these techniques. The alternative here is to use stains that help to distinguish between animal and other material (Mason and Yevich, 1967) or, better still, fluorescent dyes and longwave ultraviolet light (Hamilton, 1969).

Many different types of organisms can be persuaded to migrate out of sediment that is allowed to dry out, or is exposed to cold or heat. Usually a water filled collecting vessel can be placed beneath sediment placed over a screen and so treated. This method works well for aquatic oligochaetes, and special versions of it are used for the delicate psammon or sand grain fauna (Uhlig, 1964, 1965).

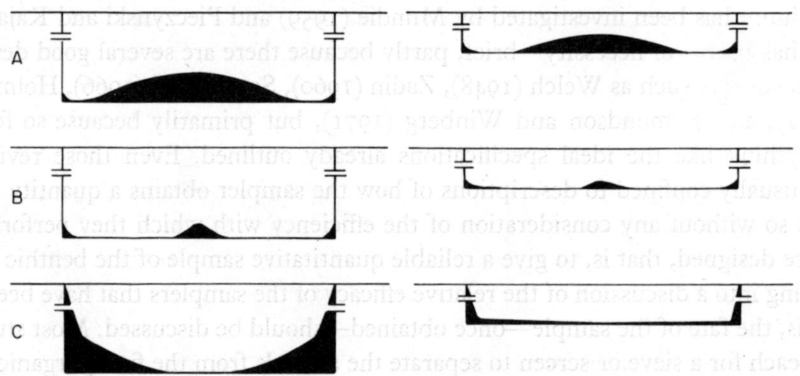

FIGURE 7.6. Biting profiles of various grabs (Gallardo, 1965). A—Petersen; B—Van Veen; C—Smith-McIntyre on hard sand (right) and soft sand (left) in air/ground trials.

Despite the extensive array of described sampling equipment, the number of serious studies of the relative efficiency of different tools is remarkably small. The increased interest in scuba diving has enabled visual examination of grabs at work on the lake bottom, but despite this there are few published accounts.

If we refer back to the theoretical requirements for samplers, it is immediately apparent that the Petersen type of gear, in which a surface scrape is picked up by the jaws, does not penetrate evenly into the sediment, nor does it penetrate deeply enough to capture the small percentage of animals living in sediment deeper than the top 6 cm. Gallardo (1965) demonstrated the biting profiles of the Petersen, Van Veen and Smith–McIntyre grabs on soft and hard substrates sampled in air rather than water (figure 7.6). The first two grabs did not cut a rectangle of sediment, but left behind a mound beneath the closing doors. The effect was more pronounced with the Petersen than with the Van Veen, both in soft and hard sediment.

The Smith–McIntyre samples an almost perfect rectangular area in hard sand, but the bite is of course quite shallow. In soft sand, better penetration has been achieved but the profile of the bite showed that large 'corners' were left unsampled at the deepest point of the bite. Northcote (1952) studied the efficacy of the Ekman grab from many points of view. As some concern had been expressed in the literature about the bite profile of this grab and the possibility that the curvature of the jaws led to an uneven sampling of the sediment when comparing material trapped in the middle of the sampler rather than at the edges, he divided the interior of a grab with vertical partitions. The results showed that central partitions contained as many animals as partitions along the outer edges when sampling in deep water in soft sediments where penetration exceeded 4 inches. At a depth of 2 feet, penetration was only 2–3 inches, and while a greater volume of sediment was initially contained in central compartments with the grab, in the final analysis fewer animals were found in these sections because of the loss of silt that occurred while the jaws finally shut as the grab was withdrawn. These differences were most apparent in oligochaetes, in which depth penetration is significant.

Another aspect of this study was revealed by Wigley (1967) who used moving pictures to reveal the disturbance to sediment and to lightly weighted table tennis balls lying on the mud surface. The Van Veen was shown to create a considerable pressure wave as it descended through water, whereas the Smith–McIntyre created much less disturbance because of the screened portion of the jaws that reduces the bow wave effect. The Ponar grab, mentioned above, uses the same screening device to avoid the same difficulty with the Petersen grab, and light doors can be used for the same purpose. The same effect, only this time with a corer, was demonstrated by Brinkhurst *et al.* (1969) in which the catch of invertebrates using a Freshwater Biological Association (FBA or Gilson corer) was substantially less than that using an Ekman even when great care was taken with samples in very shallow water where sediment wash-out could be eliminated. The virtually closed FBA corer obtains good, undisturbed looking cores but the animals

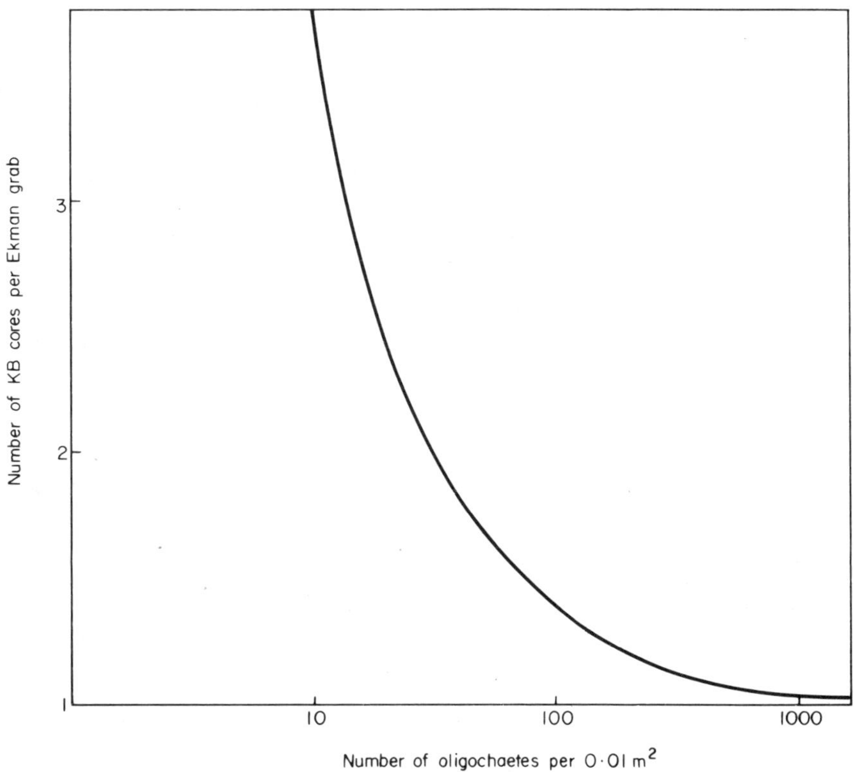

FIGURE 7.7. Number of KB core samples of oligochaetes required to obtain the same estimate of worm abundance as an Ekman grab at various population densities (Brinkhurst *et al.*, 1969).

seem to be able to avoid it during its descent, whereas trials with the KB corer showed that estimates of standing stock as good as those obtained by the Ekman could be obtained with far less effort because of the lower volumes of sediment requiring sorting. The number of core samples needed to obtain as accurate an estimate of oligochaete abundance as that obtained by a single Ekman sample is illustrated in figure 7.7. The conclusion from this study was that, unless animals are exceedingly scarce, or very large in relation to the bore of the core, a through-flow core device would be preferred to the Ekman because a six-sample series could be collected and sorted with less effort than a single 15 cm or 6 inch Ekman. Very similar conclusions were reached earlier by Kajak (1963*b*) who showed that the greatest accuracy would be obtained using a series of thirty cores of 10 cm^2 cross sectional area or ten to twenty Ekman grabs, but that the volume of sediment in the grab was up to fifteen times greater than that in the core series.

Dugdale (1955) demonstrated that the screen often attached to the top of the box frame of an Ekman reduced the 'catch' by one half, and that weights added to the grab further reduced the catch when the screen was in place. No doubt this effect is also attributable to the build-up of water pressure within the device. Prejs (1969) has commented adversely about the screen added to the Ekman. The screen is added to stop the contents from washing out of the top of the sampler when it is used in very soft sediments. The proper course of action would be to build the sampler tall enough to avoid the problem and, if need be, to use particularly light models where excess penetration is a problem. The best design for the Ekman would therefore be a tall, light device which needs neither screen nor doors at the top, but which has a variable additional weight package that can be added where needed. The Enequist sampler is just such a device with the added benefit that the sample stands little chance of escaping from the device through the bottom doors if they are made to fit closely or are provided with plastic or rubber gaskets.

Henson (1954) obtained as good results with an Orange Peel grab as with an Ekman in Cayuga Lake in which the sediment contained only 9 per cent sand. This is at variance with most trials using the Orange Peel in comparison to other samplers, so much so that Flannagan (1970) omitted the device from a trial of a series of devices. This exhaustive survey showed that different samplers performed best in different substrates. The Ponar and the Shipek were considered to be the only all purpose samplers, primarily because

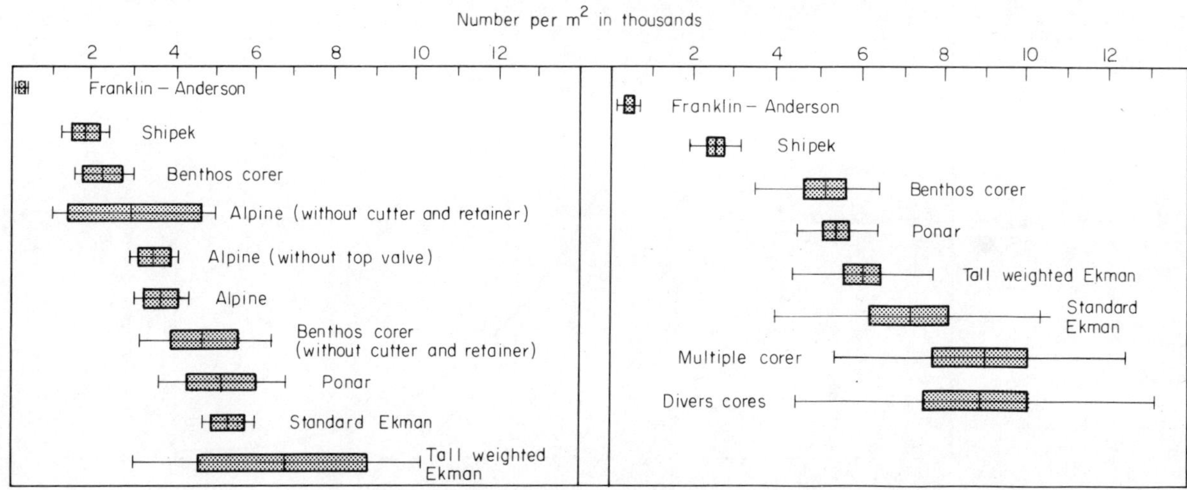

FIGURE 7.8. Means, standard deviations, and standard errors of estimates of benthos/m in Hamilton Harbour, Lake Ontario (A) and Lake Winnipeg (B), Canada using various samplers (Flannagan, 1970).

they are the only ones with which a sample could be obtained in gravel. In sand, the Franklin Anderson performed better than any other grab, in so far as the number of specimens obtained. In mud, the Ekman grab gave the highest number of specimens, but the results were not statistically different from a number of other devices where only three samples per device were taken. In later trials in Lake Winnipeg, taken through ice, twelve samples were taken with each tool. The results are illustrated in figure 7.8A–B, from which it is clear that the hand taken divers' cores, and the multiple-core FBA corer (essentially similar to the Kajak and KB corers but using a rubber ball closure system that failed on the original KB prototype) performed somewhat better than the tall, weighted Ekman, the Ponar and the Benthos corer. The Franklin Anderson and Shipek did not perform well in mud, just as in the earlier trial. Only the standard Ekman and the multiple corer obtained samples that were not statistically different to the divers' cores. In this instance the tall, weighted Ekman penetrated the sediments too deeply, and it is unfortunate that no samples were taken with the tall Ekman without the additional weights. The efficiency of the Benthos corer was reduced by adding the core cutter and core retainer, presumably because of the slight impediment to the flow of water through the device when lowered.

A further point of some interest was that the samplers did not perform in the same manner regardless of the major taxa concerned (figure 7.9). The multiple corer, for instance, caught significantly fewer chironomids than the divers' cores, whereas the standard Ekman caught significantly fewer worms. Both of these, the tall Ekman and the Ponar, caught the same number of sphaeriids as the diver, but the last two caught fewer worms and chironomids. Flannagan also computed the mechanical reliability of the samplers on the various substrates in terms of the number of successful hauls compared with number of attempts. In mud the multiple corer and Ekman worked well (1.0) and the Ponar quite well (0.86, 1.0). In sand only the Franklin Anderson obtained a 1.0 score, and in gravel the Ponar and Shipek scored 0.5 and 0.38, respectively.

Comparisons of tall and short Ekmans have been made by others, particularly by Berg (1938) who showed that the tall version got 40 per cent or more additional material. Mrs. J. Crowe (personal communication) tested a standard Ekman against the Ponar, and obtained significantly ($P<0.05$) larger samples of animals in

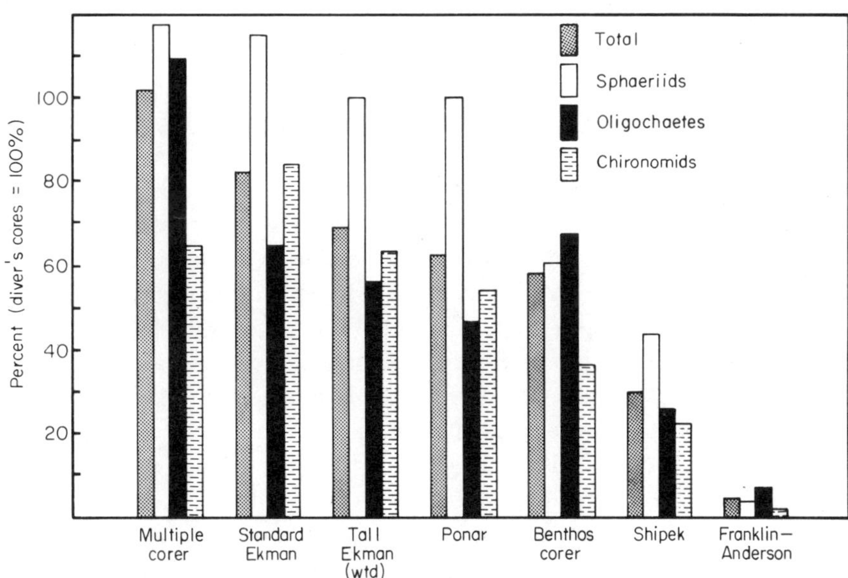

FIGURE 7.9. The abundance of benthos estimated from samples using various tools compared with diver's hand core samples (Flannagan, 1970).

a 9 inch Ekman using paired samples at twenty-six sites and sieving through a sixty-two mesh/inch screen. Rawson (1947) mentioned that an Ekman obtained five times the amount of benthos collected with the Petersen in deep water (76 m, 122 m) over soft sediment in Great Slave Lake, but that the latter was used over hard substrates. The greatest discrepancy was found to be in the number of amphipods, organisms that one would suspect to be most sensitive to the pressure wave problem. Økland (1962) demonstrated that the use of the pole attached to the Ekman in shallow, hard substrates increased the number of organisms obtained, but that at 15 m there was no significant difference. Northcote recorded the variability between samples with a 6 inch (15.25 cm) and 9 inch (22.9 cm) Ekman, and found no difference at 5 m or 8 m (approx.) but a greater variability using the smaller version at 15 m.

The variability of animals in time and space, already described, demands a rigorous sampling scheme if the true abundance of each species is to be established. Seasonal and annual variation is little understood in the freshwater benthos because of the few studies that extend throughout a whole season, and the even smaller number that extend beyond one or two seasons. The common practice of restricting the sampling scheme to a single or a pair of samples at a series of intervals along a line extending from shore to the deepest point of the lake, is familiar to us all.

The results of such studies may give an indication of the species present and tell us a little about the relative abundance of the commoner forms, but almost all of the published data is totally unreliable in terms of the standing stock of the benthos in freshwater lakes. As has already been demonstrated, few attempts have been made to isolate field problems and then to design sampling programmes to fit the problem and the known variables. Sampling stations are nearly always associated with constant depth increments and are sited along a single transect or a small number of transects. A rough general survey is often undertaken in order to substantiate the belief that the transect line is typical, but in practice this usually means no more than checking that the dominant species are the same at one particular time prior to the main study. The number of replicate samples to be taken has been discussed, and opinions have varied from the view of Deevey (1941) that a single sample should suffice, through the view that two or three are adequate (Lang, 1931; Berg, 1938; Prejs, 1969), a preference for five (Eggleton, 1931; Rawson, 1930; Miller, 1937) to the more reasoned statements by Northcote (1952), Lenz (1951) and Kajak (1963*b*) that the sample number must depend upon the particular circumstances, especially the spatial distribution of the animals and other causes of variability.

As Kajak (*op. cit.*) pointed out: Berg (1938), Deevey (1941), Mundie (1957) and others who argued for single or for paired samples, assumed a Poisson distribution of the animals, and hence required a small number of large samples so as to obtain a large number of individual animals. If we realise, as Southwood claims (1966), that few, if any, animals are so distributed, and that most are aggregated or otherwise dispersed, then a large number of small samples will be preferable to a few bulky samples. Both Northcote (1952) and Gerking (1962) cite a paper by Neyman (1934) in which it is suggested that samples on a randomly stratified design should be taken in proportion to both the area which the populations occupy and to the standard deviation to be expected in samples from each of these areas. The difficulty here is in establishing such areas of relative uniformity (see chapter 3). Mothes (1966) expressed a preference for one sample per site but for many randomly selected sites across the lake. Few people have studied the microdistribution patterns of benthic organisms, or have recognised the various parameters of distribution. A terminology developed by Macan in contribution to the Freshwater Biological Association (UK) handbooks is useful here. Macan recognised that a species might have a large or small geographical distribution, that it might be found in a few or many sites within this range and that where found it might be abundant or scarce.

Within a small area of 4.5 × 9.0 m in Lake Michigan, Alley and Anderson (1969) took eighty-eight samples in a pre-arranged pattern of quadrats and in a pattern of squares radiating around each central sample area. In contrast to the assertion by many authors that the total benthos (which was identified as consisting of oligochaetes, chironomids, sphaeriids and *Pontoporeia affinis*) was distributed according to a Poisson series, this study revealed a normal distribution (figure 7.10). The data on chironomids and tubificids obtained in Lake Michigan fitted the Poisson curve and the negative binomial respectively. In a study by Brinkhurst *et al.* (1969) the data for both groups approximated to a negative binomial distribution. According to Northcote (1952) the negative binomial, Poisson and Neyman's contagious distribution all described his observed distributions equally well, and the conclusion was that a random distribution pattern, as suggested by Miller (1941) for whole fauna, chironomids and chaoborids, gave the simplest explanation. Raverra (1966) found that the pattern obtained for data on each type of organism varied from place to place or year

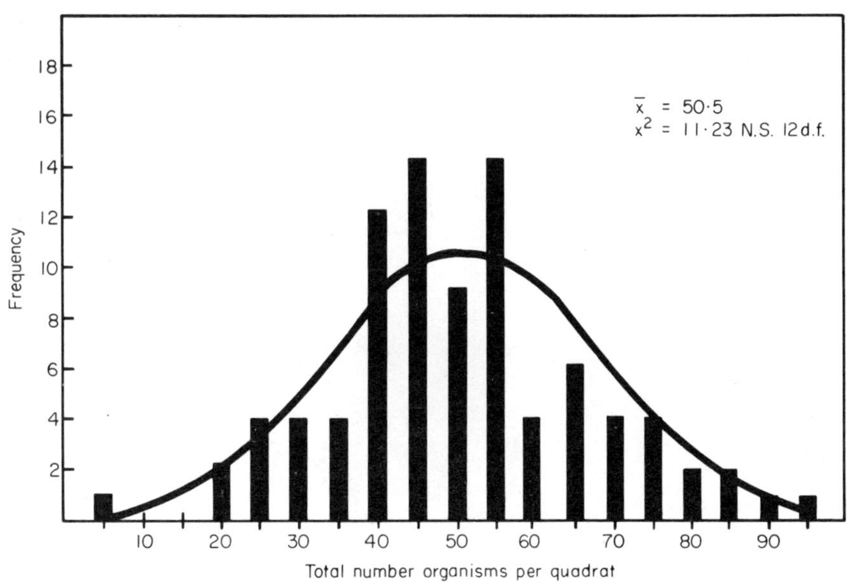

FIGURE 7.10. Frequency of occurrence of total counts of benthos per quadrat (Alley and Anderson, 1969).

to year. Until these questions of detailed distribution and the recognition of associations or biocoenoces progresses further, sampling programmes will have to allow for relatively large error terms.

The whole subject of statistical methodology in benthic studies has recently been reviewed by Elliott (1971) and Edmondson and Winberg (1971), and hence does not bear closer scrutiny here. We should emphasise, however, that for most purposes the single transect line should be abandoned, simply because depth is not necessarily the dominant variable to be considered. Patterns of samples should be taken at random across the lake or, better still, random patterns within predetermined zones. Such zones may be identifiable from major differences in sediment type, or may be established in relation to the relative abundance of benthic organisms. As changes in abundance from zone to zone are so often referable to a logarithmic progression, the zones are quite readily established and within-series variation between samples can be greatly reduced by assessing abundance zone by zone in this manner.

PART III
DISCUSSION

8 DISCUSSION AND CONCLUSIONS

The second part of this account has been, in large measure, a critique of the first section, but nevertheless it may be worthwhile outlining the current status of some of the questions raised and their potential for further study.

Classifications of lakes, and of zones within lakes, suffer from the same inherent weakness, even when classification is regarded as no more than nomenclature without evolutionary implications. To have a useful classification, we must have real discontinuities between groups of equal status, made up of recognisable discrete units. A simple consideration of morphometry of lakes and of variation in horizontal distribution of benthos within them is sufficient to enable us to recognise that some lakes are composite units unlike the small, simple basins that were initially studied by typologists. We must, at least, be prepared to subdivide lakes into their *functional* units if we are to have any sort of working classification.

It is clear that one can classify either lakes or zones within lakes for particular purposes using a few interrelated criteria, but that any attempt to create unified classifications soon falls down over the problem of lack of correspondence of the schemata based on different sets of criteria. Thus zones can be recognised along the vertical gradient in lakes in terms of physical factors, plant associations or various animal species distributions, but there is no agreement between these various systems as to the precise location of boundaries. The establishment of such zones or types of lakes may help in the search for correlated factors, but this can be done more effectively today by the use of mathematical analyses of data arranged along continua rather than assembled in blocks.

Several aspects of the old benthic classifications of lakes or zones could be improved upon before they are rejected as the basis of even benthic studies *per se*, however. Such systems must be based on properly identified units, which may be species or reasonably constant associations of species recognised by statistical evaluation, and estimates of quantity should obviously be expressed in terms of the applicable confidence limits. Seasonal and annual variation should be understood sufficiently to ensure that quantitative values represent more than some chance point along the fluctuating line relating abundance with time. Numerical estimates of quantity for this purpose are of little or no value because of variations in biomass between species, and between individuals in relation to both time and space. The chironomids are perhaps the worst species to use as indicators in this situation, subject as they are to such large fluctuations from season to season. The more permanent occupants of the sediments, such as the small clams and the tubificid worms, are probably of much more use as they are present on a year-round basis and do not emigrate from the lake in order to reproduce. The mass emergence of chironomids not only promotes strong seasonal fluctuations in their abundance, but may induce considerable year-to-year variations depending on the success or failure of the breeding swarms to lay eggs in the lake once more. A strong wind on the wrong night can have a huge impact on the next year crop of any one chironomid species. Even the statistical evaluation of community limits should, perhaps, avoid transient species.

The relationship between benthic fauna and local conditions has been roughly sketched by students of the benthos, and this has been termed an 'apparent typology' by those who consider that algal production is the true indicator of lake production—or rather that standing stocks of algae indicate lake productivity, as the early workers could not, in fact, establish production rates. A clear demonstration of the correlation between annual production of algae, benthos and fish is difficult to demonstrate, as localised bottom topography, water currents or significant allochthonous inputs may create special local conditions on the bottom, and even if these are transitory they may determine the sort of species able to colonise particular spots. The simple assumption of a one way flow of materials in a system from primary production through secondary production (often thought of as zooplankton) to fish and eventually to the sink in the lake sediment or downstream to the sea ignores both allochthonous inputs that drop rapidly to the bottom and returns to the system *via* benthic production, as well as sediment irrigation. Although a relationship of sorts clearly must exist between those components of the lake that we associate together as the benthos and other such units, there is no reason to expect it to be a simple, direct one. For one thing, the quality of the allochthonous and autochthonous food supply will play a significant role in determining the nature and quantity of benthos that they support and, conversely, the nature of the benthic forms available as potential fish food may help to determine the sort of fish present or their dependence on plankton for food. Qualitative considerations have been too long overlooked by the students of energetics, but have received too much attention from typologists who were supposedly relating to production in lakes. The fusion of the typology schemes of Thienemann and Naumann has not, therefore, been altogether successful and was, at least, premature. It is interesting to note that the same sort of difficulty applies to the correlation between stream fauna and effluent characteristics in pollution studies; while the stream fauna clearly reflects living conditions for the biota of a stream, there is difficulty in demonstrating a *statistical* correlation between biological and chemical data. Resuspension of deposited material and the rate of decomposition during descent remind us of the importance of wind exposure, ambient temperature, and morphometry in determining benthic production. Stratification and variations in the oxygen regime induced by the interplay of these factors obviously plays a determining role in benthic ecology as well as a subsidiary role in primary production, but local events at the mud/water interface may override such general water column events so far as benthos is concerned. Criteria such as Total Dissolved Solids may be useful first approximations to causal factors of some significance, but limited successful application of such crude yardsticks should promote their careful refinement rather than the slavish adoption of a series of analytical procedures sanctified by tradition.

While the emphasis on the so-called harmonic lakes has led many to forget that the eutrophic–oligotrophic series is of limited regional and morphometric application (because it refers, in effect, to temperate zone, stratified lakes) the much discussed dystrophic lake type has never really been adequately defined or incorporated into the scheme. Is there a three way, one dimensional classification of lakes or a three by three lattice with degree of eutrophy on one scale and humic influence along the other? Are we convinced that lakes of the harmonic series evolve toward eutrophy other than by the simple effect of morphometric change at their terminal stages of existence, or is this another example of the influence of cultural background on human thought? If one lives on plains surrounded by filled-in lakes, they do seem a bit more transient than, say, Baikal or Tanganyika do to their local residents.

Perhaps we must recognise that lakes exist in a number of continuous serial arrays around some generalised average state, and that the whole range can be visualised as a multi-dimensional shape with many pointed rays diverging from a central core. The core lakes may be regarded as the harmonic series, and extending from these are groups of lakes in which one criterion or another begins to dominate its ecology. Some of these extreme states can be identified, and degrees of intensity of the development of 'disharmony', or translation from the central mass, established fairly easily. Humic content then becomes just one of these disturbing factors, as does unusual morphometry, volume, surface area, depth (both minimal and maximal), salt content (with the Dead Sea as a near-terminal example of one such lake dominance or lack of a critical chemical), and position in respect to altitude or latitude. The more such constraints one can name in describing a lake, the more predictable becomes the definition of other characteristics. Classifications so based would almost certainly be of regional rather than general applicability, but our present non-systematic array is scarcely even that. Such a scheme would more nearly approach the classification of the living world by virtue of the number of terms to be used to distinguish a particular category of lake. Just as a single species of sludge worm can be referred to as:

Animalia,
  Eumetazoa,
    PHYLUM Annelida,
      CLASS Clitellata,
        ORDER Haplotaxida,
          SUB-ORDER Tuficina,
            FAMILY Tubificidae
              SUB-FAMILY Tubificinae
                GENUS *Limnodrilus*
                  SPECIES *hoffmeisteri*

which tells us that it is a triploblastic, metamerically segmented, coelomate protostome with a whole host of anatomical features associated with the ordinal, familial, generic and specific epithets used, so a lake might more meaningfully be described in relation to its latitude, altitude, surface area, depth, degree of exposure to wind, a few major ion characteristics, its dominant phytoplankton, zooplankton, fish and benthic *associations* plus macrophyte cover; possibly also its drainage basin characteristics and detention time of the water mass, and biological productivity yardsticks. No doubt considerable convergence will be discovered in relation to, say, benthic associations or production of fish. So long as one adopts a functional rather than an architectural approach, such convergences are predictive rather than confusing, as evidenced by the current success in studies on animal phylogeny in contrast to the older systems, which paid no attention to the functional significance of the proposed advances and regressions in the form of particular organs or whole organisms.

There is no real need for such a system to be based on evolutionary concepts, as each of the major latitudinal zones do not evolve rapidly from one to another (although such shifts are known to occur in geological time). While each lake must go through a process of ontogeny, there may be no need to assume that they all undergo a personal recapitulation of a phylogeny which may have more to do with change in morphometric status with age or perhaps with human interference, especially in the set of lakes that have been intensively studied in the more populated parts of the western temperate zones in the last 75 years. If lakes perpetually export materials from the water column to the sediments and over the outflow, and if nothing is done to prevent the expected decline in the contributions received from the watershed, it is difficult to see why lakes should become steadily more productive, as has normally been assumed. If they do, it would seem logical to suppose that they would not recover from the effects of eutrophication once sewage is treated at the tertiary level or diverted altogether, but instances such as the recovery of Lake Washington and the failure of fertilisation programmes to effect permanent enhancement of production suggest that lakes are driven more by input than by recirculation of internal resources.

The old, indicator-species based, benthic lake typology is probably no more useful now, after all the efforts to improve it, than it was when it was first defined in terms of *Chironomus* versus *Tanytarsus* lakes by Thienemann. If enough were known about the relative abundance of accurately named species of a number of major phyla in the soft sediments of lakes, we might be able to replace the shaky foundations of a potentially useful system with objective sets of species associations, but we would still have to recognise that large areas of lake bed would be found to be inhabited by assemblages that could at best be regarded as representing the transition between two associations (see chapter 5).

As far as intralacustrine studies go, the same approach therefore applies. The lake may not often contain a single homogeneous benthic association even at a given depth, and so the whole concept of focusing attention on one transect along the vertical axis may lead to a false assumption of uniformity. If we can work with functional associations of organisms, the littoral (or sublittoral in marine terminology) can be seen to encompass a functional benthos as well as at least two other assemblages: the stream-associated stone fauna and flora, and the inhabitants of bays that constitute a flora and associated fauna more typical of ponds. Hence the interplay of local conditions and the faunal and floral associations that have evolved as a response to them constitute the basis for study, and even the difficulty of classifying the continuous spectra of pond–lake or river–lake is de-emphasised.

We may still recognise the importance of the vertical axis in relation to physical/chemical parameters, and that there is a greater diversity of living conditions in the marginal location than in the deeper parts of the basin, if only because the physical non-conformities of the substrate are commonly obliterated by silt in places beyond the reach of wave action. Apart from that, however, the uniformity of the deep sediments is more apparent than real, and both seasonal and short term fluctuations in conditions occur (see p. 115). Even the diminution of food supply with depth that we take so much for granted may be modified by submerged rivers and other currents, the descent of large corpses or other sources of slow release of food to the macrobenthos by the bacteria or one local area, or by slumping or resuspension of sediments. The physical conditions and the nature of the nutritional resources (for those dependent upon newly deposited matter or the bacterial flora, and also for the invertebrate predators) restricts the deepest situations to relatively few animals. The time taken to develop a rich benthic fauna may be indicated by the low diversity of most benthic populations in relation to those of pre-glacial lakes of proven antiquity. Numbers of individuals biomass and even production may also be depth limited, but the quantitative evidence for this is still tenuous.

Detailed discussions of the shapes of curves relating numbers of benthic organisms to supposed lake trophy may be criticised from a number of viewpoints.

The curves should be derived from reproducible, quantitative data on biomass rather than number, and again should perhaps be based on the benthos as defined herein—possibly including only the permanent inhabitants. The various total curves discussed in the literature are made up of various organisms, each differing in life history and response to the environment. Many of them migrate within the lake or emigrate for a while. There is no single pattern of distribution of total numbers of benthic organisms which can be said to be truly representative of a given lake, and the annual average distribution is seldom available, as observations are commonly restricted to a single season. Year-to-year variations must be presumed to exist as well. The distribution of individual species depends on the interplay of the whole gamut of biotic and abiotic factors that currently apply, and which applied for a time in the past. The fact that several unrelated species show distribution patterns in common, as demonstrated in Rostherne Mere, may be of more significance than the average plots produced from combining all the data. However, there are suggestions of a consistent sigmoid disturbance in the otherwise smooth distribution of benthos with depth (referred to as the sublittoral minimum or perhaps also the concentration zone) which seems characteristic of lakes that have a demonstrable oxygen shortage below the thermocline in summer. If this correlation exists, the significance of internal seiches in producing an estuarine type of location might be investigated. While animals may adapt to strenuous situations, fluctuating conditions are more difficult to tolerate. Such an estuarine zone would move downward in a lake and become broader but less intense with time due to mixing at the shear zone between the water masses. In any event, the search for real patterns and the combinations of circumstances that create them, should be more rewarding than the sterile arguments about the precise definition of specific zones along one particular axis.

Where vertical gradients can be upset by experimentation—as in the study of El Capitan reservoir, described on p. 109—the degree to which the benthic distribution is first re-arranged and then restored (or not restored) to its original pattern as the environment is modified, gives us a real opportunity to detect causal relationships rather than simple correlations. Testing hypotheses concerning temperature tolerance of supposed stenotherms and respiratory adaptation of both oxygen limited and non-limited organisms are two other neglected methods of using the predictive value of descriptive, regional studies. Enclosure or exclosure experiments are often handicapped by the effects of the structures introduced into the system and, although the growth of bacteria may be overcome by using aluminium cages, the interpretation of results from such studies are not easy to substantiate. Nevertheless, the effort may be more worthwhile than the production of another badly planned survey of partially identified organisms based on an inadequate series of quasi-quantitative samples collected for no specific reason.

The preceding account of the achievements of benthic research, set against a consideration of the complexity of the system to be studied and the inadequate methods employed, may leave many despondent and unwilling to persevere in the face of such difficulties. We should, however, bear in mind the reasons for undertaking the study of lakes and what our expectations might be, in terms of the investment of manpower and resources available to use, before we give up hope. The critical ecological impasse which seems to threaten the future of technological western civilisation, if not the very existence of man, suggests to many an urgent need to find quick solutions to the problem of managing our aquatic (and other) natural resources, and a new appeal to empirical holistic study has been launched to counter the supposedly reductionist emphasis in ecology in the past. While recognising the urgent need for a re-appraisal of our social needs and aspirations, as indicated in an earlier volume (Brinkhurst and Chant, 1971), this panic response to an awakened interest in our study area is unwarranted for at least two reasons. In the first place, to abandon most of the hints, clues and suggestions from the existing literature in the search for new empirical correlations (as the most polarised modellers would suggest) is simply a waste, but even a more moderate approach is unlikely to produce answers to any but the most simple questions. It is, perhaps, better to admit the inaccuracy of the predictions we can make now rather than have our deficiencies revealed by others once expensive decisions have been based on them. In a field in which a handful of poorly supported scientists have worked for so short a time, we have no need to feel ashamed of our achievements even if they cannot instantly be mobilised into social action. We did not learn to travel through space by the unaided efforts of a few poorly financed academics scattered through the world with few analytical instruments designed around their needs. In any case, it would seem quite possible that we are facing a human dilemma that has many qualitative emotional components and which has to be fought in the political arena where objective facts gathered by rational men may play a relatively minor role in what we nowadays term the decision making process. The ecotactic that may bring about greatest progress is that of reduction of the problem to its ultimate components. We cannot tell a government how much of its conservation cake it can have, and how much development for industry and housing it can devour. We cannot set up standards that will allow all natural bodies of water to deteriorate to a tolerable level for human health and the maintenance of a few fisheries, because to do so would be to ignore the basic malaise-population and technological growth, *the growth that will eventually render the pressures on environment intolerable even if our new found awareness staves off disaster at great cost to what we term our living standard*. It is possible that future generations will nominate some neo-Darwinian as the originator of the concept that man is dependent upon his ecosystem—as simple a concept as that of evolution, but one equally profound in its significance to man in terms of his self-appointed status on earth. From evolution to genetics and the code of inheritance, and then to ecology, man has had to learn to devalue his own image and this will be achieved—or not achieved—as much by rhetoric as by rationalism.

The second reason for avoiding the latest of scientific fads is that the broad stream of knowledge seems to be advanced in fits and starts, but the latest breakthrough does not mean that all have to exploit its potential. There are qualitative questions to be answered as well as quantitative ones and, as Warren (1971) has pointed out in his critique of Water Pollution Biology, there has perhaps been an inordinate emphasis on quantity unrelated to quality in the use of the energetics approach to ecology stimulated by Lindeman (1942). Those who consider the productivity of lakes should, perhaps, welcome eutrophication as being the achievement of what was so often quoted as the rationale for lake studies in the recent past—the enhancement of the production of fish for the relief of human want. In our haste to condemn eutrophication we forget that we, in the developed nations, can afford unproductive (underdeveloped?) lakes for aesthetic reasons such as appearance of beaches and of water to sail upon, and we prefer the taste of energetically expensive predatory fish species. Although the treatment of water for cooking and drinking purposes may be more expensive when it is drawn from eutrophic rather than oligotrophic lakes, that argument is not often voiced by those pressing for a cleaning up of our waters. Even if our energetics studies focused on potential fish yield, we would still ask the question 'which species?'

More persuasive to the scientist, however, may be the fact that progress may arise by the interaction of disciplines—the theorist providing direction for studies by those with a narrower frame of reference, the factual information sources providing material for the initiation or refinement of still broader theoretical concepts. Either approach carried out in a vacuum rapidly becomes sterile, but even objective, rational scientists seem all too ready to judge and categorise each other in the race to divert resources to their own field of study. The denigration of whole areas of study by those in the current vogue is a repugnant affair and, anyway, unless one is nimble, it is all too easy for the advocates of one wave to be overwhelmed by the next—how many cell biologists who berated ecologists not too long ago have managed to switch fields to the more 'mission-oriented, multidisciplinary, relevant social aspects of biology' of today? Shifts in fashion may occur with increasing frequency, if we may judge from the fact that some are now suggesting that systems analysts working up models of energy flow in lakes can predict relatively stable-state future conditions, but cannot predict the effects of changes which alter the specific make-up of their systems. The key problem here is the recognition of the causal bases of the switch in successional states, and the ability to channel production into either useful or at least neutral channels. Such problems demand the skills of systematists, physiologists, ecologists and mathematicians—and they may be slow to solve. That is why this volume concerns itself with both old and (relatively) new approaches to studies on the benthos. Surely a proper holist must have an appreciation of the historical development of his field in order to direct, in some small way, its future development.

How, then, should we approach the study of benthos? We know that a lake is a part of a watershed system—it is no more than a temporary holding tank that interrupts the flow of run-off water directly to the sea (or indirectly *via* the atmosphere and other drainage systems where losses are achieved solely by evaporation). From the pools of streams and rivers through to the great lakes of the world, there is a complex of serial arrays varying in surface area, depth, detention time and other factors, many shaped by the diverse origins of lake basins. We cannot distinguish lakes from ponds, nor can we adequately decide on the limits of ecosystems within complex lake basins. We similarly recognise that the subdivision known as the benthos is an abstraction from a whole, not ideally the subject of independent study nor fully definable even in functional rather than spatial terms. Hence we begin with a set of non-operational bases, and we can perhaps learn to appreciate the fascination of this complexity as our prime motivation—indeed I suspect that no rational man would choose to become an ecologist or limnologist. The questions we may proceed to ask are then both qualitative and quantitative. What is it, when, and where is it found, how much of it is there, and how does it function, are some of the basic facts we may require to know about objects in our environment. We know, as biologists, that the living components interact with an instantly multivariate set of physical/chemical conditions around each individual that are themselves affected by the presence of that individual. We know that individuals vary, that a species may exist in local aggregations that differ from one another, anatomically and physiologically, and that these groups may become modified in time. All living things may be assumed to be more or less tenuously related to other living things by virtue of descent from some early common progenitor as well as by their interaction in ecosystems. Hence no system is the same once it has been subjected to sampling, isolation or any of the manipulations we must undertake in order to make the study feasible. Hence we are working with a few damaged pieces of a recently begun jigsaw puzzle. This is emphasised not to discourage the reader, but to encourage him to regard all our more revered theories, no matter how recent or how old, as fallible rather than sacrosanct. The basis of scientific endeavour is the painful process of accepting change, rejecting concepts that do not survive rigorous testings—but few of us enjoy seeing established or popular concepts challenged.

Our first task may then be to attempt to describe the bases of the observable variation by good regional studies, and selected long term studies of the changes in relative abundance of properly identified key species, as well as of production and other ecological parameters. If possible, such work should not be carried on in isolation without comparable coverage of all other aspects of limnology. Such a task might well be judged to lie in the province of the pure or applied limnological laboratory where such useful pursuits could be equated to the teaching efforts of the academic lacking the resources for year-round, on-site investigations in depth. The biocensus programme of the Systematics and Ecology group at the Marine Biological Laboratory, Wood's Hole, has produced a wealth of background data and should generate hosts of projects for ecologists and physiologists alike, but such endeavours are unpopular and seldom funded, and even this promising effort has now been terminated. In the whole of Canada there is no 'pure science', limnological laboratory of the type found in the classical limnological centres, despite the wealth of lakes and the number of fishery biologists, though the Freshwater Institute, Winnipeg, a Federal Government laboratory on a University Campus, is a good approximation.

Clearly, there should be a much greater emphasis on experimental studies, both in the field and in the laboratory, but these must take into account the multivariate nature of the system and the importance of rates of change. If yardsticks such as Total Dissolved Solids seem to be useful, they should be analysed more closely in order to refine correlations between them and factors of importance such as production. Closer experience with experimental procedures might help to focus the inadequacies of sampling programmes and the tools employed therein. The wasteful gathering of samples that cannot even be used to establish sound descriptive baseline data, still persists in survey programmes that appear to be 'busy work' meant to pad annual reports that justify wasting even more money in subsequent years. Huge resources are being mobilised in benthic surveys at great cost to the public, but little is achieved by them because too much is collected with too little thought as to the objectives or to the ability to analyse the samples adequately. Quantity of output cannot substitute for quality, and ingenuity may often replace dollars. Just because studies of the systematics and natural history of animals may not lead to a profound ecological theory it does not follow that such studies are complete (as some students naïvely believe) or redundant. We know of no better introduction to a sound study of aquatic systems than to begin with a study of the identity, distribution, and habits of a poorly known group, so long as the investigator retains a wider horizon than his immediate study area.

So far we have invested little talent or time in studies of the benthos of lakes, so we cannot be surprised at our modest achievements. This is one field that will provide ample opportunity for the curious for many years to come.

BIBLIOGRAPHY

ADAMSTONE, F.B. 1924. Distribution and economic importance of bottom fauna of Lake Nipigon: with an appendix on the bottom fauna of Lake Ontario. *Univ. Toronto Stud. Biol., Publ. Ont. Fish. Res. Lab.* **24**: 33–100.

ADAMSTONE, F.B., and HARKNESS, W.J.K. 1923. The bottom fauna of Lake Nipigon. *Univ. Toronto Stud. Biol., Publ. Ont. Fish. Res. Lab.* **15**: 121–170.

AHREN, T., and GRIMÅS, U. 1965. The composition of the bottom fauna in two basins of Lake Mälaren. *Rep. Inst. Freshwat. Res. Drottningholm.* **46**: 49–57.

ALLAN, I.R.H. 1952. A hand operated quantitative grab for sampling river beds. *J. Anim. Ecol.* **21**: 159–160.

ALLEN, K.R. 1951. The Horokiwi Stream. *Fish. Bull. N.Z. Mar. Dept.* **10**: 1–231.

ALLEY, W.P., and ANDERSON, R.F. 1969. Small-scale patterns of spatial distribution of the Lake Michigan macrobenthos. *Proc. 11th Conf., Great Lakes Res.* 1–10.

ALM, G. 1922. Bottenfauna och fiskens biologi i Yxtasjön samt jämförande studier över bottenfauna och fiskavkastning i vara sjöar. *Medd. Landbruksstyr.* **236**: 1–186.

ALSTERBERG, G. 1922. Die respiratorischen Mechanismen der Tubificiden. *Lunds Univ. Arsskr. N.F. Avd.* **18**: 1–175.

ALSTERBERG, G. 1924. Die Sinnesphysiologie der Tubificiden. *Lunds Univ. Arsskr. N.F. Avd.* **20**: 1–77.

ALSTERBERG, G. 1930. Die thermischen und chemischen Ausgleiche in den Seen zwischen Boden- und Wasserkontakt sowie ihre biologische Bedeutung. *Int. Revue ges. Hydrobiol. Hydrogr.* **24**: 290–327.

ANDERSON, R. O. 1959. A modified technique for sorting bottom fauna samples. *Limnol. Oceanogr.* **4**: 223–225.

ANDERSON, R. O., and HOOPER, F.F. 1956. Seasonal abundance and production of littoral bottom fauna in a Southern Michigan lake. *Trans. Am. microsc. Soc.* **75**: 259–270.

AUERBACH, M. 1953. Ein quantitativer Bodengreifer. *Beitr. naturk. Forsch. Südwdtschl. Deutschl.* **12**: 17–23.

BAJKOV, A. 1930. Biological conditions of Manitoba lakes. *Contr. Can. Biol. Fish. N.S.* **5**: 165–204.

BALL, R.C. 1948. Relationship between available fish food, feeding habits of fish and total fish production in a Michigan lake. *Bull. Mich. agric. Coll. Exp. Stn.* **206**: 1–51.

BALL, R.C., and HAYNE, D.W. 1952. Effects of the removal of the fish population on the fish-food organisms of a lake. *Ecology.* **33**: 41–48.

BARDACH, J.E. 1955. Certain biological effects of thermocline shifts. *Hydrobiologia.* **7**: 309–324.

BARDACH, J.E., MORRILL, J., and GAMBONY, F. 1951. Preliminary report on the distribution of the bottom organisms in West Lake Okoboji, Iowa. *Proc. Iowa Acad. Sci.* **58**: 405–414.

BEATTY, L.D., and HOOPER, F.F. 1958. Benthic associations of Sugar Loaf Lake. *Pap. Mich. Acad.* **43**: 89–106.

BEETON, A.M. 1960. The vertical migration of *Mysis relicta* in lakes Huron and Michigan. *J. Fish. Res. Bd Canada.* **17**: 517–539.

BEKMAN, M.Y. 1954. Biologiya *Gammarus lacustris* Sars pribaikal'skikh. *Trudy Baikal limnol. Stn, Acad. Sci. USSR.* **14**: 263–311. (The biology of *Gammarus lacustris* Sars in water bodies of the Baikal region, cited in Winberg, 1968.)

BEKMAN, M.Y. 1959. Nekotorye zakonomernosti raspredelniya i produtsirovania massovyh vidov zoobenthosa v Malom More. *Trudy Baikal limnol. Stn, Acad. USSR* **17**: 342–381. (Some regularities in the distribution and production of dominant zoobenthic species in the Baikal Malove More, cited in Winberg, 1968.)

BEKMAN, M.Y. 1962. Ekologiya i produktsiya *Micruropus possolskii* Sow i *Gmelinoides fasciatus* Stelb. *Trudy Baikal limnol. Stn, Acad Sci. USSR.* **2**: 141–155. (Ecology and production of *Micruropus possolskii* Sow and *Gmelinoides fasciatus* Stelb, cited in Winberg, 1968.)

BERG, K. 1938. Studies on the bottom animals of Esrom Lake. *K. danske Vidensk. Selsk. Naturv. Math. Afd.* **8**: 1–255.

BERG, K. 1953. The problem of respiratory acclimatization. *Hydrobiologia.* **5**: 331–350.

BERG, K., and JONASSON, P.M. 1965. Oxygen consumption of profundal lake animals at low oxygen content of the water. *Hydrobiologia.* **26**: 131–143.

BERG, K., JONASSON, P.M., and OCKELMANN, K.W. 1962. The respiration of some animals from the profundal zone of a lake. *Hydrobiologia.* **19**: 1–39.

BERG, K., and OCKELMANN, K.W. 1959. The respiration of freshwater snails. *J. exp. Biol.* **36**: 690–708.

BERG, K., and PETERSEN, I.B.C. 1956. Studies on the humic acid Lake Gribsø. *Folia limnol. scand.* **8**: 1–273.

BESCH, W., HOFMANN, W., and ELLENBERGER, W. 1967. Das Makrobenthos auf Polyäthylensubstraten in Fliessengewässern. *Annls. Limnol.* **3**: 331–367.

BOLTT, R.E. 1969. The benthos of some South African lakes. II. The epifauna and infauna of the benthos of Lake Sibayi. *Trans. R. Soc. S. Afr.* **38**: 249–269.

BONOMI, G. 1967. L'evoluzione recente del Lago Maggiore rivelata dalle conspicue modoficazioni del macrobenton profundo. *Mem. Ist. Ital. Idrobiol.* **21**: 197–212.

BONOMI, G. 1969. The use of a new version of the Tonolli mud-burrower for sampling low density benthonic populations. *Verh. Int. Verein. Limnol.* **17**: 511–515.

BORNER, L. 1917. *Die Bodenfauna des St. Mortizer-Sees.* Inaugural Dissertation. Basel. Univ. Stuttgart. 163 pp.

BORUTZKY, E.V. 1935. Vertikalnoe raspredlenie bentosa v tolsce ozernych otlozeniji znacenie etogo faktora. *Trudy Limnol. Stn. Kossino.* **20**: 129–147.

BORUTZKY, E.V. 1939*a*. Dinam ika biomassy *Chironomus plumosus* profundali. Belogo ozera. *Trudy Limnol. Stn. Kossino.* **22**: 156–195. (Dynamics of the biomass of *Chironomus plumosus* in the profundal water of Lake Beloye.)

BORUTZKY, E.V. 1939*b*. Dynamics of the total benthic biomass in the profundal water of Lake Beloye. *Trudy Limnol. Stn. Kossino.* **22**: 196–218.

BOYSEN-JENSEN, P. 1919. Valuation of the Limfjord. I. Studies on the fish pond in the Limfjord, 1909–1917. *Rep. Danish Biol. Stn, Copenhagen.* **26**: 1–44.

BRINKHURST, R. O. 1964. Observations on the biology of the lake dwelling Tubificidae. *Arch. Hydrobiol.* **60**: 385–418.

BRINKHURST, R.O. 1965. The biology of the Tubificidae with special reference to pollution in Biological problems in water pollution. *Proc. 3rd Seminar. Environmental Health Ser., Water Supply and Pollution Control Cincinnati, Ohio.* 57–66.

BRINKHURST, R.O. 1967. Sampling the benthos. *Great Lakes Inst. Univ. Toronto PR/32.*

BRINKHURST, R.O. 1969. A zoologist looks at eutrophication problems in relation to the ecology. *Water and Pollution Control*, Sept. 1969, 15–17, 40–41.

BRINKHURST, R.O. 1970. Distribution and abundance of tubificid (Oligochaeta) species in Toronto Harbour, Lake Ontario. *J. Fish. Res. Bd Canada.* **27**: 1961–1969.

BRINKHURST, R.O. 1972. The role of sludgeworms in eutrophication. *E.P.A. terminal report* 16010 *ECQ.*

BRINKHURST, R.O., and CHANT, D.A. 1971. *This Good, Good Earth: Our fight for survival.* Macmillan of Canada, Toronto. 174 pp.

BRINKHURST, R.O., CHUA, K.E., and BATOOSINGH, E. 1969. Modifications in sampling procedures as applied to studies on the bacteria and tubificid oligochaetes inhabiting aquatic sediments. *J. Fish. Res. Bd Canada.* **26**: 2581–2593.

BRINKHURST, R.O., CHUA, K.E., and KAUSHIK, N.K. 1972. Interspecific interactions and selective feeding by tubificid oligochaetes. *Limnol. Oceanogr.* **17**: 122–133.

BRINKHURST, R.O., and JAMIESON, B.G.M. 1971. *The Aquatic Oligochaeta of the World.* Oliver and Boyd, Edinburgh. 860 pp.

BRINKHURST, R.O., and KENNEDY, C.R. 1965. Studies on the biology of the Tubificidae (Annelida, Oligochaeta) in a polluted stream. *J. Animal. Ecol.* **34**: 429–443.

BRINKHURST, R.O., and WALSH, B. 1967. Rostherne Mere, England, a further instance of guanotrophy. *J. Fish. Res. Bd Canada.* **24**: 1299–1313.

BRITT, N.W. 1955*a*. Stratification in western Lake Erie in summer of 1953: Effect on the *Hexagenia* (Ephemeroptera) population. *Ecology.* **36**: 239–244.

BRITT, N.W. 1955*b*. *Hexagenia* (Ephemeroptera) population recovery in western Lake Erie following the 1953 catastrophe. *Ecology.* **36**: 529–522.

BROOKS, J.L. 1950. Speciation in ancient lakes. *Q. Rev. Biol.* **25**: 30–60.

BRUNDIN, L. 1942. Sur Limnologie jämtländischer Seen. *Mitt. Anst. Binnenfisch. Drottningholm, Stockholm.* **20**: 1–104.

BRUNDIN, L. 1949. Chironomiden und andere Bodentiere der Südschweden Urgebirsseen. *Rep. Inst. Freshwt. Res. Drottningholm.* **30**: 1–914.

BRUNDIN, L. 1951. The relation of O_2 microstratification of the mud surface to the ecology of the profundal bottom fauna. *Rep. Inst. Freshwat. Res. Drottningholm.* **32**: 32–44.

BRUNDIN, L. 1956. Die bodenfaunistischen Seetypen und ihre Anwendbarkheit auf die Südhalkugel. Zugleich ein Theorie der produktionbiologischen Bedeutung der glazialen Erosion. *Rep. Inst. Freshwat. Res. Drottningholm.* **37**: 186–235.

BRYCE, D. 1962. Chironomidae (Diptera) from fresh water sediments, with special reference to Malham Tarn (Yorks.). *Trans. Soc. Br. Ent.* **15**: 41–54.

BRYSON, R.A., and RAGOTZKIE, R.A. 1955. Rate of water replacement in a bay of Lake Mendota, Wisconsin. *Am. J. Sci.* **253**: 533–539.

BURKE, J.C. 1969. A sediment coring device of 21 cm diameter with sphincter core retainer. *Limnol. Oceanogr* **13**: 714–718.

BUT, V.I. 1938. Kolicestvennaja draga dla issledovanija bentosa zarosley v vodemach. *Dokl. Akad. Nauk SSSR.* **21**: 147–151.

CARR, J.F., and HILTUNEN, J. 1965. Changes in the bottom fauna of western Lake Erie from 1930–1961. *Limnol. Oceanogr.* **19**: 551–569.

CASSIE, R.M. and MICHAEL, A.D. 1968. Fauna and sediments of an intertidal mud flat: a multivariate analysis. *J. Exp. Mar. Biol. Ecol.* **2**: 1–27.

CATELL, R.B. 1965*a*. Factor analysis: an introduction to essentials I. The purpose and underlying models. *Biometrics.* **21**: 190–215.

CATELL, R.B. 1965*b*. Factor analysis: an introduction to essentials II. The role of factor analysis in research. *Biometrics.* **21**: 405–435.

CHUA, K.E. and BRINKHURST, R.O. 1973. Evidence of interspecific interactions in the respiration of Tubificid Oligochaetes. *J. Fish. Res. Bd. Canada.* **30**: 617–622.

COFFEE, C.E. 1968. A new technique in sand coring. *Under Sea Technology.* **35**: 1–37.

COLBORN, L.G. 1966. The limnology and cutthroat trout fishery of Trappers Lake, Colorado. *Spec. Rep. Dept. Game, Fish, Parks, State of Colorado*. 26 pp.

COLE, L.C. 1949. The measurement of interspecific association. *Ecology*. **30**: 411–424.

COOK, D.G. 1971. The Tubificidaes (Annelida, Oligochaeta) of Cape Cod Bay. II. Ecology and systematics, with the description of *Phallodrilus parviatriatus* nov. sp. *Biol. Bull. mar. biol. Lab. Wood's Hole*. **141**: 203–221.

COOPER, G.P. 1939. A biological survey of the thirty-one lakes and ponds of the Upper Saco River and Sebago Lake drainage systems in Maine. *Maine Dept. Inland Fish. Game, Fish. Surv. Rep.* **2**: 1–147.

COOPER, G.P. 1940. A biological survey of Rangeley Lakes, with special reference to the trout and salmon. *Maine Dept. Inland Fish. Game, Fish. Surv. Rep.* **3**: 1–182.

COOPER, G.P. 1941. A biological survey of lakes and ponds of the Androscoggin and Kennebec River drainage systems in Maine. *Maine Dept. Inland Fish. Game, Fish. Surv. Rep.* **4**: 1–238.

COOPER, G.P. 1942. A biological survey of lakes and ponds of the central coastal area of Maine. *Maine Dept. Inland Fish. Game, Fish. Surv. Rep.* **5**: 1–185.

COOPER, G.P., and FULLER, J.L. 1945. A biological survey of Moosehead Lake and Haymock Lake Maine. *Main Dept. Inland Fish. Game, Fish. Surv. Rep.* **6**: 1–160.

COOPER, W.E. 1965. Dynamics and productivity of a natural population of a fresh-water amphipod *Hyalella azteca*. *Ecol. Monogr.* **35**: 377–394.

CORBET, P.S. 1964. Temporal patterns of emergence in aquatic insects. *Can. Ent.* **96**: 264–279.

CRAIB, J.S. 1965. A sampler for taking short undisturbed marine cores. *J. Conseil*. **30**: 34–39.

CRONK, M.W. 1932. The bottom fauna of Shakespeare Island Lake, Ontario. *Univ. Toronto Stud. Biol., Publ. Ont. Fish. Res. Lab.* **43**: 30–65.

DARNELL, R.M. 1968. Animal nutrition in relation to secondary production. *Am Zool.* **8**: 83–93.

DAVIS, G.E., and WARREN, C.E. 1968. Estimation of food consumption rates. In *Methods for Assessment of Fish Production in Fresh Waters*. (Ed. W.E. Ricker). IBP Handbook No. 3. Blackwell Scientific Publ., Oxford and Edinburgh. Pp. 204–225.

DEACON, G.E.R. 1962. *Oceans*. P. Hamlyn, London. 297 pp.

DECKSBACH, N.K. 1929. Uber verschiedene Typenfolge der Seen. *Arch. Hydrobiol.* **20**: 65–80.

DEEVEY, E.S. 1940. Limnological studies in Connecticut. V. A contribution to regional limnology. *Am. J. Sci.* **238**: 717–741.

DEEVEY, E.S. 1941. Limnological studies in Connecticut. VI. The quantity and composition of the bottom fauna of thirty-six Connecticut and New York lakes. *Ecol. Monogr.* **11**: 413–455.

DELLA CROCE, N. 1955. The conditions of the sedimentation and their relationship with Oligochaeta populations of Lake Maggiore. *Mem. Ist. Ital. Idrobiol. Suppl.* **8**: 39–62.

DENDY, J.S. 1944. The fate of animals in stream drift when carried into lakes. *Ecol. Monogr.* **14**: 333–357.

DIXON, W.J., and MASSEY, Jr., F.J. 1957. *Introduction to Statistical Analysis*. 2nd ed. McGraw-Hill, New York. 487 pp.

DRZYCIMSKI, I. 1967. A tube sampler for collecting bottom samples. *Ekol. Pol. Ser. B.* **13**: 273–275.

DUGDALE, R.C. 1955. Studies on the ecology of the benthic Diptera of Lake Mendota. *Ph.D. Thesis*, Wisconsin Univ.

DUNN, D.R. 1961. The bottom fauna of Llyn Tegid (Lake Bala) Merionethshire. *J. Anim. Ecol.* **30**: 267–281.

DUSSART, B.H. 1963. Les grands lacs d'Europe Occidentale. *Annls. Biol.* **11**: 500–572.

DUSSART, B.H. 1966. *Limnologie. L'étude des Eaux Continentales. Géobiologie-Ecologie Aménagement*. Gauthier Villars, Paris. 676 pp.

EDMONDSON, W.T. 1959. *Fresh-water Biology*. Ward and Whipple (2nd ed.). John Wiley and Sons, New York–London. 1248 pp.

EDMONDSON, W.T., and WINBERG, G.G. 1971. *A Manual of Methods for the Assessment of Secondary Productivity in Fresh Waters*. IBP Handbook No. 17. Blackwell Scientific Publ., Oxford and Edinburgh.

EDWARDS, R.W. 1958. The relation of oxygen consumption to body size and to temperature in the larvae of *Chironomus riparius* Meigen. *J. exp. Biol.* **35**: 383–395.

EDWARDS, R.W., and LEARNER, M.A. 1960. Some factors affecting the oxygen consumption of *Asellus*. *J. exp. Biol.* **37**: 706–718.

EFFORD, I.E. 1960. A method of studying the vertical distribution of the bottom fauna in shallow waters. *Hydrobiologia*. **16**: 288–292.

EGGLETON, F.E. 1931. A limnological study of the profundal bottom fauna of certain freshwater lakes. *Ecol. Monogr.* **1**: 233–331.

EGGLETON, F.E. 1935. A comparative study of the benthic fauna of four northern Michigan lakes. *Pap. Mich. Acad.* **20**: 609–644.

EGGLETON, F.E. 1937. Productivity of the benthic zone in Lake Michigan. *Pap. Mich. Acad.* **22**: 593–611.

EGGLETON, F.E. 1939. The role of the bottom fauna in the productivity of lakes. Problems of lake biology. *Publ. Am. Ass. Adv. Sci.* **10**: 123–131.

EGGLETON, F.E. 1952. Dynamics of interdepression benthic communities. *Trans. Am. microsc. Soc.* **71**: 189–228.

EKMAN, S. 1915. Die Bodenfauna des Vättern, qualitativ und quantitativ untersucht. *Int. Revue ges. Hydrobiol. Hydrogr.* **7**: 146–425.

EKMAN, S. 1917. Allgemeine Bemerkungen über die Tiefenfauna der Binnenseen. *Int. Revue ges. Hydrobiol. Hydrogr.* **8**: 113–124.

EKMAN, S. 1920. Studien über die marinen Relikte der nordeuropäischen Binnengewässer. VI. Die morphologischen Folgen des Reliktwerdens. *Int. Revue ges. Hydrobiol. Hydrogr.* **8**: 477–528.

EKMAN, S. 1959. En översikt av de maringlaciala relikternas historia med ledning av. S.G. Segerstrala senaste arbete. *Ymer*. Stockholm. **1**: 68–74.

ELGMORK, K. 1962. A bottom sampler for soft mud. *Hydrobiologia*. **20**: 167–172.

ELLIOTT, J.M. 1971. Some methods for the statistical analysis of samples of benthic invertebrates. *Sci. Publ. Freshwat. Biol. Ass.* **25**: 1–144.

ELSTER, H.J. 1958. Lake classification, production and consumption. *Verh. Int. Verein. Limnol.* **13**: 101–120.

ELSTER, H.J. 1962. Seetypen, Fliessgewässertypen und Saprobiensystem. *Int. Revue ges. Hydrobiol. Hydrogr.* **47**: 211–218.

ENEQUIST, P. 1941. Ein neuer Zerteiler-Bodenstecher für Sedimentanalyse zu ökologischen Zwecken. *Zool. Bidr. Upps.* **20**: 461–464.

ENGELMANN, M.D. 1966. Energetics, terrestrial field studies and animal productivity, pp. 73–115. In *Adv. Ecol. Res.*, Ed. J.B. Cragg, Academic Press, London–New York.

ENGELMANN, M.D. 1968. The role of soil arthropods in community energetics. *Am. Zool.* **8**: 61–69.

ERIKSEN, C.H. 1963. Respiratory regulation in *Ephemera simulans* Walker and *Hexagenia limbata* (Serville) (Ephemeroptera). *J. exp. Biol.* **40**: 455–467.

FAGER, E.W. 1957. Determination and analysis of recurrent groups. *Ecology*. **33**: 586–596.

FAGER, E.W. 1964. Marine sediments: effects of a tube dwelling polychaete. *Science*. **143**: 356–359.

FAGER, E.W., and MCGOWAN, J.A. 1963. Zooplankton species groups in the North Pacific. *Science*. **140** (**3566**): 453–460.

FAGER, E.W., and LONGHURST, A.R. 1965. Recurrent groups analysis of species assemblages of demersal fish in the Gulf of Guinea. *J. Fish. Res. Bd. Canada*. **25** (7): 1405–1421.

FAGER, E.W., FLECHSIG, A.O., FORD, R.F., CLUTTER, R.I., and GHELARDI, R.J. 1966. Equipment for use in ecological studies using scuba. *Limnol. Oceanogr.* **11**: 503–509.

FAST, A.W. 1968. Artificial destratification of El Capitan Reservoir by aeration. I. Effects on chemical and physical parameters. *Dept. Fish. Game. Resources Agency of California. Fish. Bull.* **141**: 1–97.

FERENCZ, M. 1968. Vorstudium über die Vertikale Verteilung des Zoobenthos der Theiss. *Tiscia (Szeged).* **4**: 53–58.

FERLING, E. 1957. Die Wirkungen des erhöhten hydrostatischen Druckes auf Wachstum und Differenzierung submerser Blütenpflanzen. *Planta.* **49**: 235–270.

FINNISH, I.B.P. GROUP. 1969. Quantitative sampling equipment for the littoral benthos. *Int. Revue ges. Hydrobiol. Hydrogr.* **54**: 185–193.

FLANNAGAN, J.F. 1970. Efficiencies of various grabs and corers in sampling freshwater benthos. *J. Fish. Res. Bd Canada.* **27**: 1691–1700.

FORBES, S.A. 1887. The lake as a microcosm. *Illinois nat. Hist. Surv. Bull.* **15**: 537–550.

FORD, J.B., and HALL, R.E. 1958. A grab for quantitative sampling in stream muds. *Hydrobiologia.* **11**: 198–204.

FRANKLIN, W.R., and ANDERSON, D.V. 1961. A bottom sediment sampler. *Limnol. Oceanogr.* **6**: 233–234

GALLARDO, V.A. 1965. Observations on the biting profiles of three 0.1 m^2 bottom samplers. *Ophelia.* **2**: 319–322.

GERKING, S.D. 1957. A method of sampling the littoral macrofauna and its application. *Ecology.* **38**: 219–266.

GERKING, S.D. 1962. Production and food utilisation in a population of Bluegill Sunfish. *Ecol. Monogr.* **32**: 31–78.

GERKING, S.D. (ed.). 1966. *The Biological Basis of Freshwater Fish Production.* Blackwell Scientific Publs, Oxford–Edinburgh. 495 pp.

GESSNER, F. 1952. Der Druck in seiner Bedeutung für das Wachstum submerser Wasserpflanzen. *Planta.* **40**: 391–397.

GILLESPIE, D.M., and BROWN, C.J.D. 1966. A quantitative sampler for macroinvertebrates associated with aquatic macrophytes. *Limnol. Oceanogr.* **11**: 404–406.

GITAY, A. 1968. Preliminary data on the ecology of level-bottom fauna of Lake Tiberia. *Israel J. Ecol.* **17**: 81–96.

GLEASON, G.R., and OHLMACHER, F.J. 1965. A core sampler for in situ freezing of benthic sediments. *Ocean Sci. Ocean Eng.* **2**: 737–741.

GOLDSPINK, C.R., and SCOTT, D.B.C. 1971. Vertical migration of *Chaoborus flavicans* in a Scottish Loch. *Freshwat. Biol.* **1**: 411–421.

GOLLEY, F.B. 1968. Secondary productivity in terrestrial communities. *Am. Zool.* **8**: 53–59.

GORHAM, E. 1958. Observations on the formation and breakdown of the oxidized microzone at the mud surface in lakes. *Limnol. Oceanogr.* **3**: 291–298.

GOULD, H.R., and BUDDINGER, T.F. 1958. Control of sedimentation and bottom configuration by convection currents, Lake Washington, Washington. *J. mar. Res.* **17**: 183–197.

GOULDEN, C.E. 1964. The history of the Cladoceran fauna of Esthwaite Water (England) and its limnological significance. *Arch. Hydrobiol.* **60**: 1–52.

GREZE, B.S. 1951. Produktsiya *Pontoporeia affiinis* i metod ee opredelenyia. *Trudy vses. Gidrobiol. Obshch.* **3**: 33–43. (The production of *Pontoporeia affiinis* and methods of determining it, cited in Winberg, 1968.)

GRIMÅS, U. 1963. Reflections on the availability and utilization degree of bottom animals as fish food. *Zool. Bidr. Upps.* **35**: 497–503.

GRIMÅS, U. 1967. Bottenfaunan i Mälaren. *Zool. Revy.* **1**: 19–23. (In Swedish.)

GRIMÅS, U. 1969. The bottom fauna of Lake Vättern, central Sweden, and some effects of eutrophication. *Rep. Inst. Freshwat. Res. Drottningholm.* **49**: 49–62.

HAMILTON, A. L. 1965. An analysis of a freshwater benthic community with special reference to the Chironomidae. *Ph.D. Thesis*, Univ. British Columbia. 94 pp.

HAMILTON, A.L. 1969. A method of separating invertebrates from sediments using long wave ultra violet light and fluorescent dyes. *J. Fish. Res. Bd Canada.* **26**: 1667–1672.

HAMILTON, A. L., BURTON, W., and FLANNAGAN, J. F. 1970. A multiple corer for sampling profundal benthos. *J. Fish. Res. Bd Canada.* **27**: 1867–1869.

HANSEN, K. 1962. The dystrophic lake type. *Hydrobiologia.* **19**: 183–191.

HARGRAVE, B.T. 1969. Epibenthic algal production and community respiration in the sediments of Marion Lake. *J. Fish. Res. Bd Canada.* **26**: 2003–2026.

HARMSWORTH, R.V. 1968. The developmental history of Blelham Tarn (England) as shown by animal microfossils, with special reference to the Cladocera. *Ecol. Monogr.* **38**: 223–241.

HAYES, F.R. 1957. On the variation in bottom fauna and fish yield in relation to trophic level lake dimensions. *J. Fish. Res. Bd Canada.* **14**: 1–32.

HAYNE, D.W., and BALL, R.C. 1956. Benthic productivity as influenced by fish predation. *Limnol. Oceanogr.* **1**: 162–175.

HEALD, E.J., and ODUM, W.E. 1970. The contribution of mangrove swamps to Florida fisheries. *Proc. Gulf and Carib. Fish. Inst.* **22**: 130–135.

HENSON, E.B. 1954. The profundal bottom fauna of Cayuga Lake. *Ph.D. Thesis*, Cornell Univ. 108 pp.

HESTER, F.E., and DENDY, J.S. 1962. A multiple plate sampler for aquatic macroinvertebrates. *Trans. Am. Fish. Soc.* **91**: 420–421.

HILSENHOFF, W.L., and NARF, R.P. 1968. Ecology of Chironomidae, Chaoboridae, and other benthos in fourteen Wisconsin lakes. *Ann. ent. Soc. Am.* **61**: 1173–1181.

HOLME, N.A. 1964. Methods of sampling the benthos. *Adv. mar. Biol.* **2**: 171–260.

HOLME, N.A., and MCINTYRE, A.D. 1971. *Methods for the Study of Marine Benthos.* IBP Handbook No. 16. Blackwell Scientific Publ., Oxford and Edinburgh.

HOLMQUIST, C. 1959. Problems on marine-glacial relicts on account of investigations on genus *Mysis*. *Ph.D. Thesis*, Lund Univ. 270 pp.

HRUSKA, V. 1961. An attempt at a direct investigation of the influence of the carp stock on the bottom fauna of two ponds. *Verh. Int. Verein. Limnol.* **14**: 732–736.

HUGHES, R.N., and THOMAS, M.L.H., 1971. The classification and ordination of shallow water benthic samples from P.E.I., Canada. *J. Exp. Mar. Biol. Ecol.* **7**: 1–39.

HUMPHRIES, C.F. 1936. An investigation of the profundal and sublittoral fauna of Windermere. *J. Anim. Ecol.* **5**: 29–52.

HUNT, O.D.A. 1926. A new method for quantitative sampling of the sea bottom. *J. mar. Biol. Ass. (U.K.).* **14**: 529–534.

HURLBERT, S.H. 1969. A coefficient of interspecific assocation. *Ecology.* **51** (**1**): 1–9.

HUTCHINSON, G.E. 1957. *A Treatise on Limnology. Vol.* 1. John Wiley and Sons, New York. 1015 pp.

HYNES, H.B.N. 1954. The ecology of *Gammarus duebeni* Lilljeborg and its occurrence in freshwater in Western Britain. *J. Anim. Ecol.* **23**: 38–84.

HYNES, H.B.N. 1959. On the occurrence of *Gammarus duebeni* Lilljeborg in freshwater and of *Asellus meridianus* Racovitza in Western France. *Hydrobiologia.* **13**: 152–155.

HYNES, H.B.N. 1960. *The Biology of Polluted Waters.* Liverpool Univ. Press. 202 pp.

HYNES, H.B.N. 1970. *The Ecology of Running Waters.* Univ. Toronto Press. 555 pp.

HYNES, H.B.N., and WILLIAMS, W.D. 1965. Experiments on competition between two *Asellus* species (Isopoda Crustacea). *Hydrobiologia.* **26**: 203–210.

INLAND FISHERIES BRANCH. 1970. Effects of artificial destratification on distribution of bottom organisms in El Capitan Reservoir. *Dept. Fish. Game, Resources Agency of California. Bull. Fish.* **148**: 1–30.

IVLEV, V.S. 1934. Eine Mikromethode zu Bestimmung des Kaloreingehalts von Nahrstoffen. *Biochem. Z.* **275**: 49–55.

IVLEV, V.S. 1945. The biological productivity of waters. *Vspekhi Sovremennoi Biologii.* **19**: 98–120. (Transl. W. E. Ricker in *J. Fish. Res. Bd Canada.* **23**: 1727–1759.)

JARNEFELT, H. 1925. Zur Limnologie einiger Gewässer Finnlands. 1. *Ann. Soc. zool-bot. fenn. Vanamo.* **2**: 185–356.

JARNEFELT, H. 1929. Ein kurzer Uberblick über die Limnologie Finnlands. *Verh. Int. Verein. Limnol.* **4**: 1–401.

JARNEFELT, H. 1953. Die Seetypen in Bodenfaunistischer Hinsicht. *Ann. Soc. zool-bot. fenn Vanamo.* **15**: 1–38.

JOHNSEN, P., MATHIESEN, H., and RØEN, U. 1962. Sorø-søerne, Lyngby sø, og Bagvaerd dø Limnologische studier over fem kulturepavirkende sjaellandske søer. *Sewage Comm. Inst. Danish Civ. Engineers.* **14**: 1–135.

JOHNSON, M.G. 1970. Production, energy flow and structure in benthic communities of Lake Ontario. *Ph.D. Thesis*, Univ. Toronto. 182 pp.

JOHNSON, M.G., and BRINKHURST, R.O. 1971*a*. Associations and species diversity in benthic macroinvertebrates of Bay of Quinte and Lake Ontario. *J. Fish. Res. Bd Canada.* **28**: 1683–1697.

JOHNSON, M.G., and BRINKHURST, R.O. 1971*b*. Production of benthic macroinvertebrates of Bay of Quinte and Lake Ontario. *J. Fish. Res. Bd Canada.* **28**: 1699–1714.

JOHNSON, M.G., and BRINKHURST, R.O. 1971*c*. Benthic community metabolism in Bay of Quinte and Lake Ontario. *J. Fish Res. Bd Canada.* **28**: 1715–1725.

JONASSON, P.M. 1954. The relationship between primary production and production of profundal bottom invertebrates in a Danish eutrophic lake. *Verh. Int. Verein. Limnol.* **15**: 471–479.

JONASSON, P.M. 1955. The efficiency of sieving techniques for sampling freshwater bottom fauna. *Oikos.* **6**: 183–207.

JONASSON, P.M. 1961. Population dynamics in *Chironomus anthracinus* Zett. in the profundal zone of Lake Esromsö. *Verh. Int. Verein. Limnol.* **14**: 196–203.

JONASSON, P.M. 1963. The growth of *Plumatella repens* and *P. fungosa* (Bryozoa Ectoprocta) in relation to external factors in Danish eutrophic lakes. *Oikos.* **14**: 121–137.

JONASSON, P.M. 1964. The relationship between primary production of profundal bottom invertebrates in a Danish eutrophic lake. *Verh. Int. Verein. Limnol.* **15**: 471–479.

JONASSON, P.M. 1965. Factors determining population size of *Chironomus* in Lake Esrom. *Mitt. Int. Verein. Limnol.* **13**: 139–162.

JONASSON, P.M., and KRISTIANSEN, J. 1967. Primary and secondary production in Lake Esrom. Growth of *Chironomus anthracinus* in relation to seasonal cycles of phytoplankton and dissolved oxygen. *Int. Revue ges. Hydrobiol. Hydrogr.* **52**: 163–217.

JUDAY, C. 1921. Quantitative studies of the bottom fauna in the deeper waters of Lake Mendota. *Trans. Wis. Acad. Sci. Arts Lett.* **20**: 461–493.

JUDAY, C. 1924. Summary of quantitative investigations on Green Lake, Wisconsin. *Int. Revue ges. Hydrobiol. Hydrogr.* **12**: 2–12.

JUDAY, C. 1942. The summer standing crop of plants and animals in four Wisconsin lakes. *Trans. Wis. Acad. Sci. Arts Lett.* **34**: 103–135.

Juget, J. 1967. La faune benthique du Léman: modalites et determinisme écologique du peuplement. *Thesis*, Univ. de Lyon. 360 pp.

Kajak, Z. 1963*a*. The effect of experimentally induced variations in the abundance of *Tendipes plumosus* L. larvae on intraspecific and interspecific relations. *Ekol. Pol. Ser. A.* **11**: 355–367.

Kajak, Z. 1963*b*. Analysis of quantitative benthic methods. *Ekol. Pol. Ser. A.* **11**: 1–56.

Kajak, Z. 1964. Experimental investigations of benthos abundance on the bottom of Lake Sniardwy. *Ekol. Pol. Ser. A.* **12**: 11–31.

Kajak, Z. 1967. Remarks on the methods of investigating benthos production. *Ekol. Pol. Ser. B.* **13**: 173–195.

Kajak, Z. 1968. Remarks on the present state and requirements of research on secondary production in freshwater ecosystems. *Ekol. Pol. Ser. B.* **14**: 99–117.

Kajak, Z. 1972. *Analysis of the Influence of Fish on Benthos by the Method of Enclosures.* Proc. IBP-UNESCO Sym. Prod. Prob. Freshwaters. Eds. Kajak and Hillbricht. Ilkowska. Pp. 781–793.

Kajak, Z., Dusoge, K., and Prejs, A. 1968. Application of the floating technique to assessment of absolute numbers of benthos. *Ekol. Pol. Ser. A.* **16**: 607–620.

Kajak, Z., Kacprzak, K., and Polkowski, R. 1965. Chwytacz rurowy do pobierania prób dna. *Ekol. Pol. Ser. B.* **11**: 159–165.

Kajak, Z., and Pieczynski, E. 1966. The influence of invertebrate predators on the abundance of benthic organisms (chiefly Chironomidae). *Ekol. Pol. Ser. A.* **12**: 175–179.

Kajak, Z., and Wisniewski, R. J. 1966. An attempt at estimating the intensity of consumption of Tubificidae by predators. *Ekol. Pol. Ser. B.* **12**: 181–184.

Keast, A. 1965. Resource subdivision amongst cohabiting fish species in a bay, Lake Opinicon, Ont. *Publ.* 13. *Great Lakes Res. Div., Univ. of Michigan.* Pp. 106–132.

Kennedy, C. R. 1969. Tubificid oligochaetes as food of dace *Leuciscus leuciscus* (L.). *J. Fish. Biol.* **1**: 11–15.

Knight, W., and Tyler, A.V. 1973. A method for compression of species association data by using habitat preferences, including an analysis of fish assemblages on the southwest Scotian Shelf. *Fish Res. Bd Can. Tech. Rep.* **402**: 1–15.

Knudsen, M. 1927. A bottom sampler for hard bottom. *Meddr Kommn Havunders. Kbh. Ser. Fisk.* **8**: 1–4.

Kolkwitz, R., and Marsson, M. 1908. Okologie des pflanzlichen Saprobien. *Ber. dt. bot. Ges.* **26**a: 505–519.

Kolkwitz, R., and Marsson, M. 1909. Okologie des tierischen Saprobien. Beiträge zur Lehre von des biologischen Gewässerbeurteilung. *Int. Revue ges. Hydrobiol. Hydrogr.* **2**: 126–152.

Lang, K. 1931. Faunistische-Okologische Untersuchungen in einigen seichten oligotrophen bzw. dystrophen Seen in Sudschweden mit besonderer Derücksichtigung der Profundalfauna. *Lunds Univ. Arsskrift N.F. Avd.* **27**: 1–175.

Larkin, P.A. 1964. Canadian lakes. *Verh. Int. Verein. Limnol.* **15**: 76–90.

Lasenby, D.C. 1971. The ecology of *Mysis relicta* in an arctic and temperate lake. *Ph.D. Thesis*, Univ. Toronto. 119 pp.

Lastockin, D. 1931. Beiträge zur Seetypenlehre. *Arch. Hydrobiol.* **22**: 546–579.

Lauff, G.H., Cummins, K.W., Eriksen, H., and Parker, M. 1961. A method for sorting bottom fauna samples by elutriation. *Limnol. Oceanogr.* **6**: 462–466.

Lawley, D.N., and Maxwell, A.E. 1963. Factor analysis as a Statistical Method. Butterworths, London. 117 pp.

Leentvaar, P. 1967. Observations in guanotrophic environments. *Hydrobiologia.* **29**: 441–489.

Lellak, J. 1957. Der Einfluss der Fresstätigkeit des Fischbestandes auf die Bodenfauna der Fischteiche. *Z. Fisch.* **6**: 621–633.

LELLAK, J. 1965. The food supply as a factor regulating the population dynamics of bottom animals. *Mitt. Int. Verein. Limnol.* **13**: 128–138.

LELLAK, J. 1966. Influence of the removal of the fish population on the bottom animals of the five Elbe backwaters. *In* Hydrobiological Studies. (Ed. Hrbacek). *Academia*. Prague. 323–380.

LENZ, F. 1925. Chironomiden u. Seetypenlehre. *Nátúrwissenschaften*. **13**: 5–10.

LENZ, F. 1928*a*. Chironomiden aus Norweyischen Hochgebirgsseen. Zugleich ein Beitrag zur Seetypenfrage. *Nyt Mag. Naturvid.* **66**: 111–192.

LENZ, F. 1928*b*. Okologische Chironomidentypen. *Biol. Listy*. **14**: 413–422.

LENZ, F. 1931. Untersuchung über die Vertikalverteilung der Bodenfauna im Tiefensediment von Seen. Ein neuer Bodengreifer mit Zerteilungsvorrichtung. *Verh. Int. Verein. Limnol.* **5**: 232–261.

LENZ, F. 1933. *Das Seetypenproblem u. seine Bedeutung für die Limnologie*. IV. Hydrologische Konf. Balt. Staat. 1–13. Leningrad.

LENZ, F. 1951. Probleme der Chironomiden-Forschung. *Verh. Int. Verein. Limnol.* **11**: 230–246.

LENZ, F. 1954. Die Bodenfauna des Lago Maggiore und ihre Lebensbedingungen. *Mem. Ist. Ital. Idrobiol.* **8**: 273–322.

LIE, U., and KELLEY, J.C. 1970. Benthic infauna communities off the coast of Washington and in Puget Sound: identification and distribution of the communities. *J. Fish. Res. Bd. Canada*. **27** (**4**): 621–651.

LINDEMAN, R.L. 1942. The tropho-dynamic aspect of ecology. *Ecology*. **23**: 399–418.

LISITSIN, A.P., and UDINCEV, G.B. 1955. Novaja model dnocerpatela. *Trudy Vses. Gidrobiol. Obsnch.* **6**: 217–222.

LOFFLER, H. 1961. Vorschlag zu einem automatischen Schlammverfahren. *Int. Revue ges. Hydrobiol. Hydrogr.* **46**: 288–291.

LUNDBECK, J. 1926. Die Bodentierweld Norddeutscher Seen. *Arch Hydrobiol. Suppl.* **7**: 1–473.

LUNDBECK, J. 1936. Untersuchungen über die Bodenbesidlung der Alpenrandseen. *Arch. Hydrobiol. Suppl.* **10**: 208–358.

MACAN, T.T. 1958. Methods of sampling the bottom fauna in Stony Streams. *Mitt. Int. Verein. Limnol.* **8**: 1–21.

MACAN, T.T. 1963. *Freshwater Ecology*. Longmans, Green Co., London. 338 pp.

MACAN, T.T. 1966. The influence of predation on the fauna of a moorland fishpond. *Arch. Hydrobiol.* **61**: 432–452.

MACAN, T.T. 1970. *Biological Studies of the English Lakes*. American Elsevier Publishing Co., New York. 260 pp.

MACKERETH, F.J.H. 1965. Chemical investigation of lake sediments and their interpretation. *Proc. R. Soc. B.* **161**: 295–309.

MACKERETH, F.J.H. 1966. Some chemical observations on post-glacial lake sediments. *Phil. Trans. R. Soc. B.* (Lond.). **250**: 165–213.

MALUEG, K.W., and HASLER, A.D. 1966. Echo sounder studies on diel vertical movements of *Chaoborus* larvae in Wisconsin (U.S.A.) lakes. *Verh. Int. Verein. Limnol.* **16**: 1697–1708.

MANN, K.H. 1956. A study of the oxygen consumption of five species of leech. *J. exp. Biol.* **33**: 615–626.

MANN, K.H. 1964. The pattern of energy flow in the fish and invertebrate fauna of the river Thames. *Verh. Int. Verein. Limnol.* **15**: 485–495.

MANN, K.H. 1969. The dynamics of aquatic ecosystems. *Adv. Ecol. Res.*, Academic Press. **6**: 1–81.

MANN, K.H. 1972. Ecological energetics of the seaweed zone in a marine bay on the Atlantic coast of Canada. II. Productivity of the seaweeds. *Marine Biol.* **14**(**3**): 199–209.

MANN, K.H., and BREEN, P.A. 1972. The relation between lobster abundance, sea urchins, and kelp beds. *J. Fish Res. Bd Canada*. **29** (**5**): 603–605.

MARGALEF, R. 1969. Diversity and stability: A practical proposal and a model of interdependence in diversity and stability in ecological systems. *Brookhaven Symposium in Biol.* No. **22**: 25–37.

MARKOSYAN, A.K. 1948. Biologiya gammarusov ozera Sevan. *Trudy sevan Gidrobiol. Stn* **10**: 40–74. (The biology of Lake Sevan *Gammarus*, cited in Winberg, 1968.)

MARZOLF, G.R. 1965. Vertical migration of *Pontoporeia affinis* (Amphipoda) in Lake Michigan. Great Lakes Res. Div., Michigan Univ. Publ. **13**: 133–140.

MASON, W.T., and YEVICH, P.P. 1967. The use of phloxine B and Rose Bengal stains to facilitate sorting benthic samples. *Trans. Am. microsc. Soc.* **86**: 221–223.

MENDIS, A.S. 1956. A limnological comparison of four lakes in central Saskatchewan. *Rep. Dept. Nat. Res. Sask.* **2**: 1–23.

MIKULSKI, J., and GISINSKI, A. 1961. Bottom fauna of Wdzydze Lake (Polish with English Summary). *Roczn. Nauk. roln.* (*Warszawa*). **93 D**: 141–157.

MILBRINK, G. 1968. A microstratification sampler for mud and water. *Oikos.* **19**: 105–110.

MILBRINK, G. 1969. Microgradients at the mud-water interface. *Rep. Inst. Freshwat. Res. Drottningholm.* **49**: 129–148.

MILLER, R.B. 1937. A preliminary investigation of the bottom fauna of five Algonquin Park lakes. *M.Sc. Thesis*, Univ. Toronto.

MILLER, R.B. 1941. A contribution to the ecology of the Chironomidae of Costello Lake, Algonquin Park, Ontario. *Univ. Toronto Stud. Biol., Publ. Ont. Fish. Res. Lab.* **49**: 1–63.

MILLER, R.J., MANN, K.H. and SCARRATT, D.J. 1971. Production potential of a seaweed lobster community in eastern Canada. *J. Fish. Res. Bd. Canada.* **28**: 1733–1738.

MILLS, E.L. 1969. The community concept in marine zoology, with comments on continua and instability in some marine communities: A review. *J. Fish. Res. Bd. Canada.* **26**: 1415–1428.

MIYADI, D. 1932. Studies on the bottom fauna of Japanese lakes: V. Five lakes at the north foot in Mt. Hudi and Lake Asi. *Jap. J. Zool.* **4**: 81–125.

MIYADI, D. 1933. Studies on the bottom fauna of Japanese lakes: X. Regional characteristics and a system of Japanese lakes based on the bottom fauna. *Jap. J. Zool.* **4**: 417–437.

MONARD, A. 1919. La faune profonde du Lac Neuchâtel. *Thesis*, Univ. Neuchâtel.

MOON, H.P. 1935. Methods and apparatus suitable for an investigation of the littoral region of oligotrophic lakes. *Int. Revue ges. Hydrobiol. Hydrogr.* **32**: 319–333.

MOORE, G.M. 1939. A limnological investigation of the macroscopic benthic fauna of Douglas Lake, Michigan. *Ecol. Monogr.* **9**: 537–582.

MORDUKHAI-BOLTOVSKOI, F.D. 1958. Usoversenstvonnaja sistema trubcatoge dnocerpatela. *Byull. Inst. Biol. Vodokchr.* **1**: 47–49.

MORGAN, N.C., and WADDELL, A.B. 1961. Insect emergence from a small trout loch and its bearing on the food supply of fish. *Dept. Agric. Fish.* (*Scotland*) *Freshwat. Salmon Fish. Res.* **25**: 1–39.

MORTENSEN, T. 1925. An apparatus for catching the microfauna of the sea bottom. *Vidensk. Meddr. dansk. naturh. Foren. Kbh.* **80**: 445–451.

MORTIMER, C.H. 1942. The exchange of dissolved substances between mud and water in lakes. *J. Ecol.* **30**: 147–201.

MORTIMER, C.H. 1971. Chemical exchanges between sediments and water in the Great Lakes. Speculations on probable regulatory mechanisms. *Limnol. Oceanogr.* **16**: 387–404.

MOTHES, G. 1966. Beitrag zur Methodik der quantitativen Bearbeitung von makroskopischer Bodenfauna in Stehenden Gewässern. *Limnologica.* **4**: 343–350.

MOYLE, J.B. 1946. Some indices of lake productivity. *Trans. Am. Fish. Soc.* **76**: 322–334.

MUNDIE, J.H. 1956*a*. A bottom sampler for inclined rock surfaces in lakes. *J. Anim. Ecol.* **25**: 429–432.

MUNDIE, J.H. 1956*b*. Emergence traps for aquatic insects. *Mitt. Int. Verein. Limnol.* 7: 1–13.

MUNDIE, J.H. 1957. The ecology of Chironomidae in storage reservoirs. *Trans. R. ent. Soc. Lond.* **109**: 149–232.

MUNDIE, J.H. 1959. The diurnal activity of the larger invertebrates at the surface of Lac La Ronge, Saskatchewan. *Can. J. Zool.* **37**: 945–956.

MUUS, B.J. 1964. A new quantitative sampler for the meiobenthos. *Ophelia.* **1**: 209–216.

MCLEAN, J.H. 1962. Sublittoral ecology of kelp beds of the open coast area near Carmel, California. *Biol. Bull.* **122**: 95–114.

MCLEESE, D.W. 1956. Effects of temperature, salinity and oxygen on the survival of the American lobster. *J. Fish Res. Bd Canada.* **13**: 247–272.

NAUMANN, E. 1919. Nagra synpvnkter angaende planktons ökologi Medd. sarskild hänsyn till fytoplankton. *Svensk. bot. Tidskr.* **13**: 129–158.

NAUMANN, E. 1931. *Limnologische Terminologie.* Urban and Schwarzenberg, Berlin. 776 pp.

NAUMANN, E. 1932. Grundzuge der regionalen Limnologie. *Binnengewasser.* **11**: 1–176.

NÉAVE, F. 1932. A study of the Mayflies (Hexagenia) of Lake Winnipeg. *Contr. Can. Biol. Fish.* (*N.S.*). **7**: 177–201.

NEES, J., and DUGDALE, R.C. 1959. Computation of production for populations of aquatic midge larvae. *Ecology.* **40**: 425–430.

NEYMAN, J. 1934. On the two aspects of the representative method. *Jl. R. statist. Soc.* **97**: 558–625.

NILSSON, N.A. 1967. 'Interactive segregation between fish species' *in The Biological Basis of Freshwater Fish Production.* New York. 295–313.

NORTH, W.J. 1965. Urchin predation. In *Kelp Habitat Improvement Project*, annual report 1964–65. Calif. Inst. Technol., pp. 57–61.

NORTHCOTE, T.G. 1952. An analysis of variation in quantitative sampling of the bottom fauna of lakes. *M.Sc. Thesis* (*Unpublished*), Univ. British Columbia.

NORTHCOTE, T.G., and LARKIN, P.A. 1956. Indices of productivity in British Columbia lakes. *J. Fish. Res. Bd Canada.* **13**: 515–540.

NOVOTNA, M., and KORINEK, V. 1966. Effect of the fishstock on the quantity and species composition of the plankton of two backwaters. *In Hydrobiological Studies*, Prague. Ed. by Hrbacek. **1**: 297–322.

NYHOLM, K.G. 1952. Points de vue sur les recherches concernant la faune des sédiments marins. *Vie Milieu Suppl.* **2**: 157–164.

OCKELMANN, K.W. 1964. An improved detritus-sledge for collecting meiobenthos. *Ophelia.* **1**: 217–222.

ODUM, E.P. 1971. *Fundamentals of Ecology.* W.B. Saunders. 574 pp.

ODUM, H.T. 1957. Trophic structure and productivity of Silver Springs, Florida. *Ecol. Monogr.* **27**: 55–112.

OHLE, W. 1956. Bioactivity, production and energy utilization of lakes. *Limnol. Oceanogr.* **1**: 139–149.

OHLE, W. 1960. Fernsehen, Photographie und Schallortung der Sedimentoberflaeche in Seen. *Arch. Hydrobiol.* **57** (**1**/**2**): 135–160.

ØKLAND, J. 1962. Litt om teknik ved innsamling og konservering av ferskvannsdyr. *Fauna.* **15**: 69–92.

ØKLAND, J. 1964. The eutrophic Lake Borrevann (Norway)—an ecological study on the shore and bottom fauna with special references to gastropods, including a hydrographic survey. *Folia limnol. scand.* **13**: 8–337.

OLIVER, D.R. 1960. The macroscopic bottom fauna of Lac La Ronge, Saskatchewan. *J. Fish. Res. Bd Canada.* **17**: 607–624.

ORLOCI, L. 1967. An agglomerative method of classification of plant communities. *J. Ecol.* **55**: 193–206.

PAINE, R.T. 1966. Food web complexity and species diversity. *The American Naturalist.* **100** (**90**): 65–75.

PAINE, R.T. 1969. The Pisaster-Tequla interaction; prey patches, predator food preference, and intertidal community structure. *Ecology*. **50** (**6**): 950–961.

PAGAST, F. 1943. Uber die Bodenchironomiden des Lunzer Untersees. *Int. Revue ges. Hydrobiol. Hydrogr.* **43**: 470–479.

PEARSALL, W.H. 1921. The development of vegetation in the English lakes, considered in relation to the general evolution of glacial lakes and rock basins. *Proc. R. Soc.* **92**: 259–284.

PENNAK, R.W. 1953. *Fresh-water Invertebrates of the United States*. The Ronald Press, New York. 769 pp.

PESTA, O. 1929. Der Hochgebirgssee der Alpen. *Binnengewässer*. **8**: 1–156. Stuttgart.

PETERSEN, C.G. 1911. Valuation of the sea. *Rep. Danish Biol. Stn.* Copenhagen. **20**: 1–76.

PIECZYNSKI, E., and KAJAK, Z. 1965. Investigations on the mobility of the bottom fauna in the lakes Taltowisko, Mikolajskie and Śniardwy. *Bull. Acad. Pol. Sci. Cl. II Sér. Sci. biol.* **13**: 345–353.

PODDUBNAYA, T.L. 1962. The consumption of tubificids by fish. (Russian text). *Vopr. Ichtiol.* **2**: 560–562.

POR, F.D. 1968. The invertebrate zoobenthos of Lake Tiberias. I. Qualitative aspects. *Israel J. Zool.* **17**: 51–79.

POR, F.D., and MASSY, D. 1968. Survival of a nematode and an oligochaete species in the anaerobic benthos of Lake Tiberias. *Oikos*. **19**: 388–391.

POWERS, C.F., and ROBERTSON, A. 1967. Design and evaluation of an all-purpose benthos sampler. Great Lakes Res. Div., *Mich. Univ. Spec. Rept.* **30**: 126–131.

PREJS, A. 1969. Differences in abundance of benthos and reliability of its assessment in several lake habitats. *Ekol. Pol. Ser. A*. **17**: 133–147.

RANDALL, J.E. 1961. Overgrazing of algae by herbivorous marine fishes. *Ecology*. **42** (**4**): p. 812.

RANDALL, J.E. 1965. Grazing effect on sea grasses by herbivorous reef fishes in the West Indies. *Ecology*. **46** (**3**): 255–260.

RAVERA, O. 1966. Stability and pattern of distribution of the benthos in different habitats of an alpine oligotrophic lake. *Verh. Int. Verein. Limnol.* **16**: 233–244.

RAWSON, D.S. 1930. The bottom fauna of Lake Simcoe and its role in the ecology of the lake. *Univ. Toronto Stud. Biol., Publ. Ont. Fish. Res. Lab.* **34**: 1–183.

RAWSON, D.S. 1934. Productivity studies in lakes of the Kamloops region, British Columbia. *Bull. Biol. Bd Canada*. **42**: 1–31.

RAWSON, D.S. 1939. Some physical and chemical factors in the metabolism of lakes. Problems of lake biology. *Am. Ass. Adv. Sci. Publ.* **10**: 9–26.

RAWSON, D.S. 1942. A comparison of some large alpine lakes in western Canada. *Ecology*. **23**: 143–161.

RAWSON, D.S. 1947. An automatic closing dredge and other equipment for use in extremely deep water. *Limnol. Oceanogr. Spec. Publ.* **18**: 2–8.

RAWSON, D.S. 1952. Mean depth and fish production of large lakes. *Ecology*. **33**: 513–520.

RAWSON, D.S. 1953*a*. The limnology of Amethyst Lake. A high alpine type near Jasper, Alberta. *Can. J. Zool.* **31**: 193–210.

RAWSON, D.S. 1953*b*. The bottom fauna of Great Slave Lake. *J. Fish. Res. Bd Canada*. **10**: 486–520.

RAWSON, D.S. 1957. Limnology and fisheries of five lakes of the upper Churchill drainage, Saskatchewan. *Rep. Dept. Nat. Res. Sask.* **3**: 1–61.

RAWSON, D.S. 1959. Limnology and fisheries of Cree and Wollaston Lakes in northern Saskatchewan. *Rep. Dept. Nat. Res. Sask.* **4**: 1–73.

RAWSON, D.S. 1960. A limnological comparison of twelve large lakes in northern Saskatchewan. *Limnol. Oceanogr.* **5**: 195–211.

RAWSON, D.S., and ATTON, F.M. 1953. Biological investigation and fisheries management at Lac La Ronge, Saskatchewan. *Rep. Dept. Nat. Res. Sask.* **1**: 1–40.

RAWSON, D.S., and MOORE, J.E. 1944. The saline lakes of Saskatchewan. *Can. J. Res.* **22**: 141–201.

REIMERS, N., MACIOLEK, J.A., and PISTER, E.P. 1955. Limnological study of the lakes in Convict Creek Basin Mono County, California. *Fish. Bull., Fish. Wildl. Serv. U.S.* **56**: 437–503.

REYNOLDSON, T.B. and BELLAMY, L.S. 1970. The establishment of interspecific competition in field populations with an example of competition in action between *Polycelis nigra* (Mull.) and *P. tenius* (Ijima) (Turbellaria, Tricladida). *Proc. Adv. Study Inst. Dynamics Numbers Popul. (Oosterbeek* 1970): 282–297.

REYNOLDSON, T.B. and BELLAMY, L.S. 1971. Intraspecific competition in lake-dwelling triclads. *Oikos.* **22**: 315–328.

RICHMAN, S. 1958. The transformation of energy by *Daphnia pulex*. *Ecol. Monogr.* **28**: 273–291.

RICKER, K.E. 1959. The origin of two glacial relict crustaceans in North America, as related to Pleistocene glaciation. *Can. J. Zool.* **37**: 871–893.

RICKER, W.E. (ed.). 1971. *Methods for Assessment of Fish Production in Fresh Waters.* 2nd ed. Blackwell Scientific Publs. Oxford–Edinburgh. 326 pp.

RYDER, R.A. 1965. A method for estimating the potential fish production of north-temperate lakes. *Trans. Am. Fish. Soc.* **94**: 214–218.

RZOSKA, J. 1931. Bemerkungen über die quantitative Erfassung der Litoralfauna. *Verh. Int. Verein. Limnol.* **5**: 261–269.

SANDBERG, G. 1969. A quantitative study of chironomid distribution and emergence in Lake Erken. *Arch. Hydrobiol. Suppl.* **35**: 119–201.

SAPKAREV, J. 1965. Die Oligochaetenfauna des Ohrida-Sees. *A. Fac. Sci. Univ. Skopje.* **1965**: 5–161.

SCHMASSMANN, W. 1920. Die Bodenfauna hochalpiner Seen. *Arch. Hydrobiol. Suppl.* **3**: 1–106.

SCHNEIDER, J.C. 1965. Further studies on the benthic ecology of Sugarloaf Lake, Washtenaw County, Michigan. *Pap. Mich. Acad.* **50**: 11–29.

SCHNEIDER, R.F. 1969. A coring device for unconsolidated lake sediments. *Water Resources Res., U.S. Dept. Interior.* **5**: 524–526.

SCHUMACHER, A. 1963. Quantitativ Aspekte der Beziehung zwischen Stärke der Tubificidenbesiedlung und Schichtdicke der Oxydationszone in den Süsswatten der Unterelbe. *Arch. Fishereiwiss.* **14**: 48–50.

SCOTT, W., HILE, R.O., and SPEITH, H.T. 1928. A quantitative study of the bottom fauna of Lake Wawasee (Turkey Lake). *Invest. Indiana Lakes Streams.* **1**: 5–25.

SEGERSTRALE, S.G. 1957. On the immigration of the glacial relicts of Northern Europe, with remarks on the prehistory. *Soc. Sci. Fenn. Comment. Biol.* **16**: 1–117.

SEGERSTRALE, S.G. 1962. The immigration and prehistory of the glacial relicts of Eurasia and North America. *Int. Revue ges Hydrobiol. Hydrogr.* **45**: 1–25.

SHAPIRO, J. 1958. The core freezer, a new sampler for lake sediments. *Ecology.* **39**: p. 758.

SLACK, H.D. 1965. The profundal fauna of Loch Lomond, Scotland. *Proc. R. Soc. Edinb. B.* **69**: 272–297.

SLOBODKIN, L.B. 1962. Energy in animal ecology. Pp. 69–101. *In* J. B. Cragg (ed.), *Adv. Ecol. Res.* Academic Press, New York.

SMITH, M.W. 1952. Limnology and trout angling in Charlotte County Lakes, New Brunswick. *J. Fish Res. Bd Canada.* **8**: 383–452.

SMITH, M.W. 1961. A limnological reconnaissance of Nova Scotia brownwater lake. *J. Fish. Res. Bd Canada.* **18**: 463–478.

SOKAL, R.R. 1961. Distance as a measure of taxonomic similarity. *Systematic Zool.* **10**: 70–79.

SOKOLOVA, H.Y. 1968. The methods for estimation of production of aquatic animals. Ed. G.G. Winberg. *Soviet National Comm. of IBP of Acad. Sci. USSR, Minsk.* **2**: 226–239.

SOUTHWOOD, T.R.E. 1966. *Ecological Methods with Particular Reference to the Study of Insect Populations.* Methuen, London. 391 pp.

SPRAGUE, J.B. 1963. Resistance of four freshwater crustaceans to lethal high temperature and low oxygen. *J. Fish. Res. Bd Canada.* **20**: 387–415.

SPARROW, R.A.H. 1966. Comparative limnology of lakes in the southern Rocky Mountain Trench, British Columbia. *J. Fish. Res. Bd Canada.* **23**: 1875–1895.

STAHL, J.B. 1959. The developmental history of the chironomid and *Chaoborus* faunas of Myers Lake. *Invest. Indiana Lakes Streams.* **5**: 47–102.

STAHL, J.B. 1966. Characteristics of North America *Sergentia* lake. *Gewässer und Abwässer.* **41/42 S**: 95–122.

STANKOVIC, S. 1955. La zone profonde du lac d'Ohrid. *Mem. Ist. Ital. Idrobiol. Suppl.* **8**: 281–380.

STEINBOCK, O. 1953. Ein neurer seentyp: der Kryoeutrophe See. *Mem. Ist. Ital. Idrobiol.* **7**: 153–163.

STEINBOCK, O. 1958. Grundsäzliches zum 'kryoeutrophen' See. *Verh. Int. Verein. Limnol.* **13**: 181–190.

STEINMANN, P. 1906. Geographisches und Biologisches von Gebirsbachplanarien. *Arch. Hydrobiol.* **2**: 186–217.

STEINMANN, P. 1907. Die Tierwelt der Gebirgsbäche, eine faunistischbiologische Studie. *Ann. Biol. Lac.* **2**: 30–162.

STRASKRABA, M. 1965. The effect of fish on the number of invertebrates in ponds and streams. *Mitt. Internat. Ver. Limnol.* **13**: 106–127.

SUBLETTE, J.A., and DENDY, J.S. 1959. Plastic materials for simplified tent and funnel traps. *S.W. Nat.* **3**: 220–223.

SUTCLIFFE, D.W. 1967*a*. Sodium regulation in the amphipod *Gammarus duebeni* from brackish-water and fresh-water localities in Britain. *J. exp. Biol.* **46**: 529–550.

SUTCLIFFE, D.W. 1967*b*. A re-examination of observations on the distribution of *Gammarus duebeni* Lilljeborg in relation to the salt content in fresh water. *J. Anim. Ecol.* **36**: 579–597.

SUTCLIFFE, D.W. 1970. Experimental populations of *Gammarus duebeni* in fresh water with low sodium content. *Nature*. Lond. **228**: 875–876.

SUTCLIFFE, D.W., and SHAW, J. 1968. Sodium regulation in the amphipod *Gammarus duebeni* from freshwater in Ireland. *J. exp. Biol.* **48**: 339–358.

SZCZEPANSKI, A. 1953. Analiza dynamiki populacji skaposzczetów dna Wisly pod Warszawa. *Polskie Archwm Hydrobiol.* **1**: 227–250.

TEAL, J.M. 1957. Community metabolism in a cold temperate spring. *Ecol. Monogr.* **27**: 283–302.

TEAL, J.M. 1962. Energy flow in the salt marsh ecosystem of Georgia. *Ecology.* **43**: 614–624.

TEBO, L.B. 1955. Bottom fauna of a shallow eutrophic lake, Lizard Lake, Pocahontas County, Iowa. *Am. Midl. Nat.* **54**: 89–103.

TERBORGH, J. 1971. Distribution on environmental gradients: Theory and a preliminary interpretation of distributional patterns in the avifauna of the Cordilla Vilcabamba, Peru. *Ecology.* **52** (**1**): 23–40.

THIENEMANN, A. 1913. Der Zusammenhang zwischen dem Sauerstoffgehalt des Tiefenwassers und der Zusammensetzung der Tierfauna unserer Seen. *Int. Revue ges. Hydrobiol. Hydrogr.* **6**: 243–249.

THIENEMANN, A. 1918. Untersuchungen über die Bezeihungen zwischen dem Sauerstoffgehalt des Wassers und der Zusammensetzung der fauna in Norddeutschen Seen. *Arch. Hydrobiol.* **12**: 1–65.

THIENEMANN, A. 1925. Die Binnengewässer Mitteleuropas. Eine Limnologische Einführung. *Binnengewässer.* **1**: 1–255.

THIENEMANN, A. 1927. Der Bau des Seebeckens in seiner Bedeutung für den Ablauf des Lebens in See. *Verh. zool.-bot. Ges Wien.* **77**: 87–91.

THIENEMANN, A. 1931*a*. Tropische Seen und Seetypen. *Arch. Hydrobiol. Suppl.* **9**: 205–231.

THIENEMANN, A. 1931*b*. Productionsbegriff in der Biologie. *Arch. Hydrobiol.* **22**: 616–621.

THIENEMANN, A. 1954. Chironomus Leben. Verbreitung und wirtschaftliche Bedeutung der Chironomiden. *Binnengewässer*. **20**: 1–834.

THORSEN, G. 1957. Sampling the benthos. *Mem. geol. Soc. Am.* **67**: 61–73.

UHLIG, G. 1964. A simple method for the extraction of the vagile mesopsammal microfauna. *Helgoländer wiss Meeresunters.* **11**: 178–185.

UHLIG, G. 1965. Untersuchungen zur extraktion der vagilen Mikrofauna aus marinen Sedimenten. *Verh. deutsch. zool. Ges. Jena. Zool. Anz. Suppl.* **29**: 151–157.

ULOMSKI, S.N. 1952. Opyt kolicestvennogo uceta bentosa na plotnych recnych gruntach. *Trudy Vses. Gidrobiol. Obshch.* **4**.

VALLE, K.J. 1927. Okologische-Limnologische Untersuchungen über die Boden und Tiefenfauna in einigen Seen nördliche vom Lagoda-See. *Acta zool. fenn.* **4**: 1–231.

VEAL, D.M., and OSMOND, D.S. 1969. Bottom-fauna of the western basin and near-shore Canadian waters of Lake Erie. *Proc. 11th Conf. Great Lakes Res., Int. Ass. Great Lakes Res.* 151–160.

VERBEKE, J. 1957. Recherches écologiques sur la faune des grands lacs de l'est du Congo Belge. *Mém. Inst. r. Sci. nat. Belg.* **3**: 1–177.

VON HOFSTEN, N. 1911. Zur Kenntnis der Tiefenfauna des Brienzer und des Thuner Sees. *Arch. Hydrobiol.* **7**: 162–229.

WALKER, B. 1967. A diver-operated pneumatic core sampler. *Limnol. Oceanogr.* **12**: 144–146.

WALSHE, B.M. 1950. The function of haemoglobin in relation to filter feeding in leaf-mining chironomid larvae. *J. exp. Biol.* **28**: 57–61.

WARREN, C.E. 1971. *Biology and Water Pollution Control.* W.B. Saunders Co., Philadelphia–London–Toronto. 434 pp.

WATERS, T.F. 1969. The turnover ratio in production ecology of freshwater invertebrates. *Am. Nat.* **103**: 173–185.

WAVRE, M., and BRINKHURST, R.O. 1971. Interactions between some tubificid oligochaetes and bacteria found in the sediments of Toronto Harbour, Ontario. *J. Fish Res. Bd Canada.* **28**: 335–341.

WEBER, C.A. 1907. Aufbau und Vegetation der Moore Norddeutschlands. *Beiblatt zu den Botanischen Jahrbuchern.* **90**: 19–34.

WEEREKOON, A.C.J. 1956. Studies on the biology of Loch Lomond. II. The repopulation of McDougall Bank. *Ceylon J. Sci.* 7 (**1** new series): 95–133.

WELCH, H. 1967. Energy flow through the major macroscopic compartments of an aquatic ecosystem. *Ph.D. Thesis*, Univ. Georgia.

WELCH, P.S. 1935. *Limnology.* McGraw-Hill Book Co., New York–London. 471 pp.

WELCH, P.S. 1948. *Limnological Methods.* McGraw-Hill Co., New York. 382 pp.

WESENBERG-LUND, C. 1908. Die Littoralen Tiergesellschaften unserer grösseren Seen. *Int. Revue ges. Hydrobiol. Hydrogr.* **1**: 574–607.

WESENBERG-LUND, C. 1917. Furesöstudier. En bathymetrisk botanisk zoologisk. Undersögelse af Mölleaaens Söer. *K. danske Vidensk. Selsk. Skr., Naturv. Math. Afd.* 8. *Raekke.* **3**: 1–209.

WESENBERG-LUND, C. 1943. *Biologie der Süsswasserinsekten.* Kopenhagen (Gyldendalske Boghandel-Nordisk Forlag). 682 pp.

WHITTAKER, R.H. 1967. Gradient analysis of vegetation. *Biol. Rev.* **49**: 207–264.

WHITTAKER, R.H. 1970. *Communities and Ecosystems.* The Macmillan Co., Collier-Macmillan Ltd., London. 158 pp.

WIGLEY, R.L. 1967. Comparative efficiencies of Van Veen and Smith–McIntyre grab samplers as revealed by motion pictures. *Ecology.* **48**: 168–169.

WINBERG, G.G. 1968. Methods for the estimation of production of aquatic animals (Transl. by Annie Duncan, 1971) *Adv. Ecol. Res.* Academic Press, London–New York. 175 pp.

WOOD, K.G. 1963. The bottom fauna of Lake Erie. *Publ. Great Lakes Div., Michigan.* **10**: 258–265.

WOOD, L.W., and CHUA, K.E. 1973. Glucose flux at the sediment-water interface of Toronto Harbour, Lake Ontario, with reference to pollution stress. *Can. J. Microbiol.* **19**: 413–420.

WUHRMANN, K., and WOKER, H. 1955. Influence of temperature and oxygen tension on the toxicity of poisons to fish. *Verh. Int. Verein. Limnol.* **12**: 795–801.

YABLONSKAYA, E.A. 1947. *Opredelenie produktsii lichinok* Chironomus plumosus *Medvezk'ikh ozer*. Kaud. Diss. (Determining the production of *Chironomus plumosus* larvae in the Medvezh'e Lakes, cited in Winberg, 1968.)

YAMAGISHI, H., and FUKUHARA, H. 1971*a*. Note on the swimming behaviour of *Chironomus plumosus* larvae in Lake Suwa. *Jap. J. Ecol.* **20**: 256–257.

YAMAGISHI, H., and FUKUHARA, H. 1971*b*. Ecological studies on chironomids in Lake Suwa. I. Population dynamics of two large chironomids, *Chironomus plumosus* L. and *Spaniotoma akamusi* Tokunaga. *Oecologia*. **7**: 309–327.

YOUNG, D.K., and RHOADES, D.C. 1971. Animal-sediment relations in Cape Cod Bay, Mass. I. A transect study. *Marine Biology*. **11(3)**: 242–254.

ZABOLOCKI, A.A. 1936. O bespruznom stangovom dnocerpatele. *Trudy leningr. Obshch. Estest.* **65**: 262–265.

ZADIN, V.I. 1960. Metody gidrobiologiceskogo issledovanija. *Vyssz. Szk. Moskva.* 191 pp.

ZSCHOKKE, F. 1900. Die Tierwelt der Hochgebirgsseen. *Neue Deukschr. allg. Schweiz. Ges. Naturw.* **37**: 1–400.

ZSCHOKKE, F. 1911. Die Tierseefauna der Seen Mitteleuropas. *Int. Revue ges. Hydrobiol. Hydrogr.* **4**: 1–246.

SUBJECT INDEX

GEOGRAPHIC INDEX

TAXONOMIC INDEX